Indian Philosophy of *Nāda* and Its Vocal Applications

JUSTICE B.S. RAIKOTE

MOTILAL BANARSIDASS PUBLISHERS
PRIVATE LIMITED • DELHI

First Edition: Delhi, 2016

ISBN : 978-81-208-3691-4

Also Available at

MOTILAL BANARSIDASS

41 U.A. Bungalow Road, Jawahar Nagar, Delhi 110 007
8 Mahalaxmi Chamber, 22 Bhulabhai Desai Road, Mumbai 400 026
203 Royapettah High Road, Mylapore, Chennai 600 004
236, 9th Main III Block, Jayanagar, Bangalore 560 011
8 Camac Street, Kolkata 700 017
Ashok Rajpath, Patna 800 004
Chowk, Varanasi 221 001

MLBD Cataloging-in-Publication Data
Indian Philosophy of Nada and its Vocal Application
by Justice B.S. Raikote
Includes bibiliography and index
ISBN : 978-81-208-3691-4
I. Indian Philosophy II. Nada (Sound) III. Linguistics
IV. Raikote, B.S.

Printed in India
by RP Jain at NAB Printing Unit,
A-44, Naraina Industrial Area, Phase I, New Delhi-110028
and published by JP Jain for Motilal Banarsidass Publishers (P) Ltd,
41 U.A. Bungalow Road, Jawahar Nagar, Delhi-110007

Dedication

This book is dedicated to my paternal uncle
late **Rachayya Raikote**,
an eminent violinist, well-versed in
both Hindustani and Karnataka styles
of Indian classical music, who was
my first music *guru*, during
my childhood.

CONTENTS

ACKNOWLEDGEMENT

The concept of *śabda*, in the sense of a "word", has found extensive investigation by a number of research scholars, from linguistic point of view, grammatical point of view and also from the point of view of "testimony" as *pramāṇa* in logic and epistemology; but it has received little attention, in the sense of *dhvani* or *nāda* (sound). Moreover, there appears to be no attempt to deal with this *nāda* from the philosophical point of view. Hence, in this thesis, I have attempted to deal with it from the point of view of the Indian philosophical systems, right from the pre-Vedic and Vedic period. I have also indicated the "vocal applications", of such *nāda* on the basis of the ancient Indian texts, so as to make them available for use to the present day generations. This thesis, in short, attempts to deal with *nāda* as an independent research subject by highlighting its important aspects.

The work was executed and completed under the guidance of Prof. R.I. Ingalalli, Chairman (*Rtd.*), Department of Philosophy and Former Dean of Faculty of Social Sciences, Karnataka University, Dharwad. Prof. Ingalalli has been my friend, philosopher and a guide, in letter and spirit. He helped me by foregoing his own research activities, so much so that, this work could not have been completed but for his able assistance and guidance. In the beginning, due to my old age, I was a bit diffident, but Prof. Ingalalli, encouraged me and stood by me until the completion of this work. Hence, I profoundly thank him.

My thanks are due to all the members of my family for their co-operation and encouragement, particularly, to my daughter Shashikala and to my daughter-in-law Pratibha who helped me in preparing many of the drawings and sketches, as per my instructions. Many thanks are due to my wife, Sarvamangala Raikote, whose untiring help and assistance enabled me to devote fully for this kind of research work for a period of five years.

I am also grateful to Sri Sadheep Sivanandan and Shivarudrappa Hartikote, drawing teachers, for preparing certain drawings, as per my instructions, for the purpose of this thesis.

I had to carry on my entire research work on computers and laptop, which I learnt, after my laying down my office, under the guidance of my grandson, Darshan. I am grateful to him. I am also grateful to Praveen & Vinay brothers, the proprietors of Computer Warehouse, Bangalore, for efficiently maintaining my computers with the assistance of their very competent engineers, for the last five years.

I am also grateful to the authorities of Karnataka University, and members and the staff of the Department of Philosophy and staff of the Karnataka University Library for the help they extended to me from time to time, during my research work.

Justice B.S. Raikote

ABBREVIATIONS

A. Abbreviations

Ait. A.	*Aitareya Āraṇyaka.*
Aum.	*Aumāpatam.*
AV. or A.V.	*Atharva Veda Saṃhitā.*
Br.	*Bṛhaddeśī* of Mataṅga Muni.
Br. Up.	*Bṛhadāraṇyaka Upaniṣad.*
Chā. Up.	*Chāndogya Upaniṣad.*
Dhyā. Bin. Up.	*Dhyānabindu Upaniṣad.*
Gītā.	*Bhagavadgītā*
Kā. K.Vil.	*Kāmakalāvilāsa* of Puṇyānanda Nātha
Kāśikā.	*Kāśikā* of Sucarita Misra (as referred to by Ganganatha Jha in *Ślokavārtika.*
Kaṭ. Up.	*Kaṭha Upaniṣad.*
L.T.	*Lakṣmī Tantra.*
Māṇḍ. Up.	*Māṇḍūkya Upaniṣad.*
Mī. Sū.	*Mīmāṃsā Sūtra* of Jaiminī.
Maitr. Up.	*Maitrī Upaniṣad.*
Muṇ. Up.	*Muṇḍaka Upaniṣad.*
Nā. Śā.	*Nāṭya Śāstra* of Bharata Muni.
Nā. Śi.	*Nāradīya Śikṣā.*
Nā. Bin. Up.	*Nādabindu Upaniṣad.*
Ne. Ta.	*Netratantram.*
Nyā. Su.	*Nyāya Sūtra* of Gautama.
Pā. Śi.	*Pāṇinīya Śikṣā*
Parā. Tr. V.	*Parā-triśikā-Vivaraṇa* of Abhinavagupta.

Pat. M. Bhā.	*Patañjali Mahābhāṣya.*
Pras. Up.	*Praśna Upaniṣad.*
Rig. Prā.	*Ṛgveda-Prātiśākhyam* of Śaunaka.
Ru. Yā. Tan.	*Rudra Yāmala Tantra.*
RV. or R.V.	*Ṛgveda Saṃhitā.*
S. R.	*Saṅgīta Ratnākara* of Śāraṅgadeva.
Śā. T. T.	*Śāradā Tilaka Tantram.*
Sā. V.	*Sāmaveda.*
Sān. Pr. Sū.	*Sāṅkhya Pravacana Sūtra* of Kapila.
San. Sam. Sā.	*Saṅgīta Samaya Sāra* of Pārśvadeva.
Sl. Vā.	*Slokavārttika* of Kumārila Bhaṭṭa.
Sou. Lah.	*Soundarya Laharī.*
Sva. T.	*Svacchandatantram.*
Tai. Up.	*Taittirīya Upaniṣad.*
Tatt. Sū	*Tattvārtha Sūtra* of Umāsvāti.
Taitti. Prā.	*Taittirīya Prātiśākhyam.*
V. E.	"Vedānta Explained" – Śaṅkara's Commentary on *Brahma-Sūtra's* of Bādarāyaṇa (Date V.H.-1973).
Vā.	*Vākyapadīya* of Bhartṛhari.
Vāj. Prā.	*Vājasaneyī Prātiśākhyam.*
Vai. Sū.	*Vaiśeṣika Sūtra* of Kaṇāda.
Yā. Śi.	*Yājñavalkya Śikṣā.*
Yā. Ni.	*Yāska Nirukta.*
Yā. Smṛ.	*Yājñavalkya Smṛti.*
Yo. Sū.	*Yoga Sūtras* of Patañjali.

B. Notes on Transliteration:

The system of diacritical marks used is as follows (The same system is adopted for capital letters also):

अ	आ	इ	ई	उ	ऊ	ऋ	ए	ऐ	ओ	औ	अं	अः
a	ā	i	ī	u	ū	ṛ	e	ai	o	au	ṃ	ḥ

क्	ख्	ग्	घ्	ङ्
k	kh	g	gh	ṅ

च्	छ्	ज्	झ्	ञ्
c	ch	j	jh	ñ

ट्	ठ्	ड्	ढ्	ण्
ṭ	ṭh	ḍ	ḍh	ṇ

त्	थ्	द्	ध्	न्
t	th	d	dh	n

प्	फ्	ब्	भ्	म्
p	ph	b	bh	m

य्	र्	ल्	व्	श्	ष्	स्	ह्
y	r	la	v	ś	ṣ	s	h

Chapter One

INTRODUCTION

In the tradition of Indian philosophy, the concept of *nāda* has occupied an important place in such a way that its ramifications are found in many aspects of the Indian culture and civilization. It has been part of Indian social life right from the times immemorial. Even during Vedic period, the concept of *nāda* dominated the religious practices like *yajña* and *yāga* in the form of chanting of Vedic hymns, *praṇava* and also in the form of music. The pre-Vedic *yatis* or *yogic* practitioners seem to have thought of the *nāda* as a manifestation of the ultimate reality in the form of *śiva-śakti* principle, paving the way for *upāsanā* or *sādhanā*. The relics of such pre-Vedic thought found expression in *Āgama* and *Tantra* philosophy. Vedic philosophers, on the other hand, thought of *oṃkāra* or *praṇava nāda* as the manifestation of *ṛtam* and *satyam* principles of *akṣara* (or *puruṣa*). The statements – "The first born out of *ṛta* principle is *vācaḥ* (*ṛtasya prathamajā vācaḥ* RV.164.37), and whatever is known in the form of speech is a copy of 'That' (ultimate reality) (*yat kiṃ ca vijñātam vācas tadrūpaṃ*)"[1] – indicate that *vāk* is the earliest means of "knowledge" in the "thought-form" as a cosmic concept. According to *Ṛgveda*, this "cosmic *vāk*" rests on *akṣara*

(RV.164.39) or *oṃ*. Thus an inseparable relation was conceived between this *akṣara* or *oṃ* (cosmic existence) and cosmic *vāk* (cosmic language). This cosmic *oṃ* found new expressions generally as *śabda* in *Sāṅkhya*, *dhvani* or *śabda* in *Nyāya-Vaiśeṣika*, *Mīmāṃsā* and *Vedānta*, and as *nāda* in Yoga, *Āgamas* and in musicology. However, the grammarians used both. In fact all these expressions – *śabda*, *dhvani* and *nāda*, in relation to human *vāk* – stand for "sound" in English.

The analysis of the topic of my thesis indicates three important aspects:

a. *Nāda* is the subject matter of my thesis, requiring an investigation into it.
b. Such investigation has to be based on Indian philosophical theories of *nāda*.
c. There has to be an emphasis on the vocal application of *nāda*.

The phrase "vocal application" has necessarily to mean "human vocal application" and not the voice of the animals, which they use and apply, in their communications, with their respective breeds. The kind of voice, the animals produce, is innate, instinctive and involuntary, and as such animals, perhaps, would not consciously know their respective voice and its application, except to shout in a particular way in a particular situation instinctively. In this respect, a newborn human-baby also would not be in a better position. But the concept of applications of *nāda* should necessarily mean, in the context of my topic, "conscious" applications of *nāda*, according to accepted modes in Indian systems. Such applications should necessarily be useful applications, being consistent to ethical principles. With this object in mind, let me start with the definition of Indian philosophy.

Philosophy according to *Vedānta* is known as *Brahmajijñāsā*, (or an enquiry into the reality). The object of such enquiry would be to attain *Brahmjñāna* (the knowledge of the ultimate reality). "Brahman" means a "self-existent impersonal spirit,....the divine essence and source, from which all things emanate, or with which they are identified, and to which they return, the self-existent, the absolute; the eternal (not generally an object of worship, but rather of meditation and knowledge....)".[2] Philosophy in India is called *darśana*, and a *darśana* means "an 'ascetic vision' of the highest value and truth....".[3] In the words of Prof. S. Radhakrishnan, "it is this 'synthetic vision' of India that has made philosophy comprehend several sciences which have become differential in modern times".[4] Thus "Indian philosophy has been.... intensely spiritual and has always emphasized the need for practical realization of truth".[5] Indian philosophy, in other words, stands for a way of life.

When I say Indian philosophy, I mean the philosophical thought prevalent in the territory of India. The classical name for India, however, as commonly employed in Sanskṛt literature....is *Bhārata* or *Bhārata-varṣa*. The multifaced philosophy that is born, and brought up within this region, right from the pre-*Āryan* or pre-Vedic time of Harappa and

Mohenjodaro civilization, down to the modern times, is generally called "Indian philosophy". In this view of the matter the term Indian philosophy takes within its fold, the pre-Vedic and Vedic philosophy, philosophy of *ṣaḍdarśana*, philosophy of grammarians and *Āgama*, and philosophy of *nāda* found in *Saṅgīta-Śāstra* (music literatures), etc.

The Need of the Study

My reading suggested to me that the concept of *śabda* in the sense of a word with meaning, has been extensively investigated by the scholars in *Nyāya-Vaiśeṣika*, *Mīmāṃsā* and *Vyākaraṇa*, etc., but *śabda* as *dhvani*, or *nāda* in the sense of "sound", has received little or no attention by the scholars so far, particularly on the application side of *nāda*. It may, perhaps, be due to the fact that the study of *nāda* would be a matter of interdisciplinary study, involving the knowledge of Indian philosophical systems, grammar, phonetics and music, etc. A basic knowledge of Sanskṛt would be necessary since such a research has to base on Indian Sanskṛt texts. My knowledge in Indian philosophy, Indian classical music and basic knowledge of Sanskṛt language, perhaps might have stirred my interest, thereby driving my retired life to a research of this kind. I hope that my research would lead to positive conclusions, relevant to the time. Whenever an apple from the tree fell and hit their heads, many people might have suffered head injuries prior to Newton, but it is to Newton that injury revealed the "Theory of Gravitation", only because he was at it. Hoping such revelation, with God's grace, I proceed further.

I make it clear that, it would be my duty to reveal such an investigation with figures, diagrams and sketches, (or if permissible with audio-video demonstrations) for better understanding of the subject, more so, in the face of certain conflicting theories among the scholars, regarding certain aspects. For instance, there are conflicting theories regarding the pronunciation involved in Vedic *svara-traya–udātta, anudātta* and *svarita*–in spite of the fact that our ancient seers had taken all the pains to explain and clarify them by leaving a vast literature on the subject, for the posterity. It is so because what transpires in mouth while uttering any *svara*–whether Vedic, linguistic or musical–it is difficult to reduce it to a formula, so as to convey its true nature to the listener. For instance, under the *sūtra uccairudāttam,* the *udātta svara* was misunderstood as "high tone", by both foreign and Indian scholars. In fact it is not "high tone", and such aspect requires to be demonstrated by actually accenting them by using voice, or highlighting them with reference to the diagrams and with reference to the *sūtras* found in texts. Hence, such a research, with practical demonstrations in my opinion, would be useful to the contemporary society, and as such I think it is ethical, on the part of my retired life to do so. Otherwise, my forty years of experimentations, on certain aspects of *nāda*, as matter of curiosity and inquisitiveness would go waste.

The Problem of the Research

Both *śabda* and *nāda* in Sanskṛt stand for "sound or noise" of the English language. *Amarakośa*[6], under the heading *śabdādivargaḥ,* provides seventeen synonyms of "sound" in Sanskṛt language – 1. *śabdaḥ,* 2. *ninādaḥ,* 3. *ninadaḥ,* 4. *dhvaniḥ,* 5. *dhvānaḥ,* 6. *ravaḥ,* 7. *svanaḥ,* 8. *svānaḥ,* 9. *nirghoṣa,* 10. *nirhrāda,* 11. *nādaḥ,* 12. *nisvānaḥ,* 13. *nisvanaḥ,* 14. *āravaḥ,* 15. *ārāvaḥ,* 16. *saṃravaḥ,* 17. *virāvaḥ* – each one means sound or noise. These Sanskṛt words are "synonyms" and convey almost the same sense, or a sense very near to each other.

The New Lexicon Webster's Dictionary of the English language defines "synonym" is "A word having the same meaning as another word, in the same language, in one or more of its senses; car and automobile are synonyms....".[7] The phrase "in one or more of its senses" found in this definition clearly indicates that a synonym need not convey exactly the same meaning as the other word. For example, "car and automobile" are synonyms. But the word automobile stands for not only for car but other vehicles like lorry, tempo, etc. also. In other words, they are all the vehicles, which run on machines. Being run with the aid of machines is the common factor in all these automobile-vehicles. In the same way, in spite of minor differences, if any, in all these seventeen synonyms of the word *śabda,* there is one common characteristic, and that is, each one stands for "sound" or "producing-sound" or "noise". In fact, Liṅgayasūrins commentary on *Amarakośa* itself clarifies *śabda* as *śabdate iti śabdaḥ* (sound is the one that sounds). The *śabda,* as a noun form, is derived from the action of sounding (*śabdakriyāyām*). Similarly, there are other verbs like *nadati, ninadati,* or *ninādati*, *dhvanati* which stand for "sounding, humming and resounding, etc.". Likewise, the word *rava*, *rāva*, or *ārāva* are derived from the root *ru* which mean "roar, bellow, yelp, cry, howl (like animals); or song of singing birds, hum or humming, thunder, or sound of a ringing bell, or loud sound", etc. Likewise, *svanaḥ*, *svānaḥ* means "roar of wind or roar of water, thunder, sound of bird, or song of bird or sound of any kind." The word *ghoṣa* (RV.4.4.8) or *nirghoṣa* are derived from the word *ghuṣ* meaning thereby "to sound, to cry or proclaim aloud, call out, announce publicly declare, etc." In this sense all the seventeen synonyms of the word *śabda* stand for an action of "sounding"; may be some sounds are soft and some are harsh, and some are loud and some are low; and some with some special characteristic of their own. For instance, Liṅgayasūrin, the commentator of *Amarakośa*, provides some examples of this type – *samudra ghoṣa* (the roar of sea); *marmara* (rustle; adj. rustling) is sound of leaves; the sound of garments is called *śiñjitam* (*śiñja* = to utter a shrill sound, tinkle, rattle, jingle, whirr, buzz, hum, twang, etc.). *Bhūṣanadhvanīnām* is the tinkling sound of silver ornaments of ankles or wrists." *Amarakośa* (1.7.3) also elaborates certain special sounds. The sound of musical instruments, like *Veeṇā*, etc., is described as : *nikvāṇaḥ*, *nikvaṇaḥ*, *kvaṇaḥ*, *kvaṇanam*; the sounds of *veeṇā*, in particular, is described as *prakvāṇa*, *prakvaṇa*; [*kvaṇa* = to sound, to hum or to make a sound; *kvaṇayati* = to cause sound (as a musical instrument), etc.]. The sounds of other instruments are given in Mallinātha's commentary of

Amarakośa, e.g., *mārjanā* is the sound of a musical instrument called *muraja*, and *guṇḍila* is the sound of another musical instrument *mardala*. These two instruments made up of animal skin are used as *tāla* (beat) accompaniments. *Amarakośa* also gives examples of certain special non-musical sounds such as the loud and confused noise of multitude called *kolāhala*, *kalakalaḥ* (1.7.4); the sounds of birds as *vāśitam* [*vāśyate iti vāśitam* = *vāśyate* means roar, howl, bellow, low (of a cow), or cry, shṛiek or sing (of a bird)]; the echo-voice (*pratiśrutapratidhvāne*); the sound of a song *gītam*, or the sound of a music as *gānam*.[8] In all these instances, with minor differences as to their meaning or contextual meaning, the common element is the production of *dhvani* or *nāda*, which is generally translated as "sound" in English. These are instances of individual sounds with their own special characteristics, either in the nature of sound or in its use. There is, at the same time, in all the above instances, "a general characteristic", that stands for the "sounding phenomena" as such. In this general "sounding phenomenon", all the varieties of particular sounds can be accommodated. The Naiyāyikas call such a notion, as "genus" (*jāti*); and this "genus" as "generality" stands for the comprehensive cognition of the concept that inheres all the particular instances of "*dhvanitva* or *nādatva*" (soundness).[9] The use of the words *dhvani* or *nāda*, in the course of this thesis, refers to such *dhvanitva* or *nādatva*. Dictionaries have translated *nāda* as "sound" or "noise". Out of the two English words, "sound" and "noise", I prefer "sound" because "noise" always is used to refer to a "sound" "due to irregular vibrations" (Webster's Dictionary).[10] Many-a-time, in common parlance, "noise" is referred to as a confused and chaotic sound, similar to the one prevalent in busy market place, or on a railway platform or in bus-stands. But *nāda*, as we will see later is a regulated sound. Hence I exclude the use of the word "noise" so as to avoid possible unnecessary confusion in treatment of the subject.

In Sanskṛt, there are a number of other words, generally used to convey the same meaning as "sound" in English. The most popular amongst them are: *śabda*, *dhvani* or *nāda*. Of these three, *śabda* has wider connotation than the latter two. *Śabda* means the one that is "heard" by the ears.[11] *Śabda* is generally used to indicate sound, noise, voice, tone, note, etc. It has a few other meanings like a word, speech, language, verbal communication, testimony, oral tradition, etc. In this thesis, I am concerned with *śabda*, mainly, in the sense of "sound", voice, tone, etc. In this sense, *dhvani* and *nāda* would be very near synonyms. In other words I would not be concerned with *śabda*, in the sense of a "word", while dealing with the concept of *nāda*. This kind of distinction is clearly and meticulously maintained in Indian classical literatures. For instance, in *Mahābhāṣya*, Patañjali has clarified with illustration, the distinction between *śabda* and *dhvani*. According to him: "the audible sound (*dhvaniḥ*), in the form of group of syllables used to indicate the 'objects' or 'things', in our day-to-day life, and this audible sound itself is known as *śabda* (*tasmāt dhvaniḥ śabdaḥ*), just like in the sentences – continue to utter the sounds you are making or 'This boy always makes sounds' etc."[12] But according to *Mahābhāṣyakāra*, "the true connotation of *śabda* is *sphoṭa* – that which, when manifested, enables the listener to have a clear knowledge of the object cow".[13] In this kind of distinction between two aspects of *śabda* I am concerned mainly with "sonic" (*dhvani*) aspect of it. Even according to Bhartṛhari, a *śabda* has two elements: One is meaning, which is the real cause of the word, and the other element is *dhvani* that is used to convey the said meaning (to the listener) (I.44, and 48). In this context, I must point out that I am concerned with the *dhvani* that conveys the meaning. In a *śabda* (word), there are syllables which constitute the word. I am concerned with the formation of syllables or syllabic sounds. But *śabda* in the sense of word denoting meaning is a matter for other disciplines like grammar, and hence outside the scope of my thesis. In music also, there are musical-notes or musical-syllables used in the presentation of a *rāga* (a musical melodic pattern) with a poetic composition. Thus a *rāga* has two aspects which musicologists call *dhātu* (sound-substance) and *mātu* (word or composition). Here *dhātu* falls within the scope of my subject matter whereas *rāga* and its composition (*mātu*) aspect fall within the scope of the musicologists.

There is one more sense in which the word *śabda* is used, though it is akin to the sense the grammarians "word", but with slightly different emphasis on "testimony" (*pramāṇa*) aspect. The logicians and some of the metaphysicians take the word *śabda* in this sense. For instance, a logician, though like a grammarian, uses the word *śabda* in the sense of "a word", still he uses it to verify the authenticity of the statement of the speaker. When a boatman says – In this river water is very deep – the logician worries himself to know whether boatman's statement can be taken as a *pramāṇa* (testimony) like the statement of *Āyurveda* that a particular plant is poisonous. The word *śabda* in the sense of "oral testimony," as used by the logicians, is also outside the scope of my thesis. But for the purpose of my thesis, *śabda* in the sense of *dhvani* as clarified by Patañjali, is the one that is the most relevant. In this context, I hasten to add that I am not also concerned with *dhvani* in the sense Ānandavardhana, suggests in his *Dhvanyāloka*. Ānandavardhana uses the word *dhvani* in a technical sense to mean a suggestive meaning, which acts as a manifester (*vyañjaka*) of "sentiment" or *rasa*. In other words, *dhvani* is a sequence of sounds emanating from vocal organs expressing a meaning which is different from the actual meaning conveyed by individual words (*vācaka*). In the words of Ānandavardhana, "From the series of expressed words, the charming unexpressed manifests which are called *Vyaṅgyārtha* or suggested sense".[14] *Dhvani* is explained as one that expresses or manifests (*dhvanati*) or gets expressed (*dhvanyati*) (a separate hidden meaning which is different from what the words denote as per the linguistic convention). Such a meaning, causing an aesthetic appeal is called *rasa* (sentiment). For example, a statement – A person afraid of dogs does not enter the forest infested by lions – suggests a hidden meaning that such.person is "timid" and not an adventurist. Even in the English language there are similar expressions. For example, "The place where the sunlight does not enter a doctor must" means, a place not exposed to sunlight would be unhealthy inviting the services of a doctor. I am not concerned with *dhvani* in this sense of implied or suggestive meaning.

There is one more word in Sanskṛt standing for sound and that is *svara*. This word is the noun form of the verb root *svṛ* which means "to utter a sound, sound, resound, to pronounce," or "sound, noise, accent or tone in music, etc."[15] The word *svara* is also used to indicate *svara* (vowel), as against *vyañjana* (consonant) in accentuation or pronunciation of a syllable or a word. For that purpose, there is an independent *śāstra* (science) in Sanskṛt classical literature called *dhvanividyā*, *dhvaniśāstraṃ*, or *svaravidyā*, etc., similar to phonetics of the West, which deals with accentuations or pronunciations of syllables and words in linguistic structures. For example, in the English language– the rule that when a consonant is followed by another consonant, the former consonant would be silent (e.g., in the word "walk" the syllable "l" being followed by another consonant "k" is silent) – is a rule of phonetics. In Sanskṛt the rule – that when a vowel of the same nature is followed by another vowel in conjunction – earlier vowel (*svara*) becomes long (*dīrgha*) (e.g. *svara*+*aṣṭaka* become *svarāṣṭaka*). I must make it clear that my consideration of philosophy of *nāda* as *svara* would not be in the sense of *svara*, which the phoneticians use.

The word "sound" in the English language also has more than one meaning. The New Lexicon Webster's Dictionary of the English language, gives the meaning of "sound" as – "to cause to emit sound, to sound a trumpet.... to pronounce, give sound to, articulate; sound your consonants clearly", etc.[16] This "Sound", according to me, is the one that calls for serious scrutiny to find out whether by itself it is *nāda* or not.

I must, again, make it clear that though I am not dealing with my topic as a grammarian, as a logician, or as a phonetician, etc., yet the study of these disciplines would be necessary to know different aspects of *nāda* so as to distinguish *nāda* from other allied concepts. A research of this type has got to be a matter of inter-disciplinary study. There cannot be any watertight compartment like approach. For instance, I do investigate into the nature of *śabda* with its meaning as grammarians and logicians do, but only to extract and emphasize the "sonic element" of that *śabda*. The thrust of my thesis would be on the "the sonic aspect" of that *śabda*, emphasizing its ontological source and its epistemological means to knowledge. For example, on the linguistic side – after seeing a *gauḥ* when one utters – *gauḥ*; the subject matter of my thesis, requires to find out as to what is the nature of that "sound" used in uttering *gauḥ*; and as to what transpired in the mouth, while pronouncing the word *gauḥ*; and also to find out, on the applications side, whether there can be a better mode of pronouncing *gauḥ*, in order to have a correct pronunciation and accordingly a correct meaning, which leads to the "cognition" or "knowledge", that "it is a cow", as an epistemological means. On the musical side when one sings *svaras* of music, the subject matter of my thesis requires to find out as to what is the nature of that "sound" used in voicing the musical tones; and as to what transpired in the mouth while pronouncing such *svaras* and also to find out, on the applications side, whether there can be a better mode of producing voice, in order to have a better aesthetic appeal, or for better communicative or meditative value in spiritual practices. Thus the subject matter of my thesis requires that I should attempt to explore the nature of that sound on its theoretical side and also on its application side, basing my investigation on traditional literature, and to suggest the improvements in the pronunciation of the word *gauḥ*, so that, on the epistemological side, the meaning of the word *gauḥ* is not lost; and on the musical side the melody of the music is not affected, so as to lose its aesthetic value.

In this kind of background, this thesis intends to find answers to the following questions :

1. Are these concepts *nāda* and *dhvani* the same or different ?
2. Wherefrom *nāda* originates ? What exactly is the nature of *nāda* according to classical theories in Indian philosophy ?

3. Is *nāda* a "substance," or a "quality" of some other substance or an "action" ? Is it eternal or non-eternal and transitory ?
4. Can *nāda* be an epistemological means of cognition or communication?
5. Can it assure better understanding and better aesthetic and spiritual means of communication, if its production is improved through vocal chord ?

Questions nos. 1 to 3 relate to the ontological aspects, as to origin and nature of *dhvani* and *nāda* involving the study of the Indian philosophical systems right from the pre-Vedic and Vedic times like *Upaniṣads, Ṣaḍdarśanas,* grammatology, *Tantrāgamas,* and musicology, etc., and the question nos. four and five relate to its epistemological, aesthetic and spiritual applications, involving the study of Indian *Sikṣāśāstras, Prātiśakhyās,* music, and *Tantrāgamas,* etc.

The Scope of the Study

The scope of the study consists in analytical review of the theories of *nāda* propounded by Indian philosophical systems, like Vedas, *Ṣaḍdarśanas, Tantrāgamas,* grammar, *Prātiśākhyas, Śikṣās,* musicology, etc. I also relied on the secondary material, in the form of books and journals, by modern thinkers like Dr. S. Radhakrishnan, Prof. Hiriyanna, Sir John Woodroff, V.N. Jha etc. clarify certain matters that were not clearly expressed in original *sūtras.* I also make it clear that while dealing with different aspects of *nāda* found in a particular system of philosophy, I propose to give the philosophical framework of that system, so as to ascertain the position of *nāda* in that system, for appreciating its ontological nature and its epistemological utility.

The Method Applied in My Research

I have adopted philosophical analysis as a method for analyzing and exploring the principles involved, in the evolution of the concept of *nāda*, with the help of the theories enunciated by Indian ancient classical thinkers and philosophers by using, as far as possible, the original Sanskṛt *sūtras* (aphorisms)[17] and commentaries (*bhāṣyās*)[18] and other Sanskṛt texts, with or without translations, in the concerned subjects, as my basic material.

Plan of the Research Work

The thesis attempts a philosophical analysis of *nāda* as spelt out in major Indian philosophical systems, including the philosophy of *Tantrāgamas*, grammarians, and musicologists and phoneticians, etc., in so far as they deal with *nāda* and its applications. The analytical structure of the research design is divided in twelve chapters as under:

1. Introduction – dealing with
   a. The meaning and definition of *nāda*
   b. The problems of *nāda* within the framework of Indian philosophical systems, relating to ontology, epistemology, aesthetics and spiritual realization.

2. Pre-Vedic and Vedic views on *vāk*, *nāda* and *dhvani*.
3. The concept of *nāda* or *śabda* in *Sāṅkhya*-Yoga systems.
4. *Nyāya-Vaiśeṣika* theories of *nāda*, *śabda* or *dhvani*.
5. The doctrines of *nāda* or *śabda* in *Mīmāṃsā* and *Vedānta*.
6. *Tantrāgama* theory of *nāda* or *śabda*.
7. The concept of *nāda* or *dhvani* in grammatical systems.
8. The theory of *nāda* according to musicology.
9. The theories of *śabda*, *dhvani*, *nāda* in heterodox schools – Cārvāka, Jainism and Buddhism.
10. Critical evaluation of different theories of *nāda*.
11. Vocal applications of the accepted theory of *nāda*.
12. Conclusion.

Keeping the above outlines in mind, I proceed with my investigation from the pre-Vedic and Vedic philosophy.

Notes and References

1. *Bṛhadāraṇyaka Upaniṣad*, 1.5.8.
2. Williams, Sir Monier Monier (1997), p. 738 & p. 549.
3. Swami Prajñananda (1973), pp. 3, 4 and 7.
4. Radhakṛshnan, S. Prof. (1997), p. 24.
5. Sharma, Chandradhar (2000), p. 13.
6. Ramanathan, A.A. (ed.) (1971), Vol. I; (1.7.1-4) ; Vol. III (1983).
7. *The New Lexicon Webster's Dictionary of the English Language* (1987), p. 1003.
8. Williams, Sir Monier Monier (1997).

9. Nyā. Su. II.ii.66.
10. *The New Lexicon Webster's Dictionary of the English Language:* (1987), p. 948.
11. *śrotragrahaṇo yorthaḥ sa śabdā*. - Jhalakīkara Bhīmācārya (1996), p. 860.
12. ....*pratītapadārthako loke dhvaniḥ śabda ityucyate. tadyathā - sabdam kuru, mā śabdam kārṣīḥ - śabdakāryayaṃ māṇavakaḥ, iti dhvaniṃ kurvannevamucyate - tasmāt dhvaniḥ śabdaḥ*- Śastri, Subramanya, P.S. (1944), Vol. I, p. 16.
13. Śastri, Subramanya, P.S. (1944), Vol. I, p. 17.
14. Gangopādhyāya, Dr. Anantalal (*tr.*) (1984) : *Dhvanyāloka*, p. 124.
15. Williams, Sir Monier Monier, (1997), p. 1285.
16. *The New Lexicon Webster's Dictionary of the English Language;* (1987), p. 948.
17. An undisputable gist in limited words of a universal rule or statement is called a *sūtra* (aphorism)

    "*alpākṣaramasandigdhaṃ sāravadviśvatomukham |*
    astobhamanavadyaṃ ca sūtraṃ śāstravido viduḥ"||

    Abhyankar K.V. (ed.) : (1967); 'Introduction' p. 1; Webster's Dictionary has also explained aphorism as "short, concise statement of a principle or a short, pointed sentence expressing a wise or clever observation or a general truth; maxim; adage."
18. *Bhāṣya* has been explained as

    '*sūtrārtho varṇyate yena padaiḥ sūtrānusāribhiḥ* |
    svapadāni ca varṇyante bhāṣyaṃ bhāṣyavido viduḥ ||

    "The *Bhāṣya* is that which explains the meaning of the *sūtra* by means of words in accordance with the *sūtra* and which also offers explanations of its own statements." - Jhā, Ganganatha (1982) : Introduction, p. iii.

* * *

Chapter Two

PRE-VEDIC AND VEDIC VIEWS ON *VĀK*, *NāDA* AND *DHVANI*

Pre-Vedic Concepts Relating to *nāda*

Indian philosophical thought, usually, was traced from the Vedas, due to lack of availability of necessary material, to assert the existence of the pre-Vedic civilization and its philosophy. But, as observed by Ramkumar Tripathi– "Archaeological discoveries at Harappa in the Montgomery district and Mohenjodaro in the Larkana district, besides other sites in the Punjab, Sind (like Canhudaro, Jhūkadaro), and Balochistan (e.g., *Nāl*, Kelat state), make it abundantly clear that several centuries before the period of the *Ṛgveda* there were busy centres of life and activity along the course of the river Indus. They show that people possessed a high degree of social life and culture, which was similar to, and in many respects more advanced than that of contemporary Mesopotamia, Elam, and Egypt." He further stated that "It has been suggested that they were the pre-Vedic people (probably Dravidian)....".[1]

In fact the credit of discovering Harappa and Mohenjo-daro civilization, religion and its philosophy should necessarily go to Sir John Marshall who was the Director-General of Archaeological Survey of India during the early part of the twentieth-century. His publication of "Mohenjodaro and the Indus civilization", in three volumes proved a turning point in the ancient Indian history, religion and philosophy. Sir John Marshall found adequate evidence for yogic cult, on the basis of image of meditating Śiva. He has found that the practice of Śiva-*yoga* including a deep devotion to Mother Goddess. On the basis of copper tablets, terracotta figurines, statutes, phallic objects, ritual vassals, metals and other structural remains found at the sites, John Marshall also recorded a number of other findings relating to the nature of civilization and religion and philosophy of Harappa and Mohenjodaro people. Majority of the subsequent researchers did not, broadly speaking, dispute his observations on the nature of their religion and their mode of worshipping tree, animals, and their worship of Goddess, etc.

In fact Marshall is amply quoted with approval by many of the subsequent writers. Regarding the nature of religion of Harappan times, Marshall observed that "....all the material of a religious nature recovered at Mohenjodaro and Harappa appears to be characteristically Indian. Although relatively meagre in proportion to the extent and importance of the sites, this material is sufficient at any rate to make it clear that iconic and aniconic cults existed side by side, and were just as compatible five thousand years ago as they are in the Hinduism of today. It exhibits to our eyes, on the one hand, the worship of the Mother Goddess, who still occupies a foremost place among the teeming village population of India; and side by side with her a god whom we have seen a good reason to recognize as the ancestor of the historic Śiva, the principle male deity of the Hindu pantheon....".[2]

Sudhakar Chattopadhyaya, an eminent scholar in ethnic elements of Indian traditions, accepted these findings of Marshall.[3] Prof. N.N. Bhattacharyya, an eminent Indologist and an authority on *Tantric* religion and philosophy, observes: "From the circumstantial evidence it, therefore, appears that the pre-Vedic religion of India consisted of the cult of Mother Goddess, worship of *linga*.... i.e., the concept of *Puruṣa* and *Prakṛti* the male and female principles of creation, and the practice of *yoga* in which the human body was conceived of as the abode of all mysteries of the universe. All these principles stood in reciprocal relation, being components of an undifferentiated religious and ritualistic complex, which subsequently came to be known as the *Tāntric* tradition".[4] This *Tāntric* tradition is also known as *Āgama* tradition.

From the above conclusions of the two eminent professors it follows that the *śiva-śakti* philosophy of *Tantrāgamas* in later years inherited in its "genes" from the Harappa Mohenjodaro culture, discovered by Marshall. Some scholars have described Vedic tradition as *Nigama* as against *Āgama* traditions. Both these, are said to be parallel traditions, from time immemorial, and many times, complementary to each other. One has influenced the other on many aspects.[5] For instance Śankarācārya, one of the most brilliant Advaitic philosopher of Vedic tradition that India has ever produced, gave vent, in the opening verse of his famous *stotra*, in *Saundarya Laharī* to his *Āgama* philosophy when he exclaimed :

śivaḥ śaktyā yukto yadi bhavati śaktaḥ prabhavituṃ
na cedevaṃ devo na khalu kuśalaḥ spanditumapi.

"Only if conjunction with Śakti would Śiva earn the privilege to become overlord; otherwise the God is not able even to stir."[6] In fact it is this *śiva-śakti* philosophy of *Tantrāgamas*, as we will see later, that has very much contributed the concept of *bindu* to the philosophy of *nāda*. *Nāda* and *bindu* are considered to be inseparable, just like Śiva and his *Śakti*. *Nāda* without *bindu* is soundless, just as Śiva without *Sakti* is powerless.

Vedic Views on *Vāk*, *Nāda* and *Dhvani*

Vedic seers, on the other hand, left the seeds of innumerable metaphysical concepts including the concept of *puruṣa*, *ṛtam*, *satyam*, *akṣara*, and *vāk*, etc., for the future to ponder over, reflect and develop further. Their enquiry left no stone unturned on every possible aspect of the universe and the life therein. Their approach to "....the object of their investigation, in no way differs much from that of the modern scientists. Whenever they faced the challenges in their search for truth, they tried to find out discoveries made by earlier thinkers on the problems that taxed their mind. They expressly mention how the modern intellectuals of their time, who are referred to in the Vedas as *dhīras*, *manīṣins*, etc., meaning the bold rationalists, proceed on their research in the field of hidden mysteries taking into account the progress in their investigations already made by their predecessors in the field".[7] Later thinkers also followed this Vedic methodology.

The investigations of Vedic seers proceeded on the basis of framing certain fundamental questions both of ontological nature and of epistemological nature for recording their findings. These questions are important for the purpose of this thesis, since the answers so provided by them would be important for my analysis of *nāda* or *dhvani*, in relation to the theories of later philosophical systems.

Ontological Questions

First I will take up the question of ontological nature. For instance, Ṛṣi Prajāpati Parameṣṭi, looking at this wonderful creation, raised a number of skeptic queries as to its ontological source and antiquity. But for my purpose it would suffice, if I take note of the following question only:

"Who verily knows and who can here declare it, whence it was born and whence comes this creation? The Gods are later-than this world's production. Who knows then whence it first came into being?"[8]

Ṛṣi Nārāyaṇa, pondering over the issue, replied that the omniscient and omnipresent and omnipotent divine being, *Puruṣa*, is the author of this creation. By describing the said *Puruṣa* he said:

"*Puruṣa*, who has a thousand heads, a thousand eyes, a thousand feet.

Investing the earth in all directions, exceeds (it by a space) measuring ten fingers".[9]

Here *Puruṣa* is conceived as an architect of the entire universe and the one who manifests it in the form of cosmic *vāk*. For this reason only, He is called Viśvakarman (The author of the universe) and the lord of speech (Vācaspati) RV.10.81.7); etc. Here the description of *Puruṣa* as being, "beyond ten fingers" indicates that the creator is not the sum total of the universe. He transcends it. Devichand interpreting a similar hymn in Atharvaveda (AV.9.6.1) stated that *daśāngulam* indicates that "the world is made up of ten parts: gross five : sky (*ākāśa*), air (*vāyu*), fire (*agni*), water (*jala*), earth (*pṛthvī*); five subtle elements: speech (*śabda*), touch (*sparśa*), sight (*rūpa*), taste (*rasa*), smell (*gaṇdha*). It may also mean ten quarters : four main, four intervening, above and below. It may mean heart, souls, abode in the body. Griffith translates it as a space of ten fingers, which is inappropriate in view of the infinite immensity of God."[10]

Ṛṣi Nārāyaṇa further adds :

"Such is his greatness; and *Puruṣa* is greater than this;
all beings are one-fourths of him; his other three-
fourths, (being) immortal, (abide). in heaven.
'Three-fourths of *Puruṣa* ascended;
the other fourth that remained in this
world proceeds repeatedly, and,
diversified various forms, went
to all animate and inanimate creation.

'From him was born Virāṭ and from
Virāṭ *Puruṣa*, he, as soon as born,
became manifested, and afterwards
(created) the earth (and) then corporeal forms".[11]

From the above description of *Puruṣa* it is clear that the ultimate reality conceived of by the vedic philosophers is an absolute reality, which consists of both transcendental and cosmic or phenomenal world. *Puruṣa* is called, Brahmaṇaśpati, Hiraṇyagarbha, Viśvakarmā, Prajāpati, etc., emphasizing His different functions. Atharvaveda calls Him *Kāla* (19.53.1) regulator of time. "He is one, but sages call Him by many names" (*ekam sat viprā bahudhā vadanti* – RV.1.164.46).

Then the next question that was posed for enquiry was: Is this creation chaotic or orderly?

For Ṛṣi Aghamarṣaṇa this Creation is orderly and regulated to the core. To quote:

"From fervour kindled to its highest,
Eternal law (*ṛtam*) and truth or existence
(*satyam*) were born:
Thence was the night produced, and thence
the billowy flood of sea arose.
From the same billowy flood of sea the year
was afterwards produced
Ordainer of the days and nights, Lord
Overall who close the eyes

Dhātar, the great Creator, then formed in
due order the sun and the moon
He formed in order heaven and earth, the
regions of the air, and light."[12]

From the above hymns of Aghamarṣaṇa, it is clear that the Creator (*dhātar* or *dhātṛ*) first created *ṛtam*, a body of universal principles to regulate His own creation (*satyam*) so that He may be free (or close His eyes). The phrase "who closes the eyes" indicates that these two principles – *satyam* and *ṛtam* being His own manifestations – by themselves would constitute the entire creation (the Creator remaining latent in them). The word *satyam* comes from the root *as* to be or to exist. *Sat* is the present participle, "being". *Satya* is "beingness", "the quality of existence", "the state or condition of Reality". It has come to mean, "Truth".[13] Thus, *satyam* accordingly would mean or in the present context, "the ultimate reality". On the other hand the word *ṛtam* comes from the root *"ṛ"* "to move" "to act". It means, therefore, "of truth movement" or 'movement towards truth" or "truth action". It is not merely amoral as some have interpreted it; it is the power of self-existent truth working out its purpose or end, spontaneously. The significance of *ṛtam* is seen in the word *ṛtu*, the inevitable but regular and spontaneous succession of time. It has come to mean "seasons". *Ṛtam* can therefore mean the omnipotence of the divine working out its purpose in the cosmos; it is the dynamic aspect of the truth.[14] In the words of Prof. S. Radhakrishnan, *"Ṛtam* is a unifying principle that determines ....course of things. It stands for law in general and the immanence of justice. This conception must have been suggested by the regularity of the movements of the sun, moon and stars, the alternations of day and of night, and of the seasons. *Ṛta* denotes the order of the world. Everything that is ordered in the universe has *ṛta* for its principle. It corresponds to the universals of Plato.... The universal is prior to the particular and so the Vedic seer thinks that *ṛta* exists before the manifestation of all the phenomena.... So *ṛta* is called the father of all.... Gradually it became the path of morality to be followed by man and the law of righteousness observed even by gods.... The whole universe is founded on *ṛta* and moves in it.... What law is in the physical world that virtue is in the moral world. The Greek conception of the moral life as harmony or an ordered whole is suggested here....".[15] To put it differently *ṛtam* is "form" and *satyam* is its "content". Hence, according to the Vedic *ṛṣis* they were born together (RV.10.190.1). It appears that *śiva-śakti* principles, out of which this universe has emerged, according to pre-Vedic philosophy, have taken the form of *ṛtam* and *satyam* principles in Vedic philosophy to discharge the same functions.

How exactly was the Creation evolved?

Ṛṣi Bṛhaspati Angīrasa described the process of this creation by saying that *Brahamaṇaspati* (i.e. *Puruṣa*) produced the existence with blast and smelting like a smith, from out of non-existence (*asataḥ sat jāyate* – RV.10.72.2) (similar to the Big-Bang Theory of the West). Thereafter the regions and earth sprang from the productive power– "Dakṣa was born from Aditi, and afterwards Aditi from Dakṣa", "....After her, Gods were born."

Pausing here for a moment, it is necessary to notice the notes appended by Wilson as a reply to Sāyaṇa's criticism that ".... there is contradiction here, since a self-produced effect cannot be the cause of itself." To which Yāska gave an answer that "Either they were born together or by divine law they reciprocally gave birth to each other and shared each other's nature" (Nir, xi.23). Griffith further adds that "Aditi is infinity or infinite, Dakṣa is force personified".[16] In my opinion Yāska's solution seems to be apt and justified. Vedic literature bears ample evidence to this kind of solution. Dakṣa and Aditi, here, may be personification of the *satyam* and *ṛtam* principles which are two aspects of the *Puruṣa* Himself.

Here Aditi is considered to be the mother of all the gods, viz., Indra, Varuṇa, Agni, Āditya, etc. Regarding the nature of these gods Max Mullar says: "....The process on which originally all gods depended for their existence, the personification of, or activity attributed to the great natural phenomena, while more or less obscured in all other religions, takes place in the *Ṛgveda* as it were in the full light of day. The gods of the Vedic, and indirectly of the Aryan people, were the agents postulated behind the great phenomena of nature...." (p. 36). And "they were distributed into three classes as gods of the sky, of the earth, and of the clouds" (p. 37 - last line).[17] It appears that these gods, which were natural forces personified as gods, took the form of *pañca mahābhūtas* during *upaniṣadic* time. For instance, *Taittirīya Upaniṣad* asserted that from *Brahman*, five basic elements arose – "From this Self (*Brahman*) verily ether arose: from ether, air; from air, fire; from fire, water; from water, the earth, etc., ... (*tasmādvā etasmādātmana ākāśaḥ sambhūtaḥ, ākāsādvāyuḥ, vāyuragniḥ, agnerāpaḥ, adhyaḥ pṛthvī* .... Tai. Up. 2.1). Even the human body is composed of five elements. Such elements are of two types – subtle and gross. (*Maitrī Upaniṣad* 3.2.2). These aspects are further clarified by Prof. S. Radhakrishnan as follows:

"In regard to the development of the universe, the *Upaniṣads* look on the earliest state of the material world as one of extension in space, of which the characteristic feature is vibration represented to us by the phenomenon of sound. From *ākāśa*, *vāyu* (air) arises. Vibration by itself cannot create forms unless it meets with obstruction. The interaction of vibrations is possible in air which is the next modification. To sustain the different forces, a third modification arises, *tejas*, of which light and heat are the manifestations. We still do not have stable forms and so the denser medium of water is produced. A further state of cohesion is found in earth. The development of the world is a process of steady grossening of subtle *ākāśa* or space. All physical objects, even the most subtle are built up by the combination of these five elements. Our sense experience depends on them. By the action of vibration comes the sense of sound; by the action of things in a world of vibrations the sense of touch; by the action of light the sense of sight; by the action of water the sense of taste; by the action of earth the sense of smell".[18]

Prof. Radhakrishnan also noted another theory, according to which Agni was the first element to be born and from Agni other elements were born. But he noticed that the very few accepted this theory.

Thus emerged the entire creation as duly determined and constituted out of fundamental Holy Law (*rtam*), which is the source of all laws like "Law of Gravitation", "Law of Motion", etc., that govern the physical world (*satyam*), consisting of five great elements (*pañca bhūtas*), viz., *pṛthvi*, *vāyu*, *āpa*, *teja*, *ākāśa*, which, in turn, regulate the entire phenomenal world and all its plants, animals, including man. It is these *pañca mahābhūtas*, which are the immediate ontological sources of "sound" or *nāda* according to later philosophers, as we will see, in the chapters to follow.

Epistemological Questions

Our forefathers, finding themselves as part of this wonderful creation, have been asking a number of epistemological questions also, in order to know one's relationship with the creation, including the one relating to the efficacy of one's knowledge of it, right from Vedic times. For instance Dīrghatmā Aucathyārṣi raised the following question:

"Ignorant, I inquire of the sages who know (the truth): not as one knowing (do I inquire), for the sake of (gaining) knowledge".[19]

"....What is the supreme heaven of (holy) speech (*vācaḥ*)?"[20]

His own reply is that – "this Brahmā is the supreme heaven of (holy) speech." (RV.1.164.35). According to Griffith, Brahmā here is "the highest heaven where speech abideth". Ṛṣi Dīrghatamā believed that Brahmā "....the lord and steadfast protector of all beings consigned me, (though) immature (in wisdom)...." [21], i.e., our intellect is yet too immature to grasp the reality. The man or the individual soul, being a product of the cosmic father (*pitaram*), partakes of His intellect, but of immature type. Such a person cannot share the fruits of the earth (sweet *pippal* fruit) unless he understands his protecting father (i.e., the ultimate reality) (RV.1.164.22). But Ṛṣi Dīrghātmās cosidering himself a person of the limited intellect, again raised a question:

"What thing I truly am I know not clearly:
mysterious, fettered in my mind I wander.
When the first-born of Holy Law (*ṛtam*)
approached me, then of this speech.
I first obtain a portion". [22]

I must note here that the text – *prathamajā ṛtasya ādidvācaḥ,* etc. – found in this hymn is being interpreted differently by Wilson and Griffith. According to Wilson's translation, based on Sāyaṇa's commentary it means....the first-born (perceptions) of truth reaches me, then immediately shall I obtain a portion (of the meaning) of the (sacred) word. But according to Griffith, "....When the first-born of Holy Law (*ṛtam*) approached me, then of this speech I first obtain a portion." But according to me the phrase *ṛtasya prathamajā* (the first-born of *ṛtam*), as a third alternative, can also be taken as the sun's rays, which cause visual "perception" of the external phenomena, serving as the first source of knowledge – though of a limited type. The word *ṛta* also means the sun [*ṛtamādityaḥ* – *ṛtam* means *āditya* (sun)].[23] In fact the preceding hymn (i.e. RV.1.164.36) speaks of Viṣṇu's ordinance (the laws of the sun). Here Viṣṇu is taken as the sun by both Wilson and Griffith. The sun through his rays or light causes our perceptions, as the first seed of our "thought". Our language or thought starts from such sensual perceptions. As Griffith interprets, this *vāk* can also be taken as the first manifestation of *ṛtam*, or Holy Law. However *ṛtasya prathamajā* equally admits the interpretation as 'perception' ('truth' means *satyam* or reality), as interpreted by Wilson. In all these interpretations, one thing is certain that *vāk* or *vacaḥ* is taken as the means of knowledge. If *ṛtam* stands for the "Universal Fundamental Law" that governs the "existence" (on the ontological side), then *vāk* stands as the means of apprehension of that law or reality, on epistemological side. Even if Wilson's interpretation of *vāk*, as "the first-born perception of truth" (*prathamajā ṛtasya*), is taken, then also my interpretation of *vāk* as the epistemological means of the knowledge of that "reality" stands fortified (may be due to his limited intellect, man may obtain a limited knowledge under the clause "of this speech I obtain a portion" found in the said hymn). It also suggests that with more maturity, man may obtain better knowledge. The hymns of all the four Vedas clearly reveal that the Vedic philosophers were optimistic in their approach.

I must emphasize that here the *vāk* or *vacaḥ* is used as "cosmic speech" or "cosmic-thought". Heavenly bodies by regularity in their movements, or by their uniform behavior, as determined by *ṛtam*, convey certain definite idea or meaning, as if they are talking among themselves. The *Ṛgveda* itself says: "The gods (of the three worlds : *Sūrya*, heaven, *Agni* earth and *Vāyu* sky) on the summit of the sky speak together in speech all-knowing but not all-impelling".[24] Wilson's translation clarifies it – "....in a language all-comprehending (but) not extending to all." The behaviors of the cosmic bodies are so co-ordinated so as to make us understand them, as if they are speaking amongst themselves or speaking to us. Sāyaṇa's illustration of the nature of this cosmic language, by an example of thunder–*vācam garjitalakṣaṇām* (i.e., thunder has the character of speech), is a very apt analogy in this context. Thus this *vāk* is the epistemological counterpart of the ontological rules or laws (*ṛtam*) which assures such predictable cosmic regularity. Hence *vāk*, in this sense, is the language or thought of the cosmic manifestations. In the words of *Ṛgveda*, "The fifteen chief forms (are found) in a thousand places; as heaven and earth are, so verily in that; the thousand great (functions) are in a thousand places; as Brahmā is variably developed, so is speech[25]." According to this hymn, thousands of "activities" or "functions" take place every moment in the universe, and by virtue of such activities in thousands of places in the universe, the entire reality (*Brahman*) has evolved. In this way the cosmic language (*vāk*), as the manifested phenomena of such reality has also accordingly developed, along with reality. Thus cosmic *vāk* is co-extensive with cosmic reality (*yāvad brahma viṣṭhitaṃ tāvatī vāk*–RV.10.114.8). In other words cosmic *vāk* stands for the totality of such "functions" or "activities" of the universe. As per Sāyaṇa, in this hymn, "there is perhaps a reference to the notion of the identity of the first cause and all created effects" and "each action or function (as sight, hearing, etc.) has its own *viṣaya* or object".[26] What perhaps Sāyaṇa meant by that was all such objects or functions of the cosmos being the manifestations of that primordial transcendental cause, are comprehensible by human intellect, through the senses of "sight," "hearing," etc., and each such object or its function is the *viṣaya* or object in "human thought" and thus every thing is nameable on the basis of the *nāma-rūpa* principle.

If it is so, then an important question arises: What is the extent of that reality that is comprehensible by "human intellect?"

According to *Ṛgveda*, the whole of the universe consists of four parts – "Three-fourths of *Puruṣa* (reality) ascended; the other fourth that remained in this world proceeds repeatedly, and diversified into various forms, went to all animate and inanimate creation".[27] If that is so, then corresponding *vāk* of that hidden three-fourth reality would necessarily lie beyond human comprehension. From that it follows that, on its epistemological side, *vāk* as a means of knowledge has to confine itself to that remaining one-fourth reality only, which "proceeds repeatedly" and which is "diversified in various forms" which is nothing but "phenomenal world" in Western philosophical term. Even regarding this part of the "diversified cosmic phenomenon", according to *Ṛgveda* (RV.1.164.45), men can have only one-fourth knowledge of that world. *Ṛgveda* said, "Four are the definite grades of speech, those *brāhmaṇas* who are wise know them: three, which are deposited in secret, indicate no meaning, men speak the fourth grade of speech (*turīyaṃ*)".[28] Even though the learned men may "think of" the existence of four divisions in cosmic speech, yet they can comprehend that one-fourth portion only, since the other three-fourth of it is "deposited in secret, indicating no meaning" (RV.1.164.45–Tr. by Wilson). In that view of the matter humans obtain a portion of the meaning (*bhāgamasyāḥ*) of that (sacred) word (*vacaḥ*). (1.164.37)

It is necessary to clarify here that the clause *catvārī vākparīmitā*, indicating the four divisions in cosmic *vāk*, is related or applicable to the fourth division of the reality conceived by *Ṛgveda* (in hymn 10.90.3 & 4) which is "diversified in various forms" which "went to all animals and inanimate creation i.e. in the cosmos." The four divisions of speech (*catvāri vākparimitā*) contemplated by *Ṛgvedic* hymn (RV.1.164.45) are accordingly related to this fourth part of the divisions of reality (contemplated by hymn 10.90.3&4) which is "diversified in various forms" which, "went to all animals and inanimate creation i.e., in the cosmos." This takes with it both the inarticulate language of inanimate objects and animals and the articulate language which the men speak. The concept of Vedic *vāk*, includes behavioral phenomena of the physical objects as determined by the laws of the physical world (*ṛtam*). For instance, an object not supported falls down. As if the "object" speaks to us saying "I will fall down, if there is no support to me (as per the law of gravitation)." Wittgenstein put the same idea in modern terminology – "The laws of physics, with all their logical apparatus, still speak, however indirectly, about the objects in the world."[29] According to Sāyaṇa, thunder has the characteristic of a language (*vācam garjitalakṣaṇam*). This kind of phenomenal behavior is taken as "inarticulate language" just like the language of animals expressed through their behavior and sounds. Out of the four divisions of language (*catvāri vākparimitā*) the three which are hidden in secret (*guhā nihitā*) are knowable by the experts (*maniṣin*), *ṛṣis* and yogis, and the last and fourth part called *turīyaṃ* (*turīyṃ vācaḥ manuṣyā vadanti*, a common man speaks – 1.164.45). *Brāhmaṇas* referred to here, according to Sāyaṇa, are the learned men (*manīṣinaḥ*) who are well-versed in *śabdabrahma* (i.e. experts in phonetics and language).

Commenting on the clause *catvāri vākparimitā padāni*, Sāyaṇa, following Yāska, explains that ".... the four '*padas*' may be a) *oṃ*, and the three sacred words *bhur*, *bhuvar*, *svar*, or b) the four parts of speech – nouns, verbs, prepositions and particles (as grammarians do); or c) the language of the *mantras*, the *kalpa* the *brāhmaṇa* and *laukika*, or current speech; (as taken by the *yājñikās*, i.e., the priests of sacrifices); or d) the languages of serpents, birds, insects, and man, or e) they may be *parā*, audible; *paśyanti*, visible, audible only to sages and saints; *madhyamā*, intelligible or expressive, proceeding from the heart; and *vaiśavarī*, articulate, as residing in the mouth and enunciated by the palate, lips, tongue (as the phoneticians think), etc., or f) again, they may be the languages of the three upper worlds and of the world of man".[30] (The bracketed portion are inserted by me by way of clarification.)

For the purpose of this thesis, the fourth and the fifth categories noted by Yāska are relevant. According to Yāska's fourth category, there can be four types of language: 1) snakes, 2) birds, 3) insects, and 4) man. But the language of snakes, birds and insects together may be classified as inarticulate language, and the language of man as articulate. *Ṛgveda* also distinguishes between inarticulate speech of the animals and articulate speech of man. For instance the hymn RV.8.100.11 states that thc major portion of *vāk* has gone towards speech of the animals of every kind, which they utter and use in their day to-day communications: "The gods produced the goddess *vāk*; here do animals of every kind utter".[31] Here the hymn contains a clause: "animals of every kind utter", Śāyaṇa comments: "whether their utterances be articulate or inarticulate." There are some *Ṛgvedic* hymns to show how the cow and calf communicate with each other by their inarticulate sounds.

"The cow bellows for her calf, (who stands) with winking eyes, and lows as (she) proceeds to lick his forehead: she utters a cry, as anxious, she sees the moisture in the corners of his mouth, and nourishes him with her milk."

"He, (calf) too, bellows, and the cow utters inarticulate sounds, as, encompassed by him, she repairs to her stall; (influenced) by her instincts, she acts like a human being, and, radiant, manifests her nature."[32]

By conducting research on the same lines, as *Ṛgveda* did, modern scientists have found that animals and insects do communicate with each other by sending "sounds" of different frequencies, for varied purposes, like inviting for courtship, alarm calls warning impending danger, fear and distress calls, navigation calls for locating obstacles and to locate and evade predators, etc., etc. Humans do not hear most of the communications of insects because of inaudible frequencies of sounds they emit through a particular part of their body, like wings, legs, etc. Even in the case of audible communications, unless one is an expert (or *maniṣin*, in the words of . *Ṛgveda*), in the mode and purpose of communication of particular species of animal, it is difficult to follow such communication or language.[33] All such inaudible languages, or audible but unintelligible languages, of the animals are the one which fall within that three-fourth of the *vāk* hidden in the phenomenal world and accordingly are outside the scope of my thesis. But the "articulate part of language" as spoken to by Sāyaṇa, in his phrase "whether their utterances be articulate or inarticulate", falls within the scope of the investigation of this thesis.

In relation to the "articulate language", the other four divisions spoken of by Sāyaṇa, (commenting on RV. 1.164.45) like: *para*, *paśyanti*, *madhymā*, and *vaikharī* have got to be the parts of that one-fourth of the *turīyam*.[34] This one-fourth of the reality relatable to the world – that "proceeds repeatedly and diversified in various forms" – may be described as phenomenal as against three-fourth transcendental reality, (as per RV.10.90.3-4), which is hidden in the heaven (universe). Of the four divisions of phenomenal language, it is only *vaikharī* ("colloquial language") that is spoken by a common man, the other three being hidden in the human body,[35] or hidden with animal kingdom (of course knowable by the experts and by *ṛṣi's* and yogis). The word *vaikharī* in Saṅskṛt means "articulate utterance", that means the utterance in "sounds or words consisting of full and intelligible sentences."[36] The other three which are hidden in human heart, (or in human body) being imperceptible and inaudible are considered as *anāhata nāda* (inaudible sound), by the phoneticians, and the fourth one, which is being expressed or uttered in audible sounds is called *āhata nāda* or *vaikharī*. A point to be born in mind, in this context is that, as in the case of cosmic *vāk*, the other three-fourth, relatable to three-fourth of the universe is hidden in the heaven (or cosmos). In the case of human *vāk* relatable to *turīyam* also, the other three-fourth is hidden in the human body or human heart or in the animal kingdom. If that is so, the remaining one-fourth of cosmic *vāk*, which is amenable to human comprehension (*turīyam vāco manuṣyā vadanti*–1.164.45), becomes "human *vāk*", with further four divisions as *parā*, *paśyantī*, *madhyamā* and *vaikharī*. Out of these four, the first three are comprehensible only by *maniṣin* or the *pandits*, who are experts in phonetics; and a common man knows only the fourth one, i.e., *vaikharī*. From this it follows that the *vaikharī* would be one-fourth of human *vāk*; and human *vāk* itself is one-fourth of the cosmic *vāk*. It means that an ordinary man, who knows, only *vaikharī*, knows one-sixteenth of the cosmic language. Please note that according to Vedic seers, the human *vāk* in this manner is ultimately a part of cosmic *vāk*.

Another aspect of the cosmic *vāk* is in this context that should command our attention is that the concept of cosmic *vāk* mainly stands for the cosmic phenomena that is reflected in "human thought" which human language manifests. The "thought" or "the meaning" one conceives can be conveyed to others through human language (*vāk*), to make them understand also the same. In human language this is the basic feature of the language. If so, a question may arise: "Wherefrom is the 'meaning' or 'thought' conveyed, in cosmic *vāk*, to call it a 'speech' (*vacaḥ*), on the analogy of our own language? My answer is that it is *ṛtam* that conveys the meaning by assuring the cosmic regularity. The function of *ṛtam* is, just like the conventions in human language, to provide rules to cosmic *vāk* in order to make it a 'cosmic-language.' The regularity assured by *ṛtam* itself provides meaning to the cosmic *vāk*. For example, the presence of thick and dark clouds accompanied by thunder means that it may rain shortly; if not, here at least somewhere else. This is being observed by humans, everywhere and at every time; or the nature has taught us this eternal relation between phenomenal behavior and its meaning, from times immemorial. If that is so, the principle of *ṛtam* makes us to understand this cosmic phenomena on the basis of observable "causal relations" in the cosmos or in the "external world." For example, our understanding of "logical relation" is nothing but a comprehension of the "causal relation" amongst the cosmic or physical objects. In the words of Ludwig Wittgenstein – "The exploration of logic means the exploration of everything that is subject to law."[37] "Wherever there is smoke, there is fire" (*yatra yatra dhūmaḥ, tatra tatra vahniḥ* – is a logical proposition). It is based on the "causal relations" amongst the physical objects i.e., the fire always causes smoke and as such "fire" is the cause, and the "smoke" is the effect; and on the basis of that we infer the existence of "fire" on the basis of the "smoke" it has emitted. This is so, according to the law of nature (*ṛtam*). Thus the laws of nature and laws of logic are two aspects of the same reality. "One might say, using Hert'z terminology, that only connections that are subject to law are thinkable (Tractatus)".[38] Because of this principle of *ṛtam*, the Vedic thinkers found an inseparable relationship between *vāk* and "thought." The

Taittirīya Saṃhitā explains this kind of relationship between *vāk* and "thought" as under:

"Thou art thought", he says; for what one thinks in the mind one expresses in speech. "Thou art meditation" he says; for one meditates with the mind one expresses in speech.[39] In other words, "We cannot think what we cannot think; so what we cannot think we cannot say either" (Tractatus).[40] In this context the observation of Prof. Max Muller is also worth noting:

"Some of the Brahmanic thinkers say in so many words that speech is Brahman (Satap. Br. II.1.4.10 – *Vāg vai Brahma*), and the co-existence of Brihaspati and *Brahmaṇas* could hardly have failed to suggest to them the identity of *Brahman* and *bṛh* in the sense of speech, just as every thoughtful Greek must have known that there was a reason why Logos meant both word and thought."[41] Hence it is clear that Vedic *vāk* stands for a concept, which combines in itself both "speech and thought." Just like "logos" in Greeks, we can describe Indian *vāk*.... as.... "thought-word" or "word-thought." At least I can think of no better expedient.[42]

From the above discussion, it is clearly established that, we understand cosmic world through cosmic *vācaḥ* or *vāk*, which is the first manifestation of *ṛtam*, (*prathamajā ṛtasya*). *Ṛgvedic* thinkers did not stop there. They also wanted to know "where from and how the cosmic language itself is manifested", and in order to probe on these lines they posed another question:

"I ask you, what is the supreme heaven of (holy) speech ?"[43] *Ṛgveda* answered the question by saying ".... This *Brahmā* (the reality) is the supreme heaven of (holy) speech".[44] Ṛṣi Dīrghatamas further asked another question: "How this *vāk* (cosmic language) is manifested?" Their answer to that was the *vāk* rest on *akṣara* (imperishable entity) which manifests it : "Even gods (*pañca bhūtas,* etc., natural forces) have taken their seats upon this Supreme Heaven, the imperishable *akṣara* and even Veda itself rests on that *akṣara* (*ṛco akṣare parame vyoman*); and those who know this principle would understand Vedas and those who understand Vedas are perfect persons" (RV.1.164.39).

Of the phrase *"ṛco akṣare parame vyoman"*, found in the above hymn, Yāska in his *Nirukta* has an enlightening explanation. According to him *akṣara* is *oṃ* on which all the gods repose. "Those who do not know this Supreme word; what can they do with *ṛcaḥ* only, and those who know it are well placed" is the advice of the learned.

What is that word *akṣara*? Yāska says "It is *oṃ*, in the opinion of Śākapūṇi".[45] (Śākapūṇi was an ancient Grammarian.)[46] Therefore, here, *oṃ* is the ultimate reality (*Brahman*) on which everything, including *vāk*, rests.

Even *Upaniṣads*, pursued their enquiry on the basis of the above propositions, and stated that *oṃ* itself denotes "the ultimate reality." *Taittirīya Upaniṣad* declares that "*oṃ* is Brahman; *oṃ* is this all" (*omiti brahma, omitidam sarvaṃ*).[47] For *Brahmavidyopaniṣat*: "A single syllable *oṃ* itself is Brahman or reality".[48] The same is also the statement in

Bhagavadgītā (Bha. Gītā 8.13). *Muṇḍaka Upaniṣad* asserts the same, though in a different manner, when it says: "One should know that this *akṣara* by itself is *Puruṣa* and the reality".[49] *Māṇḍukya Upaniṣad* elaborating the transcendental nature of that *AUM* states : "*AUM*, this syllable is all this. An explanation of that (is the following). All that is the past, the present and the future; all this is only the syllable *AUM*. And whatever else there is beyond the three-fold time, that too is only the syllable *AUM*."[50] According to this *Upaniṣad* there are four parts in this syllable – A, U, M and *Turīya* : a). *Vaiśvānara* (waking state) (represented by letter "A"), b). *Tejasa* (dreaming state) (represented by letter "U") and c). *Prajñā* (deep sleep) (represented by letter "M") and transcending all these three states there is the fourth one called *turīya*. The *turīya* is the non-dual state of the reality. In this state ".... syllable *AUM* is the very self." Prof. Radhakrishṇan offers his own comments on this statement: "This soundless, partless, supreme reality is the very self.... In this experience of '*turīya*', there is neither subject nor object.... It is pure consciousness without any state of duality; it is unfailing light".[51]

Thus this syllable *oṃ* is the transcendental reality, which is a state of pure "consciousness" that manifests this world of animate and inanimate objects. In this view of the matter "The entire world and the entire animal kingdom is dependent on it".[52] Even human soul is part of it. Bhartṛhari also meant this kind of "Cosmic consciousness" when he said: "The speech (or word) exists within and outside all living beings in the form of consciousness (*caitanya*)".[53] According to him the consciousness within enables the man to understand cosmic consciousness of the external world. This kind of metaphysical theory is commonly shared by almost all the Indian philosophical systems. It means that the ultimate reality (*Praṇava*) is knowable through human consciousness and human speech. Even human syllable *oṃ* or *praṇava* (or speech emanated by it) is itself the manifestation of cosmic *praṇava*. This cosmic *praṇava* is nothing but cosmic *śakti* or cosmic creative force. In view of this commonly accepted metaphysical principle Bhartṛhari asserted that – "Almost all Indian (schools) without contradiction, accepted that the God's creation is capable of being grasped through one word in the form of *praṇava* (*AUM*)".[54] Having regard to this theory only even Patañjali said that the *praṇava* is the manifesting word for Brahman (*tasya vācaka praṇavaḥ*).[55]

Agreeing with Prof. Fatah Singh, it may be concluded that "When *vāk* came to mean *śakti* (consciousness) evolving into, and lying at the root of all manifold creation, *oṃ* as the essence of *vāk* was thought to be co-extensive with it and hence pervading the whole temporal creation."[56] On this *akṣara* (*oṃ*) the entire universe with all its cosmic bodies (*devatās*) and their *vāk* rest according to *Ṛgveda* (R.V.1.164.39). Hence, Aitareyabrāhmaṇa rightly said: "neither the sea nor the *vāk* can ever be exhausted".[57]

But the nature of this "cosmic *vāk*" is entirely different from "human *vāk*." Madhusūdana Sharma, a Vedic scholar, referring to *Ṛgveda* (RV.1.164.42) (*tasyāḥ samudrā* ....etc.), and *Taittirīya Brāhmaṇa* (T.B.2.8.8.5 *vāgākṣaraṃ prathamajā ṛtasya*), observes that "there is no ear perceptible sound" in this kind of "cosmic *vāk*" similar to the sound in human *vāk*. Hence it cannot be heard by the human ears, like any other phenomenal sound. Hence this "cosmic *vāk*" being without sound cannot be equated with *vāk* which the humans speak. According to him, here the word *vāk* is used (with reference to "cosmic *vāk*") in a figurative sense (*aupacārika*). The author takes support from the statement of *Manusmṛti*, which says that the said vedic-*vāk* is without sound (*nirmame*) (*vedaśabdebhya evādau pṛthak saṃsthāśca nirmame*–1.21). He further states that soundless holy speech (*deva vācaḥ*) is the cause of the world.[58] Even according to Gandharva tantra, *praṇava* referred in the three Vedas has no sound.[59] Here sound is used in the sense of sounding-phenomena perceptible to ears. But the cosmic-sound (*praṇava*) as the manifesting transcendental reality or the "cosmic *vāk*" the manifested phenomena of the reality has no "sound". *Praṇava*, thus, stands for such a totality of "transcendental manifestation of consciousness" of reality on which *vāk* rests (RV.1.164.34-35). The external world (manifestation of transcendental consciousness) communicates through stimuli and man comprehends through senses (attached to the consciousness of the soul through mind). In this way cosmic *nāda* is the manifester of cosmic *vāk*. This *praṇava* in its subtle form is "non-sounding" (*anāhata*) cosmic energy or *śaktī* that causes vibrations or spanda which in turn causes "physical sound" (*āhatanāda*). According to Kullūka

Bhaṭṭa, the commentator of *Manusmṛti*, this cosmic *vāk* stands for the totality of all the means (*pramāṇas*) like perception, inference, etc., which man uses to comprehend the reality (*Manusmṛti* -1.21). In this view of the matter, in my opinion, *praṇavá* stands for a metaphysical "category" by which the totality of "stimuli", the reality manifest, and also for the totality of all senses, which man possesses, in order to comprehend it. *Praṇava*, by itself is the ultimate reality, from the ontological point of view, and it is also a means of human knowledge from the epistemological point of view.

The importance of *vāk* in *Ṛgveda* is heightened in the personification of *vāk* sometimes as *Vācaspati* (Brahma) and sometimes as Goddess Saraswati. In fact, the Goddess of *vāk* declares:

"I, verily, myself announce and utter the 'Word' that Gods (creative forces of the nature) and men alike shall welcome".[60]

So far as the men are concerned they speak "*turīyam* (*turīyaṃ vāco manuṣyā vadanti*)"[61]. As I have noted above this *turīyaṃ vācaḥ* has gone to the part of the world that "proceeds repeatedly," which is "diversified in various forms" and which, "went to all animate and inanimate creation (of the cosmos)" (RV.10.90.3 & 4). Wilson notes the comments offered by both learned commentators of *Ṛgveda*–Śāyaṇa and Mahīdhara–according to whom the phrase "proceeds repeatedly" means "either in individual by death or by birth, or in the world by its temporary dissolution or renovation", and the word *sāśanānaśane* means "those who eat and those who do not; that is, the two classes of created things, those capable of enjoyment, etc., as gods, men, animals, or incapable thereof, as mountains and rivers, conscious (animate) and unconscious (in animate) creation".[62]

From this kind of description, it is clear that this part of world to which the last part of *vāk* called *turīyam vācaḥ* has gone to the world we live in, this is normally called "phenomenal world" by the Western thinkers. According to *Ṛgveda* the fourth part of the cosmic language called *turīyam vācaḥ* has gone to men (RV.1.164.45) who live in this "phenomenal world."

This *turīyam vācaḥ* was known as the "articulate language" during the post-Vedic time. So far as the human language is concerned (unlike cosmic *vāk*) it necessarily manifests through this *vaikharī dhvani*, a sound produced by vocal organs. In fact *Ṛgveda* itself explains the sound phenomenon, that manifests itself, when someone utters "Gauri":

"(When the word) Gaurī is uttered (*gaurīmimāya*), once, (the sound that manifests) in space (*salila*) by multiplying twice, four times, eight times, nine times, etc. (*ekapadi, dvipadi, catuṣpadi, navapadi*) becomes thousand letters (*sahasrākṣaro babhūva*) (or particles) in the infinite sky (*parame vyoman*)" (RV.1.164.41); this is how sound travels, in all directions, even according to modern physics.

I pause here to emphasize a point that the Vedic *ṛṣis*, also used the word *nāda*. But they used it, sometimes in the sense of sound (*dhvani*) and sometimes in the sense of human voice.[63]

Ṛgveda also noticed that in the utterance of human language (*vacaḥ*) thousands of functions take place in the human body, just like thousands of functions taking place in thousands of places, in fifteen chief forms, in cosmos (RV.10.114.8). Śāyaṇa's commentary clarifies those fifteen chief forms or actions in *vāk* that take place in human body such as: *cakṣuḥ* (eyes), *śrotraṃ* (ears), *manaḥ* (mind), *vāk* (speech), *prāṇa* (life)–these five (*pañcendriyās*–sense organs) and the other five, (*pañca mahābhūtas*–gross elements) that support like parents: *pṛthvī* (earth), *āp* (water), *tejas* (fire), *vāyu* (air), and *ākāśa* (space), and the five objects of senses (*tanmātras*–subtle elements) speech (*śabda*), touch (*sparśa*), sight (*rūpa*), taste (*rasa*), smell (*gandha*)–all of them together manifest thousands of objects, to whom the learned give thousands of names. In other words, five *pancendriyas*, supported by five *pañca mahābhūtas* and five *tanmātras* manifest the world and its objects in human speech.[64]

According to *Ṛgveda*, the "human-*vāk*" started by giving names to the objects of the world, which is "diversified in various forms" (RV.10.90.4), which are generally described as *nāma-rūpa* (name and form) principle. *Ṛgveda* says, "When men like Bṛhaspati, giving names to objects, sent out *vāk's* first and earliest utterances...." (Griffith's Tr.), (RV.10.71.1). Later the *ṛṣis* cleaned it, just like corns are cleaned of husk, etc. While using this language in Vedic sacrifices, they made it sweet and musical by employing the seven notes. Vedic scholars treated language as man's best friend. A person using language without knowing the true importance of it would be like a blind husband to whom his fond and beautiful and well-dressed wife reveals herself. (RV.10.71.1-5). Emphasizing the importance of language *Ṛgveda* said that a person who does not know language would always be in delusion without knowing "the path of a righteous action".[65]

From the entire above analysis, it is clear that the Vedic *ṛṣis* used *Vāk* or *Vacaḥ* both for "cosmic *vāk*" and for "human *vāk*", as pointed out by Yāska in his *Nirukta*. "Therefore *brāhmaṇās* speak of *vāk* both for cosmic *vāk* (*devānām*) and for human *vāk* (*manuṣyāṇām*) (*tasmād brāhmaṇā ubhayīṃ vācam vadanti yā ca devānām yā ca manuṣyāṇām)* (Yāska's *Nirukta* -13.9).[66] But as I have explained above, the "cosmic *vāk*" is different from "human *vāk*". They operate it in two different spheres, one in cosmos (as transcendental or as "*a priori*" cosmic principle) in the form of varied predictable laws (*ṛtam*), the other in human body, (as empirical or "*a posteriori*" principle). The "cosmic *vāk*" is manifested through "cosmic *omkāra*" (the totality of the transcendental phenomena) and the human *vāk* is manifested through sound produced in vocal chords. But, by confusing one for the other the later scholars, propounded conflicting theories in Indian classical philosophical systems, generally known as *ṣaḍdarśanas*.

The *ṣaḍdarśanas* alongwith non-orthodox schools, like Jainism and Buddhism, etc., set a new trend in Indian philosophical thought. They are acknowledged as Indian philosophical systems, as counterparts of the systems of the West. Each one of these systems made use of a new technique called *nyāya* or logic for justifying its own "premises" or denying the "premises" of others.

The main aim of the propounders of the *ṣaḍdarśanā* schools, was to positively justify Vedic philosophy and its authority. Hence they retained certain basic concepts of Veda like *ṛtam* and *satyam*. In fact *Taittirīya Upaniṣad* had directed both the teachers and the students: "Let the learning of *ṛtam* and *satyam* principles be part of your teaching and study" (*ṛtaṃ ca svādhyāya pravacane ca, satyaṃ ca svādhyāya pravacane ca*–1.9.1). Hence they could not avoid them. In the circumstances *ṣaḍadarśanā* schools used them either by suitably modifying them or by giving them new names or new terminologies to avoid the confusion already created by varied meanings and interpretations assigned to such concepts in Vedic literature. For instance as pointed out by A.B. Purani, Sāyaṇa himself assigned, not less than twenty-one meanings to the word *ṛtam*, as "sacrifice, truth, speech, water, sun, *ṛta*-god, true action, hymn, home, prayer, etc., etc., and this increased.... the uncertainty and confusion in the minds of the student."[67] Likewise the word *satyam* or *satya* was also used in a number of senses as "being", "existence", "truth", "sun", etc.[68] In these circumstances, the thinkers of the classical schools avoided using the terms like *ṛtam*, or *satyam* but nevertheless made use of the principles underlying these concepts under different new terminologies. For instance, *Mīmāṃsā Sūtra* of Jaimini used *dharma*–in the sense of duty or law in the place of *ṛtam*. Likewise, *adṛṣṭa* in *Nyāya-Vaiśeṣika* and in *Mīmāṃsā*; *avyakta* in *Sāṅkhya*-Yoga, etc., are the concepts embodying *ṛtam* principle only. The same is the position regarding the concept of *satyam*. The orthodox schools used *satyam* principle in their systems under new terminologies like *prakṛti, dravya, sat*, etc. In the course of discussion I will be highlighting these aspects, wherever it is found to be feasible. However, it is also seen that *ṣaḍadarśanā* thinkers during the course of their investigation, adopted the principles of some other system on varied aspects. *Nyāya-Vaiśeṣika* systems are the classical instances. *Vaiśeṣika* developed a metaphysical system and used the logical apparatus developed by *Nyāya* as its companion. Likewise, *Nyāya* used *Vaiśeṣikas* ontological theories for developing its own epistemological techniques for application. The same is true for *Sāṅkhya*-Yoga and *Mīmāṃsā-Vedānta*. Having regard to their interrelationship, the majority of the writers on Indian philosophy have discussed them as twins. I also adopt the same method to avoid repetition of the common aspects found in the twin systems. So far as heterodox systems, like *Cārvāka*, Jainism and Buddhism are concerned, I refer to them, with a view to notice their "counter-point of view", to the contentions raised by the orthodox schools, wherever it is necessary, as done by some of the orthodox schools themselves, in their respective systems. I will also consider them as indepenent systems. In addition there are other theories of *nāda* or *dhvani* enunciated by *Tantra* and *Āgama* systems; by the grammarians and phoneticians; and by the musicologists, etc., I am going to consider them also. With this background, I now proceed to consider these systems with a special emphasis on the concept of *nāda*, *śabda* or *dhvani* (sound) as expounded by each one of them, in order to ascertain the philosophical concepts of *nāda* in Indian philosophical tradition.

* * *

The gist of the Pre-Vedic and the Vedic Views on *Vāk, Nāda* and *Dhvani*

The outstanding contribution of the Vedic seers, from ontological point of view, were the concepts *ṛtam* and *satyam*, and from epistemological point of view the concept of *vāk* or *vācaḥ*. *Ṛtam* is a regulatory mechanism of the *Satyam* (the existence). They are similar to *śiva* and *śakti* principles of the pre-Vedic times the relics of which are found in later *Tantrāgama* systems. *Vāk*, being the first manifestation of *ṛtam* principle, rests on *akṣara* or *oṃkāra nāda* or *Puruṣa* (the ultimate reality).

The concept of *praṇava* is critically examined with reference to *Upaniṣads*.

Vāk is the "cosmic language" expressed in an inarticulate mode through the cosmic activity. In the words of Sāyaṇa "the thunder" has the characteristic feature of language that it would rain shortly (*vacogarjit lakṣaṇam*). On the other hand, human language started on the basis of articulate language by naming the objects on the basis of *nāma-rūpa* (name and form) principle. Thus there emerged two kinds of languages: Vedic cosmic language (*Deva Bhāṣā*) being manifested by *akṣara* or *oṃkāra nāda* and the colloquial *Sanskṛt Bhāṣā* expressed in human voice or *dhvani*. But the later learned scholars, used the word *vāk* or *vacaḥ* in both the senses, without appreciating the difference between these two. Such confusion gave rise to the conflicting theories, in Indian philosophical systems, like *ṣaḍdarśanas,* etc., as we will see hereunder.

Notes and References

1. Tripathi, Rama Shankar (1992) : p. 16 and p. 24.
2. Marshall, John Sir (1931) : p. 76.
3. Chattopadhyaya, Sudhakar (1979) : pp. 22-23.
4. Bhattacharyya, N.N. (1999) : p. 159.
5. Iyengar Srinivasa, P.T. (1909) : pp. 130-31.
6. Sastri Subrahmanya, S. and Ayyangar Srinivasa, T.R. (2000).
7. He quotes: *pūrvesām panthām anudṛshya dhīrā anvalebhire rathyo na raśmin* (RV. 10.130.7) - (Viewing the path of the *ṛṣis* of bygone age the modern intellectuals have taken up reins like chariot-drivers) - Sharma, B.R. (1991): pp. 108-09.
8. RV. X.129.6; Griffith, R.T.H. (1973).
9. RV. 10.90.1; Wilson, H.H. (2001) : p. 423.
10. Devichand (*tr.*) (1997) : p. 727.
11. RV. 10.90.2-5 (Wilson).
12. RV. 10.190.1, 2 & 3 (Griffith).
13. Purani, A.B. (1963) : p. 101.
14. — (1963) : p. 101.

15. Radhakrishnan, S. Prof. (1997), Vol. I, pp. 78-79.
16. R.V. 10.72.4-5 (Wilson).
17. Muller, Max K.M. (1998) : pp. 36-37.
18. Radhakrishnan, S. (1994) : pp. 55-56.
19. R.V. 1.164.6 (Wilson).
20. R.V. 1.164.34 (Wilson).
21. R.V. 1.164.21 (Wilson).
22. R.V. 1.164.37 (Griffith).
23. Bhaṭṭācārya, Tārānātha Tarka Vācaspati (2003) : p. 1429.
24. R.V. 1.164.10 (Griffith).
25. R.V. 10.114.8 (Wilson).
26. Wilson, H.H. (2001) : Vol. IV, p. 490.
27. R.V. 10.90.4 (Wilson).
28. R.V. 1.164.45 (Wilson).
29. Wittgenstein, Ludwig (1961).
30. Wilson (*tr.*): p. 433.
31. R.V. 8.100.11 (Wilson).
32. R.V. 1.164.27–28 (Wilson).
33. Sarkar, Bharati (1999) : p. 31.
34. R.V. 1.164.45; (Wilson), Vol. I: p. 433.
35. *trīṇi-parā paśyanti madhyamā etāni padāni guhāyām śarīramadhye nihitāni sthāpitāni vartante–Dharmkosha* (1950): p. 349.
36. Williams, Sir Monier Monier (1997) : p. 1020.
37. *Tractatus* 6.3.
38. *Tractatus* 6.3431; p. 141.
39. Keith, A.B. (*tr.*) (1914) : Part II, Kaṇda vi. 1.8, p. 495.
40. *Tractatus* 5.61 (Wittgenstein).
41. Muller, Max (1998) : p. 69.
42. — (1887) Preface - page ii.

43. R.V. 1.164.34 (Wilson).
44. R.V. 1.164.35 (Wilson).
45. Yāska's *Nirukta* (13.10).
46. Williams, Sir Monier Monier : p. 1062.
47. *Taittirīya Upaniṣad* (1.8.1) : Radhakrishnan, S. (1994): p. 535.
48. *Om̐ iti ekākṣaram brahma* (*Brahmavidyopaniṣad*) (Verse No. 2) Paṇḍita, Jagadīśa Śāstri (1996): p. 292.
49. *yenākṣaram puruṣam veda satyam* (*Muṇḍaka Up.* 1.2.13.). Radhakrishnan, Prof. S. (1994) : p. 695.
50. Mā. Up. 1. Radhakrishnan, Prof. S. (*tr.*) (1994) : p. 695.
51. *turīyaḥ sarvadṛk sadā* : Kārikā 1.12; Radhakrishnan, Prof. S. (1994): p. 702.
52. *Omkāram prabhavam sarvam trailokyam sacarācaram* (*Dhyānabindu Upaniṣad*, verse 16) – Paṇḍita Jagadīśa Śāstri (1996): p. 286.
53. *Vākyapādīya* 1.41 (Korada Subramanyam).
54. *Vākyapādīya* 1.9 (Korada Subramanyam).
55. Patañjali's *Yoga Sūtra* (*Samādhipāda*), (verse 27).
56. *Omityetadakṣaramidaṃ sarvaṃ tasyopavyākhyānaṃ bhūtaṃ bhavad bhaviṣyāditi sarvamoṅkāra eva* (Mā. Up.2); Singh, Prof. Fatah : p. 115.
57. *na vai vākkṣīyate na ca samudraḥ* – *Aitareyabrāhmaṇa*, verse 23.1. (Pandeya, Devendra Nath; 1997)
58. Śarma, Madhusūdana (1996) : p. 30.
59. *vedatrayātsamuddhrutya praṇavaṃ nirmame purā*–*Gandharva Tantra*, Verse 18.57; Rai, Rāmkumāra : p. 140.
60. R.V. 10.125.5 (Griffith). Note : Bible also said : "In the beginning was the word and the word was with God and the Word was God" (3:14); referred in, AUM - *The Essence of the Veda* (1993); Kendra Worker.
61. R.V. 1.164.45.

62. Wilson, H.H. (2001) : p. 424; Vol. IV.
63. For instance, see the statements like "Raising my voice in praise of Agni" (*yoṣaṇā nadasya nāde pari pātu me manaḥ* etc. (R.V. 10.11.2); and also a statement – "Enfeeble the artificial high soundings of the enemy" etc. – *arasaṃ kutrimam nādamarasāḥ sapta visrasaḥ* (R.V. 19.34.3); Devi Chand (1997).
64. Muller, F. Max (1983) : (R.V. 10.114.8): p. 382, Vol. IV.
65. R.V. 10.71.6. (Griffiths) : p. 584.
66. *tasmād brāhamaṇā ubhayīṃ vācam vadanti yā ca devānām yā ca manuṣyāṇām* – Yāska's *Nirukta*, Verse No. 13.9.
67. Purani, A.B. (1963) : Ch. III; p. 50.
68. — (1963) : Ch. III; p. 101.

* * *

Chapter Three

THE CONCEPT OF *NĀDA* OR *ŚABDA* IN *SĀṄKHYA*-YOGA SYSTEMS

Sāṅkhya is famous for its theory of cosmic evolution and *Yoga* for its meditative techniques. Both *Sānkhya* and Yoga share common ontological theory.

Sāṅkhya is ".....so called because it enumerates twenty five *tattvās* or principles. Of the twenty-five principles, *Puruṣa* and *Prakṛti* are the first principles, from the associations of which, the entire creation evolves on the basis of cause and effect relations. *Sāṅkhya Pravacana Sūtram* enumerates those twenty-five principles as under:

Prakṛti is the state of equilibrium of three *guṇas–sattva, rajas* and *tamas*. From *Prakṛti* evolves *mahat*, from *mahat*, *ahaṅkāra*, from *ahaṅkāra*, the five *tanmātras* and the two sets of *Indriyas* (five *jñānendriyas* and five *karmendriyas*); from the five *tanmātras*, the gross elements. (Then there is) *Puruṣa*, (in whose company (*sānidhya*) only) *Prakṛti* can evolve. Such is the group of the twenty-five (principles)" (Sān. Pr. Su. 1.61).[1]

Mūla Prakṛti is conceived as the first uncaused cause in order to avoid the principle of "infinitesimal regression."

The evolvent is the cause having capacity to produce some other substance and the evolute is the effect or product. *Mūla Prakṛti* is only an evolvement. She evolves herself into *mahat*. From *mahat*, *ahaṅkāra*, is evolved. *Ahaṅkāra*, in turn, causes the production of ten *indriyas* and five *tanmātras*. As such this *ahaṅkāra* is both evolute (from *mahat*) and evolvement (for *tanmātras*). In the same manner, all the *pañca mahābhūtas* are evolutes, evolved out of *pañca tanmātras*, their immediate causes. Thus, the objects like "go" (cow), *ghaṭa* (pot), etc., which are amenable to our sensations are the ultimate evolutes (*pariṇāma*) of *Mūla Prakṛti*. In the same manner, *ākāśa* is evolved out *śabda-tanmātra* and accordingly, the "sound" (*śabda*), with which I am concerned in this thesis, is an evolute from *ākāśa* (ether) principle. Thus, *Mūla Prakṛti* is the uncaused cause of all things in the cosmic and in the phenomenal world. An effect is present in the cause latently and hence all the things, including the *śabda* (sound), are effects already present in the *Mūla Prakṛti* (or *pradhāna*), a primordial cause. If that is so, in order to have a better understanding of *pañca mahābhūtas*, one has to understand the respective *pañca tanmātra* out of which a particular *bhūta* (element) or an "object" has evolved. If that is so, in order to understand the nature of *śabda* as "sound", we should try to understand *śabda tanmātra*, out of which has evolved *ākāśa* (ether) whose quality is *śabda* or sound.

Sāṅkhya Pravachana Sūtram of Kapila says that these *tanmātras*, which are not amenable to our sense perceptions are, therefore, matters of inference on the basis of the phenomenal gross elements only.[2] Pātañjali's *Yoga Sūtra* (2.19) also suggests such an inference of unspecialized, undifferentiated (unknown) qualities of noumenal (*tanmātras*) is possible from specialized, differentiated (known) qualities of phenomenal (*bhūtas*). These *bhūtas* are matters of stages of "the qualities". The *Sāṅkhya Pravacana Bhāṣya*, a commentary authored by Vyāsa, explains the *sūtra* by stating that the *bhūtas* are different, due to the difference of nature shown by "the qualities" which constitute the "knowable". The specialized, the unspecialized, undifferentiated phenomenal and the noumenals are the matters of stages of "the qualities." "Here the elements known as *ākāśa* (ether), *vāyu* (invisible gas), *tejas* (light or heat), *āpa* (water), *pṛthvī* (solid) are specialized modifications of the unspecialized soniferous, tangiferous, luminiferous, gustiferous and odoriferous measures thereof (*tanmātras*, the subtle elements)".[3] Iśvara Kṛṣṇa, who lived much prior to Kapila, representing earlier classical school of *Sāṅkhya*, has a slightly different explanation of the subtle elements, in relation to gross objects. In *Sāṅkhya Kārikā*-38, Iśvara Kṛṣṇa provides that : "The subtle elements are non-specific; those five subtle elements precede the five gross elements : known as specific, (being variously) tranquil, terrific, and delusive."[4] *Yukti Dipika*, an ancient commentary on *Sāṅkhya Kārikā* of Iśvara Kṛṣṇa, whose author is unknown, commented this *kārikā*, and explained the term *tanmātra* as signifying "absence of species" (*aviśeṣa*). *Aviśeṣa* is further explained as ...."that in which there exists not a distinction (*tasya guṇasya sāmānyam evā'tra na viseṣa iti*), in the shape of calmness (*śāntā*), fierceness (*ghorā*) and dullness (*mūḍhā*), etc." In the words of S.S. Surya Narayaṇa Śastri, "The gross elements....are perceived as distinct, being possessed of different qualities, according to the prominent constituent–*satva, rajas,* or *tamas.* Thus they are specific."[5]

According to *Sāṅkhyatattvakaumudi* of Vācaspati Miśra, from the five *tanmātras* (subtle elements), the five *bhūtas* (gross objects) arise. He says that the *tanmātras* are *aviśeṣa* (indistinguishable), from which, the gross elements arise as specific (*viśeṣa*) by taking respectively, one, two, three, four, five *tanmātras.* According to him, in the case of gross-*ākāśa,* there is only one *tanmātra,* (i.e., *śabda tanmātra*); likewise in the case of *Vāyu* two (*vāyu* + *śabda*); *Agni,* three (*agni* + *śabda* + *vāyu*); *Āpa* four (*āpa* + *śabda* + *vāyu* + *agni*), and *Pṛthvi* five (*pṛthvi* + *śabda* + *vāyu* + *āpa* + *agni*).[6] From the above analysis it is clear that as per the older school of *Sāṅkhya* as reflected in *Sāṅkhya Kārikā* of Iśvara Kṛṣṇa, Sound (*śabda*) by itself is a *tanmātra* of which *ākāśa* is the effect. But in *Sāṅkhya Pravaçana Sūtra* of Kapila, as we have already seen, *ākāśa* is treated as effect and sound is its quality. Moreover in *Pañcīkaraṇa* principle, as accepted by ancient *Sāṅkhya, śabda tanmātra* which is common element in all gross elements, not only constitutes *ākāśa* but all the *mahābhūtas.* If it is so, as observed by S.S. Sūrya Nārāyaṇa Śāstri : "If it is said, however, that whatever is grasped sound (i.e., the gross element, ether) enters as a constituent, then we have the doctrine of quintuplication, according to which every element enters in some measure into everything that is."[7] In that case, even in the case of the other gross objects, which are constituents of less than five *tanmātras*, should share the quintuplication principle. But *Kārikā*-38, by itself, does not spell out any kind of combination of the *tanmātras* in any gross element, similar to the one, suggested by the commentators. It simply states that five gross elements arise from the five indistinct *tanmātras* (*tanmātrāṇi aviśeṣāḥ : tebhyaḥ pañcabhyaḥ pañcabhūtāni*). But according to the commentators the gross elements arise owing to different kinds of combination of the *tanmātras*, as seen above, two, three, four, five, etc. The gross element of *ākāśa* arises out of *śabda tanmātra* alone and other gross elements arise out of the compounding of two, three, four and five *tanmātras*, of which *śabda tanmātra* is a common factor. From this, it appears that the *kārikā* provides the quintuplication principle (*pañcīkaraṇa*), in the sense that all the gross elements are compounds of all the *tanmātras*, except *ākāśa*. It appears that the commentators, perhaps, thought that if such compounding of all the five *tanmātras* is of the same numbers, in all the gross elements, on the basis of such quintuplication principle, it would be difficult to account for their different natures of external objects. For example, if the same five *tanmātras* constitute the gross element of *Vāyu* and *Āpa*, then there cannot be any difference between *Vāyu* and *Āpa*, and the same cannot be countenanced by our experience, since admittedly they are of different natures – the former is of gaseous nature and the latter is liquid. Perhaps in view of this kind of difficulty they must have thought of different kinds of combinations of those *tanmātras*, in the constitution of gross elements, as stated above, in terms of two, three, four *tanmātra*, as done, for instance, in *Sāṅkhyatattvakaumudi* of Vācaspati Miśra. Whatever be the reason, there would be apparent inconsistency between the quintuplication principle provided by *kārika*, on one hand, and the principle of "one, two, three, four, and five *tanmātra* combinations" provided for different elements, on the other, as explained by the commentators. Sri S.S. Sūrya Nārāyaṇa Śāstri with an attempt to wriggle out this kind of situation, while translating *Kārikā*-35, regarding *karmendrīyas*, (relating to gross objects) observed, in his enlightening foot-note as follows: "....speech (*vāk*) manifests (gross) sound alone in five ways, *varṇa*, *pada*, *vākya*, *śloka*, and *grantha*; the rest operate on forms which are aggregates of sound, touch, colour, taste and smell; but they function even in respect of smaller aggregates, e.g., water, which is an aggregate of four alone; the mention of five is to show the possibility of operating on five, not to exclude aggregates of two, three, or four. In the light of this, some statements in earlier editions, about *pañcīkaraṇa*, have had to be changed....".[8] But his explanation of "the possibility of operating on five, not to exclude aggregates of two, three, or four", etc., has not solved the difficulty. Also no authority is cited in support of this kind of guess work. The explanation given by *Yuktidīpikā* that "in order to avoid possible meaningless situation, during earlier time only, the five aggregate elements composition was modified into four, three, etc., elements composition" – (*sambhavānartham apipañca-viṣayāṇy etāni, prāg eva catus-triviṣayāṇiti*) – amounts to avoiding the problem, rather than solving it, as observed by Sūrya Nārāyaṇa Śāstri himself. (p. 65)

Having this kind of difficulty only, the principle of *Pañcīkaraṇa* accepted in ancient *Sāṅkhya*, regarding all gross elements including *ākāśa* was slowly given the go-by, by the later *Sāṅkhya* philosophers. Perhaps it was no more acceptable during the time, when Kapila wrote his *Sāṅkhya Pravacana Sūtra*, in which *pañcīkaraṇa* principle was specifically refuted by stating that (some people say) "The (gross) body is formed of the five elements (Sān. Pra. Sū. 3.17); but "the body is not made of five elements, because many (heterogeneous things jointly) are unfit to be the material cause of anything." (Sān. Pra. Sū. 5.102); and the body has only one element and that is "Earth."[9]

However, it is seen that, at a later point of time, Ādi Śaṅkarācārya has reconstructed the *Pañcīkaraṇa* theory, with a different formula of composition of the five gross elements (*pañca mahābhūtas*) alongwith the composition of five subtle elements (*tanmātras*) in his small treatise called *Pañcīkaraṇa*.

According to *Pañcīkaraṇa* of Śaṅkarācārya also all the independent (*apañcīkṛta*) five gross elements join together (*pañcīkṛta*) in order to become a compound of quintuplication (*pañcīkaraṇa*) of the five *tanmātrās*, but in such a composition the *tanmātrā* of the concerned element would be predominant (taking a major share at half of its own *tanmātra* as against one-eighth share of the other *tanmātras*), and as such it can maintain its own identity. For instance, in the gross element of earth (*pṛthvī*) all the five *tanmātras* would join to become *pañcīkaraṇa*, but the *tanmātra* of *pṛthvī* would constitute half and the rest take one-eighth share. In such a composition, each gross element (*bhūta*), including *ākāśa*, maintains its own identity though constituted on the quintuplication principle. As such the anomalous situation emerging in ancient *Pañcīkaraṇa* Theory of *Sāṅkhya* philosophy is avoided successfully. This aspect will be considered again in Chapter five on *Mīmāṃsā* and *Vedānta* systems. However this kind of discussion takes us to the deeper relationship between *tanmātras* (subtle bodies) and *sthūla śarīra* (gross bodies) and their interrelationship.

Kapila in his *Sāṅkhya Pravacana Sūtram* hints at such a intrinsic relationship between them by stating that:

"The gross (body) is the one usually produced from the father and the mother; the other (*itarat*) one, is the one not so produced (*na tathā*)".[10] *Bhāṣya* of Vijñāna Bhikṣu comments on this aphorism by stating that "*itarat*, the subtle body, *na tathā* is not the one produced from father and mother, because of its having been produced at the beginning of the creation" (p. 283). Goudapāda, the commentator of *Sāṅkhya Kārikā* of Īśvara Kṛṣṇa, commenting on *Kārikā* No. 39, elaborated and differentiated the imperceptible *sūkṣama śarīra* (subtle body) from perceptible *sthūla śarīra* (gross body), in his *Sāṅkhya Kārikā Bhāṣya* :

"The subtle body is made up of intellect, egoity, mind, the sense capacities, the action capacities, and the five subtle elements (*tanmātras*). The gross body is the body produced from the mixture of seminal fluids .... The gross body is sustained by gross elements. Similarly, the subtle body is nourished and sustained by food provided to the organism through the umbilical cord of the mother. In this fashion the embryo (made up of subtle body, gross body, and gross elements) slowly begins to develop.... During the gestation period the embryo is wrapped in six sheaths. When the gestation period is finished, a baby is born from the mother's womb.

Of these specific forms (that is, subtle body, gross body and gross elements), only the subtle body is permanent and transmigrates from life to life....gross bodies and gross elements perish at the moment of death and merge again into undifferentiated gross elements".[11]

According to *Sāṅkhya* philosophy, such transmigration of the subtle bodies from one life to another, takes place with its own accumulated *sanskāras* (predispositions) (good or bad). Commenting on *Kārikā* No. 43 of *Sāṅkhya Kārikā* of Iśvara Kṛṣṇa, *Yukti Dīpikā* states that "According to Iśvara Kṛṣṇa, the basic predispositions (*bhāva*) are (a) innate (*sāṃsiddhika*), (b) natural (*prākṛtika*) and (c) acquired (*vaikṛta*)" (*ibid.*, p. 266). The virtues or vices are acquired dispositions according to one's good and bad deeds; and being born out of sperm and ovum, on the basis of cause and effect, is natural disposition. From their characteristics, it appears that the natural dispositions are similar to hereditary characteristics and they migrate from one life to another alongwith such "predispositions" (*sanskārās*). Precisely what "genes" do according to Genes Theory.

Now another aspect of the problem is: What does the gross body consist of according to *Sāṅkhya Pravacana Sūtra* (Sā. Pr. Sū.III.17)? The gross body is formed of the five elements, viz., earth, water, fire, air and ether. It does not agree with the theory that such gross body consists of either four elements (Sā. Pr. Sū.III.18) (by excluding "ether" (*ākāśa*) as pointed out by *Vṛtti* of Aniruddha) or one element, (Sā. Pr. Sū.III.19), as pointed out by Vijñāna Bhikṣu and *Vaiśeṣikasūtram*. (Vai. Sū.4.2.2-4). But the consciousness not being present in these insentient gross elements, they could not produce "consciousness" (*caitanya*) in the body. On the other hand the subtle body (*linga śarīra*) consists of eighteen elements (*buddhi*, *ahaṅkāra*, and five subtle elements, and ten *indrīyas*, plus *manas*) and as such could be the cause for "consciousness." Vijñāna Bhikṣu elucidates aphorism by stating that the gross elements "....are the *adhiṣṭhāna*, i.e., a vehicle of that *lingam* (subtle body). The *linga śarīra* (subtle body) cannot stand by itself. In other words the gross body and the subtle body are co-existent like the object and its shadow" (Sān. Pr. Sū.III.12).

In fact the subtle body (*linga śarīra*) is of the atomic size only. "....it is constituted by *sattva* which is light; hence it must be associated with the *bhūtās* or gross elements, and it is further suggested under aphorism" (Sā. Pr. Sū.III.22) that this subtle body is responsible for the consciousness in the gross body. But the subtle body, which is responsible for consciousness, continues to exist even after the death of the body. If the consciousness were to be innate in the gross body, there would not have been death.

The concept of *tanmātra* has not missed the attention of the modern thinkers. C. Dwarakanatha did examine the concept of *tanmātras* in relation to *pañca mahābhūtas* (five basic elements). According to him, the *tanmātras* are "active energy possessing different sensory potentials, which cause elementary quantum of action. By elementary quantum, he means the unit or quantity of protons (radiant energy) required to produce just minimum sensation." He further states that "the term elementary quantum refers to the unit of quantity of protons (radiant energy) required to produce just the minimum sensation of light. Borrowed from modern physics, this term is used to stimulate the respective sensory organs to sense the bare awareness (minimum sensation of their respective sensations, viz., sound (*śabda*), touch (*sparśa*), light (*tejas*), taste (*rasa*) and smell (*gandha*)" (p. 87). "In this sense, *tanmātras* represent specific unit of stimuli of the senses" (p. 88).... "It is seen that *śabda tanmātra* which is the lightest of the five, from all accounts, has one property, viz., the capacity to evoke the sensation of sound, i.e., *śabda*. The kinetic involved in this phenomenon relates to disturbance caused by it which impinges on all the sense-organs but evokes response only from the organ of hearing. The disturbance caused by the movements of this *tanmātra* in the air is propagated in the form of waves, described often in terms of wavelengths" (p. 88-89).[12]

Dwarakanatha appears to be right in his conclusion that the *tanmātras* are "ultimate energy units" or "quantas of specific mode of energy" which cause both our sensations and the gross elements. Almost a similar theory of *tanmātra* is also expressed by a renowned vedic scholar, Sri Surendranatha Dasgupta who says: "....The *tanmātras* then are infra-atomic particles charged with specific potential energies. First, the potential of sound stimulus is lodged in one class of particles, *tanmātras* which possess the physical energy of vibration (*parispanda*) and serve to form the radical of the ether atom (*ākāśaparamāṇu*), then the potential of the tactile stimulus is lodged in another class of *tanmātras*, particles which possess the physical energy impact or mechanical pressure ...."[13] But Surendranatha Dasagupta offers slightly a different explanation of *tanmātras* in his another book–*A Study of Patañjali*. In this book he states that "....from *bhūtādi* comes five *tanmātras* which can be compared to the *Vaiśeṣika* atoms, as they have no parts and neither grossness nor visible differentiation....The next one, the *paramāṇu*, which is gross in its nature and is generated from *tanmātras* which exist in it as parts (*tanmātrāvayava*), may be compared with the *trasareṇu*, of the *Vaiśeṣikas* or with atoms of Dalton...."[14]

But according to me, these explanations offered by the learned scholars are deficient in not highlighting the "mental element" of the *tanmātrās*. All these explanations of *tanmātra* may be alright, viewed from merely the physical element or physical energy in them. But according to the *Sāṅkhya* Theory, these *tanmātra* are also evolutes of *ahaṅkāra*, "the cosmic mind" and as such they should also possess "insentient" element, or the "psych." According to me, *tanmātras* are supposed to evolve both mind and matter, which may indicate the "mind-body relation" which bears testimony in the external world. The three guṇ*as* – *sattva, rajas, tamas* – constitute the necessary ingredients in *tanmātras*, since *Mūla Prakṛti* in its primary status represents the equipoised status of these *guṇas*. These *guṇas* represent pleasant, unpleasant or passive state of mind in day-to-day life. It is, perhaps, to emphasize this aspect only, Surendranath Dasgupta further observes : ".... I believe, it has been made clear that, when the inner and the outer proceed from one source, the ego and the external world do not altogether differ in nature from the inner; both have been formed by the collocation of the *guṇas* (*sarvamidaṃ guṇānāṃ sanniveśaviśeṣamātram*)."[15]

The resultant conclusion, according to me, would be that, according to *Sāṅkhya*-Yoga, the subtle element (*tanmātras*), which is of atomic size (*aṇuparimāṇam*– Sān. Pr. Su.III.14) is not a mere physical atom like that of *Vaiśeṣikas* but a psycho-physical-organic-cosmic-gene, which is responsible both for the existence (*prakṛti*) and transformation (*vikāra*), of which this universe is the resultant entity (*pariṇāma*) and for the transmigration of soul. Thus the human body, for instance, is not composed of five gross elements only. It consists of "vehicular" subtle body also, which is not gross.[16] This subtle body pervades the whole of gross body. The gross body is the seat of the master, i.e., (*manas*), the seat of reflection of *Puruṣa* (*Bhāṣya*). Under the superintendence of *prāṇa* (the experiencer), his building, i.e., the body connected with senses, comes into existence.[17]

Senses (*indrīyas*), according to *Sāṅkhya*-Yoga, are attached to the body. The objects are manifested through senses. In the case of the manifestation of objects, there is modification of senses.[18] "For the manifestation of objects, the senses must reach them. In reaching the objects, they must not quit connection with the body. So that, while their connection with the body is maintained, their connection with objects has to be explained. And this can be possible only by means of a peculiar modification of the senses themselves, which is technically called *vṛtti* (modification)."[19] These senses do not illuminate what they do not reach.[20] In the case of senses what is necessary is that the stimuli of the external object and the sense-organs should come in contact with each other so that there is the "modification" (*vṛtti*) of that senses (so as to send message to the mind).

What is the nature of sound we hear, and what happens in the case of cognition of sound?

To start with, one should note that, according to *Sāṅkhya*-Yoga, the sound is not direct evolute of *śabda tanmātra*. As we have seen above, from *śabda tanmātra* the gross element that evolves is *ākāśa*. This *ākāśa* has sound as its quality because the sound, as the quality is latently present in *śabda tanmātra*, though in an undifferentiated or unmanifested form. For *ākāśa* could not have sound as its quality, if that were to be not present, latently, in *śabda tanmātra*. According to *Sāṅkhya Pravacana Sūtra* (II.12) "space" and "time" are not the qualities of *ākāśa* but are only *upādhis* (external conditions) of that *ākāśa* and accordingly appear to be limited by limiting objects. *Bhāṣya* of Vijñāna Bhikṣu further clarifies that - "Although limited space and time are (in reality, not the products of *ākāśa*, but) *ākāśa* itself as particularized by this or that limiting object, still they have been stated here the effects of *ākāśa*. Similarly, as in the *Vaiśeṣika* system, the sense of hearing has been stated to be the effect of *ākāśa*, following the custom admitting the thing particularized as separate and additional entity" (Nandalal Simha, pp. 246). In fact, *ākāśa* is all pervading unobstructed medium (*anāvaraṇam*), and, as such, is everywhere, including inside the pot, but it appears as separate in the pot, because of obstruction caused by the pot only. This *ākāśa* is substance, like that of *ākāśa* in *Nyāya-Vaiśeṣika*, and not a vacuity as Buddhists believe it to be. (I will consider this concept in detail in the next chapter.). Even Aphorism forty of *Yoga Sūtra* states that there is the relationship between "power-of-hearing" and *ākāśa*. Its commentator, Vyāsa, in his *Bhāṣya*, elucidated this principle, as under:

"In *ākāśa* abide all powers of hearing and all sounds. To all those whose organs of hearing are similarly situated, the situation of hearing is the same.... The power of hearing is the means of perceiving sound. Of a deaf and not-deaf, one senses the sound, and the other does not. Therefore, the "power of hearing" is the sphere for the "action of sound." "Whoever performs *samyama* (concentration) with reference to the relation between the power of hearing and the *ākāśa*, evolves the power of higher audition (means may hear *anāhata nāda*)."[21] The gloss of Vāchaspati Miśra further clarifies that the relation between the "power of hearing" and *ākāśa*, is of the type of – "the thing supporting and the thing supported." All the powers of hearing, even though they have their origin in the principle of egoism, reside in the *ākāśa*, placed in the hollow of the ear. It is in this place where the power of hearing is located. When soundness or defect is noticed therein, soundness or defect, as the case may be, is noticed in the power of hearing also. Further, when the sounds working in unison with the power of hearing, the sounds of solids & c., are to be taken in, then the power of hearing located in the hollow of the ear, stands in need of the capacity of resonance residing in the substratum of the ear. "....This sense of hearing then, having its origin in the principal egoism, acts like iron, drawn as it is by sound originate and located in the mouth of the speaker, acting as loadstone, transforms them into its own modifications in sequence of the sounds of the speaker, and thus senses them.... Further, the *ākāśa* in which the power of hearing is located is born out of the soniferous *tanmātra*, and has therefore the quality of sound inherent in itself. It is by this sound acting in unison that it takes the sounds of external solids, & c. This then establishes that the *ākāśa* is the substratum of the power of hearing, and also possesses the quality of sound....

Further the absence of obstruction is an indication of *ākāśa*. If there were no *ākāśa*, the forms would be in such close contact with one another that even a needle point would not find room between them. Everything would thus be obstructed by everything."[22]

The mode of the cognition of senses (in the context of sound) is made clear by Sān. Pr. Sū.V.104, that a lamp not reached by the eye cannot reveal itself. In the same way unless the sound reaches the ears the same cannot be perceived. In recognition of sound there is modification of sense of hearing in unison with *ākāśa* in the ear (which ultimately reaches brain), on the principle : "In reality, however, by means of modification, that is, through connection, is the accomplishment thereof, that is, is the proof of the objects of recognition".[23] Sān. Pr. Sū.(V.106), further adds that "Through the mark (*linga*) of the manifestation of the objects reached to, (there is) proof of the modification (of the senses)." The author, Nandalal Simha, adds by reading between the lines of the *Sūtra* and the commentary of *Bhāṣya*, has provided a note which clarify the position: "Note: The reasoning, indicated here, may be exhibited as follows: For the manifestation of objects, the senses must reach them. In reaching to objects, they must not quit connection with the body. So that, while their connection with the body is maintained, their connection with the objects has to be explained. And this can be possible only by means of a peculiar modification of the senses themselves, which is technically called *vṛtti*, i.e., modification. Thus, the existence of *vṛtti* is proved".[24] Commenting on Sān. Pr. Sū.V.107, *Vṛtti* of Aniruddha, clarifies that "this modification (*vṛtti*) is a different principle which is formed of *ahamkāra*, (and this does not run counter to our enumeration of twenty-five principles)...." Since the recognition of unconnected (objects) is impossible, (unless there is) the favourable influence of *adṛṣṭam*, (the causes of enlightenment of connected objects). According to me, this *adṛṣṭam* principle (Sān. Pr. Sū.2.39) is nothing but Vedic *ṛtam* principle. My opinion stands fortified by *Bhāṣya* which says: "....the activity of the instruments, which also for the sake of *Puruṣa*, proceeds only from the manifestation of the *adṛṣṭam* of *Puruṣa*".[25]

What is the nature of this *vṛtti* or "modification of senses" conceived by *Sāṅkhya*-Yoga in terms of modern psychology?

To my surprise, I find that the modern psychologists have also attempted to answer similar questions as to how the stimuli cause the modification of senses and in turn how they send message to the brain. "What are these 'messages'? What does the nerve conduct or transmit?" – are the questions framed in this context and answered by Robert S. Woodworth and Donald G. Marquis in their textbook on psychology by stating that: "We call it the nerve impulse and as far known it is an electrochemical wave in the nerve fibre, which is very weak and consumes very little energy, but still is capable of arousing a muscle or a nerve centre to action." (p. 238).... "The activity going on in the brain and cord is modified by the incoming nerve impulses. We should think of the system as constantly active and constantly receiving stimuli which modify its activity (p. 244)".[26] If that is so, there is substance in the theory of "modification" suggested by *Sāṅkhya*-Yoga.

Perception, accordingly, is cognition which, coming into contact with the thing cognized (Vijñāna Bhikṣu), or being produced by means of relation to the thing cognized (Aniruddha), portrays the form thereof (i.e., of the thing cognized).[27] According to *vṛtti* of Aniruddha perception is sensual cognition of "form" (*ākāra*) of the object like a water-pot. It is *nirvikalpa* or indeterminate without the help of memory. He does not agree with the theory of the Buddhists which holds that the cognition of an object (cow) is always with the help of memory (of cowness), as such it is determinate or *savikalpa*. Aniruddha further points out that though memory of cowness is helpful in cognition but it is not opposed to be the authority of direct sensual perception with the eyes.[28] In the same way, sound also is cognized with the ears.

In this background *Sāṅkhya Pravacana Sūtram* does not accept the doctrine of *sphoṭa*, enunciated by the *Mahābhāṣya* of Patañjali and other grammarians, while determining the relationship between word and its meaning. According to it, either on the basis of intuition or non-intuition, a "'word' is not of the nature of *sphoṭa*."[29] According to *Bhāṣya* the collection of letters, arranged in a particular manner, one after another, the object is manifested, and if that is so, then the supposition of *sphoṭa* is useless and unnecessary. (See Nandalal Simha, p. 441). *Sāṅkhya Pravacana Sūtram* forbids the identity of word and objects. Word acts as a signifier of the objects signified. When someone says jar, such jar is cognized by the word heard in the ear and cognized by the figure of *jar* seen with the eyes. Here both the word – jar, and the image –jar signify the object jar. Thus "the relation of word and object is the relation of the thing to be signified and that which signifies (Sān. Pra. Sū.5.37) and nothing more. In the object (*artha*) lies the power called signifiability and in the word (*śabda*), significativeness. It is that (power) which constitutes their relation, as is the case with the adaptability of one thing to another. And through the cognition thereof becomes possible the presentation of objects by means of words. Such is the meaning."[30] Thus *Sāṅkhya Pravacana Sūtram* does not accept the *Sphoṭa* theory, which the *Yoga Sūtra* of Patañjali and the *Yoga Sāra Sangraḥ* of Vijñāna Bhikṣu accepted. However, according to both, it is the convention that determines the relation between the word and its meaning. A word gets meaning by being referrable to an object as per the convention.

According to *Yoga Sūtra*, the sacred word *Praṇavaḥ* itself conveys the meaning of *Iśvara*. "It denotes Him (i.e. *Iśvara*) *tasya vācakaḥ praṇavaḥ*."[31] By commenting on this aphorism, *Vyāsa Bhāṣya* says that by virtue of the convention the word *Praṇavaḥ* (*AUM*) itself is the sign (*sanketa*) of *Iśvara* (*tat sanketaḥ Iśvarasya*). "His relation with sign is inherent and thus ever present.... As the relation already existing between father and son, is only expressed by convention, this is the father, this is the son".[32] Vijñāna Bhikṣu, in his *Yoga Vārtika* further adds that "Those who are well-versed in the scriptures (*āgaminaḥ*) know that the relationship between the word and its meaning is permanent because of the permanency of similar usages (in successive generations)".[33]

According to *Yoga Sūtra*, "By its repetition (*japa*) there is understanding of its meaning (*tat-japaḥ tadartha bhāvanam*- I.28). According to *Vyāsa Bhāṣya*, the relation between word, *Praṇavaḥ* and its meaning (*Iśvara*) being eternal, and ever co-existing, by constant repetition of it, it manifests the essence of its meaning to the *yogis*. The gloss of Vācaspati adds that by such constant repetition of it, *praṇava* becomes "the very substance of the mental existence" (of such *yogi*), and by such repetition "the mind feels bliss in the One Lord alone....The Lord then becomes gracious to him up to his attaining the faculty of trance (*samādhi*) and its fruit".[34] This state of mind is usually described as *nādānusandhāna* or absorption in *nāda* – meditation, which is the highest means of salvation. Of the many kinds of *yogas*, *nāda yoga* is considered to be very important, as *Haṭha Yoga Pradīpikā* states "Adinātha propounded one and one-fourth crore methods of trance, and they are all extant. Of these, the hearing of *anāhata nāda* (*nādānusandhāna*) is the only one, the chief, in my opinion (*nādānusandhānamekameva mānyamahe mukhyatamam*)".[35]

Is sound eternal ?

According to the *Sāṅkhya* philosophy, as we have seen above, sound ultimately the effect of *ākāśa* only. The *Sāṅkhya Pravacan Sūtra* declares that "Sound (*śabda*) is not eternal, because it is seen to be an effect" (of *ākāśa*).[36] Likewise according to *sūtra* the letters or syllables (*varṇas*) and word (*śabda*) (formed of such sound or sounds) are also not eternal.

But this sound, as the quality of *ākāśa*, is the "physical sound" a pre-stage of *nāda*, by taking *nāda* as a "modulated or modified sound" (*vaikṛtadhvani*), in the sense Bhartṛhari uses. Vijñāna Bhikṣu in his *Yogasārasangraḥ* clarifies the subtle distinction between sound and *nāda* by elaborating three kinds of sounds: "(1) The object of the sense of hearing (*vāgindriyaviṣayaḥ*), (i.e. the sound characterised by different parts of mouth – throat, palate, etc.,– is the object of the sense of speech, being its effect; (2) the object of the sense of hearing (*śrotrendriyaviṣayaḥ*), (i.e. the Sound produced by sound, removed from the sense of speech and located in the ear, is the object of sense of hearing, being perceptible by it; and (3) the object of the intellect alone (*buddhimātra viṣayaḥ*), like the concept *ghaṭa* (jar) (i.e. *śabda* or word), etc."[37] In this kind of three sounds, *Sāṅkhya's śabda* is the sound of the first kind. Whereas, Bhartṛhari's *nāda* is of the sound of the second kind. The sound of the third kind by itself is *sphoṭa* which *Sāṅkhya* does not accept. Keeping aside "the sound of third kind" (in the sense of *sphoṭa*), amongst the remaining two sounds, *Sāṅkhya's* description of "sound" belongs to the first kind. Yet the "letters" as constituting word nevertheless, are the instances of the "sounds of the second kind," accordingly, belong to the concept of *nāda* as clarified Bhartṛhari (see Ch. Seven). At any rate *Sāṅkhya*, does not accept the eternality of sound, in either sense.

Ontologically also, except *Puruṣa* and *Mūla Prakṛti*, (with the equilibrium of her three *guṇās*) the rest are effects and non-eternal, and at the time of *pralaya* or dissolution, they simply recede back into that *Mūla Prakṛti*. Likewise, the relation (of the name and the named) is non-eternal, since both are non-eternal.[38] "Eternality does not belong to the Vedas, because it is heard that they are effects."[39] Aniruddha has commented on this aphorism by stating that, "He practiced penance; from that penance having been practiced, the three Vedas were produced", would show that the Vedas were the product, and as such they are also not eternal. However, according to *Sāṅkhya Pravacana Sūtra*, "the verbal testimony of the Vedas is still acceptable like the books of medicine on the basis of their own intrinsic truth based on objective observations. From (seeing) the manifestation of the power inherent in the Vedas, their authoritativeness follows from themselves."[40] *Bhāṣya* of

Vijñāna Bhikṣu elucidates and says : "Of the Veda what is *nija* or natural or innate *śakti* or power of producing cognition corresponding to objective realities, of that, since there is observation of manifestation in the case of ...., the *Āyurveda*, etc., therefore, all the Vedic declarations, without exception, prove the authoritativeness of the *mantras* by themselves, and not by means of their having their origin in cognition, corresponding to objective realities on the part of their speaker."[41] This kind of proof is accepted on the basis of the word-meaning relation of the vedic *mantras* (*mantrārthavādayoḥ prāmāṇyam*)[42] described as "scriptural testimony" by Prof. R.I. Ingalalli.[43]

* * *

The Gist of the Theories of *Sāṅkhya* and Yoga :

Nāda or śabda is a quality (guṇa) of ākāśa (ether)–
(Cosmic theory of Sound)

Sāṅkhya-Yoga adopted the concept of vedic cosmic *vāk* to explain human language or human *dhvani* or *nāda*. Their *Prakṛti* and *Puruṣa* are only eternal cosmic principles. In the presence of *Puruṣa*, *Prakṛti* evolves into the entire creation; and at the time of dissolution the said creation recedes into her. Except *Puruṣa* and *Prakṛti*, the other material substances and their qualities go on changing and, as such, are non-eternal. The qualities inherent in substance change in the process of modification, in the course of evolution. According to them, sound as "quality" subsists in *ākāśa*, which itself is evolved out of *śabda-tanmātra*, in the course of cosmic evolutionary process from *Mūla Prakṛti*. In the words of Surendranath Dasgupta, *śabda-tanmātras* are "infra-atomic particles charged with specific potential energies" (inherited from *Mūla Prakṛti*). Out of such *śabda-tanmātra*, *ākāśa* arises, whose only potential quality is sound. Sound, in the sense of "physical sound" arising as quality of *ākāśa* is non-eternal.

Sāṅkhya does not use the word *nāda*. A word is a group of letter-sounds (*varṇas*) signifying an object (or meaning), according to convention. These letters sound by virtue of their modulation would be of the form of *nāda*. But these letters and the words, constituted of these letters, are non-eternal. The Veda expressed in such non-eternal words is also non-eternal. However, the Vedas is acceptable as an authority just like the books on medicine.

Notes and References

1. Sinha Nandalal (2003) : p. 94.
2. Sān. Pr. Sū. I.62.
3. Prasāda, Rāma (1995) : (Verse 2.19); pp. 129-30.
4. Sāstri, S.S.; Sūrya Nārāyaṇa; (*tr.*) (1948) : p. 70.
5. ____ (*tr.*) (1948) : p. 70.
6. Musulgaonkar Gajānana Śāstri, Dr. (2000).
7. Śāstri, S.S. Sūrya Nārāyaṇa (*tr.*) (1948) : foot-note at page 65.
8. ____ (*tr.*) (1948), foot-note at page 64.
9. Sān. Pra. Sū. V.112 - (*tr.*) Sinha, Nandalal.
10. Sān. Pr. Sū. III.7 - (*tr.*) Sinha, Nandalal.

11. Larson & Bhattacharya : Potter, K.H. (Vol. IV); pp. 219-20.
12. Dwarakanatha, C. (1996).
13. Dasgupta, Surendranatha (2001): p. 89.
14. ____ (2001): p. 56.
15. ____ (2001): p. 57.
16. Sān. Pr. Sū. V.102, 103.
17. Sān. Pr. Sū. V.114.
18. Sān. Pr. Sū. V.106.
19. See Editors Note to Sān. Pr. Sū.V.106; Simha, Nandalal: p. 488.
20. Sān. Pr. Sū.V.104.
21. Prasāda Rāma (1995) : p. 240.
22. ____ (1995) : *Pātañjali's Yoga Sūtra*, pp. 240-41; (the author uses the symbol '&c.' to translate '*ityadi*', to indicate similar things of that category.
23. *Vṛtti* of Aniruddha on Sān. Pr. Sū.V.105 : (*tr.*) Simha, Nandalal; p. 487.
24. Simha, Nandalal: p. 487.
25. ____: p. 269.
26. Woodworth Robert, S. and Marquis Donald, G. (1955).
27. Sān. Pra. Sū I.89. Simha, Nandalal: p. 138.
28. Sān. Pra. Sū I.89. Simha, Nandalal: p. 139.
29. Sān. Pra. Sū. V.57. Simha, Nandalal: p. 441.
30. *Bhāṣya of* Vijñāna Bhikṣu : Simha, Nandalal; pp. 419-20.
31. *Yoga-Sūtra* I.27 : Prasāda, Rāma; p. 49.
32. *Yoga-Sūtra* Prasāda, Rāma: p. 49.
33. *Aphorism 27* - Rukmani, T.S. (1981) : (Vol. I); p. 157.
34. *Yoga-Sūtra* - Prasāda, Rāma: p. 51.
35. *nādanusandhānamekameva mānyamahe mukhyatamaṃ* (verse - 65); Sinha, Pancham (1992) : p. 58.

36. Sān. Pr. Sū.V.58. : (1992) Simha, Nandalal; p. 442.
37. Jha, Ganganath (2004) : p. 127.
38. Sān. Pr. Sū. V.97.
39. Sān. Pr. Sū. V.45; Simha, Nandalal: p. 428.
40. Sān. Pr. Sū. V.51.
41. Simha, Nandalal: pp. 432-33.
42. *mantrārthavādayoḥ prāmāṇyam* : Triathi, Kedarnatha (1974).
43. Ingalalli, Prof. R.I., (1988) : "Consequently scriptural testimony as a set of true (credential) sentences qualifies itself as a source of knowledge" at p. 146.

* * *

Chapter Four

NYĀYA-VAIŚEṢIKA THEORIES OF *NĀDA*, *ŚABDA* OR *DHVANI*

The ontological theory of *Nyāya-Vaiśeṣika* is characterized as philosophy of atomism. According to *Nyāya-Vaiśeṣika*, the ultimate substancc out of which all other substances emerge in atom (*aṇu*). Out of nine, the first five substances viz. earth, water, fire, air and *manas* are atomic substances and the rest four viz. time, space, *ākāśa* and *ātma* are pervasive (*vibhu*) substances.

According to the *Vaiśeṣika Sūtra* of Kaṇāda, there are six categories (*padārthas*), which require investigation as a means of enlightenment or liberation or to relieve the soul from pain and misery. The word *padārtha* means a "meaning" of word. But *Nyāya-Vaiśeṣika* thinkers use *padārtha* as a category of investigation. Such categories are six: 1) *Dravya* (substance), 2) *guṇa* (quality), 3) *karma* (action), 4) *sāmānya* (the generality of a thing to its genus), 5) *viśeṣa* (differentia), and 6) *samavāya* (inherence).[1] (Vai. Sū.1.i.4). Later thinkers considered *abhāva* (non-existence) as the seventh category.

Dravya (substances) is without any distinguishing mark[2] (Vai. Sū.1.4 and 17). It serves as a substrate (*ādhāra*) for qualities and actions. There are only nine *dravyās* (substances): earth (*pṛthvi*), water (*āpa*), fire (*tejaḥ*), air (*vāyu*), ether (*ākāśa*), time (*kālaḥ*), space (*dik*), Self or Soul (*ātma*) and mind (*manas*).[3] (Vai. Sū.1.5). Substances are not annihilated either by cause or by effect.[4] (Vai. Sū.1.i.12).

Quality inheres in substance and it is without any other quality. It is not a cause for any conjunction or disjunction. An action is destroyed by its effect[5] (Vai. Sū.1.i.14). The characteristics of action (*karma*) are that it inheres in one substance. It is without qualities. It is the sole cause of conjunctions and disjunctions.[6] (Vai. Sū.1.i.17, 30). The categories like *sāmānya* (genus), *viśeṣa* (species) and *samavāya* (coherence), are not amenable to perception. They are only conceptual (*buddhyapekṣam*)[7] (Vai. Sū.1.ii.3)

Substantiality (*dravyatva*), qualitativeness, (*guṇatva*) and activity (*karmatva*) are both general and specific. (And so all others) except ultimate specific, (atoms, etc.).[8] (Vai. Sū1.ii.5-6). *Samavāya*, the last category, is generally translated as 'coherence' or 'inherence'. For example, the relation of threads in cloth is a matter of '*samavāya*' but not a matter of '*samyoga*', like milk placed in the pot.

According to *Vaiśeṣika*, the ultimate substances belong to two classes : *aṇu* (atom) and *vibhu* (pervasive or extensive). When we go on dividing the substance, it cannot go on ad infinitum, but stops at a point when it cannot be divided further. Such a substance is atom (*paramāṇu*). A combination of two atoms is called dyad (*dvyaṇuka*). For being perceptible to our senses it should be a combination of at least three atoms called triad (*trasareṇu*). A particle, visible, in the sunbeam, entering a dark room, is a triad.

"The action of fire and the action of air are explained by the action of earth. The initial upward flaming of fire, the initial sideward blowing of air, the initial actions of atoms and of mind or egress and ingress (of life and mind, from and into body) conjunctions (i.e. assimilation) of food and drink and conjunctions and disjunction of other products, etc., are caused by *adṛṣṭam*."[9] This *adṛṣṭam* is an invisible creative force. As "I" have already suggested in Chapter two, that this is a new term coined for the same Vedic *ṛtam* principle.

Of all the substances, *ātman* (or soul) is the most important substance, since it is this substance that enables cognition of other substances. The existence of soul is proved not only on the basis of revelation but also on the basis of sensuous cognition or perception in the form of "I", such as "I am *Devadatta*, or I am *Yajñadatta*", etc. (Then there is no need of inference)[10]. Every individual has different experiences of breathing, winking of eyes, life, the movements of the mind and the effect of the other senses and also pleasure, pain, desire, aversion, and volition as marks of (existence) of his soul. Hence there are as many souls, as there are individuals. Soul is a substance which serves as substratum for sense-organs which produce cognition and knowledge.

Time (*kāl*), space (*dik*) and *ākāśa* are the other remaining ultimate substances. The existence of Time is proved by its marks (i.e. the cognitions or the notions of): "Posterior", or "later", "simultaneous", "slow", "quick".[11] Likewise, *dik* (space) is also an ultimate substance. This is remote from a mark of space.[12] The unity of time and space are due to unity in existence. But they appear manifold on account of the accidental qualities added to them as the result of effects. Like "soul", both of them are *vibhu* (pervasive) and infinite, unlike *aṇu* (atom). *Akāśa* is the last substance, with sound as quality attached to it. It is also *vibhu* (pervasive).

Dik and *ākāśa* as substances are always confusing to the students of philosophy. Many of the modern philosophers translate *ākāśa* as space and *dik* as direction, but in my opinion, they are not correct. Encyclopedia Britannica has given the definition of "space" as "a boundless, three-dimensional extent in which objects and events occur and have relative position and direction." This definition of space includes both *dik* and *ākāśa*. The scientists have conceived "space" as a receptacle or a container or directional. Encyclopedia of Indian philosophy, explaining the difference between space (*dik*) and *ākāśa*, as found in Indian systems, states: ".... *ākāśa* is not exactly ubiquitous, since it does not penetrate atoms of the first four substances, whereas, of course, "space" as normally conceived does. Furthermore, the *Nyāya-Vaiśeṣika*, as opposed to *Bhaṭṭa Mīmāṃsaka* and *Vaiyākaraṇas*, believes that *ākāśa* cannot be perceived, whereas space, one might suppose, can be."[13] Thus they translate *dik* as space, and use the word *ākāśa* as it is. I also propose to do the same. In fact, the *ākāśa* of *Nyāya-Vaiśeṣika* is a substituted term for Vedic term *śalila*. Hence, if it is necessary to translate it in English, it can be translated only as "ether", as many have done. Hence this "....*ākāśa* is not a vacuum, a mere absence of objects, but a substance, which is conceived to be a physical matter as the other four gross elements. It corresponds to the ancient Greek conception of space as a gas-like 'ether'. In India it is thought to be the material medium of sound."[14] It has been said in the *vaiśeṣika-sūtra* that "the distinguishing feature of *ākāśa* is that it enters into (all empty spaces) and it quits (them when they are filled), (*niṣkramaṇam praveśanam iti ākāśasya liṅgam* – Vai. Sū. II.i.20).[15] Therefore, *sūnyatā*–void or vacuity–cannot go with the *Nyāya-Vaiśeṣika* concept of *ākāśa* but such *sūnyatā*, conceptually, may go with their *dik* or space. Their *dik* is an extensive space, alright, but is empty so as to accommodate all other substances, including *ākāśa* (ether) within itself. Thus, in *Nyāya-Vaiśeṣika* their *dik* (space) and *ākāśa* coexist. The most important difference between them is that *ākāśa* is regarded as one of the five elements (*pañca mahā-bhūtas*), whereas *dik* has no such status. Sound (*śabda*) is a quality or a property of the substance called *ākāśa* and not that of *dik* or space.

Each of the five elements (*pañca mahābhūtas*), as substances, inheres certain quality or qualities. The sound is a quality that inheres in *ākāśa*. The sensation of touch inheres in air. Likewise, Fire inheres two qualities: colour and touch;

Water, three: colour, taste and touch; Earth four: colour, taste, smell and taste. These five elements (*pañca mahābhūtas*), in turn, produce perishable phenomenal objects, as their effects (*kārya*). These phenomenal objects derive their qualities on account of the *samavāya* (coherence) relationship between such qualities and their basic elemental substances. The nature of the effect is already present in its cause (in the atom).[16] (Note: For this part I have followed the translations of Madan Mohan Agrawal with necessary modifications, if found necessary.)[17]

Gautama, in his *Nyāya Sūtra*, accepted the Atomic theory of Reality of *Vaiśeṣika* of Kaṇada. His contribution consists in his attempt to develop an epistemological theory to prove, with logical apparatus, the *padārthas* and *dravyas* which are identified by *Vaiśeṣika*. But for the purpose of his epistemological analysis he identifies different objects of investigation (*prameyas*) and proof. Accordingly, he says: "Soul, body, senses, objects of senses, intellect, mind, activity, fault, transmigration, fruit, pain, and release are the objects of right knowledge."[18] (Note : For this part of analysis I have adopted the translation of *Sūtras* by M.M. Satish Chandra Vidyābhūṣaṇa with the necessary modification whenever required.)[19]

The "soul (*ātman*) is not body, though this body is a site for the operation of the soul, through its gesture, sense and sentiments.[20] The soul is different from body and when the body is burnt, the soul is released.[21] The soul is beyond senses because the right eye recognizes what the left eye sees. When body is burnt, the soul continues to exist, since it is eternal. The soul is required to be admitted, as eternal on account of joy, fear, and the grief arising in a child from the memory of the things previously experienced. The child's desires for milk in this life are caused by the practice of his having drunk it in the previous life."[22] Thus remembrance is really a quality of soul.

There are five elements : earth (*pṛthvī*), water (*āpa*), light (*teja*), air (*vāyu*), and ether (*ākāśa*).[23] The sense-organs viz., "nose, tongue, eye, skin, and ear are the senses produced from elements."[24] Smell, taste, colour, touch, and sound are the objects of the senses and qualities of earth, etc.[25] Intellect, apprehension and knowledge are not different from each other.[26] The mark of the mind is that there do not arise (in the soul) more acts of knowledge than one at a time.[27] Activity is that which makes the voice, mind and body begin their action.[28]

The elements (*pañca mahābhūtas*) are found both in the objects of senses and in the sense-organs. The senses are essentially identical with the elements in consequence of the possession of their special quality.[29] "Sense" is really called as such when it is attended by its respective quality. Moreover, an object is never perceived by itself.[30]

Perception depends upon the special character of the substance and its quality. A colour is perceived only when it abides in things intimately, and when it is perceived through the unperceived ray of our eyes, when such a ray reaches the objects through the aid of external light.[31] There must be ray in the eye of man as we see it in the eye of animals that move about in the night (Nyā. Sū.3.1.44). The "senses are essentially identical with the elements in consequence of the possession of their special quality."[32] But their cognition is possible through the mind (*manas*). The cognition (or knowledge) of an object cannot take place when the mind is drawn away by another object.[33] Desire and aversion belong to the soul in as much as they are the causes of its doing an act or forbearing from doing the same.[34] Therefore, knowledge, etc., must be admitted to be the qualities of the soul by the principle of exclusion and on account of arguments already adduced. Thus even "memory belongs to the soul which possesses the character of a knower."[35] Transmigration is possible, since soul is eternal.[36]

Our false apprehension is destroyed by a knowledge of the truth just as our concept of objects in a dream comes to an end on our awakening. Gautama says that perception, etc., are the right means of knowledge and without admitting them, their denial is impossible.[37] They are established in the manner that drum is proved by its sound. "It is through convention that the meaning of a 'word', like 'drum, sound', '*nāda*', etc., is understood".[38] Vātsyāyana points out that when *sūtra* states that a *śabda* (word) is an assertion of a reliable person. (*āptopadeśaḥ śabdaḥ*—Nyā. Sū. 1.1.7). It means that it is a particular qualified word (*śabda*) that can be an instrument of right cognition which implies that there are several kinds of *śabdaḥ*. In this sense, *śabda* can be divided into letter –

sounds (*varṇātmaka*) and sound in general (Noise) (*dhvanyātmaka*).[39]

What is "Sound" then?

As per the *Tarka Sangraha* of "Annam" Bhaṭṭa, "The quality that is apprehended by the organ of hearing (*sotra*) is sound (*śabda*), it resides in ether only (*srotragrāhyo guṇaḥ śabdaḥ, ākāśamātravṛttīḥ*). It is twofold – inarticulate and articulate. Inarticulate sound like that of the sound of drum, etc., and articulate sound is in the form of letters of Sanskṛt and other languages".[40]

Inarticulate sound (*dhvanyātmaka śabda*) means a sound in general that is produced by human voice or by musical instruments, or sound in nature. This sound is quality of *ākāśa* (ether), according to *Nyāya Sūtra.* Articulate sound (*varṇātmaka śabda*), as explained by *Bhāṣya* of Vātsyāyana, commenting on Nyā. Sū. 2.2.13, is in the form of "word" "which represents a particular combination of sounds".[41] Even Viśvanātha, commenting on Nyā. Sū. 2.2.39 of Gautama stated that "there are two kinds of sounds: syllabic sound and only sound".[42] (Note : The discussion that I have considered hereinafter is an extraction or summary from Gangānātha Jhā).[43]

Now let us see the nature of these two kinds of sounds:

A. "Sound in general" (*dhvanyātmaka śabda*)

What is the nature of the "Sound in general" (*dhvanyātmaka śabda*)?

Is it eternal or non-eternal?

The "sound-in-general" is a non-syllabic sound like the sound of "drum" or the sound one hears, when some body were to simply shout loudly or the sound of a musical instrument.

What is the nature of this kind of sound-in-general?

Gautama accepts the view of *Vaiśeṣikas*, that is – "sound is the quality of *ākāśa* liable to production and destruction."

According to *Nyāya-Vaiśeṣika* philosophy each of the five elements (*pañca mahābhūtas*), as substance, inhere certain quality or qualities. The sensation of sound is a quality that inheres in *ākāśa*, and "sound" is the quality of *ākāśa* liable to production and destruction. "Sound is non-eternal, because it has a beginning and is cognized by our senses, and is spoken of as artificial (or product)."[44]

The non-eternality of sound is sought to be proved by Naiyāyikas, on the basis of three grounds:

1. That it has a beginning (*ādi*). Since it has a beginning, it is caused or produced by something else. It is caused by conjunction or disjunction. Once it is caused, it is liable to destruction. Hence it is not eternal.

2. It is apprehended through sense-organs and is not a matter of mere "manifestation" as contended by *Mīmāṃsakas*. The colour on the "jar", which is already there, is manifested. But in the case of "sound", it is apprehended by sense-organs after it is

produced by contact, i.e., when there is conjunction or disjunction. "For instance", says *Bhāṣya* of Vātsyāyana, "when a piece of wood is being cut, the 'sound' that arises from the impact of the axe with the wood is heard by the person at a distance and after that impact has ceased the sound also ceases to exist...." (Jhā - Vol. II, p. 905)

3. The "sound", being the product, is not the one "manifested." The product is normally spoken of as acute or dull, like acute pain or dull pain, etc. In the case of sound it is spoken of as "acute sound" or "dull sound." In modern days also we often find terminologies like "bass-sound" or "treble-sound" in the musical field. In order to have this kind of thing, it must be a product. One may still assert, in support of *Mīmāṃsaka*, that "acuteness" or "dullness" belongs to the manifester, just as one can speak of painting as being in "fast colour" or "dull colour", etc. Thus these qualities are of the manifester. But this kind of analogy does not hold good in the case of the "sound". Because in case of "sound" there is suppression, in the sense that the louder sound produced suppresses the weaker sound, just like a lamplight in the light of the sun. And such suppression of "weaker sound" by louder sound is possible only when such sounds are produced differently, as it happens in the case of the sound of violin in the present sound of bugle. In the case of

painting, though the painting is the same, it may manifest "bright" or "dull" colour as per the intensity of light to which it is exposed. Thus sound is "produced" not "manifested" like the colour of a painting. At the same time, it is possible that "the series of sounds (produced in each case) being distinct, it becomes possible for only a certain dull sound to be suppressed by a certain acute sound – this being dependent upon their reaching the auditory organ, at the same time. In the case of suppression of one sound, when, being otherwise audible, it is rendered inaudible by another sound" (*Bhāṣya* of Vātsyāyana).[45] Thus according to Gautama, eternal thing is one which is not destroyed (viz. atom, soul etc.). If so, all other things which are produced and destroyed are non-eternal. Sound having a beginning (produced) and an end is non-eternal.

Sāṅkhya also believes in the non-eternality of sound; but, according to Naiyāyikas this non-eternality of sound is of a different kind. For *Sāṅkhya* "non-eternal" means: "When it is found that all the conditions of the perception of a certain thing are present, and yet in its own form, the thing, having completely disappeared from the view, is absolutely not perceived...." (*Vārtika Uddyotakara*).[46] At the same time, according to *Sāṅkhya*, "everything" in the world is an evolutionary product of *prakṛti* (primordial matter), as such it is not different from that primordial matter. Thus, a thing is neither produced nor destroyed. According to them the so-called destruction is only a transformation of the known form to something else. When a pot is destroyed, it simply takes the form of pieces or dust. Such being the case, as a matter of fact, it is not possible that at any time no product of primordial matter should be perceived; that is, some product or the other is sure to be perceived always, as all are non-different from the original matter, no product can be said to be absolutely "not perceived."[47] If this is so, their statement, "....the thing, having completely disappeared from the view, is absolutely not perceived – that thing is called 'non-eternal'", is not consistent with their own basic theory.

The sound is characterized by both a beginning (cause) and an end (effect), and hence it is non-eternal. It is a product. It is amenable to senses, when it is found to be perceptible by means of proximity (contact) of an organ of perception. It is not possible for the auditory organ (of the hearer) to move up to the place (in the speaker's mouth) where sound appears. From this, it follows that the sound is produced, not simply manifested in the mouth of the speakers. At the same time, it is not possible for the sound to move up (to the auditory organ) of the hearer, since sound has no motion. *Ākāśa*, whose quality the sound is, being all-pervasive, also has no motion, and it cannot move up to the ears of the hearer. But unless sound reached the auditory organ of the hearer, no apprehension of that sound is possible. If such apprehension were to be possible, notwithstanding that, both the sound and *ākāśa* have no motion; there would be possibility of all sounds being apprehended by all men.

However, this does not happen, as our experience tells us. For instance, the same sound heard in Bangalore cannot be heard in Mysore. According to *Vārtika* of Uddyotkara, in these circumstances, only the hypothesis left is that (in case of every sound) "there is a 'series' of sounds; of this series, the first sound is produced by conjunction and disjunction; and from that initial sound proceed other sounds proceeding in all directions, like the filaments sticking out of the '*kadamba*' flower, (or when a stone is thrown into a pond circles of waves in water spread out, just like that) from each of these latter sounds, there proceeds another, and thence another, each of these being duller than its predecessor; and this series of sounds goes on being produced until there is an obstacle in the way of their vehicle (air); the last sound of this series, having become too attenuated, loses the capacity of producing a further sound, by reason of some sort of obstacle; thus the series of sounds comes to an end. Of these series of sounds that alone which approaches the *ākāśa*, in the ear-cavity (of the hearer) becomes apprehended (heard), and none other is so apprehended. It is so in view of the fact that sound is regarded as 'apprehended through a sense-organ'; and thus sound has to be regarded as 'non-eternal'; as otherwise the said apprehension through a sense-organ would not be possible (the 'production' of the series of sounds being impossible), if sounds were to be eternal."[48]

Vārtika of Uddyotkara, in view of their above theory, rejects the theory of *Mīmāṃsāka* that "there is only one sound" occupying the entire *ākāśa*, or when heard by the hearer a part of it is heard, etc., on the ground that, if there was to be only one sound occupying the entire *ākāśa*, then all the people of the world should hear it, but it does not happen like that. Their further theory that the hearer hears the sound, manifesting at the place of source, also cannot be accepted, because, the sound occupying the entire *ākāśa*, would be also all-pervasive like *ākāśa*, and a part of it (or its severance) is not conceivable; or such modification of sound, being a quality of *ākāśa*, also is unthinkable, (or even if sound is taken as substance (representing the view of Bhaṭṭas), there cannot be its modification, unless there is a cause of conjunction or disjunction in *ākāśa* but such a thing is not found). Even if it is assumed that such a part of sound can be manifested, (*śabdasya ekadeśaḥ abhivyajyate*,) then what the hearer hears at that place would be a part of the sound that would be unintelligible. For instance, a "letter" of a word cannot convey the meaning of the word. Moreover, *ākāśa*, being all pervasive, is indivisible. Hence this theory is liable to be rejected as untenable.[49]

The other theory of *Mīmāṃsākas* that in the case of wood cutting what happens is – "the air is produced by the stroke of the axe on the wood; this air is produced in the form of a current; so that this air-current reaches the *ākāśa* in the ear-cavity; and the sound subsisting in that *ākāśa*, becomes heard." This also is rejected by *Vārtika* of Uddyotkara. It is pointed out that *Mīmāṃsākas* believe that "the sound is eternal, in eternal all pervasive *ākāśa*, and whatever sound is manifested by the manifester in the form of 'air-current' (i.e., stroke of the axe), would manifest all sounds at the same time (in jumble), and if so, there could be no restriction for a particular sound being heard, as we do and hence this theory of *Mīmāṃsāka* also is untenable." But as already pointed out, the "sound" is neither eternal nor is it all-pervading, as being thought of by *Mīmāṃsākas*.[50]

Vārtika of Uddyotkara also rejected the Theory of Vibration. According to this theory, "what manifested sound is, not air, but a particular quality of air, called *nāda* vibration; but vibration cannot be accepted as the 'manifester' of sound; because even when the 'vibration' is perceived by a man at a distance, he does not (even though he hears the sound) hear or perceive it at the spot where the vibration has been perceived" (Jhā). Thus, this theory (of vibration) is rejected on the same grounds used, for rejecting the theory that "sound is manifested by the conjunction and disjunction of air" (as propounded by *Mīmāṃsākas*).[51]

However, *Vārtika* of Uddyotkara also took note of Sāṅkhya's serious objection to Naiyāyika's theory of sound, "If it be true that sound proceeding in a series and reaches the *ākāśa* enclosed in tympanum and becomes heard, then there could be no notion of direction in regard to sound" that a particular "sound" is being heard from the East or from the North, etc. (for example the direction of "odor" is not being experienced). His reply is that such direction of sound, we do experience in life and it is due to the sources of sound, located in different directions like in the East or in the North etc. and not due to the sound-series itself, and the notion of direction is not the same to all sounds having their sources in different directions. The source is the place where conjunction or disjunction takes place (the axe falling on the wood). Uddyotkara further clarified that "when the sound series first reaches (the auditory organ), it does so always from the direction of its source.... sound of this series, that reaches the *ākāśa* in a particular tympanum, is recognized as reaching that part of this *ākāśa* which lies in the direction of the sound, then there arises the notion of direction (in regard to the sound itself); but in cases where this first sound of the series cannot be discerned (and all sounds of the series of crowd at once), no notion of direction can arise. "But to this kind of objections *Vārtika* of Uddyotkara said "No". "Experience is otherwise".[52]

However some are of the opinion that notion of direction arises only when the object concerned is perceptible by the eye and as such persons born blind cannot experience the direction of sound; the direction of sound is always known with the help of both "eye" and "ear." P.F. Strawson, a Western philosopher also believes that "A pure auditory concept of space,....is an impossibility.... without 'visual, kinaesthetic, tactual phenomena' and 'congenitally blind' man can have concept of space with hearing combined with 'tactual with kinetic sensations.'" If it is so, according to Strawson, one can have sense of space like, above or below, left or right, nearer or farther, etc., through sense of hearing combined with "tactual with kinetic sensations" but without "visual" perception.[53] But to this kind of objections *Vārtika* of Uddyotkara said - "No". On the ground that human "Experience is otherwise".

Another important aspect of sound as highlighted by *Nyāya Sūtra* (2.2.18) is that the sound is known after it is "uttered" or "pronounced" (*ucchāraṇāt*). In other words, there is no sound before its utterance. But for *Mīmāṃsaka* sound being eternal, either as eternal quality of eternal *ākāśa* or as an independent eternal substance, exists even before its manifestation through vocal utterances. It is not comprehended because it is veiled; and the "utterance" with the help wind striking different parts of mouth, lifts the veil. "Thus the sound which was covered by veil was uncovered".[54] But according to Vātsyāyana, in fact such "impact of the wind with particular spot of mouth" caused the production of the sound, and it is not a matter of only manifestation. Naiyāyikas further add that there is no veil so as to cover the sound. Since sound is non-eternal, such a phenomena like a veil is conspicuously not perceptible; and such non perception consist in the absence of its perception[55] (in the sense that such veil does not exist so as to be perceived). Still objectors persist and say that sound is intangible accordingly it must be eternal, *Nyāya Sūtra* replied and said that though atom is eternal, still it is intangible.

B. Articulate sound (*varṇātmaka dhvani*)

Articulate sound is the one that takes the form of the "letters" (*varṇa*) and "words" (*śabda*) in language. If so, a question may be raised–What is the nature of the "sound" in a letter and consequently in "word"?

Viśvanātha in his *Bhāṣya-Paricceheda* explained the nature of syllabic sounds as – "Sounds such as *ka* that are produced by the conjunction of the throat, etc., are regarded as articulate (*kaṇṭhasaṃyogādijanyā varṇāste matāḥ*) (165) and the sound is transitory, because we have the notion that (the sound) *ka* is produced, and the sound *ka* is destroyed." As for the recognition, "This is that *ka*, it apprehends its belonging to the same class"(167)[56]. In *Siddhānta-Muktāvali*, his own commentary on *Bhāṣya-Paricceheda*, he further clarified that the sound is non-eternal being produced and destroyed. So also the sounds of syllables like *ka*, etc., are produced and destroyed. However it may be urged that sound is eternal, since we recognize that this is the same *ka*, and so on. But his explanation is that, in such instances we recognize the sound *ka* as belonging to the same class of *ka* and not that of its identity with first individual *ka*, and, in these circumstances even though sound *ka* is produced and destroyed but its recognition as belonging to the same class also is there, as in the case – "The very medicine that I had made was made by another also".[57]

Praśastapāda commenting on Vai. Sū.2.1.27 and 2.2.21, in his *Padārthadharmasaṅgraha* explains how this kind of process takes place. According to him 'the sound in the form of letters ...proceeds from the contact of the mind and soul as influenced by remembrances (p. 612). What constitutes such 'remembrances', *Nyāyakaṇḍalī* of Śrīdhara offers as further explanation: "the recognition of that 'this' is the same sound that I had heard yesterday"– can be explained as being similar due to similarity; as in the case of the flame, (which is regarded to be the same, while as a matter of fact there is only a series of continually appearing and disappearing series of distinct flames); specially as the fact of each sound (though similar) being distinct is proved by the differences in the degree of loudness or fairness of each individual sound.[58] I may emphasize here that the syllabic sounds proceeding from the contact of the mind and soul as influenced by remembrances, as explained by Praśastapāda and *Nyāyakaṇḍalī*, are modified or modulated sounds with the help of mind are of the description of *nāda*, similar to theory of Bhartṛhari. Hence *varṇātmaka dhvani* of Naiyāyikas is by itself *nāda* though they have not used the word *nāda*, nor they accept the theory of Bhartṛhari.

How do these letters manifest cognition?

Vārtika of Uddyotkara points out that the theory of Naiyāyika, is in contrast to the "*Sphoṭavāda*"of grammarians. According to *Sphoṭavāda*, "Things are not signified by 'letters'; as letters cannot have any connection with anything, either singly or collectively. Nor can things be held to be signified by letters as aided by the impressions left by the preceding letters; because impressions can pertain to their own objects, and not to other things; hence the impressions of letters could bring about the cognition of letters only, and not of 'things'. And yet it cannot be denied that when the letters *ghaṭaḥ* are pronounced, there comes about the cognition of the jar."

Hence the conclusion is that the letters concerned bring about the manifestation of a peculiar entity in the shape of *sphoṭa*–a kind of conglomerate sound–which in its turn brings about the cognition of the jar. That several letters should give rise to one *sphoṭa* is just like several words forming a sentence. Hence there is no such thing as "word," denoting things. This theory of *sphoṭa* is refuted by *Vārtika* of Uddyotkara by observing that - "In answer to this view we have the *sūtra* laying down that the 'word'–by which things are denoted–consists of the letters themselves, and 'not' of any such thing as *sphoṭa*. As a matter of fact, when a thing is spoken of by means of verbal expressions, we do not perceive anything except certain letters.... And so long as we can explain the phenomena of verbal expression on the basis of the directly perceptible letters, there can be no justification for assuming of a super physical and purely hypothetical entity in the shape of *sphoṭa*."[59]

Sphotvādins' further objection is that – "if the letters are the only thing perceived then cognition of the thing signified by them may not be possible." Meeting this objection *Vārtika* of Uddyotkara, stated that the perception of the last letter aided by "representative cognition" of foregoing letters makes such a cognition possible.[60]

According to *Tātparya* of Vācaspati Miśra, *"antyavarṇa-pratyayāt"* means "the later (*antya*, in relation to the first perception of each letter) cognition of letters (*varṇapratyaya*), the comprehensive cognition in the form of 'remembrance', that follows after the perception of each of the letters." In other words, according to the theory of Naiyāyikas, on the basis of the memory of their conventional denotative potency, the series of sound-letters, perceived (in a word) from beginning to end, (as represented by the last letter), signify the things they denote. They are established in the manner that a drum is proved by its sound. "It is through convention that the meaning of a word, like drum, sound, *nāda*, etc., is understood".[61] "There is no universal uniformity of connection between word and its meanings".[62] That is to say connection between a word and its meaning is not everywhere uniform. However, there is necessity for the classification of Vedic speech differently.[63]

According to the *Bhāṣya* of Vātsyāyana, on this *sūtra*, "Vedic texts must be regarded as an 'instrument of right recognition'; just as is done in ordinary parlance where every word serving a useful purpose is accepted as an instrument of right cognition." Vācaspati Mishra's *Nyāya-Vārtika-Tātparyaṭīkā* gives the following examples: "Fire is the antidote for cold (which is quite true)." Vedic texts are trustworthy, "because there is a classification of them on the basis of their purpose. Vedic texts also are found to be serving diverse purposes, these should be trustworthy.[64] Veda is thus reliable like the spell and the medical science because of the reliability of their authors."[65]

Is there a modification of sound?

Gautama proceeds to investigate in order to find out whether there can be modification of sound or not; since "there is a doubt, because there is mention of both 'modification' (*vikāra*) and 'substitution' (*ādeśa*), in the injunctions (*upadeśāt*) of the *śāstras*".[66] For instance, the conjunction of two words, viz., *dadhi* and *atra*, according to Grammarians, becomes *dadhyatra* because *i* of *dadhi* in conjunction with *a* of *atra* gets modified and becomes *ya* so as to read *dadhyatra*. But according to some others *i* of the word *dadhi* and *a* of *atra* are in juxtaposition and *i* of *dadhi* stands replaced by *ya*, and as such there is substitution of *ya* in the place of *i*.

According to *Bhāṣya* of Vātsyāyana, there is substitution. There cannot be modification for the reason that:

a. No continuity or persistence of letter-sound *i* is perceived so as to cause modification of *i* sound into *ya*.

b. The two letters, *i* and *ya*, are uttered with independent effort (*prayatna*) at different parts of mouth: in the case of *i* there is open articulation like any other vowel but in the case of *ya* there is "slightly touched articulation" as is the case with semi-vowels. Hence there is no modification of letter *i* into letter *ya*. It follows that the letter *ya* is substituted in the place of *i*.

Would it not violate the rule of the grammar that *ik* followed by *ach* becomes *yan* (Pāṇini, 1.1.45 & 6.1.77) and as such there is modification? But Vātsyāyana says "no."

According to him, the grammatical rule (*iko yanchi*) itself means that "when *i* and *a* are in juxtaposition, we should use *ya* in the place of *i* and 'not' that *i* is 'modified' into *ya*. As pointed out by Ny. Su. II.ii.41, if the letters underwent modification, an increase of the bulk in the original material would have caused a corresponding increase of the bulk in the modification. In the instant case both short *i* and *ya* are of the same bulk. Moreover the modification always follows the original base, e.g. the banyan seed gets modified into banyan tree. A coconut tree cannot emanate out of a banyan seed. *Bhāṣya* of Vātsyāyana further states that the letters cannot have modifications like gold into ornaments. In case of gold ornaments, gold subsists as constancy. Hence, ornaments can be converted back into gold. Moreover, no such conversion is possible, if the thing converted takes altogether different qualities or properties. For instance, curds cannot be reconverted into milk. Thus, curds is altogether a different substance from milk. This illustration makes it clear that no 'constancy' (*nityatva*) subsists in milk and curds, (like gold in gold-ornaments) so as to convert one from the other. In the same way *ya* is altogether a different bundle of qualities than *i*. Hence there is no modification of *ya* into *i* or vice-versa. Hence the letter *ya* in *dadhyatra* is only a substitution to *i*. *Vārtika* of Uddyotkara further clarifies that in all the cases of 'so-called modification' there is 'either coming in of fresh properties' or 'suppression', but not any modifications of letters, as such."[67]

But according to Bhartṛhari and other grammarians, there is modification of sound in syllables and words. (See Ch. seven). I will be considering both the theories critically in Chapter ten.

What is the nature of "perception of sound" according to *Nyāya-Vaiśeṣika* philosophers?

According to *Nyāya-Vaiśeṣika* philosophers, sound being the quality of *ākāśa* it inheres in it. It is produced by the causes like conjunction and disjunction. For example, sound is produced (in the case of sound of the drum) by the conjunction of *ākāśa* with drum; and this conjunction is aided by (and hence dependent upon) the force with which the stick is struck. Sound also is produced by disjunction as in the case of separation of bamboo fiber. In both the cases the "contact" (*sannikarṣa*) in the form of "inherence" of the inherent (the genus inhering in sound which inheres in the *ākāśa* of the auditory organ is necessary.[68]).

In all cases of perceptions including that of sound the contact of sense-organs with mind also is necessary and it is this mind which, in fact, establishes contact between the sensation of the sense-organs with the objects of the external world. According to the notes appended by Vacaspati Miśra's *Nyāya Vārtika Tātparyaṭīkā*, just as "the axe and such other instruments operate on their objects (wood, etc.,) only by getting at them, and the sense-organs are instruments, therefore the sense-organs must be operative by getting at their object".[69] The sense-mind contact is similar to the mind-soul contact.[70] Thus according to Naiyāyikas, there cannot be perception of the objects unless the sense-organs get at their objects. "Thus then it is established that 'perception' is the 'cognition' produced by the contact of the sense-organ with the object".[71] In the circumstance, *Nyāya Sūtra* defines perception as : "Perception is that knowledge (*jñānam*) which arises from the contact (*sannikarṣe*) of a sense with its object, which is determinate (*avyabhicāri*), unnameable and non-erratic (unerroneous) (*indriyārthasannikarṣotpannaṃ jñānamavyapadeśyamavyabhicāri vyavasāyātmakaṃ prayakṣam*)."

An objection is raised: "For what purpose is the word 'cognition' introduced into the definition of perception?"

The Naiyāyikas offer more than one reason by way of reply. Their strongest reason for including "cognition" in the definition of perception is to avoid "erroneous cognition." *Bhāṣya* of Vātsyāyana explains such "erroneous cognition" with the help of "mirage" experienced during summer. (During summer it often happens that the sun's rays mixed up with the heat-rays radiated from the earth's surface; and the two together flickering at a distance come into contact with eye of the observer, who apprehends them as water.)[72]

What "erroneous"? Does the error lie in the "object" or in the "cognition"?

Some Naiyāyikas say, "The 'error' lies in the object: it is the object that appears as what is not; and it is on account of this wrong appearance of the 'object' that the cognition is called erroneous." According to *Bhāṣya,* this explanation is not correct. Because the object all the while remains the same as what it actually is. In regard to the flickering rays of the sun, when there arises the cognition of water, there is no error in the object; it is not that the "rays" are not the "rays", nor that the "flickering" is "not flickering"; what the error lies in it the "cognition" as it is the "cognition" which, instead of appearing as the "cognition of flickering rays", appears as "the cognition of water", i.e., the cognition of a thing as something which is not; there being no water there.... It has been so "by reason of some defect in the perceiving organ; hence it is in the 'cognition', not in the object, that the error lies."[73]

How is it that the mind is not included in the definition of perception?

According to Naiyāyikas, the "mind" is in fact an effective means of right recognition, but the nature of "mind" is different from other sense-organs. While other sense-organs are effective on only certain particular objects, the mind is effective on all objects. [This affords the reason for mind not being mentioned in the *sūtra* along with the other sense-organs.][74] In the result, we find that, according to Naiyāyikas there are six sense-organs with six kinds of senses, viz., 1. the eye (colour, etc.), 2. the ear (sound), 3. the nose (odour), 4. the tongue (savour), 5. the tactual surface (touch of warmth, coldness, hardness, softness, etc.,) and 6. the mind (feeling of pleasure, pain etc.). Corresponding with the senses there are six kinds of senses with six kinds of knowledge (perception), viz., the visual, auditory, olfactory, gustatory, tactual and mental (internal).

The contacts (*sannikarṣa*), translated as "intercourse" by Vidyabhusana, is of the nature of the connection of the senses with its object, and it is of six kinds as follows:

"1. Union (*saṃyoga*), e.g., in the visual perception of a jar there is union of our eye with the jar.

2. United-inherence (*saṃyukta-samavāya*), that is, inherence in that which is in union, e.g., in the visual perception of the colour of a jar there is a union of our eyes with the jar in which colour inheres.

3. United-inherent-inherence (*saṃyukta-samaveta-samavāya*), that is, inherence in that which inheres in what is in union, e.g., in the visual perception of the 'colourness' (the generic nature of colour) of a jar there is union of our eye with the jar in which inhere colour wherein again abides 'colourness' in the relations of inherence.

4. Inherence (*samavāya*), that is, in the auditory perception of sound there is the inherence of sound in the ether which pervades the cavity of our ear.

5. Inherent-inherence (*samaveta-samavāya*), that is, inherence in that which inheres, e.g., in the auditory perception of 'soundness' (the generic nature of sound), there is the inherence of 'soundness' in sound which again inheres in the ether of our ear-cavity.

6. Particularity (*viśeṣaṇatā*), e.g., in the perception of non-existence of a jar on the ground, there is a union

of our eye with the ground which is possessed of non-existence of the jar."[75]

Since I am concerned with perception of sound, the type of contact (*sannikarṣa*) that is applicable would be vide item nos. four and five. If somebody were to utter sound *gha,* the same is heard by the listener because the sound *gha* that inheres in *ākāśa* (in *samavāya* relation as its quality) produces the soundness (that inheres in sound by way of *samaveta-samavāya* relation) in the *ākāśa* of the ear-cavity of the listener. As a result the listener "perceives" the sound *gha* that inheres in the *akāśa* of his ear-cavity. This sound *gha* in linguistic convention is recognised as a letter-sound (*varṇa*). This letter-sound along with another letter-sound *ṭa* takes the form of a word *ghaṭa.* In addition, according to convention, it means a "pot". If a person, knowing the meanings of these words, utters a sentence *ghaṭaḥ asti* (there is a pot), it would be a means of valid knowledge. In this manner "....the means by which or the process through which the valid knowlege is derived, is called verbal testimony (*śabda pramāṇa*).... Any knowledge derived from a speech is called verbal knowledge (*śabda-bodhaḥ*)."

Vidyābhūṣaṇa explains the nature of this speech process as under:

"In a speech–*ghaṭaḥ asti* (there is a pot)–are to be noted the following:

i. At first there is *hearing of* (*śabdasya śravaṇam*) words in the speech, viz., *ghaṭa+ḥ+as+ti'* (there + is + a + pot).

ii. Then there is the *recollection of things* (*arthasya smaraṇam*) signified by the words, viz., the recollection of 'pot' signified by the word *ghaṭa*, of 'one' signified by *ḥ* (a modification of the first-case-ending *su*) of 'existing' signified by *as* and of 'the state of abiding' signified by *ti* (a verbal termination of the third person, singular number, present tense).

iii. Afterwards there is the knowledge of the *mutual connection of things* thus recollected (*saṃsarga-bodhaḥ*), that is, the knowledge that a 'pot' as qualified by oneness is an abode of existence. The knowledge in this third step is specially called a verbal knowledge.

iv. Lastly there is *self-consciousness* (*anuvyavasāya*) of the knowledge in the following form : I am the possessor of the knowledge of pot which as qualified by oneness is an abode of existence."[76]

The Gist of the theory of *Nyāya - Vaiśeṣika* philosophers:

Nāda is a quality (_guṇa_) of _ākāśa_ (ether) which is an extensive atom (Phenomenal theory of Sound)

Nyāya- Vaiśeṣika philosophers also adopt the principles of Vedic cosmic *vāk*, like *Sāṅkhya*-Yoga, but they proceed from the phenomenal world to the cosmic world, in keeping with their theory of "atomism."

In *Nyāya-Vaiśeṣika* theory, sound is a "quality" of *ākāśa*. *Ākāśa* is one of the nine substances (*dravyas*). Of all the atoms, *ākāśa* is *vibhu* (an extensive and all pervasive substance). Qualities inhere in substance. The phenomenal objects derive their qualities from the *samavāya* (inherence) relationship between the qualities and their basic substances. Even actions inhere in substance. They cause conjunction and disjunction, etc., because of the *adṛṣṭa* principle (*ṛtam* principle as explained in Chapter two). Time and space (*dik*) are other substances. "Posterior", or "later", "slow" and "quick", etc., indicate time, and "this" and "that" indicate *dik*. *Ākāśa* is similar to Greeks "gas like ether" (similar to vedic *śalila*) which functions as a material medium of sound. Sensation of sound is also a quality that is inherent in *ākāśa*. Perception, as a right means of knowledge, depends on the special character of the substance and its quality. Sound is caused by conjunction, disjunction, etc., and gets destroyed by any kind of obstruction. Hence, sound, being a quality of *ākāśa*, is produced and destroyed, and, as such, it is non-eternal. However, Veda can be an instrument of right recognition, as a statement of a reliable person just like the statements of the persons in medical science.

Naiyāyikas use *śabda*, for physical sound which is considered the quality of *ākāśa*. This sound is divided into: *Dhvanyātmaka* (physical sound) produced by drum (*bherī*) and *Varṇātmaka dhvani* (syllabic sound). The syllabic sounds consciously produced by an effort in vocal organ in their application) would be of the nature of *nāda*. The syllabic sound is the basic material for a letter, and, ultimately for the word. A word is a "particular combination of sound." Sound is a quality of eternal *ākāśa*, and, as such, there cannot be any modification of such sound but only a substitution; and *ya* is a substitution in the word *dadhyatra* for *i* and *a*, and not a modification. Hence they do not accept the theory of modification sound of Bhartṛhari. Each letter is destroyed by succeeding letter but with the help of the last letter; in a series, a comprehensive cognition is obtained, based on the memory of their conventional denotative potency.

Notes and References

1. Vai. Sū. 1.i.4.
2. Vai. Sū. 1.4 and 17.
3. Vai. Sū. 1.5.
4. Vai. Sū. 1.i.12.
5. Vai. Sū. 1.i.14.
6. Vai. Sū. 1.i.17, 30.
7. Vai. Sū. 1.ii.3.
8. Vai. Sū. 1.ii.5-6.
9. Vai. Sū. ii.12, 13 &17.
10. Vai. Sū. III.ii.10 and 18.
11. Vai. Sū. 2.2.6.
12. Vai. Sū. 2.2.6.
13. Potter, Karl H. (1995): Vol. II; p. 90.
14. Baumer, Bettina (ed.) : Vol. III; p. 125.
15. *Kalātattvakośa* - Vol. III; p. 126.

16. Vai. Sū. 4.1.2 & 3.
17. Agrawal, Madan Mohan (2001).
18. Nyā. Sū. 1.1.9.
19. Vidyābhūṣaṇa, Satish Chandra M.M. (1990).
20. Nyā. Sū. 1.1.11.
21. Nyā. Sū. 3.1.4.
22. Nyā. Sū. 3.1.18 & 3. 1.18 & 21.
23. Nyā. Sū. 1.1.13.
24. Nyā. Sū. 1.1.12.
25. Nyā. Sū. 1.1.14.
26. Nyā. Sū. 1.1.15.
27. Nyā. Sū. 1.1.16.
28. Nyā. Sū. 1.1.17.
29. Nyā. Sū. 3.1.70.
30. Nyā. Sū. 3.1.71III.i.71.
31. Nyā. Sū. 3.1.35, 36, 41.
32. Nyā. Sū. 3.1.63.
33. Nyā. Sū. 3.2.7.
34. Nyā. Sū. 3.2.34.
35. Nyā. Sū. 3.2.38-40.
36. Nyā. Sū. 4.1.10.
37. Nyā. Sū. 2.1.12.
38. Nyā. Sū. 2.1.55.
39. *dvidhascayaṃ śabdo varṇātmako dhvanimātrāsca*, p. 638: Tarkatirtha Amarendramohan (2003).
40. *srotragrāhyo guṇaḥ śabdaḥ, ākāśamātravṛttīḥ, sa dvividhaḥ dhvanyātmakaḥ varṇātmakaśca, tatra dhvanyātmakaḥ bheryādau, varṇātmakaḥ śaṃskṛtabhāṣādirūpaḥ*, verse 15; *Tarka Sangraha*

with the Dīpika Annambhaṭṭa and Notes; p. 67: Swami Virupakshananda (*tr.*) (1994).

41. Jhā, Gangānātha (1999) : Vol. II (foot-note, at page 903).
42. *dvividhaścāyaṃ śabdo varṇātmako dhvanimātrāśca;* p. 638: (in his Vṛtti) Tarkatirtha Amarendramohan (2003).
43. Jhā, Gangānātha (1999) : Vol. II .
44. Nyā. Sū. 2.2.13.
45. See Nyā. Sū. Vol. II; pp. 904-07 : Jhā, Gangānātha.
46. Nyā. Sū. Vol. II; p. 910 : Jhā, Gangānātha.
47. *Tatparya* - Foot Note No. 3 at page 915 - Vol. II - Nyā. Sū. : Jhā, Gangānātha.
48. See p. 923, Nyā. Sū.; Vol. II : Jhā, Gangānātha.
49. See pp. 921–23, Nyā. Sū.; Vol. II : Jhā, Gangānātha.
50. pp. 923-30, Nyā. Sū.; Vol. II : Jhā, Gangānātha.
51. Nyā.Sū. Vol. II ; p. 931 : Jhā, Gangānātha.
52. Nyā.Sū. Vol. II; pp. 935-36 : Jhā, Gangānātha.
53. Strawson, P.F (1959) : Ch. on *'Sounds';* p. 65-66.
54. Nyā.Sū. Vol. II; p. 952 : Jhā, Gangānātha.
55. Nyā.Sū. 2.2.19-21.
56. Swami Madhavānanda (1956) : p. 266
57. ____ (1956) : p. 268.
58. Jhā, Gangānātha. (1982) : pp. 612-13.
59. Tr. para 3 of foot-note - Nyā. Sū.; p. 1010, Vol. II : Jhā, Gangānātha.
60. Tr. at Nyā. Sū. - p. 1011, Vol. II : Jhā, Gangānātha.
61. Nyā. Sū. - 2.1.55.
62. Nyā. Sū. - 2.1.56.
63. Nyā. Sū. - 2.1.61.

64. Nyā.Sū.: Vol.II; at pp. 861-62 : Jhā Gangānātha
65. Nyā. Sū. 2. 1.68.
66. Nyā. Su. 2.2.40.
67. Tr. at Nyā. Sū. Vol. II; p. 1009: Jhā, Gangānātha.
68. Nyā. Sū. Vol. I; p. 121 : Jhā, Gangānātha.
69. Nyā. Sū. Vol. I; p. 132 : Jhā, Gangānātha.
70. Nyā. Sū. Vol. I; p. 125 : Jhā, Gangānātha.
71. Nyā. Sū. Vol. I; p. 133. : Jhā, Gangānātha.
72. Nyā. Sū. Vol. I; p. 135 : Jhā, Gangānātha.
73. Nyā. Sū. Vol. I; pp. 135-36 : Jhā, Gangānātha.
74. Nyā. Sū. Vol. I; p. 140 : Jhā, Gangānātha.
75. Viḍyābhuṣaṇa, Satish Chandra (2002) : pp. 411-12.
76. ____ (2002) : pp. 444-45.

* * *

Chapter Five

THE DOCTRINES OF *NĀDA* OR *ŚABDA* IN *MĪMĀṂSĀ* AND *VEDĀNTA* SYSTEMS

From the point of view of my thesis, *Mīmāṃsā* and *Vedānta* are important schools, after *Nyāya - Vaiśeṣika.* These schools with their basic aphorisms (*sūtras*) and commentaries thereon, have developed a theory which is almost diagonally opposite to the theory of *nāda* or *dhvani* as propounded by *Nyāya - Vaiśeṣika* on one hand, and that of *Sāṅkhya* -Yoga on the other.

Many times *Mīmāṃsā* and *Vedānta* are linked up owing to their common faith in the authority and eternality of Veda, though for different reasons. Sometimes *Mīmāṃsā,* is called *Pūrva Mīmāṃsā,* as against *Uttara Mīmāṃsā* (*Vedānta*). The central theme of *Mīmāṃsā* is the desire of knowing of the duty [*athāto dharmajijñāsa*] and that of *Vedānta* "The desire of knowing Brahman" [*athāto brahmajijñāsa*] ("The desire of the knowledge of the reality"). *Vedānta* in Sanskṛt means "the end of Veda" or "culmination of the Vedic thought".

Bādarāyaṇa, the pioneer of *Vedāntic* thought, attempted a reconciliation of the inconsistent conclusions of *Upaniṣads* in his *sūtras* (aphorisms) called *Brahma Sūtras*. The commentators of *Brahma Sūtras* also contributed, very much for the development of *Vedānta* philosophy by providing different and, sometimes even divergent approaches to the said *sūtras*. Śankara, Bhāskara, Yādavaprakāśa, Rāmānuja, Nīlakaṇṭha, Madhva, Baladeva, Vallabha, Nimbārka and Vjñānabhikṣu, etc., are some of such renowned commentators. Out of these persons, the theories advocated by Śankara, Ramānuja and Madhava are quite distinct and most popular. It is very difficult for one to say which one of these theories is correct. It is also not within the scope of this thesis to examine the same. Hence I propose to examine *Vedānta* philosophy mainly on the basis of Bādarāyaṇa's *Brahma Sūtras* with the help of Śankara's *Bhāṣya*, and likewise with regard to *Mīmāṃsā*, I propose to rely heavily on *Mīmāṃsā Sutras* of Jaimini, and *Shabarabhāṣya* of Shabarasvāmin on *Mīmāṃsā Sūtras*. In turn there were two powerful commentators of *Shabarabhāṣya* : Kumārila Bhaṭṭa and Prabhākar, each with a band of followers, paved the way for two sub-schools commonly known as "*Bhaṭṭa Mīmāṃsā*" and "*Prābhākara Mīmāṃsā*" Of them *Bhaṭṭa Mīmāṃsā*, appears to be more popular. Hence, I strongly rely on "*Ślokavārtika* of Kumarila Bhaṭṭa" in order to appreciate the philosophy of *nāda* of *Mīmāṃsā* system. I will be referring to Prabhākara's theory also, whenever it is felt necessary, as counterpoint of view, amongst *Mīmāṃsākas*.

"Of the seven categories formulated in the *Nyāya-Vaiśeṣikā*", in the words of Prof. Hiriyanna, "*Mīmāṃsā* accepts five categories viz. substance (*dravya*), quality (*guṇa*), action (*karma*), universals (*sāmānya*) and non-existence (*abhāva*); and it rejects the remaining two – *samavāya* (coherence) and *viśeṣa* (differentia). ....As regards the first of these categories, viz., substance, the Mīmāṃsā admits all the nine which *Nyāya-Vaiśeṣika* does: (earth, water, air, fire, *ākāśa*, space, time, self, and *manas*); and adds two more to them. They are darkness (*tamas*) and sound (*śabda*). Of the latter, the first is explained in the *Nyāya-Vaiśeṣika* as mere absence of light and the second as a quality of *ākāśa*."[1]

Thus *Mīmāṃsā*, like *Nyāya-Vaiśeṣika*, is a realistic school; and as such it accepts the atomic theory of the external world and pluralistic souls. Mīmāṃsā considers perception (*pratyakṣa*), inference (*anumāna*) verbal testimony (*śabda*), as primary among the six *pramāṇās*, the other three being *upamāna* (comparison), presumption (*arthāpatti*), non-apprehension (*anupalabdhi* or *āpoha*), (or apprehension of "negation" (*abhāva*) as others call it).

On the other hand *Vedānta* holds that, "*Brahman* is that from which (subsistence and dissolution), beginning with the origin of this (world proceed)."[2] Interpreting the said aphorism, Śaṅkara says that *Brahman* is the only entity that is real and the three states of the world : origin, subsistence and dissolution, with their names and forms, causes and effects, depend upon him. "Even the origin of the five great *bhūtas* must be referred back to the *Brahman*, which is both omniscient and omnipotent...."[3] According to Gauḍapāda, in fact all entities like sky, etc., (called *pañca mahābhūtās*) are beginningless and eternal and enlightened, since they are nothing but *Brahman*, Himself. But due to ignorance, the mental wrecks move about in the world of duality and difference.[4] To realize this truth, *Brahmajñāna* is absolutely necessary.

Commenting on Br. Sū. 2.3.7 (*yadvikāraṃ tu vibhāgo lokavat* - "But whatever is an effect (*vikāraṃ*) is (also) a distinct entity, as is seen in ordinary life"), Śaṅkara says – *ākāśa* must have been originated. Besides, *ākāśa* must be non-eternal because it has the non-eternal quality of sound in it.[5] Commenting on Br. Sū. 2.3.8-11 he further adds that the same is the position with regard to "air", fire, water, etc., being the product of *Brahma* are non-eternal elements.[6]

According to Śaṅkarācārya, all the gross objects of this world are the combination of these five fundamental elements (*pañca mahābhūtas*), ether, air, fire, water, earth. He calls the process of such conjunction of five elements *pañcīkaraṇa*, which is translated as "quintuplication", in his small treatise, *pañcīkaraṇa*. But before the quintuplication, (i.e., *apañcīkṛta* state) these five elements have independent existence as rudimentary elements with their effects, constituting the subtle body called the *Hiraṇyagarbha* (Cosmic Egg). This material subtle body (*liṅga*) has seventeen parts, viz., five vital forces (*prāṇa*, *apāna*, *vyāna*, *udāna*, *samāna* – also called *pañca-vāyu*), five organs of perception (ear, skin, eye, tongue, nose called *pañcendriyas*); and five organs of actions, hands, legs, organs of excretion called *karmendriyas*); the mind (*manas*), and the intellect (*buddhi*). All these seventeen constitute the subtle body of the *Ātman*. But after quintuplication (*pañcīkṛta*) of *pañca mahābhūtas*, they constitute into gross elements.[7]

Sureśvarācārya explains the nature of this process of compounding of these elements as under:

"Each of the five elements, i.e. Earth, etc., must be divided into two equal parts. One of these two parts should be further split into four equal parts. Now one half of each element should be added to one quarter of each of the other four halved elements towards the formation of one gross element. Thus in Ether there will be five constituent parts. Half of it will be Ether and the other half will consist of the four parts contributed together by all the other four elements, at ratio of one-eighth each. The same would be the case in all other four elements, like Air, etc. This process is the fivefold combination according to the wise" (Verses 8-10)[8]. This principle can be put in tabular form as under:

		Ether +	Air +	Fire +	Water +	Earth
Ether (*ākāśa*)	-	**1/2**	1/8	1/8	1/8	1/8
Air (*vāyu*)	-	1/8	**1/2**	1/8	1/8	1/8
Fire (*teja*)	-	1/8	1/8	**1/2**	1/8	1/8
Water (*āpa*)	-	1/8	1/8	1/8	**1/2**	1/8
Earth (*pṛthvī*)	-	1/8	1/8	1/8	1/8	**1/2**

(Sanskṛt equivalents are inserted by me)[9]

Having regard to this kind of composition, each gross element, has the characteristics of other elements, by retaining its own individual predominant characteristic. Sound is the predominant quality of the gross element *ākāśa* but a hard substance like "bell" when struck with a hammer produces "sound" because the hard substance (metal), as "earth", has shared the quality of *ākāśa* which is constituted of one-eighth share of *ākāśa* by retaining, at the same time, its own "earth element" at the one-half share.

I pause here to point out that the other part of the commentary of Srī Sureśvarācārya states that ".... Ether has the quality of sound only. Air possesses the double qualities of sound and touch. Light or Fire is said to have the triple qualities sound, form, touch. Water is said to possess four qualities – sound, form, touch and taste; whereas the Earth is endowed with five qualities, viz., sound, touch, form, taste and smell".[10] But this "one, two, etc., principle" is inconsistent to the principle of *pañcīkaraṇa* (quintuplication) as advocated by Śrī Śaṅkarācārya. According to Śrī Śaṅkarācārya, all the gross elements share the other gross elements and their qualities, in the ratio as explained by Srī Sureśvarācārya himself (extracted above, illustrating the same with chart). Hence describing the same quintuplicated (*pañcīkṛta*) compounds (ether, air, light, fire, earth) as constituting "one, two, three, four and five *tanmātras*" respectively would be self contradictory, and also inconsistent with *pañcīkaraṇa* (quintuplication) principle of Śrī Śaṅkarācārya, explained by himself in terms of "one-half and one-eighth" principle.[11]

In fact, as we have seen in the Chapter three on *Sāṅkhya*-Yoga, on the same lines the commentators of Iśvara Kṛṣṇa (with reference to *Sāṅkhya Kārikā*, 34 and 38), provided the composition of the five gross elements, as under: "in case of gross-*Ākāśa*, there is only one *tanmātra*, (i.e., *śabda tanmātra*); likewise in case of *Vāyu* two (*vāyu* + *śabda*); *Agni* three (*agni* + *śabda* + *vāyu*); *Āpa* four (*āpa* + *śabda*, + *vāyu* + *agni*), and *Pṛthvi* five (*pṛthvī* + *śabda* + *vāyu* + *āpa* + *agni*)."[12] But finding quintuplication principle inconsistent with the theory of gross elements which are formed of one, two, three, four and five *tanmātras* respectively, quintuplication theory itself was given up by later *Sāṅkhya* philosophers. But the *Pañcīkaraṇa* of Śrī Śaṅkarācārya, with a different formula of quintuplication, in which a gross element retains its own individual character, even after quintuplication, does not suffer from the difficulty of *Pañcīkaraṇa* of ancient *Sāṅkhya* did. Therefore *Pañcīkaraṇa* theory of Śrī Śaṅkarācārya, which is based on a more rational foundation (than that of *Pañcīkaraṇa* of ancient *Sāṅkhya*), is acceptable even today to the Vedic scholars. In these circumstances, the theory of gross elements being formed of one, two, three, four and five *tanmātras* respectively, is liable to be given up in preference to *Pañcīkaraṇa* theory. Moreover *Pañcīkaraṇa* theory appears to be more plausible in view of modern scientific theories, according to which the forms of elements are changeable, i.e., from solid to liquid, from liquid to gas, etc., and this would not have been possible unless every element shared some qualities of the other elements. For instance, water (*āpa*), predominantly liquid, can be found in the form of ice [solid similar to earth (*pṛthvī*) element], and in the form of steam (gaseous, similar to air element), etc.

Moreover, in Śaṅkarācārya's scheme *ākāśa* is a substance like any other substance duly sharing the qualities of other element at one-eighth ratio. Unless *ākāśa* shared "air" element as its own fundamental quality, the sound which is said to have been produced by *ākāśa* could not have been communicated. According to modern science and its "bell jar" experiment, sound cannot be communicated without a medium like air. The birds could not fly in the *ākāśa*, as contemplated by the commentators of Iśvara Kṛṣṇa, since it is constituted of *śabda-tanmātra* only as the sole characteristic. Such instances clearly establish the plausibility of Śaṅkarācārya's theory as against the *Pañcīkaraṇa* theory of ancient *Sāṅkhya* philosophers.

But for the purpose of this thesis an important question that is required to be posed to both *Mīmāṃsā* and *Vedānta* systems would be: What is the nature of that sound (*nāda*)?

According to *Vedānta* philosophy, just like *Mīmāṃsā*, Vedas are eternal and are the sources of real knowledge of Brahman. The eternality of Veda is assured by the priority of sound (*śabdapūrvatvam*)[13]. In fact, according to the *Autpattika sūtra* of *Mīmāṃsā*[14] the Vedas have self validity, and are eternal, just like that of the relation between word and its meaning.

So far as the theory of *nāda* is concerned both Mīmāṃsā and Śaṅkara share a common thought by tracing their theory to a common ancestor by name Upavarṣa, "an ancient grammarian and *Mīmāṃsaka*."[15] Śaṅkara himself in his *Bhāṣya* of *Brahma Sūtra* (1.3.28) stated that according to the said Upavarṣa "the word is made up of letters only, in as much as there is no separate perception of *sphoṭa* over and above the perception of the letters."[16] *Mīmāṃsā* also accepted the same principle, as we see hereunder. In the present circumstance, I propose to discuss the philosophy of *nāda* in respect of both *Mīmāṃsā* and *Vedānta* together.

Regarding the nature of sound, *Mānameyodaya* of Nārāyaṇa, one of the authoritative works on *Mīmāṃsā*, following Kumārila Bhaṭṭa School, asserts as under:

"Sound is what can be apprehended by the sense of hearing alone and has the genus, soundness; it is all-pervading and eternal, and a substance (*dravyam*); so is it accepted in the system of Kumārila."

"Some scholars (Prabhākaras) say that sound is a quality of ether. This is discarded by Bhaṭṭapāda since that is in conflict with perception, etc."[17]

Nārāyaṇa further elaborates and says: "Sound is a substance, because it can be directly apprehended through a direct relation with sense-organ, like a jar; .... Sound is not a quality (of ether), because it can be apprehended through the sense of hearing, like soundness. Therefore its being as substance has to be concluded from other means of valid knowledge"[18]....Sound is all pervasive, because it is an intangible substance, or because while it is not producer, it is a substance without parts, like soul.... Since of the same sound *g*, there is simultaneous cognition by those situated in all directions, there is established its grossness."[19] Dr. Govardhana P. Bhaṭṭa, in his doctoral thesis, has also said: "According to the Bhaṭṭa, *śabda* is an eternal and omnipresent substance and the effort of a speaker does not produce but simply manifests it."[20] Because of the effort in vocal cord, sound manifests of its own (but not produced) just like water manifest of its own while digging the earth.

But a contrary theory is advocated by Sālikanātha Miśra, a close disciple of Prabhākara. He described sound, as a quality of *ākāśa*. According to him "sound as the attribute of ether should be admitted by one who advocates that the sense of hearing is possible through *ākāśa*-element, when it comes in contact with the object. Otherwise, the sense of such a sound would be impossible, without one of the two relations, viz., conjunction and inherence, and such relation would be impossible in case sound is admitted as substance, (hence) it is admitted that sound is the attribute of ether....".[21]

From this kind of description it is clear that according to Prābhākaras, the sound is the quality of *ākāśa* which is eternal, similar to the theory of *Vaiśeṣikas*. But according to them what is produced is a sound in the form of "letters" (*varṇa*) which are eternal. They don't seem to admit an indistinct, non-syllabic (inarticulate) sound as Bhaṭṭas do. In the circumstances it is clear that "The *Mīmāṃsakas* admission of eternality of *varṇātmaka śabda* is due to their recognition of it as *dravya* on par with *ākāśa*. They, however, do not recognise the sounds that manifest the letters as eternal."[22]

How is this sound perceived?

For both *Vedānta* and *Mīmāṃsā* sense perceptions do not cognize the principles of injunctions of Vedas and other *Śrutis*. For Śaṅkara the word *pratyakṣa* means intuition and not sensual perception and through such intuition only Vedic principles can be grasped. In this context *Mīmāṃsā Sūtra* of Jaimini also states that:

"Sense perception, which is the cognition of the person, brought about by the correct functioning of the sense-organs, is not the means (of knowing duty); because perception only consists in the apprehension of what already exists."[23]

Śabara Swamin explains in his commentary the meaning of this aphorism by stating that neither perception nor the other *pramāṇās*, which, in turn, are dependent on perception, can reveal the true nature of *dharma*.[24] Soul (*ātman*), according to *Mīmāṃsā* philosophers, is all pervading and eternal and it is directly cognized by *manas*. The self, through *manas* and other perceptions attached to *manas*, recognizes only the external objects. Cognition or *jñāna* of worldly objects, (that means including that of *dhvani*) for *Mīmāṃsaka* is partly perceptual (*pratyakṣa*) and partly inferential (*parokṣa*). The knowledge, that one gets immediately, through sense perception, is vague and indefinite. When a child, who had not seen a cow in his lifetime, sees a cow, for the first time, he would not recognize it as cow, but only as some animal with a tail, horns etc. This kind of knowledge is called "indeterminate" (*nirvikalpakam*) knowledge. But later being informed by the parents regarding the characteristic features of animals, that are called "cow", he would recognize it as "cow." Such a kind of knowledge is determinate (*savikalpakam*) knowledge. This is so, because according to *Mīmāṃsā* the object that exists (*sat*) has "two-fold aspects": 1) general and 2) particular. The cognition of "cow" means to cognize it as a "particular" cow and also its general character of "cow-hood" simultaneously. Here the general character of "cow-hood" (as a class character), (in the remembrance) would be the qualification for the qualificand (cow).

According to Kumārila, an object can be recognized even if it is not specified by words. Commenting of Aphorism IV (Mī. Sū. 1.1.4), he says : "Therefore even he, who does not know the word, can cognize the class of 'cow', &c."[25] Thus according to *Mīmāṃsakas*, unlike grammarians, one can have an idea of an object without knowing the corresponding word to convey it.

According to *Mimāṃsā*, such perceptual knowledge, no doubt post us with the knowledge of the objects already existing but such knowledge cannot be the means of knowing the "duty" or *dharma* (injunctions of *Śrutis*). If it is so, what is the next alternative means of knowing such vedic injunctions?

Mīmāṃsā Sūtra suggests the following means:

"Constant is the relation between the 'word' and its denotation: and the means of knowing it is the *'upadeśa'* (injunction), (which is) incapable of contradiction; it is authoritative with regard to the object not perceived (before), because it is independent–so says Bādarāyaṇa."[26]

Śabara Swāmin, explains in his *Bhāṣya*, the import of the aphorism by stating that the relation between the "word" and its "meaning" is natural (*autpattikaḥ*) and constant (*aviyuktaḥ*), and is eternal (*nityam*); it is not made by any person (with any motive) and it is beyond perception & c., and as such is free from contradictions; otherwise, it would not have been accepted as a means of human language (*na śakyate vaktum*) and hence it is taken as 'injunction' (*vidhi vākya*).[27]

The self-evidential character of Veda can easily be deciphered on the basis of the relation between the word and its denotation or meaning, which is eternal. If all kinds of relations are denied then it would not be possible to accept even the relation between the father and son, which the meanings of these words indicate.

By way of refuting the theory–that we here the entire word as a "class" (*sphoṭa*), and not as separate letters–Kumārila states that we do cognize individual letters as we cognize individual cows different from the class of cows. Hence we do comprehend the letter *gatva* (i.e. letter *ga*) in *śabdatva* (word) of *gau*, of course, the sub-divisions of *gatva* (of *gau*), may not be perceptible by the ear, since it is *gatva* that is the object of sense-perception. Hence the class of *gatva* (as *vaiśeṣika* assumes) is inconceivable, though one *gatva* may be similar to another, yet they are differently perceived. Even in the case of long *ga*, or short *ga*, there is only one "idea" of *gatva*, and the "presence of such diverse specific cognitions (as long *ga* and short *ga*), must be explained as being due to the diversity of the manifesting cause (the uttering of the letter with different degrees of effort, &c. (in vocal organ)."[28] Even in the case of consonants also, there is no question of diversity as "long" or "short", since such "long" or "short" diversity belongs to vowel accompanying them; and such diversity is also due to the exertion employed in utterance, and is due to such external influence.[29]

Question: "One, to whom both are objects of auditory perception, could have the 'dual conception'; for you, however, the tone of utterance being super sensuous, how could any specific cognition (of individuals) be brought about by means of these tones (of utterances)?"[30]

From the point of view of my thesis, this is an important question, which hits at the bulls eyes. Because in the reply to this question, I get the theory of *nāda* of *Mīmāṃsakas*, clearly explicated.

Kumārila examines more than one approach by way of reply to the above question:

1. Some people "assert that when a sound is recognized by the ear, as affected by the difference in the degree

of tone, then it is that there is comprehension of this degree of tone, brought about on account of its being mixed up with the letters."[31] Kāśikā elucidates that, according to this theory, "The degree of tone is neither airy, nor consisting of the conjunction and disjunction of air-waves; it is only a property of air, a particular form of 'sound' known as *dhvani* or *nāda* & c. Sound is of two kinds – one being an entirely undifferentiated state, and the other consisting of the various letter sounds; both of them equally belong to the class of *śabda*. Of the latter sort, are the letters *ga* & c. while the sound of the drum is of the former kind. Thus then, *śabda* in the form of *dhvani* is a property of the air; and it is this that is the manifesting agency of the letters *g* & c. Consequently, as soon as the air-waves, in the form of *dhvani*, have struck the tympanum, the ear becomes affected by them; and by means of the ear thus affected, the *dhvani* becomes perceived, and is comprehended, sometimes, as an undifferentiated sound, as in the case of drum, while at other times, it is found to manifest a certain distinct 'letter-sound' (*varṇa*); and having thereby mixed up with the utterance of the letters, it comes to be cognized as thus mixed up. Even in the utterance of letters, we are cognizant of the mere sound, as apart from the letters, especially when we differentiate the distance-sounds, through a difference in their intensity. Therefore in our case also, *dhvani* as an object of sense-perception, being perceptible by the ear; and hence even for us, a dual conception is not an impossibility."[32]

2. Kumārila then presents another view: "....Or that there is no cognizance of these *dhvanis;* it is mere cognizance of *śabda* that is brought about by means of *dhvani.* Even the *Vaiśeṣikas* becomes cognizant of the intensity, & c., of the sound only through affection (of the *dhvani*)".[33] Kāśikā says: This *kārika* presents another solution of the difficulty raised by Sl.V. 38. Even the *Vaiśeṣika,* who admits of the class of *gatwa,* accepts the presence of the different degrees of intensity – high, low, &c. But these he cannot represent as the properties of sound, which according to him is itself a property (of *ākāśa*) and as such incapable of having any property of its own.

[The *Mīmāṃsaka* holds sound to be a distinct substance.] Consequently, the *Vaiśeṣika* holds that though "highness" or "lowness" cannot belong to the "sound", yet they are cognized by means of a conception which is affected by the differences of intensity of the tone of the utterance. In the same manner, in our case also, when the *dhvani* has entered the ear, and leaves it soon after, then in that case, the affection of the ear, caused by the speedy striking and return continues for a very short time; and thereby the sound too comes to be produced, at that very time, in accordance with the aforesaid affection of the ear, and disappears soon after; and this speedy appearance and disappearance constitutes what is known as the "shortness" or "lowness" of the sound, its "highness" consisting of a longer stay in the ear of the air-waves (*dhvani*), and hence also of the sound itself. And thus, though the "shortness", & c., really belongs to the manifesting agency of the *dhvani*, yet through extreme proximity, they come to be attributed to the manifested "sound"; and the *dhvani* only becomes the means of rendering the "sound" cognizable; and as such, it can be the means of differentiating the indivisible letters, as short, long, &c."[34] According to Kumārila, people mistake the "sound of letter" (which is eternal) for the sound of "manifesting agency" (i.e., utterance or pronunciation arising from different parts of mouth which is due to the striking of the air, emanated from the chest (which is not eternal). Long, short, broad, & c. belong to the manifesting sound but not to "letter sound". Thus, ".... the letter is one, the sound is of two kinds – one serving the purpose of indicating the form of letters, and the another extending throughout the comprehension (of such forms); these two being the means of bringing about the definition (of letters) immediately and gradually (respectively). Hence 'long sound', short sound, broad sound (*dhvani* or *nāda*), etc., are due to conglomeration of the sounds of pronunciation but not due to 'letter-sound'." (This theory is similar to Bhartṛhari's theory of *prākṛta* and *vaikṛta dhvani* in regard to pronouncing sounds, *dhvani* or *nāda*.) "The letters cannot be said to bring about an aggregate 'word', because each of the "letters" is indicated by individually distinct efforts, and each of them is eternal all pervading" (Verse 65). They "should be accepted as being denotative of meaning, only according as they are known (conventionally and traditionally) to have the capability of expressing such meaning" (Verse 69); when they are uttered "by a single person, and that too in a certain definite order" (Verse 70). The simultaneous utterance of the 'letters' like four persons carrying *palkī*, is impossible, "unless there is multiplicity of speakers. But we do not find such multiplicity in the case of any denotation" (Verse 72).[35]

For those who believe in *sphoṭa* the word as a whole signifies the meaning, but for Kumārila the individual letters are capable of bringing about a meaning; and in some cases even a single letter is capable of signifying a meaning (as in the case of the letter, *ka* meaning Prajāpatī)[36], as per "the residual effect" (or *sanskāra* or convention). He further states that they would admit the cognition of the word *gauḥ* different from letters. "But the cognition of the word cannot be anything totally apart from that of the 'letters' composing it." It is also not dependent of the last letter only, as helped by the impressions left by the preceding letters as the grammarians think.[37] According to Kumārila, "The cognition of meaning proceeds from the 'letters' because it follows immediately after the cognition of these "letters";.... because these objects are always recognized on the utterance of the 'letters'; and because the "letters" are always recognized prior (to the cognition of the object)."[38] He gives an analogy. People unnecessarily mistake forest for "trees"; there is nothing like "forest", apart from trees. If all the trees are removed, the forest automatically disappears. Hence the so-called forest is nothing but the "class" of trees. According to Kumārila, it is only to this class or "commonality" (*jāti*) that the word *ākṛti* is used in *Mīmāṃsā.* Thus "class" is nothing but the collection of "individuals" or "a corporate whole". It is that which is "common" to all the individual objects and the means of a "collective idea" of all these (individuals) as forming "one composite whole"....[39] Thus, "there is mutual dependence between the individual and the class: the class belonging to the individuals, and individuals to the class".[40] According to Kumārila, this kind of "double ideas"–as "individual" and "the class" – though different, yet it is inevitable.[41] A class is a unity in diversity.

Then, next question would be: What is that factor, which establishes the "relation" between the word and its denotation (i.e. "the name and the named")?

According to Kumārila, it is the "conventional rule" that establishes the relation between the word and its denotation.

Is this conventional rule made in accordance with the requirements of each individual mortal-being, or of each utterance (of the word)? or is it made once for all, at the beginning of creation, by some one person (*Brahmā,* for instance)?

Kumārila replies that "conventional rule" cannot be by one "conventional rule" since the other may contradict it. Nor we see any co-existence of such different "conventional rules."

It cannot be by anyone individual; since such notion is inconceivable in multiplicity of individuals, as it would result in different meanings of a word with different people. As such "conventional rule" cannot be optional. If a "hearer" has a different conventional rule, he cannot understand what the "speaker" says. In other word, in order to have a communication of ideas between the speaker and the hearer both should necessarily belong to the common eternality of relation, more so in the case of multitude of hearers. "Because the relation is only a particular kind of potency (*śakti*) (or denotability); and of this (potency) there can be no different individuals. And further, the potency being only inferable from its effect (which is one only), it cannot be many."[42] If it is assumed that this denotability of the word is fixed by some people in the past from whom the later generation learnt it, then the process of finding the persons from whom the people of the past learnt would lead to "ad infinitum." Therefore such "relation" must be held to be eternal, having no beginning in time. Even here Mīmāṃsā does not wish to ascribe such eternality to the Creator of the world as it would be difficult to prove such a theory.[43] (In the case of such failure, it would be difficult for them to prove the eternality of the Veda.)

Even in our day-to-day life, use common names like "cow" which everyone understands as referring to object cow and there is no mistake "....because, in this case, the relation too is eternal. For, as a mater of fact, the application (between the word and its denotation) must be admitted to exist before all the people that are found to use it. The relation being thus established (to have existed before all persons using it, from time immemorial), there could be no beginning for the relation."[44] The "conventional rule" that – *ā* and *ai* should be used as *vṛddhi* – one can use without knowing Pāṇini who has authored it. Hence, for using a rule knowing its author would not be an absolute necessity, and the same need not be insisted upon. "The only means of comprehending the meaning of words lies in perceiving (and noticing) the repeated comprehensions by experienced people (i.e., words uttered and used by other experienced persons). And certainly this meaning is found to fail with regard to (i.e., can be no avail of to) people, who do not comprehend the relation (between words and meanings, prior to the laying down of the rule). Even such means, as gestures of the hand, & c., could not exist at the first actions (at the beginning of creation). Because the meaning of these (gestures) could not be known unless there were other persons (using them)."[45]

Is sound eternal?

This question whether sound is eternal or not, *Mīmāṃsā Sūtra* considers along with the eternality of "words" (*śabda*), in order to prove the eternality of Veda. Kumārila put the same thing aptly when he said ".... it is for the sake of the validity of the Veda, that we seek to prove the eternality of *śabda*-sound."[46]

What is that which is responsible for causing impression upon the ear (which causes the manifestation of a "word")?

According to Kumārila, such an entity, which actually causes impression on the ear (of the hearer), is the same entity which causes manifestation of the word in the utterance of the mouth of the speaker. This entity is "a power" which is "....inferable from the effects (it brings about). The only ground for believing (the "utterance" to have the power of manifestation 'word') lies in the fact of the cognition (of the word) appearing only when there is "utterance." But this entity or "power" is beyond the reach of the sense perception. "Thus then, it is by means of super sensuous 'power' alone that these (utterances) impart a super sensuous facility (power) to the sense-perception (of the ear), and thereby, become the causes of the manifestation of the "words".[47] According to me, this "unseen power" is nothing but "*ṛtam* principle" of *Ṛgveda* which causes *vāk* (*ṛtasya prathamajāvāk*, RV.1.164.37) Kāśikā adds that "....everything that brings about the perception of an object is its manifester (a lamp in the dark, as one among others), and the 'conjunction' of the 'soul' (also) is meaning of such perception; therefore this too is as good manifester as anything else)."[48] The aim of the authors appears to demonstrate the fact that, though there are heterogeneous factors causing such manifestation of word, yet all these factors are due to one homogeneous "power" (like *ṛtam*) that causes such manifestation.

Though the "word" is eternal and all-pervasive, it is not heard by all men simultaneously because the hearing by different persons is regulated by diverse factors. The *ākāśa*, the substratum of "word" is no doubt all pervasive and impartible (if left to itself), but it is capable of being partitioned with the obstruction of objects occupying it. (Hence the ear could be a part of *ākāśa* itself, or a distinct entity by itself.) Hence the change produced by the utterance of the word could only belong to the substrate of the auditory *ākāśa* of hearer only. An utterance does not affect any change in the auditory organ, if it fails to reach it; or if it is not received as in the case of a deaf person, (such deafness is situated in the body of a particular person and not in all). At any rate "....the air-vibrations, (of utterance) which are held to be manifesters (of the word), are both endowed with parts and capable of occupying different places, (i.e., are neither impartite nor all-pervading). And (of these manifesting air-vibrations) there are different classes also on which (classes) are based the changes (produced in the auditory sense).... [49]"; "....though the word is produced equally with regard to all men, yet it is not recognized by all (simultaneously), on account of ....the fact of (its cognition depending upon) the division or direction of the place & c., so, in the same manner ....when a word is affected by changes brought about by sounds produced in proximity to some men, the word is heard by these men alone, and not by those who are at distance (from the sounds)".[50]

Mimāṃsā Sūtra I.1.18 lays down that "the sound (or the word) is eternal by reason of its manifestation being for the sake of others" (*nityastusyāddarśanasyaparārthvāt*).[51] *Śābar Bhāṣya* explains the aphorism by stating that the word is uttered for the sake of others to communicate an idea of *gau* for instance, and if it ceases to exist on utterance, it would not be possible to communicate its meaning to others; and hence it must be eternal, and, as such, we would be able to utter the same word *gau* two times, three times and more.

Kumārila elaborates the underlying principle of "eternality" of word or sound, by excluding its non-eternal aspects connected with its utterance or accent. He elaborates this process by stating that the faculty or the potency in the mouth of the speaker requires "air" (for going out of throat) for the conjunction and disjunction of the (tongue with palate, & c.). Since the "air" has certain force with which it moves, along with sound particles, so long as this initial force lasts; and meanwhile, if it reached the *ākāśa* (ether) of the ear of the hearer, there the "air" imparts a certain faculty or potency to the auditory sense; and this faculty causes changes in the "sense" of the ear, and produces (in the ears of the hearer) the sound uttered by the speaker's mouth.[52] Kumārila admits that this is an imperceptible "faculty or potency" of causing changes in the "senses" by the sound received by tympanum (ear drum), but they are presuming in the circumstances. He adds that this striking of the sound against tympanum is due to "....the great force or velocity of air-current." Since the air has its own intensity and velocity which is perishable and "since it moves along in a certain order of sequence, therefore, it comes to be the sole cause of the change (in the auditory sense) of the order of sequence (in hearing of the sound), as also of the intensity and lowness, & c. (of the words)", and in the circumstances the interception of the sound caused by the wall is possible.[53]

The modification of the senses in the ear caused by such sound is called *sanskāra*, which is transitory or momentary and is non-eternal. The other eternal *sanskāra* of the ear which is its potency or power is not caused by sound. An entity, which is eternal, is not caused. For instance, *ākāśa* which is eternal is not caused. While digging the earth, when earth is dumped elsewhere, some "space" appears but such space is not created. In the same sense, the "word" is eternal.[54] "The 'word' has no parts; and as such, it cannot be cognized in parts (like any large objects). The word is always (cognized) as it exists; and it always exists in its entirety (therefore it is only reasonable that it should always be cognized in its entirety and never in parts)".[55] Kāsikā adds: "Since a word is heard in all places, it cannot be either material (corporeal) or caused or non-eternal. Because in one place having known a word, when we come across it in some other place, we at once recognize it to be the same word. Thus the 'word' is one only, and is manifested in the mouth of different people, who cannot be said to produce the 'word'. The simultaneity that we perceive, when we hear the same word pronounced by different people, belongs to the 'utterance (manifestation)' of the ever existing, all-pervading word, in the mouth of different people."[56] The sounds of utterances thus have definite space and time and are transitory and are not all-pervading. "And since these (utterances) extend over a certain definite limited space, there appears a (mistaken) notion of the limited (non-pervading) character of the 'word' (manifested by the utterances).... Since these (utterances) have motion and a certain velocity, therefore from whatever place they proceed, the 'word' (manifested by these utterances) appears, to the hearer, to come from the same place (though, as a matter of fact the 'word' exists in all places, and is only manifested or rendered perceptible to the ear, by these utterances)."[57] Likewise, even the letters are eternal and non-changing. The.... "letters having no parts and as such, being like *ākāśa*, they cannot undergo either an increase or decrease and hence the increase could not belong to the 'letters' within themselves."[58] In the example, *dadhi* + *atra* = *dadhyatra*, the letter *ya* is an independent new letter and not the modification of the letter *i*. Thus "....(the notion of the increase and decrease in the word-sounds) would depend upon the increase or decrease in the (intensity of the) 'utterance' (manifesting, or rendering perceptible, the word)".[59] (But Bhartṛhari, as we will see in Chapter Seven, holds that there is modification.)

Objection: "If either (conjunction, & c., as) properties of the air, or the air itself as possessing these properties (of conjunction, & c.), be held to be (meant by) the word 'sound' (*nāda*), then, as 'letters' alone are perceptible by the ear, the sounds could not be audible by the ear (because air is only perceptible by the sense of touch); and then, how could the sounds of the conch-shell, & c., which do not consist of 'letters', be heard?"[60] By way of reply to this question, Kumārila examines certain theories, which according to him, would be laboring under false notions.

Some people hold that sounds also (and not letters alone) are perceptible by the ear. According to these people, the sounds, which are properties of the air, are urged (uttered) along with uttering respective letters, e.g., sound *a* along with letter *a* is uttered simultaneously. This is urged, as clarified by Kāsikā, objecting to the assertion of *Śābar Bhāṣya*, that "the conjunctions and disjunctions in the air, manifesting the words, come to be known as *nāda* (sound)." In this context *Nyāya Ratnākara* of Pārtha Sārathi Misra raises an objection: "If sound be held to be conjunctions, & c., of the air, or the air itself as possessing these properties, and if it (sound or *nāda*) be not held to be in the form of a word, then the 'sound' cannot be held to consist of any letters; and it has been held by the *Mīmāṃsakas* that 'letters' alone are perceptible by the ear; therefore the 'sounds' that do not consist of letters, (e.g., those uttered by the conch-shell, &c.). How such sounds could be objects of audition? But we do 'hear' such sounds. How do you explain this contradiction?"[61]

Mīmāṃsaka replies :

"If the 'air' were to be the manifester of words, then the 'air' being amenable to the tactile sense alone, the above objection would apply; but as a matter of fact it is not the air but the sounds as properties of the air that manifest words in the manners described in the *kārikā* (of Kumārila Bhatta). Hence the objection is avoided. When people are speaking at a house at distance, we hear only the sounds and not distinct letter or word".[62]

Thus according to *Mīmāṃsakas* the word is eternal but its manifester (sound of the mouth) in the form of utterance is not eternal. The mode of utterance may vary from place to place but still the word remains the same (e.g., in some places the rustic call *gavi* for the word *go* to mean a 'cow'). A word means the same in all the places because its relation with meaning also is eternal. But such relation is not created at the time of creation of the world as some people think. "But since we have never been cognizant of this word (as created with meaning), how could we have any notion of similarity with this (original word) (of any subsequent word that we may hear as spoken?".[63] Kāsikā explains it – "Because uttering of the 'word' is not possible without the knowledge of the relation; nor is the laying down of the relation possible without the utterance of the word a case of mutual interdependence".[64]

But an objection is raised: Moreover the word is a particular arrangement of letters; and a word is not possible without such arrangement of letters; hence the letters being dependent on arrangement, are non-eternal.

Mīmāṃsakas reply is that "arrangement" is subordinate to those to which it belongs (i.e. the letters). Because the arrangement is only a property of the "letters", and is not held to be a distinct entity by itself. Therefore (it must be admitted that) that which signifies the meaning is the "letters" as perceived (in a certain order of sequence). But as a matter of fact, the "arrangement" too is not caused ....Because the speaker does not use the letters (as constituting a word) in the order of his own choice; he always utters a word in the same way (following the same sequence of letters) as it is uttered by others. So we have the eternality of the (arrangement of letters) just as we have that of the relation (of words with their meanings).[65] Thus the meaning of the *sūtra* is that "word is eternal because it stands in need of its relation with its meanings, whereby it comes to be used for another's sake, which could not be possible, if the word had no relation with its meaning".[66]

According to *Mīmāṃsakas,* the eternality is the eternality of the relation between word and its meaning. Hence "even in a case where we are cognizant of eternal relations of non-eternal objects, the substrate (of the relation) is never absent; and hence the relation never ceases (to exist)".[67] "Therefore we assert the eternality of the 'word' (*cow,* for instance), which is one only (the difference lying only in the utterances that serve to manifest the already existing 'word')".[68]

"Thus, it having been proved (through recognition) that the word continues to exist (at least) during the time intervening between its first hearing and its subsequent recognition (as being the same), no other argument could prove its perishability (non-eternality). In the case of cloth, & c., we find that they are destroyed either on account of their being cut by instruments, or on account of their becoming too old; whereas, in the case of the 'word', there are no such causes of destruction."[69]

In this view of the matter, Kumārila rejects the theory put forth by Bauddhas which "asserts that the jar is recognized to be the same today as yesterday, because there is a series of destructions and reconstructions affecting the jar." Kumārila explains that "it is on account of the present shape of the jar forming part of the same series as the form perceived yesterday, that it is recognized to be the same." *Kāsikā* of Sucarita Misra clarifies that according to Kumārila there is nothing as a series of perceptions or cognitions (as Buddhists conceive). The so-called series of perception of jar is nothing but the non-difference individual "forms" of a jar.[70]

Kumārila also, likewise, rejected the theory of Jaina. According to Jaina philosophy "sound" arises out of *skandha* (molecules) principle. It is the natural characteristic (*guṇa*) of these molecules that they get organized into an atom and atoms into physical objects or *pañca mahābhūtās*, etc. Thus the physical objects are nothing but *pudgala skandha*. Sound is the product molecules or particles (*skandajanya*). Sound emanates as particles from *śabda pudgala*. *Pudgala*, for Jaina, means "material objects including atoms; and *śabda pudgala* appears to be similar to *śabda tanmātra* of *Sāṅkhya*. The *śabda pudgala*, arising from the place of its origin, travels in all directions to the end of the world in the form of *skandha* or molecules or particles. But while travelling from one stage (or place to the other), it goes on losing its characteristics (*guṇa*), and it cannot go beyond the 'air sphere', owing to its inherent disability arising out of the material object. In its mixed up form (with air), it becomes audible to the ears in the form of language, & c. Sound is heard when it is produced by striking at distance or from near. It is not the property of *ākāśa* (*ākāśa guṇa*) as thought of by *Vaiśeṣikās*. It is of the 'air principle' (*vāyuguṇa*), and it is the air that carries the sound in the form of molecules or particles".[71]

Kumārila criticizes this theory on more than one ground:

"How can there be any production (of final perceptible sound) by means of these (subtle factors), which are imperceptible (and as such incapable of producing perceptible entities). And, from what sort of diversity in the process of production would proceed the diversity of the letters (as appearing in the sound)? In the absence of 'fluidity' in these (subtle factors), how can they be said to be mixed up (into a complete whole) in the shape of the sound? And (even if such a mixing up be admitted, as in the case of a lump of flour), how is it that in travelling (from the region where the sound is produced to that where it is heard), the sound is not dissipated (and blown away) by air currents? Specially as these parts (i.e., the subtle factors making up sound) are extremely light (being subtle) and are not bound together (into composite whole) by anything. And just as a lump of clay is shattered (into fragments) by striking against trees, so would sound also (be shattered into its imperceptible component fragments by its striking against trees & c., intervening in its path, from the place of its production to that of its cognition)."[72]

Even according to this theory (of Jaina) that it is the "auditory sense that moves (to the region where the sound is produced), such motion of the 'auditory sense' is not possible. And if (it be held that) it is the function (or action of the ear) that travels, then (in that case) it would mean the assumption of two imperceptible factors (since neither of the function of the ear nor the travelling of the function is perceptible). And further, (in this theory) you would have a modification (of the 'auditory sense') by a distant object (viz., the sound, which is always produced at a certain distance from the ear)."[73]

Kumārila further points out that, as held by this theory, if the sound has all-pervading character, then all sounds of very far distance should have been heard but it is not so. "If it be held that the 'auditory sense' is modified by those (sounds) that have a (particular) relation with it; then, as shown above, non-relation being equal (in the case of sounds near and distant), there would be no spatiality in the near sound (whereby such sound would be heard, and not the one at a distance). And further, the function of the 'auditory sense', being immaterial, could not be intercepted by any material obstacles; and hence wherefore should an intercepted sound not be heard?"[74]

Kumārila further points out that, according to Jaina theory, word is being made up of atoms of air (and as such it is being made up of component parts). Such a theory is not acceptable, "in as much as people are never cognizant of any cause (productive) of the word, and as everywhere the word is found in its own complete form by itself (and not as made up of component words). Hence the word must be (admitted to be) eternal."[75]

But this theory of eternality of word or sound is not acceptable even to Śaṅkarācārya. According to him, the sound is not as eternal as *Brahman* is, but by *Brahman* he means *Nirguṇa Brahman*, who is beyond human comprehension in terms of qualification and the qualificand. He stated that, according to tradition, all attributes belong to

Ishvara or *Saguṇa Brahman. Saguṇa Brahman* is identical with *oṃ*, which is "the object of both meditations and vision." He refers to *Praśnopaniṣad*, according to which Satyakāmā, the son of Shibi, asked Pippalāda as to what world a person, who meditates on *oṃ*, attains, if he were to practise chanting *oṃ* during his life time. To that, Pippalāda replied:

"If a person, through all three elements of the sound *oṃ*, (A U M) meditates on the highest spirit, then after he has entered into the light into the sun, as a serpent is freed from its slough, so he is freed from evil; ...."[76] Śaṅkara says that "this shows us, further, that this freedom from sin must proceed as a result of meditation on the highest *ātman*, and not from meditation on any thing different from the highest *ātman*. Then, again, the man, who meditates on *oṃ* as the *saguṇa* aspect of the *ātman*, need not be said to receive a small reward by way of his being limited to Brahmaloka; rather it is his first reward. For in course of time he may get the highest reward, viz., the clear vision of the *ātman* and become free. In other words, he attains *mokṣa*...."[77]

* * *

The Gist of the Philosophy of *Mīmāṃsā* and *Vedānta* :

Nāda is an eternal substance (*dravya*)–(Transcendental Theory of sound)

Mīmāṃsā and *Vedānta* implicitly accepted "cosmic creative power" (*praṇava* or *oṃkāra*) as being manifested in the form of eternal "sound." *Mīmāṃsā* has two sub-schools:

a) Sound is an intangible and eternal substance, but manifested by non-eternal vocal sounds (as per *Kumārila Bhaṭṭa Mīmāṃsā*); b) Sound is an eternal quality of eternal *ākāśa*, in the form of letter-sounds (*varṇas*) (for *Prābhākaras Mīmāṃsā*). *Bhaṭṭa Mīmāṃsā* appears to be more popular and therefore I have followed this theory for the purpose of this thesis. According to the *Advaita Vedānta* of *Śankara*, "sound" is non-eternal manifestation of eternal *Brahman*. Both *Mīmāṃsā* and *Vedānta* follow a common tradition handed down by Upavarṣa so far as the concept of sound is concerned.

The vocal sound, that manifests letters (*varṇas*), is called *nāda* or *dhvani*. Such vocal *nāda* or *dhvani* is transitory and non-eternal, but the letters are eternal and the word composed of such letters is also eternal. Sound is the property of air and not the quality of *ākāśa*. These letters are perceived in a mixed-up form along with the vocal sound that manifests it. For instance, letter *ga*, that is conveyed by means of *air*, is perceived by the ear along with the uttered sound *ga*. What is eternal is the letter *ga*, but not the sound *ga* uttered by vocal organs. Long (*dīrgha*), short (*hṛsva*), etc., of *gatva* belong to the utterance (an external influence), owing to accumulation of vocal sound for longer duration or shorter duration, etc., but not owing to letter. If it is so, then "Is there a 'dual conception' of letter *ga* and vocal sound *ga*?" Kumārila Bhaṭṭa says "yes". "Then what is the relation between the two?" According to Kumārila, the vocal sound, (*dhvani* or *nāda*), which is transitory, is the manifester of the letters which are eternal. Letters being eternal are non-changing, and hence they cannot undergo any modification. In *daddhyatra* (*dadhi+atra*), there is no modification of *i* into *ya*, but there is substitution of *ya* in the place of *i*.

How to distinguish the letters from their sounds? Kumārila says it is difficult to perceive such distinction between the two. However, such a distinction is perceptible, when a person is speaking from a long distance, in which case what is heard is only the sound he utters but not the letters or words manifested by his voice. Thus, letter is one; the sound is of two kinds – (i) one serving the purpose of indicating the form of letters and the other (ii) extending throughout the comprehension (of such forms). (So far as the accentuated sound is concerned, this theory is similar to that of Bhartṛhari.)

Letters in the form of word convey meaning, according to conventional rule, which in the form of relation between word and its meaning which is of the nature of a particular kind of potency *Śakti* – lying beyond the reach of the sense perception (=*ṛtam* principle). Thus, not only are the letters eternal, but the 'arrangement' of such letters in a word also is eternal. On this principle, even the Vedas are eternal. But according to the *Vedānta* philosophy of Śankara, *Brahman* is the only entity that is eternal and all other things, including *oṃkāra* being created by *Saguṇa Brahman* (*Īśvara*) are non-eternal and are subject to dissolution at the time of *pralaya*. Yet one can attain *brahmajñāna* by meditating on *Praṇava*.

Notes and References

1. Hiriyanna (1995) : pp. 130-131.
2. *Brahma Sūtra* 1.1.2 9 (Date's tr.).
3. V.E. : page 11 - Date's V.H. (1973).
4. See Karmkar, Raghunātha Damodar (1973) : (4.91-94).
5. V.E. - Vol. II; pp. 9, 12.
6. V. E. - Vol. II; pp. 9, 12.
7. See *Pañcīkaraṇam* (2004) : pp. 1 & 2.
8. See *Pañcīkaraṇam* pp. 16-17 (2004) : pp. 1 & 2.
9. See Mishra, Dr. Kameshwara Nath (1962) : Introduction; p. 7.
10. *Pañcīkaraṇam* (2004) : pp. 1 & 2.
11. *Pañcīkaraṇam* (1962) : pp. 1 & 2.
12. Musulgaonkar, Dr. Gajānana Śāstri (2000) : p. 210 & p. 219.
13. Mī. Sū. 1.1.28.
14. Mī. Sū. 1.1.5.
15. Abhyankar, Kāshinath Vasudev and Shukla, J.M. : (1986).
16. V.E. (Vol. I; p. 157).
17. "*śrotramātrendriyagrāhyaḥ śabdaḥ śabdatvajātimān / dravyam sarvagato nityaḥ kumārilamate mataḥ*"|| (2.2.130). *viyadguṇatvaṃ śabdasya kecidūcurmanīṣiṇaḥ / pratyakṣādivirodhāt tadbhaṭṭapādairupekṣitam* || (2.2.131) : Raja Kunhan, C. and Śastri, Suryanarayana (1975) : p. 222.
18. *Mānameyodaya* of Nārāyaṇa; 2.2. 131; pp. 223-24.
19. *Mānameyodaya* of Nārāyaṇa; 2.2.133; p. 224.
20. Bhatt, Govardhan P. : (1962); p. 180.
21. Sharma, R.N. (*tr.*) : (1987); p. 51 (Its equivalent Sanskṛt version, at p. 71 of - The *Vākyārtha-Mātṛkā* (Hindi *Vyākhyā*) : Avasthī, Dr. Brahāmitra.
22. Goswamy, Ashok Kumar (1991) : p. 31.
23. *Mīmāṃsā Sūtrta*-1.1.4 : Jha (tr.) : Śl. Vā. (1983); p. 68.

24. Musalagānvakar, Dr. Gajānana Shāstri, (2004).
25. Sl. Vā. 176; p. 99.
26. Mi. Su. I.1.5 Jha (tr.) : Sl. Vā.; p. 113.
27. Musalagānvakar, Dr. Gajānana Shāstri, (2004) : p. 16.
28. Sl. Vā. 19-23; pp. 264-65.
29. Sl. Vā. 29-31; p. 266.
30. Sl. Vā. 38; p. 267.
31. Sl. Vā. 39; p. 267.
32. Kāsikā 39, p. 267 (foot-notes).
33. Sl. V.40; p. 267.
34. Kāsikā-40 - Sl. Vā.; pp. 267-68 (foot-notes).
35. Sl. Vā. 65, 69-72; pp. 272-73.
36. Sl. Vā. 90-94; p. 275.
37. Sl. Vā. 130; pp. 280-81.
38. Sl. Vā. 135-137; p. 281.
39. Sl. Vā. 3; p. 282.
40. Sl. Vā. 9; p. 282.
41. Sl. Vā. 7; p. 282.
42. Sl. Vā. 28; p. 352.
43. Sl. Vā. 41-44; p. 355.
44. Sl. Vā. 122-123; p. 369.
45. Sl. Vā. 138-140; pp. 373-74.
46. Sl. Vā. 7; p. 410.
47. Sl. Vā. 45 ; p. 417.
48. Kāsikā 46-48, Sl. Vā.; p. 417 (foot-notes).
49. Sl. Vā. 78-80 ; p. 462.
50. Sl. Vā. 84-86; p. 423.
51. Sandal, Mohan Lal (1999) - (*tr.*).
52. Sl. Vā. 122-126; p. 429.

53. Sl. Vā. 130; pp. 429-30.
54. Sl. Vā. 162-163; p. 435.
55. Sl. Vā. 171-172; p. 43.
56. Sl. Vā. 169-171, p. 437 (foot-notes).
57. Sl. Vā. 172-177; pp. 437-38.
58. Sl. Vā. 213-214; p. 445.
59. Sl. Vā. 215-16; pp. 429-30.
60. Sl. Vā. 222-23; p. 447.
61. Kāsikā- Sl. Vā. 222-23, p. 447 (foot-notes).
62. Sl. Vā. 224-25, p. 447 (foot-notes).
63. Sl. Vā. 264-65; p. 456.
64. Kāsikā Sl. Vā. 258-59, p. 455 (foot-notes).
65. Sl. Vā. 287-90; p. 460.
66. Kāsikā. Sl. Vā. 310, p. 463 (foot-notes).
67. Sl. Vā. 358; p. 471.
68. Sl. Vā. 359; p. 471.
69. Sl. Vā. 443-44; p. 484.
70. Kāsikā Sl. Vā. 442; p. 484 (foot-notes).
71. Jain, Hiralal and Upadhyaya, Dr. A.N.; (1944). See pp. 3 and 445 of Vol. IV.
72. Sl. Vā. 109-11; p. 427.
73. Sl. Vā. 112-13; p. 427.
74. Sl. Vā. 114-17; p. 428.
75. Sl. Vā. 445; pp. 484-85.
76. Radhakṛṣṇa, S. (1994) 5.5; p. 665.
77. V.E.-Vol.I; pp. 132.

* * *

Chapter Six

TANTRĀGAMA THEORY OF *NĀDA* AND *ŚABDA*

The theory of *nāda* found new dimensions in the philosophy of *tantras* and *āgamas*. The concept of *bindu* as the source of *nāda* is their important contribution.

Sometimes *āgama* is distinguished from *nigama* or *vedic* tradition. Both are said to be parallel traditions. "Like the Vedas, the *tantras* or the *āgamas*", in the words of Manoranjan Basu, "are....brought down to us from time immemorial through spiritual traditions."[1] As I have noted in Chapter Two, in all probability *tantrāgama* principles have been handed down to us from Harappa–Mohenjodāro civilization, as opined by Sir John Marshall and subsequent Indian scholars.

The terms *āgama* and *tantra*, broadly speaking, are one the same from philosophical point of view. However, if there is predominantly *śiva* element, that *śāstra* (science) is called *āgama* and if *śakti* element is prominent, then it is called *tantra*. Thus on the basis of *iṣṭadevatā* (Deity of ones devotion), there are *śākta-āgamas*, *śaiva-āgamas*, and *vaiṣṇava-āgamas*. *Vaiṣṇava-āgamas* are generally known as *pañcarātra āgamas*. I have used the words *tantra* or *āgama* or *tantrāgamas* to refer to them as a general term.

For *tantrāgamas* thinkers, spiritual practice (*sādhana*) in the form of *japa*, or *dhyāna* of *mantra* or *pūja* (worship) is absolutely necessary in order to put an end to the past *sanskāras* and liberate the soul from births and deaths. It is worth noting that, according to *tantrāgamas*, unlike *vaidika* traditions, all classes of people without any distinction of castes, creed and professions are entitled to be initiated in the "system". Women too are allowed to embrace *tantrāgama* way of life. For realization of *Brahmajñāna*, according to *tantrāgama* philosophers, what is required is "the purified heart". "In the purified heart the knowledge of *Brahman* grows."[2]

All the *tantrāgama* systems, believe in two *brahmans* : *sakala brahman* (with parts) and *niṣkala brahman* (without parts). The former is *"para"* (transcendental) and the latter is "*apara*" (empirical). *Niṣkala brahman* is "the Absolute and Pure Cosmic Consciousness", but described differently as Śiva, Śaktī, Viṣṇu, etc. to suit their respective faith. In *Mahānirvāṇa Tantra*, Śīva, by way of explaining the nature of *niṣkala brahman* says to Pārvatī that: "....the Lord of the Universe (*Viśveśaḥ*),.... is one. He is ever. He is the truth. He is the Supreme Unity without second. He is ever full and 'self-manifest' (*sva prakāśa*). He is 'eternal consciousness' (*cit*) and bliss (*ānanda*).... The cause of all the three worlds; He is yet beyond them and beyond the mind of men. .... He, the one Supreme Lord, is the 'cause' of all-beings, the manifestation of whose creative 'energy' in the three worlds is called *Brahmā* (or *śaktī*)....".[3]

The above description of *brahman* makes it clear that *brahman* is *cit* or "consciousness". It is generally described as *saṃvid, caitanya* or *cit*. This *cit* is supreme consciousness latent in all physical and psychic bodies. In the words of Sir John Woodroffe "*cit* is one undifferentiated, partless, all-pervading, eternal, spiritual substance".[4]

At the *niṣkala* stage there is mere "I-hood" of *brahman*. But later, with his "creative energy" inherent in him, He desired a more playful mood (*līlā*) and accordingly wished: "May I be many";[5] consequently his "creative energy" or *śaktī*, evolved Herself into *Hiraṇyāṇḍa* (Golden Egg) which hatched Ishvara or *Śabdabrahman*, an intermediate stage of three equipoised *guṇas* – *sattva, rajas* and *tamas*, with undifferentiated state of "I and this", designated by pandits as *śabdabrahman*. In the evolutionary system of *Kāśmīri śaivism*, this stage is known as *śādākhya tattva*. His inner *cetana śaktī* (consciousness) also the wise people have named differently as Brahmā, Pārvati or Lakṣmī etc.

Later because of intervention of *māyā* and *kañcukas* created by the *śaktī*, the three *guṇas* get disturbed. Consequently "I" (*ahaṃ*) gets separated from "this" (*idaṃ*), i.e., consciousness gets separated into duality as *jiva* (a *śiva* element) and *jada* (*śaktī* element). The form of *ahaṃkāra* (I-hood) is manifested in the union (*mithuna* or *sāmarasya*) of *śiva* and *śakti*. *Tantrāgama* philosopher explains this idea in a more graphic and mundane manner by stating that *śiva* takes the form of "white *bindu*" (*sita bindu*) and *śaktī* takes the form of red bindu (*sona bindu*), and the union of the two (as if in sexual union) results in a new *miśra bindu*. This *miśra bindu* is that "I-hood" (*ahaṅkāra* of the "cosmic consciousness") which is the cause of the creation of the "world" (on the ontological side) and the cause of the creation of the "word" (*śabda*) on the epistemological side, on the basis of the *nāma-rūpa* principle. This *miśra bindu* is also called *kalā* or *vimarśa śaktī* or *vidyā*. Because of these three *bindu* phenomenon, *śaktī* is known as *tribindvātmakā* or *tripura sundarī*. By virtue of "Her" power to manifest three *guṇās* (*triguṇa svarūpinī*) She assumes the "form" of a "triangle", according to *Kāmakalāvilāsa*.[6] It further says that this "triangle form" is nothing but the manifestation of *omkāra nāda*. It says: "The beautiful *śṛṅgāṭa* (triangle) which is her very self (*svātmanśṛṅgāṭa*) is made up of three *bindus* – mixed, white and red. It is ancient (*purāṇa*) and is the *praṇava* itself (*praṇavātmakam*). It can be known by the three lines (*rekhātraya*) which compose it. It is pure knowledge (*saṃvin-mātra*) and is of the nature of *śiva*".[7]

The *bindu-tattva*, when it gets ready to evolve (*ucchūnna*) it transforms and manifests as a triangle (*trikoṇa-rūpeṇa pariṇataṃ*). This (triangle) is the source of the three (*śaktīs*), namely *parā*, *paśyantī*, *madhyamā* and also three *bījas*. In dissolution She assumes the state of *bindu*. (see p. 75-76)[8].

From the foregoing description and origin of "triangle" "it is clear that the form of 'triangle' (*śṛṅgāṭa cakra*) is, in fact, the manifestation of *praṇava nāda* only. Devi, thus, assumed the form of a 'triangle' as a result of the union of the 'supreme bliss', symbolized by the letter 'a' with *icchā*, creative will, symbolized by the letter 'ī'. This is the cakra of triangular form (*śṛṅgāṭa*), which is most secret and called *sarva-siddhi-pradāyaka* or that which accomplishes all."[9] Likewise even *śrī-cakra* composed of nine "triangles (*nava-yonyātmaka*), is the manifestation (*vikāsa rūpa*) of the *śaktī's*, *parā*, *paśyantī* and the rest."[10] It is a mixture of two triangles by name *śiva* triangle and *śakti* triangle. The *śrī-cakra* thus "consists of a dot (*bindu*) at the centre surrounded by nine triangles (*trikoṇa*), of which five have their apexes downwards and the other four, upwards."[11] The nine triangles symbolize the mixture of *śiva* and *śaktī* principles in the evolution of the entire "universe". Thus both *trikoṇa* and *śrī-cakra* appear to be basically a sonic phenomenon, arising out of *praṇava*, but expressed in an esoteric language only to camouflage it so as to make it unintelligible to the uninitiated. The sonic aspects of "triangle" and *śrī-cakra* will be explained with the help of the theory of "triangle mode of voice production", as propounded by *Aumāpatam* in Chapters Eleven and Twelve.

In the course of such "cosmic evolution", according to *Lakṣmi Tantra*, two, inseparable realities come into existence– "(i) conscious or sentient reality (material creation), and (ii) non-conscious or insentient reality (sonic creation) – of the complex of the three *guṇas*".[12] Out of these thirty-six *tattvas*, according to all schools of *śaivism*, including *Kāśmīr śaivism*, eleven new categories are added to *Sāṃkhya* categories, to explain as to how *Sāṃkhya's puruṣa*, and *prakṛtī* themselves came into existence viz., *śiva*, *śaktī*, *sadāśiva*, *īśvara*, *śuddhavidyā*, *māyā* and its five *kañcukas*, which would be in addition to *Sāṃkhya's* twenty five categories – *puruṣa*, *prakṛtī*, etc., (in all there would be 11+25=36 categories).[13] Though *Śāktas* also believe in 36 categories yet there is a slight difference in their enumeration of those eleven newly added categories which are – *bhagavān* (omitted from the counting being beyond such categories) *paramavyoman*, *puruṣa*, *śaktī*, *niyati*, *kāla*, the three *guṇas* (*sattva*, *rajas* and *tamas*), *māyā*, *prasūtī*, *prakṛtī*.[14]

According to *tantrāgamas*, human body (*piṇḍāṇḍa*) is nothing but a miniature cosmos (*brahmāṇḍa*). Abhinava Gupta in his *Parā-triśikā Vivaraṇa* states that the relation between the transcendental and the phenomenal would be like *bimba* and *pratibimba*. He says:

"All the categories of existence have two aspects, viz. (i) the original orb (*bimba*) and (ii) its reflection (*pratibimba*). Their original orb is in *parāśaktī*. No reflection [in mirror] has any existence unless its original orb (*bimba*) is present in *parā*. The supreme original orb is decidedly *parā*; the bimbas of the original orbs, and *vāṇīs* (speech), viz., *paśyantī*, *madhyamā* and *vaikharī*, are also present in *parā*."[15] According to him, this is so because of the basic principle: "everything consists of everything else" (*sarvaṃ sarvātmakaṃ*).[16] Therefore the same principles operate both in "cosmic body" and "human body", but in inverted order just like reflection of an object in mirror. Hence both in cosmos and in human body we find such parallel aspects. In human body we find (a) physical body (dominated by *tāmas guṇa*) and (b) *jīva* (dominated by *rajas guṇa*) and "I consciousness" of *jīva* expresses itself in "sound" or "vibration" or *spanda*. What is in *brahmāṇḍa* (cosmic world) is the same in *piṇḍāṇḍa* (human body). Thus consciousness and the matter, both in cosmos (*brahmāṇḍa*) and human body (*piṇḍāṇḍa*), are not different existence, nor are they separable, just like *śiva* and *śakti*. What normally called matter is a substance in which *tāmas guṇa* is predominant and the other two *guṇas*, namely *rajas* and *sattva*, are also present, but in insignificant proportions. *Jīva* is the product of body (i.e. Matter), with the predominance of *rajas guṇa*, yet it is of the nature of consciousness, psychic element. Even the other two elements, viz., *tamas* and *sattva guṇas* are in *jīva*, but in insignificant proportions. Thus there are "concomitant parallel creations" within the cosmic creation, as physical and psychic or sonic creation. Arthur Avalon calls this phenomenon a "psycho-physical parallelism."[17]

According to the *Tantrāgama* doctrine, *śiva* and His Creative Energy (*śaktī*), are always latent and inseparable in this world, like fire and fuel. This idea is graphically presented by Śaṅkara in his *Soundarya Laharī* as under:

śivaḥ śaktyā yukto yadi bhavati śaktaḥ prabhavituṃ
na cedevaṃ devo na khalu kuśalaḥ spanditumapi

"If *śiva* is associated with *śaktī*, He can create the universe; if not, He is not capable of even moving His limbs".[18] Some people highlighted this principle in the form of a symbol and depicted *śiva* without *śaktī* as *śava* (=dead body).[19]

According to John Woodroffe, the so-called "phenomenal world" in terms of the Western traditions, with five great elements, "is nothing but a combination of *śiva* and *śakti* principle. *Śiva* represents the static aspect of the supreme substance, and *śaktī,* its kinetic aspect. The term *śaktī* is derived from the root *śak* which denotes the capacity of action or power" (*ibid.*, p. 191). Even if one is taken as substance and the other as motion (*kriya*), they represent two aspects of the phenomenal world, ultimately reducible to an energy, in view of the development in modern science. As observed by John Woodroffe, "The old duality of force and matter disappears, these being held to be differing forms of the same thing. The matter is relatively stable form of energy into which, on disturbance of its equilibrium, it disappears; for all forms of matter disassociate. The ultimate basis is that energy which is called in Indian philosophy as *prakṛti*, *māyā* or *śaktī*." (p. 194).[20]

"In fact, the most general phenomenon of the universe is vibration, to which the human body as all else is subject. Various vibrations affect differently each organ of sensation. When certain quality and number, they denote to the skin the degree of external temperature; others incite the eye to see different colours: others again enable the ear to hear defined sounds. Moreover, 'inertia', which is alleged to be a distinguishing quality of 'matter' is said to be the possession of electricity, which is considered to be not material." (p. 193)....Moreover, "Herbert Spencer, the philosopher of modern science, carrying the investigation beyond physical matter, holds .... that the universe, whether physical or psychical, whether as mind or matter, is play of 'force'; mind, 'life' and 'matter' – each varying aspects of the one cosmic process form the 'first cause'. (p. 196).... Both mind and matter derive from what Herbert Spencer calls the Primal Energy (*Ādyā Śakti*), and Haeckel the fundamental Spirit-Matter Substance (p. 195)."[21]

According to *tantrāgama* philosophers *śakti* (cosmic energy) manifests herself in the form of vibration (*spanda*). The ultimate reality has three important *śaktis* (powers), viz., *jñāna śakti* (power of knowledge), *icchā śakti* (will power) and *krīyā śakti* (power of action). *Jñāna śakti* and *icchā śakti* of the Brahman prompt His *krīyā śakti* into action. As a result, there is throb or vibration or *spanda* generally described as *nāda* or *nādabrahman*. This *nādabrahman* is nothing but manifestation of *śiva-śakti tattva*. *Shāradā Tilaka Tantram* explains the same principle but in different words: "From the eternal bliss, *parameśvara* who is in the form of *sat* (ever true), *cit* (ever living being) and *ānanda* (eternal happiness), *śakti* originated; from *śakti nāda* comes and from *nāda*, *bindu* comes into existence".[22]

Thus we find that *nāda* is ultimately nothing but manifestation of *spanda* or throb of *cit śakti* of cosmic reality. "Owing to the ripening of *adṛṣṭa* (according to me the same as *ṛtam* principle of *Ṛgveda*) or *karma*, creation takes place by the disturbance of this equality of the *guṇas* (*guṇakṣobha*), which then commences to oscillate and act upon one another.

It is this initial creative motion which is known in the *tantra* as 'cosmic sound' (*parāśabda*). It is through the association of *Puruṣa* with *Mūlaprakṛti* in cosmic vibration (*spandana*) that creation takes place. The whole universe arises from varied forms of this grand initial motion. So, scientific 'matter' is now currently held to be the varied appearance produced in our minds by vibration of, and in the single substance called ether. This new Western scientific doctrine of vibration is in India an ancient inheritance." [23]

The *śakti* of *śiva* manifests herself in three forms : *bindu*, *nāda* and *bīja*. It is said by some *āgama* pandits that *bindu* is *śiva*, *bīja* is *śakti* and *nāda* is the component of these two. But others say that *śiva* is *nāda* and *bindu* is *śakti* and *bija* is their other manifestation. But this kind of controversy need not hold us up here, in view of the explanation offered by Sri Raghava Bhaṭṭa, the commentator of *Śārada Tilaka Tantra*.

"It is His *icchā* (or the will) that uniformly extends to the whole of existence in the form of *bindu*, which is nothing but solidified massive energy-in-action (=*bindubhāvanam ca kriyāpradhānya lakṣaṇam*). In other words consciousness (*caitanya*) intrinsically is *kriyā*, i.e., functional or actional, (or activity of energy *śakti*)."[24]

It is true that this kind of description relates to esoteric field, which is beyond empirical verifiability. As stated by *Śarada Tilaka Tantram* (1.7-13) itself that this *nāda* arising from *śiva-śakti* principle is transcendental *nāda* in an unmanifested form. It is *śabdabrahman*. But this is not *śabdabrahman* in the sense of "sound" (*ravaḥ*) as some *āgama* scholars say, nor is it in the sense of "the word and meaning", as others think. This *śabdabrahman* is *caitanya* (consciousness) in the entire creation. The commentator of *Śarada Tilaka Tantram*, Sri Raghava Bhaṭṭa explaining the import of these verses says that this *śabdabrahman* is *akhaṇḍa* (whole) not subjected to special parts like *varṇa* or a sound component (*varṇādi viśeṣa rahitā, akhaṇḍā*), etc.[25]

Now the question that still persists is : What is the nature of the relation among *nāda, bindu* and *bīja*?

For *tantrāgama* thinkers the primordial *śakti* is an embodiment of action and her activities consist in the form of *nāda-bindu* series.[26] Bhāskararāya, in his commentary called *Saubhāgyabhāskara* on *Lalita Sahasranāma*, offers a beautiful explanation of this *nāda bindu* relation by quoting *Prapañcasāra* that the same *cit* or consciousness appears as solidified and concentrated (*ghanībhūta*), in the form of *bindu* (a densified drop of energy) (others call it *parā bindu*). The said *bindu* is also called *kāraṇa bindu* (concentrated causal energy). And from the *kāraṇa bindu* arises *kārya bindu* (energy in action), *nāda* (spanda) and *bīja* (seed) – the three in that order, which are also known as *parama* (transcendent), *sūkṣma* (subtle) and *sthūla* (gross). So far as it pertains to the individual self (*jīvātman*), the said *kāraṇa bindu* is called *śaktī, kuṇḍalani*, etc., situated in *mūlādhāra*. From *kāraṇa bindu* arises *kārya bindu*, etc., the three (i.e., *kārya bindu, kāraṇa bindu* and *bīja*), out of which is born subtle (*avyakta*) sound (*ravaḥ*) called *śabdabrahman* in Vedic literature. The said *śabdabrahman*, being *niṣpanda* (non-vibratory or imperceptible vibratory state) resides in *mūlādhāra* as *kāraṇa bindu*, but manifestable by air by effort; and if there is desire and effort, it becomes active and manifests as *parāvāk*. When it travels up to *nābhi* (naval), with the help of *manas* (mind), being joined with air, it manifests in the form of *vimarśa* and *kārya bindu* as a mild throb or non-particularized (*sāmānya spanda prakāśa rūpa*), and in this state it is called *paśyantī vāk* (*paśyati iti paśyantī*). The same *śabdabrahman* joined with air on reaching the heart, joined with the self determining *buddhi* (intellect) becomes special vibrative conscious form (*viśeṣaspandaprakāśa-rūpanādamayam*) and assumes the name *madhyamā*. It has all the characteristics of expressing *vāk* but still *avyakta* (*spuṭataranikhilāvayavā vāgrūpā madhyamā*). The same *śabdabrahman* joined with the same air reaching mouth, when it manifests (through throat, etc.,) *svaras* (vowels) like *a*, etc., which are of the nature of sound clearly audible to ear, as distinct vibrative seedling (*bījātmakam nāda*), it is called *vaikharī vāk*, (*viśeṣeṇa svaraḥ kaṭhinatasyeyaṃ vaikharī śaiva rūpaṃ*). In this form, word and its meaning are explicit. These four types of *vāk* are also called *mātṛkās* (a source) for letters (*varṇas*). *Vaikharī mātrukā* is the source of linguistic *varṇas*.[27] *Varṇa* is a letter, or vowel, which goes into formation of word and sentence.

From the above discussion it follows that it is the transcendental *nāda śakti* or *parā bindu* which "is thus a compact aspect of *śakti* wherein action or *kriyā śakti* predominates. It is compared to a grain or gram (*canaka*) which under its outer sheath (*māyā*) contains two halves of a seed (*śiva* and *śakti*) in close and undivided union...."[28] It is this *parā bindu* when unfolding into creative ideation (*śṛṣṭikalpanā*) into *śabdabrahman* (unmanifested sound) that causes (manifested) vibration or wave or *spanda* (phenomenal-*nāda*), generally known as *dhvani* or *śabda* (sound). The word *spanda* literally means a sort of movement or "throbbing, or throb, quiver, pulse, tremor, vibration, motion, activity".[29] But it is a technical term in the *tantra* system of *Kāśmīr śaivism.* Abhinava Gupta explains its technical aspect as follows:

".... it is only because of a slight pulsation [perhaps similar to heartbeat] within the essential nature (of the self) consisting of succession less wondrous delight (not because of moving from oneself to another object) that it has been indicated in the *agamas* by words, such as *ucchalatta* (jerking up), *ūrmi* (billow), *matsyodarī* (throbbing in the stomach of a fish). This is, what is said to be *spanda* (because of slight pulsation within the essential nature of the 'divine'). This *spanda* is of the nature of the union of *śiva-śaktī*."[30]

Kṣemarāja, in his *Spandnirṇaya*–a commentary on *Spandakārikā*– explaining the *kārikā* No. (I.1) said, "Thus the essential nature of the Lord is perpetual *spanda* (creative pulsation). He is never without *spanda*.... Our nature is identical with that of (Śaṅkara) who is full of *spanda śakti*, the essence of which consists in quivering light."[31] Thus it is clear from Kṣemarāja's *Spandnirṇaya* that the *spanda* is the essential nature of the "ultimate reality." It is nothing but the creative or thought force (*vimarśa śakti*) of *Brahman*, and accordingly is "causal force" (*kāraṇa śakti*) for both cosmic *nāda* (transcendental sound) and *bhautika nāda* (phenomenal sound or *dhvani*); it is so because the phenomenal world is a replica (a copy or *pratibimba*) of "cosmic world." Thus, transcendental *nāda* causes phenomenal *nāda*, which, in turn, manifests in the form of letter-sounds (*mātṛkās*). This aspect is further elucidated by *Netratantra*[32] as under:

"She who is the manifester of *sphoṭa*, etc., *dhvani* (or sounds) in eight forms and the one who determines *mātṛkās*, (the source of letter-sounds) and who is the goddess of energy-in-action (*kriyā śaktiḥ*). She who is the cause of motion, is no other than the cosmic-energy-in-action (*paramā kriyākhyā*) and the ocean of all languages (*sarva vāṅmayarūpiṇī*), and is the one called Ādi-Śaktī Maheśvarī." Regarding eight forms of *dhvani*, Kṣemarāja, the commentator of *Netratantra*, (on Ne. Ta. 21.38) points out that *parā vāk-śakti* (cosmic energy-in-action) causes all the sounds of *paśyantī*, etc., which are independently perceivable (*bodha svātantrātmā*) both subtle (*sūkṣma*) and the gross sounds (*sthūla*) of eight forms (*rūpa*) as under:

ghoṣo rāvaḥ svanaḥ śabdaḥ sphoṭākhyā dhvanireva ca
jhāṅkaro dhvaṅkṛtiścaiva hyāṣṭo śabdāḥ prakīrtitāḥ

Ghoṣaḥ, rāvaḥ, svanaḥ, śabdaḥ, sphoṭaḥ, dhvaniḥ, jhānkaraḥ, dhvankṛ are eight accepted and declared forms of "sounds" (*dhvani*).

Now another important question that arises from the point of my thesis is: What is the nature of this *dhvani* (or *nāda*)?

Shiva Chandra Vidyārṇava Bhaṭṭacārya Mahodaya, an eminent *tantrāgama* scholar, opines that "Those who are leaned in sound (*śabda*) have divided it into two classes (*dhvani* and *varṇa*) but in reality there is no such difference in sound itself...." What is expressed in the string of letters from *a* to *kṣa* is called *varṇa*, and that which is not expressed by any alphabetical marks is called *dhvani*. Thus "difference of tone (*svara*) alone is the cause of this twofold aspect of *śabda*".[33] Thus it is clear that the sound or *nāda* or *dhvani* is nothing but a vibrating phenomenon. *Dhvani* (Sound) is that, which *dhvanati* (Sounds). This sound itself takes the form of *mātṛkās*. (sound as the source from which letters arise) and, accordingly, "fifty letters of the alphabets, from *a* to *kṣa* are only the manifested state of that hissing sound or *dhvani*" (of *kuṇḍalanī śaktī* in the form of sleeping snake).[34]

The letters are called *mātṛkās* or little mothers only for the reason that such letters embody the sound produced by mother *kuṇḍalinī* which fact assures eternality to letters. (For *Mīmāṃsākas* also letters are eternal for different reasons, that we will see soon.). But the phenomenal sounds of uttering letters being pronunciations from the mouth of individuals vary and are different in intonation and, accordingly, are transitory. This kind of esoteric principle is the basis to the *tantric* theory of language. In this aspect, the *tantric* theory of sound is similar to that of *Mīmāṃsā*. But as to the nature of sound, *tantrics* differ from *Mīmāṃsā*. For *Mīmāṃsā*, the transcendental sound or *nada*, which causes phenomenal sound, is "substance", and phenomenal sound itself is not substance but only a quality of *ākāśa* (ether) and uses air for its propagation. But for *tantra* such transcendental sound, which causes phenomenal sound, is "cosmic energy-in-action" (*kriyā śaktī*), but not substance in the sense of *dravya*. In the same way even the phenomenal sound also would be "energy-in-action" (but of physical energy). But this physical energy is nothing but manifestation or reflection of cosmic energy. Thus, metaphysically speaking, as explained by *Parā-triśikā Vivaraṇa* of Abhinava Gupta, as we have seen above, on the basis of the *tantric* dictum—*sarvam sarvātmakam*—(everything is related to everything else), it is clear that the phenomenal sound ultimately is *pratibimba* (reflection) of "transcendental energy-in-action" (*kriyā śaktī*). There cannot be *pratibimba* (in mirror), unless there is *bimba* corresponding to it. Likewise, phenomenal *nāda* also should necessarily be present in cosmic *nāda*. The phenomenal *nāda* is the tree and its seed is "cosmic *nāda*." The tree is present in the seed. Likewise the cosmic *nāda* is present in phenomenal *nāda*. Even in the example of sound arising in breaking of wood, or two objects striking against each other, or ringing of bell, etc., as given by *Nyāya-Vaiśeṣika* school, are the instances of energy acting on these objects, in creating sound, and ultimately, sound would be a manifestation of an energy-in-action (*kriyā śaktī*) or *spanda*. In this sense, the *varṇas* (letters or syllables) are not only sound-units (*mātṛkās*) but energy units (*śaktī bīja*) also. It is because of this intrinsic nature, these *varṇas* are capable being the components of *mantra*, which again is a source of energy called *mantra śakti*.

In his commentary on *Lalitā-sahasranāma* called *Soubhāgybhāskara*, Bhāskararāya says : "Just as the supreme Śiva is twofold as *śaktī* and *śiva*, so this *mātṛkā devī* herself shines in two. The vowels indicate one form of *śakti*, the others (consonants) indicate *śiva*."[35] Thus, according to *tantra* philosophy, every letter is thus a manifestation of *śiva-śakti* principle. In *mantra yoga* of *Kāśmīr śhaivism*, *a* symbolises *anuttrara* or *Śiva*, and *ha* symbolizes *śakti*. The *svara a* is the most natural and primal *svara* or vowel (sound), out of which all the vowels and consonants emerge. *Ha*, on the other hand, represents expansion which is the symbol of *śakti*. The expansion from *a* to *ha* is the evolution process and it ultimately results in *ahaṃ* or I-hood; and *ṃ* in *ahaṃ* symbolizes the union of the two, resulting in *śiva-śakti* principle out of which all the *tattvas* emerge on the cosmic side; and all the letters, on the linguistic side, concomitantly. Hence the "word" and its "referent" have become universal by virtue of this inseparable association. They represent the empirical mixed condition of *parāpara vidyā* – A mixture of material and divine. The *parāvāk* has taken the form of *vaikharī* representing the gross aspect, but, at the same time, it is not separated from *parā*, *paśyantī* and *madhyamā*. Highlighting this truth, Abhinava Gupta, in his *Parātriśikā Vivaraṇa*, further says:

"Therefore, though the condensation of the phoneme becomes distinct only in the *vaikharī* or gross aspect, yet it abides primarily in the 'supreme verbum' (*parāvāk*) which is all inclusive (*sarvaṃ sarvātmaka*)."[36] Even according to *Lakṣmī Tantra*, the syllable *a* uttered in *vaikhari* is primary and self-revealed, consciousness and the root of the entire domain of speech.[37] All other letters like *ā, i, ī, u, ū, e, ai, o, au,* etc., arise out of primary letter *a*. "Thus all these (sounds, which ultimately) relate to objects of knowledge, are derived from the first (vowel *a*)."[38]

In this context, another question may be raised and that is: How does the language as a means of knowledge arise out of this gross letter-sounds, as per *tantrāgamas*?

Devi in *Lakṣmī Tantra* has given the following reply:

"Knowledge (insight, *bodha*) appears identical with sound, and sound, (as) identical with objects connoted. Considering that knowledge (insight) is one of my aspects, it follows that all the above mentioned sounds (*varṇasamāmnāya*) (are projections) of myself."[39] In other words, as per *tantrāgama* philosophy, word and objects (*nāma* and *rūpa*) and, consequently language, are a manifestation of that *śakti* only. "It is universally understood that indication of an object is invariably preceded by use of the sound (*śabda*) denoting it. The nature of the gross-form of *śabda* is that the object originates from *śabda*."[40] *Śabda* (sound) is the manifest knowledge (*bodha*), and (*artha*) is the object of *śabda* (word).[41] In the words of *Svacchanda Tantram*, "The forms of objects are revealed through the knowledge of words (*śabāvabhoda-rūpeṇa vasturūpasvarūpaḥ*."[42] In the words of *Lakṣmī Tantra*, "Words are uttered in *vaikharī vāk*. *Vaikharī vāk* is identified with the seat of effort (*prayatnasthāna*).[43] Thus the object is unmistakably revealed through utterance of the manifest sound (in the form of syllables). The fifty *śaktīs* resting in *vaikharī* make-up of (fifty syllables) (constitute) the garland of letter-sounds (*varṇamālinī*)."[44]

Even *ākāśa* (ether), which serves as a medium for the sound to travel is not a substance nor sound is its quality. In its transcendental aspect, *ākāśa* is itself *cidākāśa*, a manifestation of cosmic consciousness. Hence *ākāśa*, for *tantrāgama* thinkers, is not substance like *Sāṅkhya*-Yoga or *Nyāya-Vaiśeṣikas*, but is vacuity, coextensive with that of cosmic consciousness.

Thus the physical sound, being basically *spanda* (vibration), vibrates (*spandati*), in *ākāśa* but as the one caused by external force or the human effort or action. According to *Spandakārikā* (1.14), the actions caused by external effort are perishable:

> *avasthāyugalaṃ cātra kāryakartṛtvaśabditam*
> *kāryatā kṣayiṇī tatra kartṛtvaṃ punarakṣayam* (14)

"Of this *spanda* principle, two states are spoken about, viz., of the doer or the subject and the deed or the object. Of these two, the deed or the object is subject to decay but the doer or the subject is imperishable."[45]

It means that the deeds or something done with human effort perishes, but the "self", who is a doer, is imperishable. If it is so, the sound or *dhvani* caused by human or any other external effort (action *kriyā*) is perishable and hence it is non-eternal. Therefore sounds of letters disappear immediately after their utterance. In this respect *tantra* theory of sound is similar to the phenomenal or "accentual sound" (or *dhvani*) of *Mīmāṃsā* and accordingly is non-eternal and transitory. But letters born out of *mātṛkās*, being a manifestation of *śakti*, are eternal.

But, how about *mantra* and its efficacy since it is also composed in letter sounds?

In fact, a *mantra* is also a sound (*dhvani*), which (the adept invariably) associates (with the belief that) – "This protects me or which always protects him from fear" and an adept is a person who (knows) the secret purport (of *mantras*).[46] Every manifestation of I-hood in the graded sequence peculiar to sound based on absolute I-hood and inducive to the revelation of pure knowledge, is, according to tradition, a *mantra*.[47] *Śaktī* also evolves herself by means of *mantras* through sound combinations.[48] All *mantras* surge up like waves from her, the ocean, as it were, of consciousness. These forms (mass of sounds), lovely as concentrations of consciousness and bliss, evolve out of her as their substratum and repeatedly flow back into her (at the time of dissolution).[49] According to the level of the adept's mental realization, a *mantra* is addressed either to Lakṣmī or to some other (deity).[50]

A *sādhaka* (adept) visualizing himself as one with transcendental entity, ultimately realizes that "I am He" (*sohaṃ*); by inhaling as *so*, and exhaling as *haṃ*, thereby chants *sohaṃ* (I am He). This kind of the mental consciousness in breath is called *ajapa japa*. There can be chanting of *mantra* (*japa mantra*) like *Oṃ namo bhagavate Rudrāya* or *Oṃ namo Nārāyaṇāya*, etc. There can even be a single syllable *mantra*, like *Oṃ*, generally known as *praṇava* or *praṇava mantra*. What is important in *tantra vidyā* is devotion (*devatābhāva*). It is observed in *Rudrayāmalam* (*Uttaratantram*) (*Prathamo Bhāgaḥ*) that "It is by devotion to (Devi) one gets her grace and thereby the ultimate happiness. It is again by such devotion one obtains the knowledge of *Brahman* and from such knowledge consequently *mokṣa*".[51]

It is only such devoted adepts thereby drink the *amṛtā* (*ambrosia*) oozing (from *brahmarandra*) through palate and, accordingly, would be intoxicated, (but not with the toddy made out of joggary)[52]; at this juncture, they are in the state of bliss, like the one in sexual union; not indulging in sex as such "The bliss of sexual union by recollection (*smarānanda*)." It is only "inverted *kāma* or sexual delight."[53] Hence it is rightly said:

"There is no separate *mantra* other than *nāda*, nor there any other God except one self. There is no other *pūjā* other than *nāda meditation* (*nādānusandhāna*); there is no happiness or bliss (or spiritual benefit) other than the contentment, i.e., spiritual attainment (*paramaphalam* or *mokṣa*)."[54]

nāsti nādāt paro mantro na devaḥ svātmanaḥ paraḥ
nānusandheḥ parā pūjā nahi trupteḥ paraṃ phalam.

* * *

The gist of the Theory of *Tantrāgamas* :

Nāda is a phenomenal activity (*kriyā* or *spanda*) being the manifestation of cosmic energy (Vibration theory of Sound)

Tantrāgama thinkers also accepted the cosmic theory of *nāda*, but of different nature. Their *Niṣkalabrahman* is mere "I-hood" in the form of "cosmic consciousness" (*saṃvid*, *caitanya* or *cit*) in an indivisible "*śiva-śakti*" principle form, which in its *līlā* (playful mood) starts evolving in the form of *nāma* and *rūpa* (name and objects). In this process its first manifestation is *Nādabrahman*. *Omkāra* or *praṇava* manifests itself in three *bindus* in phenomenon of "triangular form" (*trikoṇa* or *śṛṅgāṭa*) and evolves into psycho-physical parallel creations, called "mind" (*jīva*) and "matter" (*jaḍa*). By virtue of its vibrations, it takes the form of *nāda* and *bindu*. *Nāda* takes the form of "word" and *bindu* that of the objects, (i.e., word and its meaning). The relation between *Nādabrahman* and ordinary "phenomenal sound" would be just like "a mountain reflecting in a mirror." *Śakti* manifests herself as *bindu*, *nāda* and *bīja*.

In human body the *nispanda*, situated at *mulādhāra*, as *kāraṇa bindu*, (cause) manifests by effort with the help of air as *parā*, *paśyanti*, *madhyama* and *vaikharī*. In *vaikharī* it becomes audible to ear in the form of *varṇa-mātṛkās* (source of letters).

Thus, it is the "*cosmic-nāda-śaktī*" that causes phenomenal *nāda* generally called "sound". This sound is not a substance but only an action or activity (*kriyā*) of energy (*śakti*). In a bell, the sound lasts till the energy in the bell lasts. Sound is not a substance, as *Mīmāṃsākas* think. Sound is "energy-in-action" (*śakti krīyā*). The phenomenal sound, caused by such activity (*krīyā*) is non-eternal. But the "syllables" (*varṇas*) being the manifestation of *kuṇḍalinī śakti* as *mātṛkās* (little mothers) are eternal. They cause phenomenal "sound-syllables" (*varṇas*) through the vocal sounds, which are matters of intonations, and which are transitory and not eternal. In this respect, the *tantrāgama* theory of sound appears to be similar to the theory of *Mīmāṃsā*, except that in *Mīmāṃsā* the sound is a "substance", but in *tantrāgamas* it is "energy-in-action" (*kriyā śakti*).

Notes and References

1. Basu, Manoranjan (1986) : p. 2.
2. *citte śuddhe.... brahma-jñānaṃ prajāyate* : *Mahānirvāṇa Tantram* (2004) - 7.94.
3. Woodroffe, Sir John (*tr.*) (2001) : (II.33-42); pp. 25-27.
4. Woodroffe, Sir John (2006) : p. 75.
5. *Taittirīya Upaniṣada* -2.6.1 : Radhakrishnan (1994), p. 547.
6. Kā. K.Vil. - Dwivedi, Ramayana Prasad, Prof. & Malaviya, Dr. Sudhakar, (ed. & tr.) (2003).
7. *Cidvalli* on Kā. K. Vil.; 25: pp. 80-81 *bindutrayātmakaṃ svātmaśṛṅgāṭaṃ viddhi sundaram, miśra śuklaṃ ca raktaṃ ca purāṇaṃ praṇavātmakaṃ. rekhātrayāvagantavyasaṃvitsāndra śivātmakam.*
8. *Cidvalli* on Kā. K. Vil.; at pp. 75-76.
9. Kā. K.Vil.: p. 82.
10. Kā. K.Vil.: p. 75.
11. Swami Harshananda (2000) : p. 15.
12. Gupta, Sanjukta : p. 24.

13. Singh, Jaideva (*tr.*) (2005) : p. 27.
14. Gupta, Sunjukta (2000) : Introduction at p. (xxiii) & Ch. VI.42-44.
15. L.T. : p. 125.
16. L.T. : p. 136.
17. Avalon Arthur (Woodroffe, Sir John) (2006) : p. 259 (in short *Śakti and Śākta)*.
18. Sami Ranganathananda (1996) : p. 29.
19. Avalon Arthur (2006) : p. 268.
20. Avalon Arthur (2006) : p. 194.
21. Avalon Arthur (2006) : pp. 194-96.
22. *Śārada Tilaka Tantram* (I.7) : Board of Scholars (*tr.*) (1988).
23. Avalon Arthur (2006) : p. 245.
24. Avalon Arthur (ed.) (2001) : pp. 16-17 and pp. 19-20 (in short Śā. T. T. 1.7).

    samastatatvabhāvena vivartatecchāsamanvitā

    prayāti bindubhāvañca kriyāpradhānalakṣaṇam
25. *Śārada Tilaka Tantram* : Board of Scholars; (1988); Verses 1.7-13 : pp. 1 & 2.
26. *karmarūpā stithā māyā; nādabindvātmakam kāryam*

    Dwivedi, Vajravallabha (ed.) (2004) : Vol. 2, verse 1263; pp. 302-303).
27. Pansikar, Wasudeva Laxmana Shastri (ed.) (1985) : pp. 99-100.
28. Avalon Arthur (2006) : p. 256.
29. Williams, Monier Monier : p. 1268.
30. *Parā-triśikā-Vivaraṇa* of Abhinava Gupta, pp. 190-91.
31. Singh, Jaideva (*tr.*) (1994) : p. 10.
32. Dwivedi, Vajravallabha (ed.) (1985) :

    varṇarūpāṣṭabhedena sphoṭādidhvanirūpiṇī

    mātṛkā sā vinirdiṣṭā kriyāśaktirmaheśvarī

    kriyākhyā paramā sā tu sarvavāṅgmayarūpiṇī (Ne. Ta. 21.38).

33. Woodroffe, John (*tr.*) (2002) : p. 505.
34. (2002) : p. 511.
35. Sastry, Ananthakrishna (*tr.*) (1988): p. 240.
36. *Parā-triśikā Vivaraṇa:* p. 176, Singh, Jaideva (2005).
37. L.T. XVIV. 2-3.
38. L.T. XVIV. 5-7.
39. L.T. XVIV. 45.
40. L.T. XVIII. 21.
41. L.T. XVIII. 22-23.
42. Sva. T. - 11.13.
43. L.T. XX. 30.
44. L.T. XX. 31-33.
45. *Spandakārikā*-1.14, Singh, Jaideva (1994).
46. LT. XVIII. 44-45.
47. L.T. XVIII. 44-45.
48. L.T. XXI. 8.
49. L.T. XVIII. 36-38.
50. L.T. XVIII. 46.
51. *bhāvādanugrahaprāptiranugrahānmahāukhī* (Ru.Y.T.-1.118 (1991)) *bhavena jñānamutpannaṃ jñānānmokṣamavāpnuyāt* (Ru.Y.T. 1.221).
52. Rāya, Rāmakumāra (1986), pp. 36.49-50.
53. Parā. Tr. V. : p. 210.
54. *nāsti nādāt paro mantro na devaḥ svātmanaḥ paraḥ*
    nānusandheḥ parā pūjā nahi trupteḥ paraṃ phalam.
    – Nayasaṅgītaḥ (From *Luptāgama Saṅgrahaḥ* (1983) : Vol. II; p. 98).

* * *

Chapter Seven

THE CONCEPT OF *NĀDA* OR *DHVANI* IN GRAMMATICAL SYSTEMS

The important contribution of the grammarians, to the subject of my thesis, consists in distinguishing *nāda* from *dhvani*. All along, we have seen that the thinkers were using *dhvani* and *nāda* in the sense of sound, as synonyms, but different only from *śabda*, used in the sense of "word". But the grammarians put the concept of *nāda* and *dhvani* for further scrutiny so as to ascertain the subtle shades of the connotations of the two expressions.

Vyākaraṇa is defined by Patañjali as "The science of words" (*śabdānuśāsanaṃ*).[1] "Words", here, stand for both Vedic and colloquial. The object of such science is to avoid the vulgar or corrupt words.

Unlike other countries, India has produced a galaxy of eminent grammarians who have made a great contribution on different aspects of grammar, particularly on "semantics". The most eminent amongst them were Pāṇinī (5th cen. B.C.), Kātyāyana (3rd cen. B.C.), Patañjali (150 B.C.), Bhartṛhari (400 A.D.), Bhaṭṭoji (1600 A.D.), Nāgoji Bhaṭṭa (1650), Nāgeśa Bhaṭṭa (1670 A.D.), etc.[2] However Bhartṛhari was the first grammarian who extensively dealt with the philosophical analysis of grammar. Hence I propose to rely heavily on Bhartṛhari's *Vākyapadīyam*, mainly as translated by Korada Subramanyam,[3] in addition to *Mahābhāṣya* of Patañjali, in order to ascertain the philosophy of *nāda* according to grammarians.

The transcendent reality, according to Bhartṛhari, is the beginningless and endless (*anādi*) *śabdabrahman*, who, being the cause of phonemes (*akṣara*), is of the nature of the essence of word (*śabda*) and from whom the entire creation emanates.[4] According to Bhartṛhari, almost all Indian (schools), accepted without any contradiction, that God's creation (i.e. the ultimate reality) is capable of being grasped through one word, that is in the form of *praṇava* (*aum*).[5] By virtue of His time-power (*kāla śakti*), *brahman* becomes the source of manifold transformations (*vikāra*).[6] In other words, time is the source of present, past and future and the seasons, etc. Bhartṛhari's *kāla* (Time) is of the nature of *śakti* and his *brahman* is of the nature of *śabdabrahman*.

Like Patañjali, Bhartṛhari also emphasizes "cosmic consciousness" (*saṃvit*) as the essence of the reality which enables the inner consciousness of the soul to understand it in the form of word and language. For instance, according to Bhartṛhari, "The speech (or word) exists within and outside all living beings in the form of consciousness (*caitanya*)."[7] *Śabda* is another form of *caitanya* or "consciousness."

For Bhartṛhari and other grammarians, *śabdas* are the sole guide to the objects. All classes of things depend on *śabda*, *vaidik* or secular; and all the disciplines of knowledge depend on *vyākaraṇa* (grammar). Without grammar, the truth cannot be apprehended.[8] In a nutshell, "The grammar is the gateway and royal road to liberation."[9]

The undifferentiated "Supreme Essence of Speech" (i.e., *sphoṭa*) is manifested by the signs (*cihnāni*) like "sounds" or "script", etc. Alphabets (*akṣara*), which are the antecedent of speech arise out of "signs."[10] (Vā.1.20 - translated by Korada Subramanyam). But as per the translations of K. Raghavan Pillai such alphabets arise out of "one letter scripture".[11] In this view of the matter it is clear that Bhartṛhari's *śabda*, in metaphysical terms, arises out of vedic *vāk* or vedic *oṃ* which, in the ultimate analysis, are two aspects of one and the same *Brahman*. On the phenomenal side, the same is reflected in the manifestation of "syllables" through sound or *dhvani*. As V. Krishnamacharya puts it, *dhvani* is an "air-borne sound" that manifests syllables (*dhvanirvāyurguṇo varṇavyañjaka*), and *varṇa* is a letter-substance manifested by sound (*varṇastu dravyaṃ, dhvanivyaṅgyam*).[12] The high tone and low tone, etc., are the characteristic of sound; and a *varṇa* or a "letter-sound", like *a*, is the one that is manifested by sound. In fact, *varṇa* (letter sound) is nothing but a "sound form" used in the languages vedic or non-vedic. A word is a group of letter-sounds. "Hence it is sound that is a word" (*tasmād dhvaniḥ śabdaḥ* - Patañjali).[13] Here Patañjali accepts *Śabarabhāṣya* on *Mīmāṃsasūtra*, which commenting on Mī. Sū.1.15 says - In the day-to-day transaction of the world, the ear-perceptible word is in the form of "syllable-form group sounds" (*varṇarūp pad dhvani samūha*) is accepted (*loke vyavahartṛṣu prasiddhaḥ śrotrendriyagrāhyatvād varṇarūpa-dhvanisamūha eva śabda ityarthaḥ* - 1.I.5).[14]

The meaning of a word is revealed by the object (*dravya* i.e. cow) for which the word (cow) is a symbol (*saṃjña*). To the question, "What is word (*śabda*) in *gauḥ*? Patañjali replied by saying that it is a word which when uttered (*uccāritena*) brings us a knowledge of the individuals possessing dewlap, tail, hump, hoofs and horns. In other words, the sounds which conventionally convey a particular sense is called a. word".[15]

Commenting on the definition of word as *tasmād dhvani śabdaḥ* of Patañjali, Surendranath Dasgupta says, "the word *uccāritena* has been interpreted by Kaiyaṭa not as 'pronounced' but as 'expressed' (*prakāśitena*). According to the grammarians, the denoting entity is something different from the alphabet constituting the word (*pada*) or a sentence (*vākya*). They argue that, if the letter-sounds individually denote the object then the pronouncement of the other letter-sounds constituting the word would be unnecessary. If each letter-sound has a meaning, then they jointly cannot produce the unified meaning of 'the cow'. If it is held that the manifestation (*abhivyakti*) of the meaning takes place in succession, then as the letter-sounds vanish each moment that they are produced, it has to be admitted that the combination of different letter-sounds contributing to the final manifestation takes place on the basis of memory.... It is for this reason the grammarians admit the existence of a separate transcendent whole called the *sphoṭa*".[16] The word (*pada*), with its own meaning, is entirely different from the *varṇas*.

The word *varṇa* referred to here is a "lettered-sound" (or "syllable") (*varṇātmaka dhvani*) different from an inarticulate sound *nādātmaka dhvani* (e.g., sound or noise). An inarticulate sound may be regulated like in instrumental music or unregulated like a noise on a railway platform. But an articulated sound, on the other hand, is regulated, and uttered sound to signify a particular letter (*varṇa*) in a particular "sound form"; say *a*, *la*, *ma*, etc. Though with certain differences, as to the nature of voices or intonations, all people utter *varṇa a, la* or *ma,* etc., in definite "sound-forms". Some scholars describe this kind of particular "articulatory sound-form," as "phoneme" (or "phonematic sound"), or *varṇa* in *Śanskṛt*. These *varṇas* (phonemes) in different combinations constitute different words. It is to be noted that in our day-to-day communications we utter a "sound-forms patterns" (morpheme), or word by uttering it through mouth as *ghaṭa*. Thus from time immemorial *sound* is being used as a sign (*cihna*) in languages.

A sign means "a mark, token, something that indicates a fact, quality, etc.; indication; token; black as a sign of mourning", etc. (Webster's New World Dictionary). A "sound form" or syllable *gha* is a sign (*cihna*) that can be used in different combinations. For example, *gha* with another "sound sign" *ṭa* becomes *ghaṭa*. A "sound-form pattern" (or in simpified form "sound-pattern") *ghaṭa* or a writing-*ghaṭa* as a sign-pattern would be meaningless "sound" or "script", left to itself. In other words, *dhvani* (inarticulate sound), standing by itself, is meaningless sound, as Kayyaṭa, puts it *nādo rtharahitatvād ghoṣamātrameva.* Sound by itself being without meaning is mere shouting only (*ghoṣamātrameva*).[17] But as per the Sanskṛt linguistic tradition (or convention), this "sound-sign" *ghaṭa* indicates or refers to a pot. That means a "sound-sign" *ghaṭa*, when it is always taken for "pot", becomes a "sound-symbol" (*samjña*) for the "pot". Hence "symbol" means "something that stands for, represents, or suggests another thing – the 'dove' is a symbol of peace".[18] In other words, this sound-sign (*cihna*) *ghaṭa* becomes a "sound-symbol" (*saṃjña*) or "word" for "pot" as per the Sanskṛt linguistic tradition, (but not in any other language). In the words of Bhartṛhari, "The signs (*cihnāni*) (of sound) of *prākṛta dhvani* (i.e., *katva* and *gatva*, for example) which are like the script-signs shine forth like reflections (of *sphoṭa* or meaning) in association with *śabda* antecedent to all speech".[19] In other words, a "sign", with meaning becomes "symbol" or "word". For instance, even in the case of a noun, "before the name becomes connected with the named (as *saṃjña*), such name is connected with its own form as the meaning (*artha*) (in the form of the named)".[20]

According to Bhartṛhari, all the words are situated in *prākṛta dhvani.* But a person, observing a vow of silence (*mauni*), may indicate the word *ghaṭa* in the "script-form" (*lipi*) by writing *ghaṭa* (sign) on a paper so as to serve as a symbol (for *ghaṭa*) to indicate the object *ghaṭa.* Such a "script-form" is described by some scholars as "grapheme". Here the script is used as a substituted sign for the "uttered sound-word" – *ghaṭa*. There is also a "shorthand" script used as substituted sign for the "long-hand" script. Similarly, a gesture language (communicating by bodily movements) used by deaf and dumb persons is also a substituted sign for spoken words. For example, a deaf and dumb person may indicate "two" in "visual sign" by raising two fingers pointing them at the pots to indicate two *ghaṭas*. Though the grammarians discuss *dhvani* (sound) as an important element in constituting a "word", yet they treat it as a manifester (*vyañjaka*) of *sphoṭa* or meaning. An "uttered sound-word", as a sign, assumes the status of a symbol (*saṃjña*), when it conveys some meaning (by referring to an object) according to convention. The symbol in the form of word (*ghaṭa*), and the object (*ghaṭa*) go together. "The said two aspects of *śabda* (word), viz., *grāhyatva* and *grāhakatva* which are analysed and separated by mind, act without mutual opposition as causes of different effects (like the *samjña* and *samjñi*)."[21] Korada Subramanyam clarified the verse by observing that *samjña* is an instrument in identifying a thing or a person. The person or thing identified is *samjñī*. For example Rama, Bhīma, Nala are *samjñi*. They are in the form of human beings. Thus a word has three aspects : 1) sign (*cihna*)–uttering sound-word "cow"; 2) symbol (*samjña*–this "sign" becomes symbol (*samjña*) when it refers to an object (cow); and 3) the object cow (*samjñi*). A "sound-word" as a "sign" cannot become a symbol, unless it has a referent. The referent stands for the meaning for which the symbol stands for. Thus without meaning a "sign" or "sound-word" (morpheme), (sound "cow") cannot become a symbol (word cow) for the object cow. It is worth noticing in this context that the majority of the modern scholars take sign (*cihna* or *cinha*) and symbol (*samjña*) together under *samjña* only.[22]

According to the grammarians, as noted above, the meaning of the word stands for the existence of "a separate transcendent whole" different from pronounced letter-sounds (morphemes–words), and to this they call *sphoṭa.* According to them, a word is uttered in the speaker's mouth in a series of sounds and is heard by the listener in the form of the "sound series" in the same sequence. It is also in the nature of vocal organ that it can utter only one sound at a time. It is also in the nature of a ear, that is, it can legibly hear only one sound at a time. Even if more than one sound is produced at a time, the mind selects and the ear perceives one particular sound clearly. Hence nobody can say that he or she can utter or the listener can hear all the seven *svaras* (musical notes) at a given time. Therefore, according to the grammarians, a word is uttered by the speaker and heard by the listener in a series of phonemes (letter sounds), in succession. Though earlier phonemes immediately extinguish after utterance, yet it is the last phoneme that reveals the meaning of the object. Only because the earlier phonemes extinguish it cannot be said that they were useless. In fact before extinguishing they leave impressions in memory and these impressions along with previous *sanskāras* [as to its particular meaning (*dravya vyakti*) or universal meaning (*jāti* or class, etc.,)] reveal the *sphoṭa* (or meaning).

For the grammarians, a word is primarily an "idea" in the mind (in the form of *madhyamā*) and is expressed or suggested in words in *vaikharī*, in the form of "syllabic-sounds" (*varṇas*), with the help of the articulatory organs, such as mouth, teeth, tongue, etc. It is important to note that the *vaikharī vāk* according to the grammarians is inadequate, owing to its vagaries in phonetic or sound utterances, to express the meaning conceived in *madhyamā vāk*. Therefore, they believe that they are primarily concerned with *madhyamā*, which, in fact, causes *vaikharī*. A lamp illuminates the object, *ghaṭa* in darkness, likewise *vaikharī vāk* illuminates (or suggests or manifests) the meaning of the *madhyamā vāk* hidden in the mind. Here *vaikharī* is *vyañjaka* (manifester) of *madhyamā*, which is *vyaṅgya* (manifested).[23]

Even for Bhartṛhari also, the word (in the form of idea in mind – *madhyamā*) has "neither prior nor posterior has sequence" but "the word is produced in a sequence with the gross sound (*vaikharī nāda*)."[24] The idea (*sphoṭa*) is mistaken for word only, because of its association with gross sounds; like the reflection of the moon in water.[25] It happens so, because it is through *vaikharī* that the *madhyamā* is revealed to the listener. Even according to *Nāgeśa sphoṭa* refers to the *madhyamā* type of *vāk*, while *dhvani* refers to the *vaikharī* type.[26]

Bhartṛhari uses three terms to explain his theory of *vaikharī dhvani*, and they are: *vṛtti-śabda*, *dhvani* and *nāda*. K.V. Subramania Ayer, by way of his comments, explains them by adding a note : "The first stands for the word which conveys the meaning. The *dhvanis* are conceived of as something atomic, all-pervasive and imperceptible. When amassed by the movements of the articulatory organs, they become gross and perceptible and are then called *nāda*. It is this *nāda* which suggests the word."[27]

According to Bhartṛhari, when a *vaikharī* word *gauḥ* is uttered through mouth, (*vṛtti-śabda*) it is uttered in *prākṛta dhvani*, (i.e., the one born from *prakṛti* or nature or original sound or physical sound (*dhvani*) and this original sound (*dhvani*) is distinguishable from *vaikṛta dhvani* or "modified speech-sounds" (*nāda*). Though there are other sounds like the "sounds (cries) of birds", or the "sounds of river", etc., yet those sounds are mere sounds, and not phonemes (*varṇa*). For uttering *ghaṭa*, the speaker utters *vaikharī* or speech sounds *gh-a-ṭa* which are phonemes (*varṇa*) and the said phonemes are heard by the listener, so as to have the *sphoṭa* (or meaning) of the word *ghaṭa*. These phonemes are uttered in *prākṛta dhvani* or the original sound. *Prākṛta* means "that which has come out or derived from *prakṛti* original element".[28] Thus, according to Bhartṛhari, there are two types of *dhvanis*—*prākṛta dhvani* and *vaikṛta dhvani*[29]; and this *prākṛta dhvani* exists even before *sphoṭa*, in fact it is the *prākṛta dhvani* that causes *sphoṭa* and obtains plurality and the difference in *mātrās* as "short" (*hṛsva*), "long" (*dīrgha*) and "prolated" (pluta), etc., in *vaikṛta dhvani*. The *vaikṛta dhvanis*, on the other hand, are those that take place so as to continue *prākṛta dhvani* with certain changes, such as long and short, etc. The phonemes are uttered in *prākṛta dhvani* or original or primary sound. *Vaikṛta - dhvanis* are "the secondary changed prolonged sounds (floating in the air)" which continue the *prākṛta dhvani* with certain modifications. *Vaikṛta* means "modified, derivative, secondary, changed, undergoing change", etc.[30] For example, the word *vada* (as *hrasva* (short) = to speak), is in *prakṛti dhvani* and gets modified into *vikṛtika dhvani* with *dīrgha* (long), as *vadāmi* (= I speak) without affecting the meaning of the *sphoṭaśabda vada*. In the words of *Saṅgraha* of *Vyādi*, an authority said to have been followed by Bhartṛhari, (not traced except as excerpts in different books of grammar):

> *Varṇasya grahaṇe hetuṛ prākṛto dhvaniriṣyate*
> *vṛttibhede nimittatvaṃ vaikṛtaḥ pratipādyate.*

"The *prākṛta dhvani* (primary sound) is the cause of the perception of the letters (*varṇa*) and the *vaikṛta dhvani* or the modified sound is the cause for the difference in speed of utterance (*vṛtti*)".[31] Nāgeśa or Nāgoji Bhaṭṭa, the most outstanding after Bhartṛhari, also accepted such a division of sound into *prākṛta dhvani* and *vaikṛta dhvani*. According to him "the former is the revealer of the *sphoṭa*, whereas the latter is produced from the former and keeps it (to be heard by the listener) and is responsible for such modification of the sound as to the speed of utterance (*vṛtti*).[32] I pause here to emphasize the fact that the "sound" that is described as *vaikṛta dhvani* or *nāda*, is the hero, that is the focal point of my thesis.

Bhartṛhari leaves no stone unturned in distinguishing *prākṛta dhvani* from *vaikṛta dhvani*. According to him, the air, which stirred the speaker's effort, following his desire to speak, strikes the speech centers in the mouth-organ, and produces different sounds.[33] To this, he calls *prākṛta dhvani*. The impact caused by such an effort is such that this *prākṛta dhvani* produces other sounds or vibrations called *vaikṛta dhvani* (or *nāda*). These *vaikṛta dhvani* (*nāda*) which cause modifications (*vṛttis* - *druta*, etc.,) arise after the cessation of the movements (of the organs) (*kampetūparate jātā nādā vṛttiviśeṣakaḥ*[34], in the form of magnified *śabdas*. "Even before the vibrations (*kampa*) of the speech-organs (which produced *śabda*) have subsided, the other sounds (*vaikṛta dhvani* or *nāda*) are formed from the *sphoṭa* itself, as from one flame to another (with the help of sticks placed)."[35] Just like the fact that even after the current is switched off, the fan rotates for sometime more, the *vaikṛta dhvani* or *nāda* also continues for a longer time, after *prākṛta dhvani* subsides.

According to Bhartṛhari, however, without the primary sound *sphoṭa* cannot be manifested; but, at the same time, the fact remains that the primary sound is not perceptible. "....It has been pointed out that the actual sounds uttered by the speaker and heard by the listener are the *vaikharī dhvani*, containing many irrelevant, idiosyncratic, and non-linguistic elements (of the utterer). This *vaikharī dhvani* reveals the *prākṛta dhvani* which is linguistically relevant phonematic pattern of utterance, free from variations of intonation, tempo, pitch, and so on, which do not affect the language. Of course in languages in which the tone or pitch or length is relevant, these factors will be part of the *prākṛta dhvani* itself."[36]

"The phonemes, which are factors of the sound (*dhvani*) that reveal the *sphoṭa*, seem to be part of the *sphoṭa*.... When a man utters a sentence – 'bring the pot' – it is heard by the listener, reaches his mind through the sense-organ, and reveals its meaning. As far as the speaker is concerned, the sound is produced simultaneously by the *madhyamā* and the *vaikharī*. To the listener, the *vaikharī* helps in revealing the *madhyamā* that gives *sphoṭa*, the meaning bearer."[37]

If according to Bhartṛhari what is heard is only *vaikṛta dhvani* or *nāda*, then a question arises: If so, what happened to *prākṛta dhvani*; whether the *vaikṛta dhvani* (or *nāda*, secondary sound) replaced it; or *prākṛta dhvani* itself got modified into *vaikṛta dhvani*?

According to Bhartṛhari, *prākṛta dhvani* is an important constituent of *vaikṛta dhvani* or *nāda*. (But according to me, *vaikṛta dhvani* is the same *prākṛta dhvani*, but at the time it is the one processed, modified and modulated (*vaikṛta*) in mouth, according to the intention of the speakers to express himself in such words as he chooses; or in the case of singing, in the *svara* he adopts and proposes to adopt next.)

For Bhartṛhari, both *prakṛta dhvani* and *vaikṛta dhvani* are, only the manifesters of *sphoṭa*, without being the part of *sphoṭa*. In view of this position, among others, the grammarians maintain that *sphoṭa* transcends "letter-sounds" (*varṇas*). Therefore, phonemes (*varṇas*), morphemes (words) and sentences are "only a means to the apprehension of the complete *śabda*, i.e., *sphoṭa*."[38] Korada Subramanyam explains by stating that the *śabda sphoṭa* is *akhaṇḍa* (partless). He further says that "In truth the *sphoṭa śabda* has got no sequence. The sequence is there in *dhvani*, which manifests the *sphoṭa*. Such a *dhvani* helps in the expression of meaning. Otherwise, the *śabda* cannot be grasped, nor is it capable of conveying the meaning."

From the above discussion it is clear that the sound is an important factor in the cognition of a language (*śabda bodhaḥ*).

What is the nature of this process of "cognition of a word" by means of sound?

There are three theories among those who hold that it is the primary sound (*prākṛta dhvanis*) that manifest *sphoṭa*.[39]

a. The *dhvanis* reveal the perfect (*samskāra*), the sense of hearing, for clear perception of the word, i.e. the sounds act upon the sense-organ.

b. The *dhvanis* refine the *śabda* (word), so as to enable it to become perceptible by the ear (Bauddhas), i.e., the sounds act upon *śabda* (word).

c. The *dhvanis* refine both the sense of hearing and the *śabda* (word), so that the word becomes perceptible. (*Naiyāyikas*).

Vṛṣabha, one of the commentators of *Vākyapadīyam*, says in his *vṛtti*, that the perception of the sense of hearing itself in three ways:

1. The sounds impart to the sense of hearing the power of grasping a word which was not there before.
2. The sounds only awaken the power which was already there.
3. What is called perception of the senses means the presence of sounds in the sense of hearing, favourable to its grasping the word.

"What is meant here is that the function of the sounds, whether it be the perception of the senses of hearing or of the word, does not go beyond the totality of the factors, but is part of them, just as the light of the lamp is part of the causal factors in the perception of visual objects."[40]

If that is so, in this context, another question may be raised:

What is the manner in which the sound manifests *sphoṭa*?

There are again three theories regarding the manifestation of *sphoṭa* through sound:

a. Sound is perceived along with *śabda* (word) in the manifestation of *sphoṭa*. Sound is the manifesting agent.[41]

b. Sound is not perceived, but only *śabda* (word) or *sphoṭa* is perceived.[42]

c: Sound is an independent manifesting agent of the *śabda* (word) or *sphoṭa*.[43]

Bhartṛhari, as I have already explained above, accepted the third theory. According to him the sound (*nāda*) is only a manifesting agent (*vyañjaka*) of *sphoṭa*, and *sphoṭa* exists independently. Whatever may be the theory, it is not substantially disputed by the grammarians that it is the *dhvani* or sound that manifest *śabda* (word) or the *sphoṭa*. According to Bhartṛhari, the word is manifested by the last *dhvani*, in the sequence of *dhvanis*, having regard to their intrinsic nature. These qualities of *dhvani* are sometimes falsely attributed to *śabda* (word); but *śabda* (word) by itself is partless.

If the word and the sound are thus different, and the word is manifested by the last sound, in sequence of sounds, then another question may be raised:

What is the nature of "this process of the manifestation" of the *sphoṭa* by sound?

The reply of Bhartṛhari is that

nādairāhitabījāyāmantena dhvaninā saha
āvṛtparipākāyāṃ buddhau śabdo'avadhāryate (Vā.1.84)

"Simultaneously with the last sound, the *śabda* is apprehended by the mind in which the seed (impression *sanskāra*) has been sown by the physical sounds, and in which ripening (maturity of speech) has been brought about." It means that the *sphoṭa* is manifested along with the last sound with the help of the impressions left by previous sounds.[44]

If *sphoṭa*, thus, is separate from *dhvani*, it follows that there are neither parts in phonemes nor are phonemes in word, then how to account for phonemes and words and sentences; or "Where from do *dhvani* (or *nāda*) and *sphoṭa* (or meaning) get this kind of relation as the manifester and the manifested?"

Bhartṛhari replies to this question as follows:

asataścāntarāle yān śabdānastīti manyate
pratipatturaśaktiḥ sā grahaṇopāya eva saḥ

"So far as the non-existent (illusory) forms phonemes and words, which a hearer considers as existing in interval, (i.e., between the utterance of the *śabda* and the revealing of *sphoṭa* by them) are concerned, that is merely the incapacity on the part of hearer; but they are, in fact, only a means to the apprehension (*grahaṇopāya eva saḥ*) (of the complete *śabda*, i.e., *sphoṭa*)."[45] What Bhartṛhari intends to say is this that, so far the hearer (for that matter even the speaker) has no option but to follow the linguistic convention that has already determined such relation between sound and the word, (i.e., phonemes as part of word and words as part of sentence) as the only means of comprehension (*grahaṇopāya eva saḥ*). What is intended here is that the linguistic tradition, in the course of its development, associates the relation between a word and sound. (e.g., "sound-gau" = the word *gau*).

According to Bhartṛhari, though the *sphoṭa* is "whole" (*akhaṇḍa*) without any parts yet appears to be with parts because of its association with 'sound', which has parts. "Such a *śabda* (sound)", K. Subramanyam states, "is helping in the expression of meaning of the word.".... Otherwise, the *śabda* (word) cannot be grasped, nor is it capable of conveying the meaning." They are inseparable like light and shadow. Hence there is always a false identity between the two, and the word is mistakenly taken as having parts, even though it is sound that has parts (like phonemes, etc.), but not the word. Likewise even knowledge (*jñāna*) which is partless appears to be in parts or in sequence, because of such illusory association between word (*sphoṭa*) and sound.[46]

Since the *dhvanis* are non-identical with each other how can they manifest their form in a *śabda*?

To this Bhartṛhari replies : "When in reality, the revealing units in phoneme, word, and sentence function independently to each other, they appear to function in combination, although they are entirely different. Their capacities (powers *śaktayaḥ*) seem to be complicated or covered or hidden or confused[47] – *saṃkīrṇā*".[48] The power of *dhvani* and its general characteristic is such that by breaking up its own inherent *bindu* (*granthi*) through breath, it reveals through different speech-sounds, and merge into the syllables and thus take the form of phoneme, word and sentence.[49] Moreover, "by the striking of the (air) (to the) organs of speech, the long and prolated sounds which are different, are produced. And the sounds which modify the *vṛtti* (*drut*, etc.,) (*vaikṛta dhvani*) arise after the cessation of the movements (of the organs)."[50] The object of these two verses is that there is inherent power or capacity (*śaktayaḥ*) with the sound, that it can take the form of syllable by diffusing its own *granthi* (*bindu*) with the help of breath and cause modification in *vṛtti* (*dhrut*, etc.,) of the sound after it is produced. Korada Subramanyam commenting on Vā.1.105 states that the distinctive capacity of the internal air while striking speech centers in the mouth is such that it creates vibration and "such vibration modifies in accordance with phoneme." Thus, according to Bhartṛhari, there would be modification in *dhvani* which takes the form of different phonemes and subsequently in long and short sounds in *vaikṛta dhvani*. (But this theory of modification of sound is not accepted by *Nyāya Vaiśeṣika* and *Mīmāṃsā* schools that will be considered in Chapter Ten.)

What is that that causes *sphoṭa* : Is it phoneme; a word or a sentence?

For Bhaṭṭoji Dīkṣita ,"the experience as one word or one sentence is the basis for assuming *padasphoṭa* and *vākyasphoṭa*. The phonemes (*varṇas*) suggest *sphoṭa*, which is the meaning bearer".[51] But Bharata Miśra, (in the opinion of the editors), "goes to the extent of denying the *varṇas* by making a clear-cut statement (not found in Bhartṛhari or in Maṇḍana) that it is sounds (*dhvani*) and not the phonemes (*varṇas*) (though he does not say how he differentiates the two) that manifest the *sphoṭa*...."[52] Bharata Miśra declares : "According to the grammarians it is the sounds and not phonemes, that manifest the *sphoṭa*. The sounds in the word *vṛṣa* are different from the first four in the word *vṛṣabha*.[53] Even Buddhist scholars differed on this issue. According to Vasubandhu as per *Sautrāntik* school, the sound itself reveals meaning according to convention and there is no necessity of the concept of syllables and word. But for *Vaibhāṣika* like Saṅgabhadra such syllables are necessary since "Syllables cause an utterance to be remembered by the speaker after the sound has passed away...." (see Chapter Nine)

Koṇḍa or Kauṇḍa Bhaṭṭa[54], the author of *Vaikaraṇa-bhūṣaṇa* and *Vaikaraṇabhūṣaṇasāra*, also maintains a position almost similar to Bharata Miśra's – "that sounds perceived by the listeners are not different from *sphoṭa*. The *sphoṭa* is cognized in the form of the distinctive sounds *g-h-a-ṭa*. Koṇḍa Bhaṭṭa holds the view that the object of cognition is the indivisible word *sphoṭa*, but its form is nothing else than the 'phonemes' auditorily perceived. The phoneme *g* manifested by 'sound' *g* is identified with the phoneme *g*, which appears to be part of indivisible *sphoṭa* word."[55] To this argument, there was an objection – "It cannot be argued that the sound-producing air waves reveal the *sphoṭa* collectively, because they are momentary, and each airwave perishes as soon as the succeeding one comes into existence....". Koṇḍa (or Kauṇḍa) Bhaṭṭa meets this objection by saying that the sound-producing movements reveal *sphoṭa* individually. A single air-wave, for instance, in the word *gauḥ* reveals *sphoṭa* through the medium of sound *g*, another reveals through the medium of sound *au*, and the third one reveals *sphoṭa* through the medium *visarga* (*ḥ*). Thus *sphoṭa* is more and more clearly revealed with each succeeding air-wave. In this manner, Koṇḍa Bhaṭṭa says, the *sphoṭa* word *gauḥ* is revealed by an individual wave through the medium of the order or sequence of sounds, *g-au-ḥ*. The different sounds are wrongly considered to be of non-different from the *sphoṭa* word *gauḥ*.[56]

The Naiyāyikas object to this theory by urging that the relation of immediate sequence cannot be maintained between two sounds, because the first had died out by the time the second has come into existence. The relation of priority and posterity arises only when two things exist simultaneously. There cannot be any combination of what is non-existent with what exists.

Kauṇḍa Bhaṭṭa answers this objection "by assuming that the combination of non-existing thing is possible in cognition. The combination can be maintained between two sounds, because at the time of the knowledge of the *utpatti* (production), the knowledge of *sthiti* (duration) of the first sound has not died out."[57] I also find that this kind of fusion of two visual perceptions, as a psychic phenomenon, is accepted in motion pictures. In motion pictures (or in cinema) different still pictures are presented to visual perception in quick succession. Before the earlier sensation is faded out (*sthiti*) if the second sensation occurs (*utpatti*) in a quick succession, then the possibility of "fusion in sensations" can be inferred in the same manner, the modification and movement of pictures is experienced in cinemas. Such a fusion of "senses of hearing" also can be inferred.

At any rate, for the grammarians, the phonemes and words are artificially created. The difference in the phonetic shape in revealing *sphoṭa* causes the difference in the revealed *sphoṭa*. The phonetic shape of *nadī* (river) is different from the phonetic shape of *dīna* (poor), though the same phonemes are employed in these two words. For the grammarians it is the sequence of sound waves (that are artificially created) that determines their different sound-shape with different meaning, to be learnt through convention. In the words of Bhartṛhari, "Just as there is a fixed sequence (in the stages) of the transformation of milk (into curd) and the seed (into the tree), similarly there is a fixed sequence in the series of the hearer's perceptions".[58] Commenting on this verse Korada Subramanyam observes that "The phonemes and words are no doubt created but they have got a sequence which is consistent." Even assuming the *Mīmāṃsā* theory that phonemes are eternal, it is sequence of phonemes that determines the meaning of the word.

Korada Subramanyam clearly highlighted the difference in the theories of *Mīmāṃsākas* and grammarians regarding this sequencing aspect. According to the theory of *Mīmāṃsākas*, the phonemes for themselves do not have any sequence and the form of words like *ghaṭaḥ* and *paṭaḥ* has to be described in terms of the sequence of the sounds which are suggestive. Otherwise, the word manifested by each sound cannot be decided. The phonemes by themselves do not have any sequence. In case all the sounds are suggestive at a time, since there are the same phonemes in both the words–*nadī* and *dīna*–it is not possible to differentiate between the two. Similar is the case with *kapi-pika*, *rāja-jarā*, *yāma-māyā* etc. Therefore, the sounds are suggestive. They are produced.

They have a sequence. When the sequence is attributed to the suggested phonemes, the difference among words is established. As against this theory of *Mīmāṃsākas* that the "sequence of sounds has nothing to do with *sphoṭa*," Bhartṛhari asserts that "due to the difference in time of the manifesting sound, their own time and that of the duration of their cognition are attributed to the phoneme (*varṇa*), word (*pada*) and sentence (*vākya*) which have no difference in time."[59] K.A.S. Iyer elucidated Bhartṛhari's theory of "time" in relation to phonemes and words. He clarified that for Bhartṛhari, the *sphoṭa* is, in fact, manifested by speech sounds in the form of phonemes, words, sentence, etc., which basically are manifesting sounds with time sequences, as the first sound, the second sound, the third sound, the last sound, etc. Thus, the time factors like *eka-mātra*, etc., is attributable to the kind of time factors of speech sounds as being uttered in time sequence in *prākṛta dhvani* (primary sound); having regard to the result of the relative intensity of attack of the *prākṛta* sound, at the speech centers in the mouth, after cessation of that *prākṛta* sound, the secondary sound vibrations (*kampa*) of *vaikṛta dhvani* take different forms (*vṛtti*) as short (*druta*), long (*dīrgha*), etc., (Vā.1.105). These time factors in manifesting sounds are reflected in the *sphoṭa*. Otherwise, they (these time factors) do not belong to the *sphoṭa* at all. Moreover, these time factors of manifesting sounds make the speech sounds perishable and non-eternal. But the *sphoṭa* by itself is separate and eternal. Some people consider *sphoṭa* as non-eternal by associating it with manifesting phonemes, etc., which are non-eternal. But a grammarian being primarily concerned with the scientific study of language, has to sympathize with and take into account, all the theories expressed by the learned people.

It appears, thus, that there are divergent opinions regarding the eternality or otherwise of *sphoṭa*. If it is so, then, what is the final verdict of the grammarians – Is *sphoṭa* eternal or non-eternal?

According to the grammarians, from the point of view of the intellectuals (*uttmādhikārins*) like Patañjali, *sphoṭa* is eternal. But to accommodate the non-intellectuals (*madhyamādhikārins*), grammarians, have sometimes accommodated the second theory that the *sphoṭa* being caused in vocal organs, is non-eternal (*kāryaśabdavāda*). At any rate, according to them, the eternality of *sphoṭa* is attributable to the eternality of the relation between the *śabda* or word and its *artha* or meaning. The *śabda*, in this sense, is the sole cause of all the transactions in the world. In the words of Bhartṛhari, "The power which is based on the *śabda* (*śabdeṣu āśritā śaktiḥ*) is the cause of (all transactions) in this universe. The universe which has a single intuition (*pratibhā*) as its soul, (but) is perceived as manifold through the *śabda* as the eye."[60] In other words, this relation between word and its meaning is of the type of *vācya* (the object) and *vācaka* (the word), on the basis of *sanskāra* of the last birth, and the linguistic convention in this birth, as grasped by one's *pratibhā* (intuition). The child on its birth sucks the milk without being taught, and learns the words quickly when taught due to the *sanskāra* of the last birth.[61] Nevertheless, the expression of thought, in this life has become possible only through words. "It is seen that the distinction between two things, for instance, between *ṣaḍja* and other musical notes, (*niśāda*, *ṛṣabha*, *gāndhāra*, *ṣaḍja*, *madhyama*, *dhaivata*, and *pañcama*), become clear when explained only through *śabda*. Therefore, the manner of things is determined only through *śabdas*".[62] Those, who are versed in Vedas, know that this universe is the transformation of speech[63] on the basis of the *nāma-rūpa* principle.

The speech exists within and outside all living beings in the form of consciousness (*caitanyam*) and it is preceded by speech.[64] "In this world no knowledge is possible except as accompanied by *śabda*. All branches of knowledge of arts and craft, etc., are possible only through *śabda*."[65]

It is the speech that is employed while transferring one's knowledge to others.[66] It is this speech that prompts the human beings in different actions or deeds.[67] It is this very speech that acts as an agent, in connection with an object and its meaning.[68] Even the *tarkaśāstra* (logic) adopts words and sentences in its reasoning and conclusions. Thus, "the human reasoning is the power of *śabda*. The reasoning which is given by the persons, who do not respect the power of *śabda*, or which is against the power of *śabda* cannot be authentic in deciding the purport of a *śabda* (a sentence, or a text etc.)".[69]

It is also the thesis of Bhartṛhari (just like that of Patañjali), that "those desirous of salvation or upliftment (*abhyudaya*) should employ correct words[70], with the threefold speech–

paśyantī, *madhyamā* and *vaikharī*, in three places—*udātta*, *anudātta*, and *svarita*" correctly.[71] Therefore, all types of knowledge (due to perception, inference, etc.,) shines as permeated by speech (*jñānam sarvam śabdena bhāsate*).[72] "Therefore, attainment of impeccable speech is the attainment of Brahman" (*tasmād yaḥ śabdasaṇskāraḥ sā siddhiḥ paramātmanaḥ*).[73] Thus, for Bhartṛhari, speech is the only epistemological means both for worldly knowledge and for the knowledge of the ultimate reality.

* * *

The Gist of the Theory in Grammatical System :

Nāda is an artificial sound produced by *vaikhari dhvani* of vocal chords (Positivistic Theory of Sound)

According to a grammarian philosopher, like Bhartṛhari, the transcendental reality is eternal *śabdabrahman*, the cause of phonemes and the essence of word (*vāk*), and who can be grasped through one word in the form of *praṇava* (*oṃ*). In metaphysical terms, his concept of *śabda* (word) is a manifestation of cosmic consciousness in the form of union of *oṃ* (cosmic sound) and cosmic *vāk*. On the phenomenal side, as explained by Nāgeśa Bhaṭṭa, "....*dhvani* is an air-born sound and *varṇa* is a letter manifesting sound." The high and low tone, etc., are the characteristic of sound (*dhvani*); whereas *varṇa* is a "letter-sound" like *a*, which is the only one, that is manifested by a particular sound (form). In other words, *"a" varṇa* (syllable) is a "particular sound form" different from *"i" varṇa* another sound "form".

Though the grammarians discuss *dhvani* (sound) as an important constituent of a word, still only as an "artificial manifesting agent (*vyañjaka*) of meaning." For the grammarians, a "separate transcendent whole" is different from the letter-sounds (*varṇas*) in *vaikharī dhvani* and to this they call *sphoṭa* (equated to the essence of *Brahman*).

According to Bhartṛhari, there are two kinds of sounds: one "physical original sound" (*prakṛta dhvani*) and the other, "syllabic-articulate modulated sound" (*vaikṛta dhvani*). It is to this modified or modulated sound (*vaikṛta dhvani*), Bhartṛhari calls *nāda*, and I have accepted his theory. According to his theory, there is a modification (*vikāra*) of sound in its application, as a means of human language. But the theory of "modification of sound" is denied by *Mimāṃsakas* and *Naiyāyikas*. I will discuss this aspect in Chapter Ten.

According to grammarians, the sound is non-eternal, but the relation between the word and its meaning, based on convention, is eternal; and on the basis of this the eternality of relation between "word" and its "meaning", as determined by convention, the eternality of the Veda can be established.

Notes and References

1. Chatterji, Kshitish Chandra (1957) : p. 1.
2. Joshi, Shivaram Dattatreya (1993).

3. Korada Subramanyam, (*tr.*) (1992). (In short *Vāk*)
4. Vāk. 1.1.
5. Vāk. 1.9.
6. Vāk. 1.3.
7. Vāk. 1.126.
8. Vāk. 1.13.
9. Vāk. 1.14 & 16.
10. Vāk. 1.
11. Pillai, K. Raghavan (1971).
12. Krishnamacharya (*ed.*) (1977) : Introduction; p. 6.
13. Chatterji, Kshitish Chandra (*tr.*) (1957); p. 4.
14. ____ p. 5 (the same is extracted).
15. ____ p. 4.
16. Dasgupta, Surendranath (1991) : p. 6.
17. Chatterji, Kshitish Chandra (1957) : p. 104.
18. *Webster's New World Dictionary.*
19. Vāk. 1.20 Korada Subramanyam (*tr.*) (1992) - (with my own modifications).
20. Vāk. 1.66.
21. Vāk. 1.58.
22. Raja, K. Kunjunni (1997) : Ch. 3; p. 97.
23. See Korada Subramanyam (1992) at pp. 29-30.
24. Vāk. 1.48.
25. Vāk. 1.49.
26. Raghavan, V.K.S.N. (*tr.*), Potter, K.H. (1990), Vol. V; p. 340.
27. Iyer, K.A. Subramania (1977) : p. 55.
28. Williams, Monier Monier (1997) : p. 703.
29. Vāk. 1.46-47 and 1.76-77.
30. Williams, Monier Monier (1997): p. 1020.
31. Raja, K. Kunjunni (*tr.*) (1977) : *Sangraha* of Vyādi (extracted); p. 101.

32. Raja, K. Kunjunni & Harold, G. Goward - (Potter, K.H. (1990)): Vol. V, p. 329.
33. Vāk. 1.108.
34. Vāk. 1.105.
35. Vāk. 1.106.
36. Raja, K. Kunjunni & Harold, G. Goward; Introduction - (Potter, K.H. (1990), Vol. V; p. 82).
37. Raja, K. Kunjunni & Harold, G. Goward - (Potter, K.H. (1990)): Vol. V, p. 329.
38. Vāk. 1.85 - Korada Subramanyam ; p. 57.
39. Vāk. 1.78.
40. See Vṛṣabha : *Vṛtti* : Commentary of *Vākyapadīyam* of Ayer Subramania, K.A. (*tr.*); p. 81.
41. Vāk. 1.81.
42. Vāk. 1.88.
43. Vāk 1.93.
44. Vāk. 1.84 Korada Subramanyam (*tr.*).
45. Vāk. 1.85 Korada Subramanyam (*tr.*); p. 57.
46. Vāk. 1.86.
47. Vāk. 1.88 Korada Subramanyam (*tr.*); p. 59.
48. Note: the word "*saṃkīrṇā*" means 1. mixed together, intermingled, 2. confused, miscellaneous; 3. shattered, spread, crowded etc.; Apte (2000): p. 946.
49. Vāk. 1.115.
50. Vāk. 1.105.
51. *Śabdakaustubha* of Bhaṭṭoji Dīkṣita : Potter, K.H. (1990), Vol. V, p. 242.
52. Miśra, Bharata : Potter, K.H. (1990), Vol. V; p. 231.
53. ____ p. 233.

54. His correct name was Kauṇḍa Bhaṭṭa, according to Shivaram Dattatreya Joshi (1993): Kauṇḍa Bhaṭṭa on the meaning of Sanskṛt verbs; p.1; Saṃbhāṣā : 'Nagoya Studies in Indian Culture and Bhuddhism'; Japan : Department of Indian Philosophy, University of Nagoya.
55. Koṇḍa (or Kauṇḍa) Bhaṭṭa : Potter, K.H. (1990), Vol. V; p. 303.
56. ____ Vol. V; p. 303.
57. ____ Vol. V; pp. 303-304.
58. Vāk. 1.91.
59. Iyer, K.A. Subrahmania (1977) (*tr.*) : Vāk.1.101; p. 97.
60. Vāk. 1. 118 - Korada Subramanyam (*tr.*).
61. Vāk. 1.121.
62. Vāk. 1.119.
63. Vāk. 1. 120.
64. Vāk. 1.126.
65. Vāk. 1.125.
66. Vāk. 1.124.
67. Vāk. 1.127.
68. Vāk. 1.128.
69. Vāk 1.138 : Korada Subramanyam (*tr.*).
70. Vāk 1.140.
71. Vāk 1.143 : Korada Subramanyam (*tr.*).
72. Vāk 1.123.
73. Vāk. 1.132.

* * *

Chapter Eight

THE THEORY OF *NĀDA* ACCORDING TO MUSICOLOGY

The concept of *śruti* and musical *svaras* are special contributions of the musicologists.

It is believed that the Indian classical music owes its origin to the *Sāmaveda*. The hymns of *Ṛgveda* were used as texts for *sāman* melodic singing, during Vedic sacrifices. *Omkāra*, *huṃkāra*, *hīṃkāra*, *vaṣaṭkāra*, etc., were used to add resonance to the Vedic chanting. Sometimes the Vedic text itself was modified by prefixing or suffixing the *stobhas*, sensible or non-sensible melodic words, like *ho*, *ohā*, etc., by way of embellishments or *alaṇkāra*. In addition, they also adopted different meters like, *gāyatrī*, *anuṣṭup*, etc., to make Vedic singing not only melodic but rhythmic also. As pointed out by G.U. Thite, "much significance was attached to the 'tone' (*svara*) in which recitations were rendered. A loud and open mouth recitation (outward tending) was disapproved. A recitation in loud and toneful pitch with closed lips (inward tending) was appreciated as bringing prosperity. Hence a toneful priest was much in demand for Vedic sacrifices. Since *sāman* chanting was oral, the Vedic seers had given due attention for improvising the proper voice, melodic tones and music."[1]

In this background, the musicologists, like Śāraṅgadeva[2], Śubhaṅkara[3], etc., opined that the science of music has been handed down to us from *Sāmaveda*.

But as per some other texts on musicology, music has grown along with *tantra* and *āgamas*, as part of their meditative means (*sādhanmārga*). For instance, *Aumāpatam*, an earliest book on music and musicology, after *Nāṭyaśāstra* of Bharat, amply speaks of *āgamīka* impact on musicology. Its general editor, T. Chandrasekharan, in his Introduction to *Aumāpatam*, stated that – "This work contains valuable material for research in ancient texts on music, musicology in the *tantras*, and dance literature....The work is co-eval with *śaivāgamas* and must be assigned the early centuries of the Christian Era." According to *Aumāpatam* because of Brahman, the cause of causes, *nāda* arises; and along with *nāda*, the *tāla* also is born, supported by *ākāśa*, conjoined with *vāyu* and *agni*.[4] In Saṅgītaratnākara, Śāraṅgadeva too has followed *āgama* traditions. While praising Śankara as an embodiment of *nāda* (*nādatanu*), he also refers to the origin of *nāda* out of *brahmagranthi* (*mulādhāra cakra*).[5]

Śāradatanaya in his *Bhāvaprakāśanam* followed *Kāśmīr śaivism* while expounding *śiva-śakti* principle with thirty-six *tattvas*.[6] *Saṅgītopaniṣad Sāroddhāra* of Shri Sudhākalaśa also declared that "The universe of animate and inanimate things consists of *śiva* and *śaktī* and *śaktī* does not exist without *śiva*, nor *śiva* without *śaktī*; deprived of *Kuṇḍalanī* (*śaktī*), *śiva* becomes *śava* (a dead body)."[7]

Even regarding the origin of *nāda* in human body, the musicologists followed *tantrāgamas*. According to *Aumāpatam* in the body composed of *pañca bhūtās*, as desired by Mahādeva, *nāda* arises in *mūlādhāra* in *trikoṇa* form; and this *nāda* composed of fire and air, being pushed by air, passes through an air-struck-agni-trikoṇa-cave (*pavanāhata-koṇāgni-jvālāpūrita-kandaraḥ*) – a narrow lane or a cave formed as a triangle stuffed with air and fire (energy).[8] And there sprouts *dhvani* with *bindu* (*ghanasvara*) at the heart. Having obtained the support from veins (*nāḍī*), the said *dhvani* rises higher, and with the help of mind, it ultimately gets the name *śabda*, and *svara*, the generator of *śruti*, and obtains different *svaras* like *udātta*, etc. Here the description of origin of *nāda* also is similar to that of *āgama* traditions. Mataṅga, also in his work *Bṛhaddeśī*, refers to *āgama* and says that *svaras* like *ṣaḍja*, *ṛṣabha*, *gāndhāra*, etc., with *mātras* have their base (*svaroddhāra*) in *āgamas*.[9] It is only in these circumstances that Caitanya Puṇḍarīka Desāī, the commentator of Nānyabhūpāla's *Bharatabhāṣyam*[10] stated that from the descriptions of the origin of *nāda*, given as *na nādena vīnā gītaṃ ....tasmānnādātmakaṃ jagakat, ... nādarūpomaheśvaraḥ* (Br. 16, 17, 18), etc., and from the descriptions of *nāḍis* and *cakras* (S.R. 1, 2, 120, 163), it is clear that whatever is said regarding the origin of *nāda*, they are translations of texts on *tantras* (original in Hindi). In the

Chapter pertaining to *tantrāgama*, I have highlighted such intimate relationship between *tantrāgamas* and music.

Thus Indian music has dual traditions of the Vedas and *tantrāgamas*. Indian music appears to have originated in *sāmavedic* singing, but it has grown along with *tantrāgama* traditions, as part of their philosophy and meditative techniques.

In relation to the subject of my thesis, the concept of *śruti*, in the sense the musicologists have used as part of *svara*, is the special contribution of the musicologists. The word *nāda*, according to the musicologists, is derived from the verb *nada* (to sound) and this *nāda*, according to them, consists of *śrutis* and *svara*. Then a question arises as to: What is *śruti*? What is *svara*? And what is the relation between the two?

The word *śruti* is derived from the root *śru* to hear. Thus *śruti* is that which is heard (or perceived). In the words of Simhabhūpāla, one of the commentators of Saṅgītaratnākara, "the word *śruti* is the one that is heard" (*śrūyant iti śrutaya ityarthaḥ*). Because they are audible to human ear, they are called *śrutis*. While commenting on the statement of Saṅgītaratnākara "1-3-24"[11] Simhabhūpāla said that audibility is common to both tones (*svara*) and *śrutis*, but such audibility by itself would not be a distinguishing factor. According to him, the distinguishing factor would be that the *śrutis* when produced for the first time with the help of air would be without any resonance (*anuraṇana śūnya*), and when it becomes audible (*śravaṇayogyatvam*) with sweet resonance (*snigdhaḥ anuraṇātmakaḥ*), it becomes *svara*. In other words, an audible and pleasing sound to the listener (*śrotṛcittaṃ rañjayati*) is *svara*. By clarifying what is *śruti*, Kallinātha stated that the *dhvani* made available to the ear in the earliest moment is *śruti*. (*prathamakṣaṇavarti śravaṇamātrayogyadhvani*), but the same *śrutis* when they assume the resonance they become *svara*. The word *śruti* is translated in English as "microtone."

Regarding the nature of the relationship between *śrutis* and *svaras*, there are a number of theories among musicologists. Some, like Śubhaṅkara, take it for granted that even *Bṛahman* is unable to explain the principle as to how *svaras* are situated in *śruti* (*śrutishāne svarān vaktuṃ nālaṃ brahmāpi tatvataḥ*).[12] *Aumāpatam*, on the other hand, thinks that their relationship can be understood only by God but not by men.[13] In fact, according to Nārada, the exact relation between *svara* and *śrutis* cannot be understood just like the path that is followed by the fish in the water and the birds in the sky.[14] He further added that *śrutis* do exist in *svara* just like *ghī* in curds, and fire in wood, and they can be availed of with human effort.[15]

Mataṅga[16] considered certain philosophical theories which definitely throw light on the relationship between *svaras* and *śrutis*, and they are five as under:

1. *Svaras* and *śrutis* are not perceived separately and hence they cannot be categorized. Being perceptible to the ear simultaneously, they are identical (The Theory of Identity – *tādātmya vāda*).

2. The *svaras* are projected by the *śrutis* just like a face is reflected in the mirror. Hence they have the relationship of appearance and reality (The Theory of Reflection – *vivartatva vāda*).
3. *Śrutis* are the material cause and *svaras* are the effect, just as mud is the material cause out of which the pot is made. Thus there is the relationship of cause and effect between *śrutis* and *svaras* (The Theory of Causation – *kāryatva vāda*).
4. The *śrutis* get transformed into *svaras*, like milk into curds and gold into ornaments (The Theory of Transformation – *pariṇāmita vāda*).
5. The *śrutis* are the manifesters of *svara* just like the lamp manifests the existing *ghaṭa* in darkness (The Theory of Manifestation – *abhivyañjaka vāda*).

The first three theories would not be acceptable, according to Mataṅga. It cannot be said that both *svaras* and *śrutis* are identical. Nor can it be said that *svaras* are the matters of reflection of *śruti*. There is also no *pramāṇa* to prove that *svaras* are caused by *śruti*, since both are perceptible simultaneously. In the case of cause and effect relation, the cause would not be visible in effect, just like the seed out of which the tree has grown would not be perceivable in tree. According to Mataṅga Muni, the theory of transformation (*pariṇāma vāda*) and the theory of manifestation (*abhivyañjaka vāda*) are justified proposition. He personally held the view of *tādātmya vāda*.[17]

For Mataṅga, *śrutis* arise as qualities of *ākāśa* and *svaras* are modifications, bursting out of (*bheda*) *śrutis.*[18] In this state *svara* becomes sweet (*rakta svaraḥ*) and progenitor of *rāga* (*rāgajanako dhvani svaraḥ*).[19]

From the nature of the relation between *śruti* and *svara*, it is clear that the *śruti* of musicologists is similar to *prākṛta dhvani* and their *svara* is similar to *vaikṛta dhvani* of Bhartṛhari.

The credit should necessarily go to Bharata Muni, for demonstrating such relationship between *svara* and *śrutis*, for the first time.[20] These *svaras* are seven, viz., *ṣaḍja, ṛṣabha, gāndhāra, madhyamā, pañcama, dhaivata* and *niṣāda* generally indicated by signs (*saṃjña*) as *sa, re, ga, ma, pa, dha, ni.* Bharata Muni demonstrated with the help of five *vīṇās* – one fixed and the other four adjustable with four strings (*catuḥsāraṇa*) that such *śrutis* are twenty-two in one register (*śaptaka*). He took five *veeṇas* – one with fixed wires, the other four with adjustable wires of sufficient length with a capacity that the next *svara* can be slightly lower than the earlier. If the earlier *svara* of static *vīṇā* is at *pañcama,* the next reduced *svara* should be of *madhyamā.* That means the later *svara* at *madhyam* is less from by one *śruti.* If this process is continued, one gets twenty-two *śrutis* in a spectrum of seven *svaras* (called as *śaptak*). He proved that those twenty-two *śrutis* are distributed in a *śaptak* of seven *svaras.* On the basis of the result of this experiment, others like Pārśvadeva thought that *śrutis* are sixty six (22x3) by taking three register-capacity of the human voice – *mandra, madhya* and *tāra.*[21] Yet some others thought by taking theoretically unlimited *śaptakas* that such *śrutis* are unlimited.

If that is so, the next question that naturally arises is : "How are *śrutis* related to *svaras*?"

According to Bharata, an individual *śruti* is not perceptible by the human ear, and *śrutis* become perceptible in a group in the form of *svara*. What is perceived is the *svara* consisting of *śrutis*. In other words, a *svara* is a sonic entity consisting of a group of certain number of *śrutis*. These *śrutis* stand distributed among seven *svaras* : *śaḍja, madhyamā* and *pañcama* get four *śrutis* each, *ṛṣabha* and *dhaivata* get three *śrutis* each and *gāndhāra, niṣāda* get two *śrutis* each as under:

śaḍja	–	4 *śrutis*
ṛṣabha	–	3 -do-
gāndhāra	–	2 -do-
madhyamā	–	4 -do-
pañcama	–	4 -do-
dhaivata	–	3 -do-
niṣāda	–	2 -do-

The above distribution of *śrutis* may be indicated with the help of a diagram as under:

sa	*re*	*ga*	*ma*	*pa*	*dh*	*ni*
||||	|||	||	||||	||||	|||	||
4	3	2	4	4	3	2

= 22

Fig. 8.1

(Based on Bharata's view – *Nāṭyaśāstra;* Ch. 28.24-26)

If we re-examine the five theories noticed by Mataṅga, in terms of Bharata's experiment, it would be clear that different *svaras* are constituted of different number of *śrutis*, out of the series of twenty-two *śrutis*, in a *śaptak*, and as such, *svaras* and *śrutis* cannot be identical, as opined by the first theory. It cannot be said, in terms of the second theory, that *svaras* are the appearance of *śrutis*. In the case of appearance, what is perceived is the appearance only but not the original entity. But here both *svaras* and *śrutis* are perceptible.

Even the third theory would be untenable for the reason that after causing the effect, the cause ceases to be perceptible. Though the seed is the cause for the tree yet after the tree has grown, the seed disappears, but here *śrutis* continue to be perceptible along with *svaras*. But, on the other hand, there is some substance in the fourth and fifth theories. The *śrutis* get transformed into *svaras* and, as such, *svaras* are the transformations (*pariṇāma*) of *śrutis* and, accordingly, *śrutis* manifest (*abhivyakti*) *svara*. Out of the series of twenty-two *śrutis*, the first four *śrutis* transform into *ṣaḍja*, next three into *ṛṣabha*, and thereafter next two *śrutis* into *gāndhāra*, etc., and, accordingly, they manifest *sa*, *re*, *ga*, etc.

If this is their relation now, the next question would be: how are the *svaras* distinguished from *śrutis*?

Śāraṅgadeva offers a comprehensive definition of *svara* as under:

"Immediately consequent upon *śruti* (*śrutantarabhāvī*), creamy (*snigdha*) and resonating (*anuraṇanātmaka*) sound that delights (*rañjati*) the listeners' minds by itself is called *svara*."[22] The translators, R.K. Shringy and Prem Lata Sharma, clarify the import of this definition by stating that:

"When a string of the *vīṇā* is plucked, the first sound produced is considered to be *śruti* and the next sounds following it, which would be resounding of the *śrutis* is called *svara*. In other words, *śruti* is essentially free from resonance and resonance (*anuraṇana*) is the essential characteristic of *svara*."[23]

Both *svara* of musicologists and *vaikṛta dhvani* or *nāda* of Bhartṛhari are matters of "vibrations or resonances in the air", as manifested by *prākṛta dhvani* (or *śrutis*), produced by the vocal chord. *Svara*, thus, is a suspended vibrating or resonating phenomenon of sound-waves in the air, (caused by vocal chord or musical instrument). In Shahanai, the first detachable part generally called "mouth-piece", produces *prākṛta dhvani* and the rest of Shahanai with holes, on which fingers operate causing different *svaras*, produces *vaikṛta dhvani* or *nāda*. (See Fig. 11.1). According to the musicologists, *dhvani* and *nāda* are matters of two stages of one and the same sound (*dhvani*). At the vocal chord, when a sound arises, it is called *dhvani* and this *dhvani* has twenty-two *śrutis* and with the combination of different number of *śrutis* a particular required *svara* (*nāda*) arises. (See Fig. 11.2).

A *svara* by itself has no musical significance. Its significance consists in its relation with a group of *svaras*. A minimum of five *svaras* are required to constitute a *rāga*. A *rāga* is a group of *svaras* "traditionally recognised pattern", that can be manipulated with different combinations of the constituting *svaras*, resulting in different melodic patterns, pleasing to the ears. In fact, a *svara* is a particular variety of *nāda*.

Thus, *nāda* is a generic concept and a particular *svara* is one of the species of *nāda*. In other words, the sounding effect of *svara* depends on the number of *śrutis* it has taken, either in the lower half or in the upper half of the *śaptak*. The seven *svaras* : *sa*, *re*, *ga*, *ma*, *pa*, *dha*, *ni*, with given number of *śrutis* as stated above, are called *śuddha svaras* (or *prakṛti svaras*). Out of those seven *svaras*, *ṣaḍja* and *pañcama* are considered to be unalterable (*acala*). But the rest five (*re*, *ga*, *ma*, *dha* and *ni*) are alterable. An alterable *svara*, for instance *svara "e"*, can become a lower *"re"* (*vaikṛti* or modified *'re'*) by losing its own upper *śruti* and by occupying the *śruti* of a lower *svara*. Such an altered *svara* is also called *komala ṛṣabha* and the western musicologists call it "half tone" and they are indicated by black keys in harmonium. Thus, it is the combinations of *śrutis* that is responsible for producing "seven *prakṛti svaras* (*śuddha svaras*)" and "five *vaikṛti* (or modified *svaras*" (half tones) and thus resulting in all twelve *svaras*, in a *svara-śaptak*. (That is seven *śuddha svaras* + five *komala svaras*.) This phenomena of *svara* losing its own upper *śruti* and occupying the upper *śruti* of lower *svara*, etc., is called *śrutyantarabhāvi*. *Śrutyantara* means a gap between two *śruti*.[24] A *svara* by retaining its own *śruti* or *śrutis* allows it (allows them) to overlap (*śrutis-sādhāraṇa*) with *śruti* or *śrutis* of its neighbouring *svara* (upper or lower) and thereby gets itself modified into either *śuddha* or *komal svara*.[25] This *śrutyantarabhāvi* principle helps the musicians to have modifications of *dhvani* (sound) in different *svaras* and a capacity to glide from one *svara* to another, as is in the case of a *mīṇḍ*.

On the linguistic side also, there are *svaras* (vowels), in relation to consonants, used in the formation of words and sentences. Then a question arises: How about the *svaratva* of *ṣaḍja* and the like, in relation to *svaratva* of linguistic consonant (*vyañjan*) like *ka*?

Mataṅga answered this question by saying that there is the *svaratva* of *ṣaḍja* and the like, on account of their being *asādhāraṇa* (*lit.* uncommon, special), but there would not be any such speciality in *svaratva* of consonants beginning with *ka*. What Mataṅga emphasizing here is that *svaras*, like *ṣaḍja*, etc., have special characteristics of moving upwards as *ṛṣabha*, *gāndhāra*, etc., but linguistic *svaras* (vowels) in relation to *vyañjana* (consonants), have no such special characteristic. He further stated that even these *svaras* in relation to *vyañjana* are also called *svaras* like *a*, *ā*, etc. (fourteen vowels). These *svaras*, in the sense of "vowels", are also of uncommon nature (i.e., of special character used for the pronunciation of consonants). But *svaras*, like *ṣaḍja*, etc., (because of their uncommonness of upward movements *re ga*, etc.) are also called *svaras*.... by virtue of being technical terms (*pāribhāṣā*) (a technical abbreviation or sign), that has been handed down to us by *ācāryas* (teachers).[26]

According to Pārśvadeva, such a specialty in musical *svaras* is:

a) because of *āptopadeśa* (testimony of trustworthy persons);

b) because some other people say that this name is only a *sanketa* (a preconcerted sign = an arbitrary or conventional symbol used in musical notation to indicate "tonality", "tempo", etc. Some authors use *saṃjña* instead *of sanketa*) and, according to some a matter of technical term (*paribhāṣā*).

Parśvadeva, elaborating such specialty in musical *svaras* says – "because of pronunciation (*ucchāraṇa*) of *ṣaḍja*, *ṛṣabha*, etc., seven *svaras* (in a *śaptak*) as *sa, re, ga, ma, pa, dha, ni* manifest in the ascending order, and, accordingly, their *svaratva* (sounding mode or pronunciation or utterance) stands determined. In fact 'in practice' it is like that". [27]

Question: Is it not a fact that (in the instruments) like *nissāraṇa*, *ḍamaru*, etc., "*ḍhaṇa ḍhaṇa*" *varṇa* is heard. Is it not the characteristic of *svara*?

Pārśvadeva says "No"; because of the characteristic of *svara* it is the *rāga*-generating (*janaka*) *dhvani* (*rāgajanako dhvaniḥ svara*)[28] but these "*ḍhaṇa ḍhaṇa*" *varṇas*, do not cause *rāga*, and hence they are not *svaras*.[29]

Thus according to the musicologists, *dhvani* (sound) ultimately manifests as a delightful (*rakta* or *snigdha*) *svara* as the progenitor of *rāga*. In this context, Mataṅga quotes Kohala, who says : "By the will of the *ātman*, the *vāyu* (that is) moving upward from the base of the earth (*nābhi*, *naval*), (and) is held on the 'wall' of the *nāḍīs* and in the space, is known as *svara*, the delightful sound".[30] Commenting on this verse, Pārśvadeva says : "In the context of music, *svara* itself is *śruti*. Due to striking of the *dhvani* to the places (in mouth) *dhvani* becomes a resonant *nāda*, and from it arises *svara*, as one or many, or pervasive or non-pervasive. In its pure form *svara* is only one (and) it takes many forms as *ṣaḍja*, etc." (....*tatra niṣkalarūpeṇaika eva svaraḥ ṣaḍajādirūpāṇāneka svaraḥ*).[31] Here there is a suggestion that basically there is one *svara*, namely, *ṣaḍja*, and the same *ṣaḍja* gets modified (*vaikṛta*) into *ṛṣabha*, *gāṇdhāra*, etc. Naiyāyikas do not accept this theory. For them there cannot be modification of sound, and what we think of a "modification" is, in fact, a matter of "substitution." I will discuss this aspect in Chapter Ten on critical reviews of the theories.

According to Kohala, such *svara* is said to be infinite on account of (its) combination with *jāti*, and *bhāṣā*, etc. *Jāti*, for Mataṅga, stands for various factors in music, like *mandra* (lower register), *tāra* (upper register), *auḍava* (five *svara rāga*), *ṣāḍava* (six *svara rāga*), etc. Such *jāti* in combination with *bhāṣā* (language) in the form of *padas* (syllabic units, meaningful or non-sensical) and *alaṇkāra* manifests *rasas*.

Thus the sound produced by effort, arising from *nābhi* (naval base) becomes sweet (*rakta*), pervasive (*vyāpaka*) and *para* (divine).[32] Such a delightful sound (in the space of the vocal organ) is called *nāda*.

Is the *svara* or *nāda* eternal or non-eternal?

Mataṅga, in his *Bṛhaddeśī*, said that "*Svara* is extensive (*sarvagataḥ*), pervasive (*vyāpakaḥ*), and eternal (*nityaḥ*) and indestructible (*avināśī*)." He further said that even according to Kohala, "*Svara* is pervasive (*vyāpaka*) and extensive (*sarvagataḥ*) and transcendental (*para*)".[33] This theory is similar to the theory of *Mīmāṃsakās*. According to *Mīmāṃsakās*, a letter-sound (*varṇa*) is eternal. (See Chapter Five).

Pārśvadeva, a jaina musicologist of *Digambara* sect, in his *Saṅgīta Samayasāra*, being consistent to Jaina metaphysics (see Chapter Nine) refutes this theory of Mataṅga and Kohala. According to him, *svara* is non-eternal (*anitya*) and non-extensive (*avyāpaka*), because it can project only its special meaning at a particular distance. It cannot be heard in other (far-off) places and as such, it is non-extensive. Otherwise, it should have been heard elsewhere, and it does not happen like that. A sound arising due to will to speak (*icchā*) of a person is heard only in that particular moment, not at other times; and if it were to be eternal, it should have been heard at some other time also. Hence *svara* is non-extensive and non-eternal.[34] We have already seen this kind of controversy in previous chapters.

From the above discussion, it is clear that *dhvani*, *śruti*, *nāda* and *svara* would be matters of different stages of *dhvani*. *Dhvani* is the source (*mātṛka*) of *śrutis*. *Dhvani* is the basic material. It is a basic material like mud in a pot. Due to effort it becomes a seasoned sound (*nāda*, variable with the help of *śrutis*), just like seasoned mud, which in turn, can be used to have finished products like pots or terracotta articles. From *dhvani* arise *śrutis*, from *śrutis*, *nāda* and from *nāda*, *svara*.

A *rāga* is an independent "melodic pattern" as conceived and presented with the help of a minimum of five *svaras*. It may consist of six or seven *svaras*. Mataṅga defines a *rāga* as under:[35]

"That with variety of sounds formed of *svara* (tones) and *varṇa* (a phonetic unit or melodic movement in music like *sthāī*, *ārohi*, *avarohi*, *sañcārī*, *aṇtara*), delights the mind (*rañjate*) of the good people (*saccittaṃ*), is known as *rāga*. In other words a special variety of sounds, decorated by *svaras* (tones) and *varṇa* (a melodic movement) which is delightful to the minds of the people is named as *rāga*."

A *rāga* may constitute only *śuddha svaras* or only *komala svaras* or a mixture of both, as per the structure of *rāga*.

But what still worries me is the fact that, according to musicologists, *ma* and *pa* in the middle of the *śaptak* consist of four *śrutis* each; *"re"* in the lower half and *dha* in the upper half have three *śrutis* each, and *ga* of lower half and *ni* of upper half of the *śaptak* have two *śrutis* each. If there is correlation between *svara* and *śrutis*, then what makes *ma* and *pa*, having the same number of *śrutis* produce different *svaras* with different pitches (or high or low tones). If they have the same number of *śrutis*, they should have produced the same *svaras* (tones). The same objection could be raised regarding *re* and *dha* (each having three *śrutis*) and *ga* and *ni* (each having two *śrutis*). The hard fact is that all these *svaras* produce different tones, so as to constitute seven *svaras* in *śaptak*. The question is–how could this happen?

The musicologists have not raised such a question nor have they answered it satisfactorily. In my opinion, the *trikoṇa* theory of Umāpaṭīśvārya may help us in this regard. (I will be discussing this theory in Chapter Eleven on Vocal Applications.)

According to the musicologists, there are two kinds of *svaras*; 1) produced in musical instruments (*yantraja*); and 2) produced in human body (*mukhaja* or *piṇḍaja* or *śarīraja*). The one produced by human body is considered to be primary and important (*Samayasāra*-2.6). According to Pārśvadeva even those produced by the instruments, nonetheless, are the products of human effort (*puruṣa prayatna*) and an accidental *dhvani* arising on account of the falling of a stick on the string of a musical instrument cannot be said to be a *svara* of music.[36] Here there is clear suggestion that *nāda* is not a mere physical sound. A physical sound (*prākṛta dhvani*) becomes *nāda* owing to human effort (*puruṣa prayatna*).

According to the musicologists, the combination of fire or energy (*agni*) and air (*vāyu*) is the immediate cause for the production of *nāda*. From *nāda bindu* and all the languages (*sarvaṃ ca vāṅgmayaṃ*) are caused.[37] Mataṅga also said – "From *nāda* is formed *bindu* and from *nāda*, all *vāṅgmaya* (whatever is made up of language) is born."[38] For the application of any kind, a material should be capable of being reduced to smaller bits, according to the requirements. In painting, the "points" or "dots" play a very important role. A line is considered to be a series of dots. Such a smallest sized object in Sanskṛt is called a *bindu*. "In the Veda, *bindu* is related to *indu*, the drop, spark, and also the moon. The Vedic synonym for *bindu* is *drapsa*. It figuratively means *śukra*, semen, and also the moon."[39] *Bindu* is like a drop (*binduriva binduḥ*).[40]

The musicologists have accepted this principle of *āgamas* that, according to it, from *nāda* arises *bindu* and from *bindu* arises *nāda*. According to *āgamas*, bindu is a *ghanībhūta śaktī* but according to musicologists, *bindu* is a *ghanībhūta nāda* (see Fig. 10.1). Musicologists, like Nānyadeva, Kumbha, Śāraṅgadeva explained the nature of *bindu*. For example, Nānyadeva said : When struck at one place of a string the one that produces a loud sound, vibrating for a long time, is called *bindu* (*ekasyāmeva yastantryāṃ prahāro guruvalguvān*) (Nānyadeva).[41] The music as an art causes aesthetic appeal with the help of *nāda* and *bindu* in the form of *rāgas*. Music is also called *sangita-vidyā*. A *vidyā* is a science. The science of the soul is called *ātma-vidyā* "or" *parā-vidyā*. *Sangīta* being *parāpara*, *vidyā* is both *bhoga* (enjoyment) and *yoga* (meditation).

* * *

The Gist of the Theory of Musicologist:

Nāda is the manifestation of cosmic energy (or *Kuṇḍalinī Śaktī* of body) in the form of vocal sound (Transcendental Theory of Sound)

Even for musicologists, just like *tantrāgamas*, the ultimate reality is *nāda brahman*. It is *Kuṇḍalinī Śaktī* that causes *nāda*. This *nāda*, with the support of *ākāśa* and conjoined with *vāyu* and *agni*, while exiting through mouth, generates *dhvani* or *svara*. This *dhvani*, when used in musical patterns (*rāga*), is called *svara*. The *svara* is manifested with the help of built-in *śrutis*. A *śruti* by itself is not amenable to perception. A combination of two or more *śrutis* is perceivable in the form of *svara*. For instance, *ṣaḍja svara* consists of four *śrutis*, *two ṛṣabha* and three *gāndhāra*, etc. According to Bhartṛhari, musicologists' *svara* is similar to *vaikṛta dhvani* or *nāda*.

Is this *svara* eternal or non-eternal?

Mataṅga, following the *Mīmāṃsā* theory, said that *svaras* are eternal. Pārśvadeva, expounding the Jaina theory, stated that these *svaras*, which are the manifestation of atoms or *śabda-pudgalas* are non-eternal.

But what worries me, as stated above, is that, according to the musicologists, the number of *śrutis* that constitute four *ṣaḍja*, *madhyama* and *pañcama*. But these *svaras* have different pitches. How to account for this kind of variation in pitches. The Triangle Theory as expounded by Aumapātam, which will be considered in Chapters Eleven and Twelve, may resolve this riddle.

Notes and References

1. Thite, G.U. (1997) : p. 326; (see Ś.B. XI.4.2.5 ff).
2. Shringy, R.K. and Sharma, Prem Lata (1991) : Vol. I; 1.vii.25.
3. Acharya Hariram (*ed.*) (1998) : Ch. 2; p. 58.
4. Aum. 1.3-8.
5. S.R. 1.1.1.
6. "*iha tattvāni ṣaḍtriṃśat-śivaḥ śaktiḥ sadāśivaḥ, īśvaraḥ śuddhavidyeti śuddhāt etāni pañca ca*" etc. (Bhāva Prakashanam-7.10).
7. Allyn, Miner (1998) : Verse No. 1.20 and 1.22.
8. Aum. 1.17.
9. Sharma, Prema Lata Assisted by Beohar, Anil Bihari : Vol. I; Verse 4.70; p. 47.
10. Desai, Caitanya Puṇḍarīka (1961) : p. 68.
11. *śrutyantarabhāvī yaḥ snīgdho' nuraṇanātmakaḥ, svato rañjayati śrotṛcittaṃ sa svara ucyate* - S.R., verse 1.3.24. Adyar edition Vol. 1, page 81 & 100 (1992).
12. Acharya, Hariram (*ed.*) (1998) : Ch. 4; p. 103.
13. Aum. 2.23-24.
14. Nā. Śi 1.6.16.
15. Nā. Śi. 1.6.17.
16. Bṛ III.3.28-43; (Vol. I), pp. 19-22.

17. Br. III.11.28-42; (Vol. I), pp. 19-21.
18. Br. III.11.39 - *svarajanakānāṃ gaganaguṇānāṃ svaro bhedaḥ*; p. 21.
19. Br. IV.15.
20. Nā. Śa : Ch. 28.24-26.
21. San. Sam. Sar. - Acharya, Brihaspati (1977):Verse 1.19-27.
22. S.R. 3.24; p. 134.
23. S.R. Vol I; p. 154.
24. Bandopadhyaya, S. (1985) : p. 364.
25. Shringy and Sharma, Prema Lata : 3.vi.39; pp. 141-46.
26. Br. IV-15; *Svara Prakaraṇa;* p. 29.
27. *Saṅgīta Samayasāra* 1.40; p. 12.
28. Br. IV.15.
29. *Saṅgīta Samayasāra* 1.40; p. 13.
30. Br. IV.15; p. 29.
31. *Saṅgīta Samayasāra* 1.38; p. 11.
32. Br. IV.16; p. 31.
33. Br. IV.16; p. 31.
34. *Saṅgīta Samayasāra* 1.40; p. 12.
35. *svaravarṇaviśeṣeṇa dhvanibhedena ya punaḥ rañjyate yena caḥ kaścit sa rāga sammataḥ satām - athavā yo' sau dhvaniviśeṣastu svaravarṇabhūṣitaḥ rañjako janacittānāṃ sa ca rāga udāhṛtaḥ.* (*Saṅgīta Samayasāra* - Ch.III.263)
36. *Saṅgīta Samayasāra* 2.6.
37. *Saṅgīta Samayasāra* 2.20; p. 27.
38. Bṛ. II. 17.
39. Baumer, Bettina (1996) : Vol II; p. 5.
40. Shastri, Babulal (1972) : Verse 24.

41. "*Bindu* is a concentrated *nāda*, like the one produced when the string of the musical instrument is struck with force. (*Binduvekatra tantryāṃ syātprahārah pṛthunādavān* (1951) - Kumbhaḥ); Sāraṅgadeva puts it differently when he says : "*Bindu* is the one producing loud *nāda* when struck at one place of string in a musical instrument" - (*bindurekatra tantryāṃ syātprahāro gurunādakṛt*) : Kavi, Ramakrishna M. : p. 420.

* * *

Chapter Nine

THE THEORIES OF *ŚABDA, DHVANI, NĀDA* IN HETERODOX SCHOOLS – *CĀRVĀKA*, JAINISM AND BUDDHISM

In this thesis, tracing the source of ambiguity in the concept of *vāk*, as being applicable to "vedic cosmic *vāk*" and human *vāk*, I considered the conflicting theories of *ṣaḍdarśanas*, the orthodox vedic schools; and also the theories of other schools, having similarity with vedic schools, and referred to heterodox schools like Jainism and Buddhism, as counterpoints of view, as done by some of the vedic schools themselves. Now I proceed to highlight these contra theories of heterodox schools, namely, *Cārvāka*, Jainism and Buddhism, independently, in respect of their views on *śabda*, *nāda* or *dhvani*, in their metaphysical and epistemological framework. Since these schools in one way or the other, believe in *śabda*, *dhvani* or *nāda* (meaning sound) as the "mode", "form", "quality", or "energy" of the "matter", all these schools can safely be dealt with under a common nomenclature "Materialistic Theories of Sound."

A. The concept of *Śabda*, or *Dhvani* in *Cārvāka* philosophy

Cārvāka is considered to be an Indian variety of materialistic philosophy. It appears that, it was very popular during ancient times, under different names such as *Nāstika, Cārvāka, Svabhāvavāda, Bhūtātmavāda* or *Bhūtacaitanyavāda*, etc. Bṛhaspati is considered to be the author of this school. Hence this system is also called *Bārhaspatya*. However, according to G. Tucci, Cārvāka was an ancient master of the school to whom Bṛhaspati transmitted his doctrine."[1] It is also said that the adherents of this school were a very sweet tongued scholars (Cārvāka) with a lot of acumen in argumentative technique and as such it was called *Cārvāka*. It is also admitted that no *cārvāka* text has come down to us to ascertain its exact philosophy and its author. However, the principles of this system are restored on the basis of detailed expositions as *pūrvapakṣa*, (which means a prima facie argument or point of view of a question, as stated by an opposite school) in other *brahmanical, buddhists* and *jaina* philosophical literature. One thing is certain that, on the basis of such a fragment, to construct a consistent and coherent system of *cārvākas* is an impossible task. However, Mādhvācārya in his *Sarva Darśana Saṃgraha;* and Haribhadra, a jaina scholar, in his *Ṣaḍdarśana-samuccaya*, have attempted to give a clear and succinct exposition of *cārvāka* philosophy. On the basis of the fact that the other systems have described *cārvāka* as a *darśana* (philosophy), it can be safely concluded that it was one of the developed systems during the time when *ṣaḍdarśanas* were popular.

In view of the present day western materialism, it would be apt to regard it as Indian view of materialism.

In terms of Western terminology "materialism" stands for "a set of related theories which hold that all entities and processes are composed of or reducible to matter, material forces or physical processes. All events and facts are explainable, actually or in principle, in terms of body, material objects or dynamic material changes or movements. In general, the metaphysical theory of materialism entails the denial of the reality of spiritual things, consciousness and mental or psychic states or processes, as ontologically distinct from, or independent of, material changes or processes. Since it denies the existence of spiritual beings or forces, materialism typically allied with atheism or agnosticism."[2] Keeping in view of this western concept now I will proceed to consider Indian materialism as advocated by Cārvāka.

Cārvāka darśana is very popular among the common masses hence it is also called *lokāyata*. The common mass considers the desire (*kāma*) and wealth (*artha*) as the only means of human happiness. According to Cārvāka, human body being constituted of four elements–earth, water, fire, and air–is subject to death and decay. Hence as long as one lives, one should live happily. "Therefore Cārvākas have contended that all the activity on the part of ordinary people for the attainment of the unseen (*adṛṣṭa*) (*mokṣa*, etc.), leaving aside (the enjoyment of) the seen (*dṛṣṭa*) is only extreme foolishness."[3]

It is the strong belief of *cārvākas* that, only because one has to strive at the cost of incurring pain to accomplish pleasure, such pleasure cannot be discarded. Nobody avoids eating rice only because there would be trouble of taking out the husk. "It is not therefore for us, through fear of pain, to reject the pleasure which our nature instinctively recognizes as congenial. Men do not refrain from sowing rice, because for sooth there are wild animals to devour it.... .... If one were to be so timid to forsake a visible pleasure, he would indeed be foolish like a beast."[4] They further say that if there were to be no such "happiness" people would not spend huge money on "*agnihotras*" and other sacrifices, believing false assurances of beneficial fruits by Vaidic *pundits*, for whom such futile ceremonies are sources of livelihood. Veda, on the contrary, is tainted with "three faults of untruth, self contradiction and tautology.... mutually destructive; as the authority of *jñāna-kāṇḍa* is overthrown by those who maintain *karma-kāṇḍa* and vice versa."[5] Hence it follows that there is no hell other than mundane pain produced by mundane causes, as thorns & c.; there is no supreme authority like god, etc., except the supreme mundane monarch whose authority is manifested to every one's naked eye.

According to *cārvāka* metaphysical theory "the matter is the only reality existing. Such reality consists of four elements viz., earth, water, fire and air. What really exists is only body. There is no soul as such. This body is the conjunction of those four elements. This body itself is mistaken for soul or the self.

In fact describing oneself–"I am thin", "I am black", & c. is describing the attributes of the body.

Human body is a specific kind of conjunction of the forms of matter. Due to a specific form of mixture of semen and female blood, so as the four forms of matter–earth, water, fire and air–combine in a unique way so as to make a body, etc. Life breath (*prāṇa*) and consciousness are present only in such a body. There is no life breath or consciousness in the minute particle (*kaṇa*) of matter which are basic constituent of the body, when they are in a disjointed state.... However, due to that peculiar mutual combination or mixture, there first appears life-breath and then consciousness.... Sense-organs are part of that matter.[6] Ananta Kumar Bhattacharya, further explained this aspect of the *cārvāka* theory by stating that "The doctrine of consciousness of matter (*bhūtacaitanya-vāda*) is only another name for this doctrine of "consciousness of sense-organs" (*indriya caitanyavāda*); in the *cārvāk* view of the sense-organs, visual, etc., are admitted to be made of forms of matter, the earth, etc. Elaborating this theory, he further says that "....material substances such as jar, cloth, etc., are of the nature of collections (*saṃghaṭa*)."

For *cārvāka* "an atom is proved by perception and has a distinct shape. That is, what is called triad in the *nyāya* view, would be the atom in the *cārvāka* view....According to this view, qualities like colour, taste, etc.; and actions, e.g., rising, falling, etc., are to be understood as some particular states of the four matters...."[7]

The so-called soul or consciousness or intelligence, according to *cārvākas*, arises from peculiar combination or conjunction of the four elements: earth, water, fire and air. Due to the interaction among the constituent elements, like flour (*piṣṭa*), molasses (*guḍa*), water (*udaka*) and *dhātakī*, the beverage with the power of intoxication (*madaśakti*) arises. In the same manner this consciousness of the body is the product of those four elements constituting the body. This consciousness of the body is wrongly taken for soul. The mind is also thus a product of the body. At the time of death, when the body disintegrates, this consciousness also automatically vanishes and there remains nothing.

Cārvākas do not admit any other *pramāṇa* except perception.

They do not admit *ākāśa* (ether) because it is not amenable to the senses.

Haribhadra's *Ṣaḍdarśana samuccaya*, a classical work of a Jaina thinker, states that - "(According to *cārvākas*) there is neither god (*deva*) nor liberation. Merit (*dharma*) and demerit (*adharma*) also do not exist. Nor there is any fruit of virtue and vice" (Verse 80, p. 258). One of his two commentators by name Maṇibhadra in his *Laghuvṛtti*, commenting on this Verse 81, explains that "Only those things which are manifested by the five senses really exist, and nothing else. Since the word 'world' (*loka*) has been used, here we should understand by it, the various groups of things found in this world.[8] Through the visual sense are apprehended so many groups of things, immovable and movable, such as earth, mountain, city, rampart, jar, cloth, pillar, lotus, etc., as well as man, animal, ferocious beasts, etc. Through the auditory sense one listens to sweet music, proceeding (from the lips of) a widely known wandering singer, playful and swaying, marked by proper time-beat, measure, and melodious modulation of voice."

"Thus, only things which can be known by these five kinds of perceptions would be things really established by *pramāṇa*. The other *pramāṇas*, there being no evidence of their existence, are to be rejected like flowers blooming in the sky".[9]

In this view of the matter according to *cārvākas*, *ākāśa* being not perceptible, does not exist.

The *cārvākas* do not believe in any causal relation. They do not accept any cause and effect theory, nor in any *adṛṣṭa* or *avyakta* principle, as cause of causes similar to *ṛtam* principle of Veda. The *cārvākas* believed in the doctrine of *svabhāva*.[10] This doctrine of *svabhāva*, in the words of D.R. Shastri, maintains that "the effects are self-existent and are produced neither by different things as causes nor by themselves, in as much as no cause can be found for the filament of lotus or the eye-like marks on the peacocks tail. If it cannot be found, it certainly does not exist. Such is the case with this diversified universe. Similarly, feelings like pleasure, pain, etc. have no causes, because they appear only at times...."[11]

Regarding their *bhūtacaitanyavāda* the critiques pose certain questions to *cārvākas*: During old days we still remember the events of childhood; the blind would recollect colour, etc., when the sense is destroyed - How can all these be possible unless the soul is admitted to be existing independent of the body?

The reply of *cārvākas* would be this: Though perception apprehends the things existing or happenings of events, at a particular point of time, yet those things or apprehensions would be stored in the memory of consciousness of the body. Body growing old or some part of body being destroyed would not affect the memory and that is its nature (*svabhāva*). "According to this school", as pointed out by Ananta Kumar Bhattacharya, "knowledge is generally divided into two classes, namely apprehension (*anubhāva*) and recollection. (*smaraṇa*)."[12] Hence according to this school admitting of either soul or *adṛṣṭa* principle would not be necessary.

What is the nature of *śabda* or sound?

The opponents to *cārvākas* themselves ask, "How is that 'sound' as the quality of *ākāśa* is perceived, but the said *ākāśa* itself is not so perceived." To this *cārvāka* reply is that "....we say that this is illogical, because sound is not the quality of *ākāśa*. Sound is, in fact, a quality of matter as it is perceived by the external sense, like colour, etc."[13] According to *cārvākas* qualities like colour, etc., and actions, e.g., rising, falling, etc., are to be understood as only some particular states of the four forms of matter, as already referred to "sound" also appears to be a "mode of sounding state" arising from four forms of matter – earth, water, fire and air.[14] In this view of the matter it is clear that *cārvākas* do not admit the sound as particles of *pudgala* as Jaina thinkers believe. The sound of *cārvāka* is physical sound similar to *śabda* of *sāṅkhya* philosophy.

How is the sound perceived?

Cārvākas do not admit modification of senses (*vṛtti*) as *sāṅkhya* and *nyāya-vaiśeṣika* philosophers believe. According to them, three sense-organs, viz., the gustatory, the olfactory and the cutaneous reveal their respective objects to the "consciousness" after coming in contact with them. But in case of visual and auditory senses, they may say that they reveal their objects having regard to their essential nature (*svabhāva*) with the help of consciousness of the body. The opponent may contend that "qualities like visual knowledge, etc., are found in the body. Therefore, it is only proper that the body should be qualities-possessor for them, as in the case of colour, etc., of the jar is so." But *cārvākas* deny such a theory. According to them, visual knowledge or auditory knowledge of sound, etc., "....are qualities of the consciousness of the body, and not directly connected to the body, like fair complexion, leanness, fatness, etc."[15] At the time of death, fair complexion, leanness, fatness, etc., may be present but the senses disappear along with the consciousness of that body.

B. The theory of *Śabda, Dhvani* and *Nāda* in Jaina philosophy

Jainism is traced back to the teachings of Vardhamāna. He was called Mahāvīra (Great Hero) who had become *jina* (literally means "conqueror" in the sense that one "who has become free from bondage." He is considered to be the contemporary of Gautama Buddha (the sixth and the fourth century B.C.). The founder of this school is believed to be Vṛṣabha, the first of the twenty four Jinas or *tīrthankaras*; and Vardhamāna was the last *tīrthankara*. Vardhamāna was an ascetic and reformer who based his life and teachings on the principles of his predecessor *Pārśvanātha*.[16]

There are two major sub-sects in Jainism, called *śvetāmbaras* and *digambaras*, following different sets of canonical texts (written in *pāli* or in *prākṛt* languages).

According to Umāsvati's[17] *Tattvārthasūtra*[18], the following are seven categories (*padārtha*) as gateways to enlightenment:

i. *jīva* (souls - sentient entities),
ii. *ajīva* (non-sentient entities),
iii. *āśrava* (inflow of *kārmic* particles to the soul),
iv. *bandha* (binding of the *kārmic* particles to the soul),
v. *saṃvāra* (stopping of the inflow of *kārmic* particles),
vi. *nirjarā* (the falling away of the *kārmic* particles), and
vii. *mokṣa* (liberation from the worldly "*kārmic* bondage").[19]

According to Jaina philosophy the true path of liberation consists in "enlightened world-view", "enlightened knowledge" and "enlightened conduct".[20] And to have the enlightened world-view is to believe in the above categories of truth.[21] The categories of truth are those that are laid down by scriptures or by liberated souls (*jina*) as true beliefs, the knowledge of which leads to liberation (*jina* state). The enlightened world-view may arise spontaneously through one's own intuition or through learning from enlightened ascetics, like Mahāvīra.[22]

According to Jaina theory, as explained by Nathmal Tatia, the translator of Umāsvati/Umāsvāmī's *Tattvārthasūtra*, the "*kārmic* bodies" are nothing but "the material clusters assimilated or 'bound' by the soul as *karma*. These bound particles cause the soul to vibrate in association with mind and the body. The vibrations manifest as thought, speech, and action and cause further *kārmic* particles to rush into the soul from all directions, thereby perpetuating worldly bondage. As long as it is bound by *kārma*, the soul can never be liberated from worldly existence. In liberated souls there is no vibration and therefore no accumulation of *karmic* particles".[23]

Among the seven categories, the most important category that requires to be investigated first is soul. *Karma*, as noticed above is of the material nature (*poudgalika*). *Karma* is a substantive force, or matter in a subtle form. ....It has the peculiar property of developing the effects of merit and demerit. The soul by its commerce with outer world becomes literally penetrated with the particles of subtle matter. These subtle matters become *karma* and build up a special body called *kārmaṇaśarīra* which does not leave the soul till its final emancipation. This *kārmic* matter retards the radiance of the soul. *Bhāvakarma* is immediate to the *jīva*, while *dravyakarma* belongs to the body. The two are associated together; they are distinct and separate as the conscious and the non-conscious (*cetana* and *acetana*). *Karma* works in such a way that every change which takes place leaves a mark which is retained and built into the organism to serve as the foundation for future actions. It is the actual and acting in the nature of *jīvas*.[24]

Mind, on the other hand, is the internal organ which connects the senses to the soul. It belongs to material group. It is both caused by and is dependent on the matter aggregate.[25]

Empirical knowledge consists of memory, recognition, reasoning and apprehension.[26] Empirical knowledge is produced by the senses and the mind.[27] Such knowledge could be of the mind alone or of the mind and senses conjointly. For instance, the cognition–"This is a table"–arises out of collaboration between sense of sight and the mind, whereas in the cognition table looks like, would be a matter of mind remembering the shape of a table and as such is a mind act.[28]

Articulate comprehension is understanding the object, what it is and what it is not, with reference to a "word" commonly used for the object in the spoken language, e.g. "It is a cow." The "imprint" is the retention of this comprehension in memory. Articulate knowledge arises in the wake of empirical knowledge.[29] Articulate knowledge is essentially knowledge derived from words, but according to convention, what is referred to here is the entire Jaina sacred literature. It is essentially knowledge arising out of "words", either spoken by the "Jinas" out of their clairvoyance, mind-reading or omniscient knowledge, or found in Jaina scriptures.

The domain of empirical and articulate knowledge extends to all substances, although not in all their modes.[30] According to *Sarvārthasiddhi* of Pūjyapāda Devanandi[31], there are six substances in the cosmos : 1) medium of motion, 2) the medium of rest, 3) space, 4) matter, 5) souls and 6) time. Only the omniscient souls fully know the infinite modes of all six substances. "The kind of substance that divides and decays by combination....are matter aggregates called '*kārmic* products' (*pudgala*). Since the number of atoms increases, decreases and changes quality, there is no harm in considering *kārmic* products to be modifiable."[32]

Matter functions as the material cause of body, speech, mind and breath.[33] Matter has, as already seen above, two varieties: atoms and clusters. The clusters of matter and atoms have the qualities of touch, taste, smell and colour.[34]

On the cognitive side there are five senses : touch (skin), taste (tongue), smell (nose), seeing (eye) and hearing (ear). The senses can be classified in two ways: senses as clusters of matter and senses as modes of the soul.[35] The senses as clusters of matter have a dual nature: as the physical organs themselves and as the capacity of those organs to perceive.[36]

The senses as modes of the soul are also of dual nature – sentient potential and sentient application.[37] The senses of touch and the like are objects of sentient application.[38]

The objects of the five senses are – for skin the sensation of touch, for tongue the sensation of taste, for nose the sensation of smell, for eye the sensation of colour and for ear the sensation of sound. Empirical knowledge (cognition) or articulate knowledge is within the domain of internal organ, i.e., of mind and not of the senses.[39]

Material awareness is not possible without participation of mind and senses. "Those which transform by merely touching space-point and are thus the object of sound are atoms. They are fine (subtle) and their beginning, middle and end are the same....Both atoms and aggregates are plural to indicate their many varieties. Likewise touches, tastes, smell, coolers are atoms; sounds are groups (*skandha*) of atoms."[40]

Perceptibility depends not on the number of atoms in a cluster but on the special combination of atom resulting from a process of involving integration and disintegration. These two aspects are referred to as "matter-atom" and "quality-atom." For instance, saturated integration of the qualities of touch may cause sensation of touch or saturation of qualities of hearing may cause sensation of sound, etc. Thus a quality or a mode has several aspects. Just as due to relation the same man is father, son and husband, so there are many modes of substances that are different from substance as such, while in their substantial existence they are somewhat non-different.[41] A pot may look black in the dark night and bright in day light. Thus every quality or mode according to Jainism has sevenfold perspective. An observer may highlight a particular quality or mode of an object ignoring others. In this kind of formula a Jaina thinker attempts to reconcile contradictory doctrines as a practical approach to several problems, by denying absolutism. This kind of approach is commonly known as *Syādvāda*, *Saptabhangi Nyāya* or *Anekāntavāda*. Space, for instance, according to them, is a substance in some respect[42] and is only an empty receptacle or container of other objects, in some other respect. As a substance, it cannot have its own container itself being all pervading. Likewise, "Time" is an intangible substance without occupying any space point. It is a substance since it has modes and qualities. Like "space-units" there are "time-units" also.[43]

If so, what is the nature of the sound, according to Jainism?

"The combination of atoms is known as *skandha*. Sound results when *skandhas* strike against another." Thus it has been laid down that all sounds result from the *skandh* of *pudgala* (matter).[44] According to Jain philosophy, "sound being a *kārmic* product has shape".[45] The causal body (*karmaṇaśarīra*), though without shape, is material since it gives rise to the results of material action and is thus connected with them.[46] Sound thus being made of the matter-aggregate (*kārmic* product) is regarded as *paudgalika* (material). It is one of the modes or forms of matter. Hence sound is defined as "The transformation of matter that is perceptible to the ears is sound (*śabda*). (*saṃsargāt paramāṇavaḥ pariṇatā bhāvaḥ śrutegocarāḥ / tadbhedaḥ pratilabdhavarṇapadavākyātmā bhilāpaḥ syataḥ* (*Siddhiviniścayaṭīkā* 9.1.).[47] Dr. Sagar Mal Jain has given in detail, the concept of sound, as explained by Srī Anantavīryācārya as : "*skandha śabdaḥ, mūrtatve asmadādi pratyakṣatve sati sāvayatvāt paṭādivat*" (*Siddhiviniścayaṭīkā,* p. 594). "Just like limestone bursts into the fire, the same way the matter-aggregate bursts into sound waves that spread in all the directions; the only difference is that in case of limestone there would not be any spreading of stone powder in all directions but in case of sound-*pudgala* there would be spreading of waves in all direction. This magical effect is so due to the potency of energy in sound-*pudgala*. In fact, there would be varied kinds of material energies in the matter (*pudgala*), giving rise to varied types of forms and modes. Hence in all kinds of material transformations there would not be any single type of transformation, but many. Since the principles responsible for such transformation in sound-*pudgala* are many and are very subtle and hence they are not perceptible to the ear...."[48]

Commenting on Tatt. Sū.5.24 ("The cluster of matter possess the following modes : sound, integration, subtlety, grossness, shape, disintegration, darkness, shadow, heat and light") in so far it pertains to "sound", *Sarvārthasiddhi* of Pūjapāda, says that a sound is of two kinds : linguistic (*akṣarātmaka* or *bhāṣalakṣaṇa*) and non-linguistic (*anakṣarātmaka* or *abhāṣalakṣaṇa*). A linguistic sound can further be categorized into articulate (syllabic) and in-articulate (non-syllabic).[49] In other words, in the opinion of the modern linguists also, even in the linguistic context also these kinds of sounds – both linguistic and non-linguistic sounds would be available. The sounds used in expressing emotions, e.g., *aho*!, *ahā*!' (*alas*!) and other inarticulate mode of expressions like the sounds of birds, etc. are considered as non-syllabic, in addition to the sounds used as syllables, like *e*, *ka*, *ta*, etc. Language consists of syllable, words and sentences. According to *Abhidhānarājendrakoṣa*, "A word is a regulated time sequence of syllables (*varṇas*) heard by the ears." But this definition is not complete because it does not include the "meaning" aspect of the word. A word is both regulated time sequencing of syllables and also the one which is conveying the meaning intended.[50]

The articulate variety is that of languages. Sanskṛt is an *āryan* language and there are non-*āryan* languages like *prākṛt*, *pāli*, *ardhamāgadi* etc. Human beings are very much accomplished in such articulate language. This kind of knowledge is called *śruta-jñāna* (verbal knowledge), since it necessarily arises with the help of intellect (*mati*), it is also called *mati jñāna*.[51] However, the transcendental knowledge and omniscience causing apprehension of the self is in non-syllabic. The language of birds and other animals are instances of inarticulate language. However, according to

Tattvārthasūtra-Rājavārttika, "Among birds the parrot and the mynah are capable of uttering syllabic sound".[52]

Non-syllabic sounds are of two types, experimental (*prāyogika*), made by effort and natural (*vaisrasika*). Both articulate and inarticulate languages are made with effort. The non-linguistic sound is also of two types: natural and made by effort. Sound of thunder is an example of natural arising out of collision of clouds. The non-linguistic sounds made by effort are the sounds produced by musical instruments, which are of four varieties : 1) sound produced by the instrument made of hide, e.g., drum, 2) sound produced by string instruments, e.g., sitar, 3) sound produced by metal instrument, e.g., cymbals, 4) sound produced by wind instruments, e.g., flutes, conches etc.[53] Dr. Sagar Mal Jain refers to *Anuyogadvārasūtra*, according to which such sounds (in musical literature) are classified in seven categories as *ṣaḍja*, *ṛṣabha*, *gāndhāra*, *madhyama*, *pañcama*, *dhaivata* and *niṣāda*.[54] The nature and characteristics of such seven sounds (*svaras*) are elucidated in detail by Yuvācārya Śrī Madhukara Muni in his *Sthānāṅgasūtra*.[55]

Having regard their *Anekāntavāda*, the Jaina philosophers believe that, there are a number of approaches (*anekānta*) to the sound as a concept. In the form of the knowledge of the ear (*śrutajñāna*), it is regarded as "word form" or "language form", but not as a mode of matter (*pudgala*). But the very word, in its "sound form", is considered as a modification of matter (*paudgalika*) and in its mode of conveying meaning, it is considered to be the mode of soul (*ātmā*) or consciousness, but not of matter. Since its manifestation is due to effort, it is also considered as a mode of knowledge. Since it is the result of modification, it is considered as quality (*guṇa*) but being non-different from the substance (*dravya*); it is also considered as *dravya*. An important virtue of Jaina philosophy is to accommodate varied view-points in its fold. Thus Jain sound is both *jaḍa* (a dead matter) and also "*cetanā*" a psychic element or a psychic modification.[56] Hence a word in Jaina concept is a sound-word (*dhvani*), or physical sound in the sense of *śabda* as *sāṅkhya* uses and it is also a consciously modified sound (*nāda*) in the sense Bhartṛhari uses.

Objection : Is not sound a quality of *ākāśa*?

Answer: No, since *ākāśa* an abstract thing like bliss, is not perceptible at all. Even when we recognize that hearing takes place at a particular point in space, the distance and direction of the sound is known due to the loudness and the distance of sound's origin. Sound particles of matter are extremely subtle and spread out in every direction; they can be affected by reverse air currents, walls, etc.[57] Thus sound is material and not characteristic or quality of space (*ākāśa*). According to Jaina scholars, "*ākāśa* is that which allows space to other substances." Therefore it is incorrect to infer space from the quality of sound (as, *sāṅkhya* and *nyāya vaiśeṣika* thinkers have done).[58] Even Akalaṅka and Abhayadeva, the two eminent logicians of Jaina system have stoutly denied *śabda* (sound) as quality of *ākāśa*. For instance, Abhayadeva, refuting the *nyāya* view of sound (*śabda*) as the special quality (*viśeṣaguṇa*) of partless *ākāśa*...points out that ".... even the usage (*vyapadeśa*) that a particular sound prevails only at a particular place would be against the conception of a partless *ākāśa*." Besides even the established fact of the transitoriness of *śabda* would militate against the *nyāya* conception of an all-pervasive (*vibhu*) *ākāśa*. "....Hence, according to Abhayadeva, the *nyāya* view of *ākāśa* points, to the Jaina thesis of the *sāvayava* (*pradeśas* = space-points) nature of *ākāśa*."[59] Sky or space, in relation to sound in Jaina theory is only instrumental cause. "Just as birds fly in the sky, so the sky is the instrumental cause (*nimitta kāraṇa*) here."[60]

How is the sound perceived?

Regarding the perception of sound, *vaiśeṣika* philosophers say that the area of space in the ear is the hearing medium. This, conditioned by *adṛṣṭa*, gains the ability to hear. But it is pointed out by Jaina thinkers that "If the space-points are not stipulated, the entire space will have to be an ear. In that case every being should be able to hear every sound. ....If, however, a specific area is called the hearing organ, then labelling the space without separate points is refuted. Or else, does one atom get connected with all space? Then one atom will have to be as large as space. And if not, then it is clear that space has primary points."[61]

Jaina thinkers further hold that "the material cause of the physical sense-organs is a particular kind of *pudgala*, i.e., a particular kind of physical substance (*jaḍa-dravyaviśeṣaḥ*), while the psychical sense-organs are of the nature of consciousness. They have two capacities which are called *labdhi* and *upayoga*. *Labdhi* is the power of the sense-organ due to which the object is apprehended. If there is no *labdhi*, the sense-organ cannot apprehend its objects. And *upayoga* is the activity of consciousness towards the object. If there is no activity towards the object (say sound here), the object cannot be apprehended. Thus *labdhi* and *upayoga* are the psychical elements; the senses would not materialise in their nature and would not be able to produce knowledge. In this way the Jainas escape from the difficulty arising from materialistic account of the sense-organs".[62] Faced with this problem, *Nyāya Vaiśeṣika* tried to explain the sense experience through sense-organs made up of five *bhūtas* with the help of *adṛṣṭa* principle. But according to Jainas, if the "Material aggregate are unconscious, they can have no *adṛṣṭa*. If *adṛṣṭa* is considered to be instrumental in motion and stasis, then material particles will not be able to move or remain fixed."[63]

Should the linguistic awareness also be called sensory perception?

Answer: "Sensory perception is merely instrumental in linguistic awareness, not a material cause. The material, in this case, is the self that transforms itself into the mode of linguistic awareness. The presence of the potter's wheel or stick cannot make a mud-pot out of sand, clay is the necessary material. Linguistic awareness cannot occur in a self that has not yet unveiled the barriers of *kārmic* adhesions, i.e., without releasing (*kṣayopāśmika*) linguistically related *karma*.

Question: 'Whatever has a beginning has an end. So linguistic awareness should not be termed beginningless (*anādi*), and since humans are its authors, it may not be valid.

Answer: Compared to ordinary substances, language is without beginning, since no one else has seen the time when it was absent. However, each piece of linguistic awareness has a beginning and an end, and may not be true. Even lack of human authorship is not sufficient to prove language validity. Otherwise stealing and adultery would be valid since they have no first-known advocate. Immediate awareness may be transitory but that does not raise a doubt about its validity."

Question: On hearing the word "pot" the first awareness of the pot occurs, followed immediately by a second awareness (say) of its ability to hold water. That second awareness is not sense-related. Similarly, if smoke is seen and fire is inferred, the inference is not sense-related.

Answer: In heard awareness, at first the sense-organ is involved, and even later the related sense-organ is understood to be operative because of the word (in the text) "*matipūrvaka*" (i.e., "preceded by thought"). Thus whether it is direct or through tradition, in any case linguistic awareness is termed "heard" (*śruta*).[64] This sound employed in such linguistic awareness, being psycho-physical concept, is *nāda*, in the sense Bhartṛhari has used it and as I have explained in Chapter Ten.

Is sound eternal?

Regarding eternality or otherwise of sound, *Tattvārtha-sūtra - Rājavārttika* first takes note of opponents view (as *pūrva pakṣa*): "According to *Mīmāṃsaka* (in fact, according to me grammarians would have been more appropriate in the context) sounds are momentary (non-eternal), caused in succession and destroyed at next moment. They get weakened in expressing their own nature. So, they are themselves not capable of meaning. If sounds are capable of conveying meaning, then like a substance, each letter or syllable would be meaningful. If one syllable could convey meaning, then another would not be necessary as a material cause to form a word. Syllables in succession being allocated and thus becoming meaningful are also not possible. Therefore, in the expression of these sounds one has to recognize the eternal essence *sphoṭa* of a word expressed through sounds, an essence capable of expressing intangible and abstract, eternal, transcending the senses, without parts and inactive.

Answer: This view is not correct, since sound and meaning cannot be related as expresser-expressed. .... If the essence of words is not present and stable intrinsically, then meaning cannot be implied, nor are sounds capable of implying meaning; on the contrary, due to being available due to the sound-configuration it will be considered a function of those sounds. Besides, if the first sound reveals the *sphoṭa* of the word then what is the purpose of the subsequent sounds? If they reveal the areas filled with the word, then it will become a whole having parts and not remain division-free. Again, if sounds were capable of revealing the *sphoṭa*, then do they help the *sphoṭa* or the ear or both? The sounds cannot help the *sphoṭa* (as the scent of the earth is revealed on watering the earth) because a sound is eternal and nothing can modify or increase it in that case. The abstract, eternal and suddenly revealed *sphoṭa* cannot have any modifications. A *sphoṭa* also cannot be compared to *kohl* (equivalent to '*kajal*' or 'surma' in Hindi) that aids the eyes, since in deaf ears the *sphoṭa* cannot cause sound or meaning. A healthy ear may be helped so that it will hear the word. And if this function is possible also by sound, the postulation of *sphoṭa* becomes unnecessary. Thus neither of the two is aided. Then again, if a sound can reveal a momentary *sphoṭa*, where is the problem in their directly revealing meaning? Since they get destroyed immediately, how can they reveal a *sphoṭa*? Even the lamp is not momentary, as locations/substances distant from it are also lit. We do not accept difference in substance and function, and from substantial point of view we accept it as abiding, not momentary. Also sound and *sphoṭa* cannot exist separately. A concrete and functional lamp is able to light up concrete and active pots, etc., but neither sounds nor their essence are concrete or functional. Also, if the *sphoṭa* is not separate from the sounds, then too, being the same, it will not have the capacity to reveal meaning. If different, then it should not be available to the organ of hearing. No example is available which can be both abstract, eternal and yet concrete, non-eternal and with parts. Therefore it should be accepted that a word is of the nature of sounds, both eternal and non-eternal (as per relative pluralism). It is eternal from material substance point of view, and non-eternal in its modal forms as being temporarily available to the organ of hearing in its changing modes".[65]

C. The concept of *Śabda*, *Dhvani* or *Nāda* in philosophy of Buddhism

Since Buddha, the founder of Buddhism, maintained silence on certain metaphysical questions, two views are prevalent:

"1. Buddha did not propound any system of metaphysics; 2. Buddha can be credited with the authorship of a systematic system of metaphysics." But the consensus appears to be in favor of a view that Buddha "did not stand for a single self-consistent system".[66] As a matter of fact there are a number of sects and sub-sects in Buddhism. Prof. Radhakrishnan divides them into two categories, as falling under i) earlier Buddhism and ii) later Buddhism. The schools falling under the category of earlier Buddhism are generally known as *Hīnayāna* schools and later schools are grouped as *Mahāyāna* schools. *Hīnayāna* developed from primitive *Therevāda*. The term *Hīnayāna* means lesser vehicle (of salvation) (as coined originally by *Mahāyāna* followers), ..."adheres to the doctrine as expounded in *pāli* canon." *Mahāyāna* did not deny *Hīnayāna* principles, but opined that they were deficient in not recording certain teachings found in the *Mahāyāna* scriptures.[67] *Hīnayāna* paved the way for two important sub-schools, viz., *Vaibhāṣika* and *Sautrāntika*. Likewise *Mahāyāna* tradition gave birth to two important sub-schools viz., *Śūnyavāda* and *Yogācāra*. In fact, Mādhvācārya, in his "the *sarva-darśana-saṅgraha*", refers to these four schools as advocating four important standpoints of Buddhism. Hence the Buddhist philosophical schools which I propose to highlight are four as under:

1. *Vaibhāṣika* – External objects exist and are perceptible. (realism)
2. *Sautrāntika* – (External objects exist with their own nature (*svabhāva*)) are only inferable, with our ideas. (Let me call it as qualified realism.)
3. *Vijñānavāda* – (What exists is only consciousness amenable to our senses and intuition.) (Idealism)
4. *Mādhyamika* – Neither there is existence nor there is phenomenal. They appear to be so in their "dependent origination" and as such neither exists. (*Śūnyavāda* – *Nihilism*)

I will be considering these four schools in order to ascertain their philosophical concept of sound (*śabda* or *nāda*).

From the point of view of this thesis, *Vaibhāṣika* and *Sautrāntika* are very important schools. They are the off-shoots of an ancient realistic school by name *Sarvāstivāda*, according to which "all exist." Everything, whether material or mental exists. According to *Sarvāstivādins* the ultimate reality, (*dharma*) is a subtle force rather than a substance or a substantial entity and such a "subtle force" can well have (to carry) its past effectiveness in its present transitory state. Now, these "subtle forces" may well be compared with sub-atomic particles of the modern physics like electrons, protons, etc. .... or taking these "items of becoming" as atoms, one may speak of the atomism of *Vaibhāṣikas*.[68]

In this kind of background, both *Vaibhāṣika* and *Sautrāntika* being offshoots of *Sarvāstivāda* were realists. But they were realists of different kinds. As K.K. Mittal puts it: "The former holds belief in the theory of direct perception of the external reality (*Bāhyāt Pratyakṣavāda*) while the latter considers the external reality to be only hypothetical in character (*Bāhya Anumeyavāda*)."[69] I will now consider them separately as under:

I. The *Vaibhāṣikas*

They believe in pluralistic realism. They are called *Vaibhāṣikas*, because they "consider themselves attached to the *vibhāṣā* or the commentary on *abhidharma*".[70] According to them, perception is the primary means of experience of the world. By perception, they mean "contact of senses" with the objects. Without perception we cannot derive universal proposition (*vyāpti*) nor can we have inference. Thus perception and inference are the only means of our cognitions and knowledge. They believe in the independent existence of the matter and mind and thus are natural dualists. "Epistemologically", Prof. Radhakrishnan says, "their theory is a naive realism. The mind is conscious of objects. Our knowledge, or awareness of things, is not mental, ... but only a discovery. Things *are* given to us. The substance of things has a permanent existence throughout the three divisions of past, present and future."[71]

Permanent substances are not transitory phenomena, but the elements which underlie them. According to them "the cause and effect" refer to two phases of one thing. Water is common substance of ice and steam. The phases are momentary but the substratum is permanent. Āryadeva puts this view of cause and effect in the following words: "The cause never perishes, but only changes its name, when it becomes an effect having changed its state. For example, clay becomes the jar, having changed its state, and in this case the name clay is lost and the name jar arises."[72]

There are four elements: earth which is hard; water which is cool; fire, which is warm; and air which is mobile. The fifth element *ākāśa* is not recognized as a composite element or an aggregate like earth, etc. It is recognized as non-composite element. *Ākāśa* is free from all distinctions and is limitless. It is eternal, all pervading positive substance. It is devoid of forms (*rūpa*), it is not material thing (*vastu*). The external objects are the results of gathering together of the ultimate atoms according to their capacity. The *Vaibhāṣikas* recognize the permanent existence of atoms or the *skandhas.* Thus the *Vaibhāṣikas* and the *Sautrāntikas* believe in atomic theory. According to them atoms can be perceived in a mass. Atom is the smallest particle of *rūpa* according to Vasubandhu. It is indivisible. The objects of senses are the aggregates of atoms. They are collection of the fourfold substrata of *rūpa*—color, smell, taste and touch. The perceptible atomic unit is *aṇu* which is a combination of *paramāṇu.* Atoms are the same in all the elements possessing the qualities of earth, air, fire and water. However, some elements display their active energy while others are in a potential condition. In hard metal the earth, liquid, water and burning element, the fire element predominates. Materiality is common in all these elements.[73]

The perceiver (*upalabdhṛ*) is *vijñāna* and the substratum of consciousness (*citta* or mind) is permanent. Memory is *cittadharma,* a quality of *citta.* The sense-objects are: i) *rūpa* (colour or form), ii) taste, iii) smell, iv) touch and v) sound. Answering to these five sense-objects, we have five sense-organs : eye, tongue, nose, skin and ear. After grasping the external objects, *indriyas* (sense-organs) arouse the *citta* or mind and excite *vijñāna* or consciousness. These *indriyas* which grasp the object are material in their nature....By means of the sixth sense or mind, we know not only the particular colour, but colour as such, or sound as such (the sound of bugle, etc). *Citta,* according to Vasubandhu, is one with mind, *vijñāna* or discrimination. There is no soul distinct from *vijñāna* or *citta.* According to this school, the Buddha is an ordinary human being, who, after attaining the qualified *nirvāṇa* by his death, lost his being. The only divine element in the Buddha is his intuitive knowledge of the truth, which he attained without the aid of others.[74]

What is the nature of sound?

According to *Vaibhāṣikas* the "self" is an aggregate of consciousness and human body (*pudgala*) consists of five elements (*skandhas*) : earth, water, fire and wind (composite elements) and *ākāśa,* all pervading (non-composite) eternal element. It is not material thing (*vastu*) or a substance. They are all the objects of our sense-organs (*vijñāna dhātu*), through mind (*citta*). Sound is *śrotra vijñāna dhātu* (sound consciousness). From the above description it is clear that, the "sound", with which I am concerned in this thesis, is a sensation (awareness) of hearing caused by external objects. Another *Vaibhāṣika* text by name *Tattvasiddhi* of Harivarman criticizes *Vaiśeṣaika* theory of sound as the quality *akāśa* (ether). According to *Tattvasiddhi* it is not the quality of *ākāśa.* Being momentary it cannot produce another sound as *Vaiśeṣaikas* say. It cannot be produced by disjunction also as they say for no sound issues when one removes his hand from the wall. "A sound is produced by something striking something. A subsequent sound is not thus produced." (As *Vaiśeṣaikas* opine).... Odour does not travel to the nose to get smelt any more than sound goes to the ear to get heard. What happens is that the flowers "smell scents a portion of the air, which then scents another portion until the series arrives at the nose."[75] According to *Tattvasiddhi,* the same thing happens even in case of sound.

The opponent says - "When things strike each other they produce sound."

Answer: "Not always. Anyway relationship is different. It is a matter of perception that sounds arise from the great elements, and in accordance with usage – we say that the sound of the bell or of the drum, where the kind of sound is identified through the matter causing it (unlike color, whose kinds may occur in any locus). *Ākāśa* is not the cause of sound, since it is not regularly accompanied by sound."[76]

For *Abhidharmakośa* of Vasubandhu[77] consciousness is "awareness" of something manifesting (*prativijñapti*). Sound is one of the sense objects (awareness) of the sense-organs just like *rūpa* (or color or form), taste, smell and touch. It is consciousness of the physical-object of the sense-organ of the "ear". In other words, sound is an element. Sound is *śrotra vijñāna dhātu,* that is consciousness element. From this angle a *dhātu* is not mere physical object but is a psycho-physical complex[78] but sound is non-tangible element. "Sound does not cut, cannot be cut, and has no weight." It has no resistance. For example, in the case of sound arising in "wood-cutting" it is the axe that cuts the wood but not the sound. The other consciousnesses are the consciousness of material or tangible objects as such are tangible elements. "The five internal-bases are the result of *kārmic* maturation and grow through nourishment. Sound is never the result of *kārmik* maturation."[79] Here *śabda* (sound) is a "psycho-physical concept" and as such is *nāda* in the sense Bhartṛhari has used it.

Vasubandhu in his *Abhidharmakośabhāṣya*, a commentary on *Abhidharmakośa* has put forth *Sautrāntika* view-point and said that "Sounds may grow through nourishment, as vocal powers are diminished in a famished series....Sound may be the result of *kārmic* maturation, because that pleasant voice called 'sound of brahma' is the result of complete avoidance of harmful language." But *Vaibhāṣikas* may still insist that "This sound does not result immediately from the action of which you suppose it is the maturation; thus it is not the result of *kārmik* maturation."[80] But according to me, external sound (like the one arising in cutting of a wood, may be the result of non-*kārmik* maturation not being appropriated to human body, but "human voice" may be the result of *kārmik* maturation, since it definitely improves by nourishment. For example musicians take milk and honey to maintain the sweetness of their voice.

What is the nature of perception of sound?

According to *Vaibhāṣika* for perception of the vision, the eye should necessarily "come in touch with object." But some distance is necessary between the eye and visible thing for sight to take place.

But for *Sautrāntika* like Vasubandhu: The ear may hear sounds within itself (just like listening through earphone): thus the same kind of distance from the object (as in the case of eye), is not necessary.

What is the meaning of "coming directly in touch with?"

Vaibhāṣika : It means that there is no object coming in between the object and the organ. According to Badanta Dharmatrāta (a *Sautrāntika*), it means that there is no interval between them, but this interpretation is erroneous, because atoms do not enter into direct contact with one another. If atoms touched (one another) completely, they would merge. If atoms touch them partially, there would be parts of atoms; but atoms have no parts. Atoms form an aggregate, but though they do not merge each other but the wind element gives them cohesiveness.[81]

Vasubandhu: Bhadanta Dharmatrāta is right. There is no contact between atoms. One merely says there is nothing coming in between them.[82]

Then the next question that arises would be: How is sound different from "word"?

Vasubandhu: Are not all three collections speech (*vāc*) and consequently sound (*śabda*), and thus belong among the material aggregates, not conditioning factors?[83]

Vaibhāṣika: If there were only sound, there would be no way to distinguish meaningless from meaningful sounds.

Vasubandhu: When I say speech "I don't mean just sound, but sounds which human beings have agreed to mean certain things. But once this agreement has been made, the vocal sound itself gives rise to an understanding of the meaning. So there is no necessity for a special entity 'word'."

Vaibhāṣika: We say that vocal sound produces a word, which is something separate.

Vasubandhu: But it is absurd to assume that vocal sounds produce an entity "word", for the vocal sounds making up a word don't at all exist at the same time. The sounds are heard successively, and if the word is an entity it can't be produced by parts.[84]

What Vasubandhu would like to emphasize here is that there is no word as such apart from a series of sounds uttered in succession. Since linguistic convention has given meaning to the sounds, either as a single or in a group, they convey meaning directly, or the concept of "word" would be unnecessary.

But this theory of speech of Vasubandhu is refuted by Saṅghabhadra of *Sarvāsti-Vaibhāṣika* School of Kaśmir, in his *Nyāyānusāra* as under:

"Collection of words" refers to the collection of identification. Identification grasp a factor through conceptual constructions, and names, issued from syllables, correspond to those ideas. Names are manifested by sound and are then able to manifest the object. They are commonly established specifications that indicate both the intention of the speaker and the essential nature of the object that is known. "Collection of phrases" refers to the collection of sentences. A sentence is an explication, which brings the desired meaning to completion. Phrases are able to explicate, from both a cursory and detailed perspective, the object-referent in terms of its phonemes such as *a, ā, dī, ka, kha* and so on. Syllables cause an utterance to be remembered by the speaker after the sound has passed away, maintaining this utterance without doubt, and allowing it to be transmitted to another. Both 'name' and "phrase" have their origin in syllables.

Question: Then how is one's understanding of any word not a misunderstanding?

Answer: The relationship between words or ideas and the objects referred to is established provisionally by consensus at the beginning of each world cycle. These words are then handed down and used conventionally. Others suggest that utterances refer to the object indirectly, because speech issues forth a word, and a word manifests the object. There exists no factor that is without a name. If there were, that factor would not be known. How then could it be said to exist?

Vasubandhu: Word, phrase and syllable have speech as their essential nature, and therefore should be included among factors of material form and thought.

Answer: Numerous scriptural passages indicate that these three–word, phrase, and syllable–are distinct from sound. Logical arguments may also be offered. One may hear sound and not understand the phoneme, as one does not understand the object-referent to which sound, as one reads lips. Or, one can understand the name of an object-referent through odour, and so on. Therefore, word must be distinct from sound. Sound, phoneme, word and object exist separately in successive dependence. The distinctions within intelligible sound depend upon phonemes, and these phonemes combine in a particular order to produce a name. This is alone able to manifest the object.

Vasubandhu: Speech is not mere sound, but only "articulated sound" that refers to object. Since a word only manifests the object through speech, why imagine that the word exists distinct from speech?

Answer: Certain phonemes are established in common with regard to certain objects. Words that specify the objects are then evolved from these phonemes. When speakers are about to speak, they must first reflect upon these specifying words in order to understand the object indicated in their own speech, or in that of others. Therefore, the object can only be indicated through this succession from sound to words; each component has a distinct function in the process, and therefore exists.

Vasubandhu: If we assume that syllables actually exist, words and phrases are only collections of these syllables; they would not exist as distinct actual entities. Further, a name can consist of a single phoneme. What would be the difference between a word and a phoneme to be in this case?

Answer: This interpretation is untenable because there is not a moment in which the syllables of a name operate simultaneously. In the case of a word consisting of a single phoneme, this phoneme is alone without meaning; it requires meaning only when it serves as the condition for the arising of a word. Further, if sound or speech alone were to be able to specify an object, any grouping of articulated sounds should specify the object, or, a particular grouping of sounds should have the ability to specify an object without being established by prior common consensus.

Vasubandhu: Indeed, the various syllables of which a word consists cannot be uttered in one moment, and a single factor cannot be produced part-by-part. How then would the string of syllables of which a word consists be able to produce it? If you respond that the last syllable of a word, which depends upon the previous syllables, produces a word, that last syllable alone should be sufficient to produce the word.

Answer: Since you reject the existence of past factors, how, in your view, could a string of syllables constitute one word? Further, how could you establish any relation of successive dependence among the syllables since you deny the existence of factors in the past or future? In that case, one would be unable to understand a word upon hearing the last syllable, as one was when hearing the first. Precisely because we accept the existence of past and future factors, a word can be produced by last syllable in dependence upon the previous ones.

Śrīlāta: People speak without recognizing these sets of words, phrases, and syllables as factors disassociated from thought. Why then should we assume that they exist?

Answer: Certainly, we cannot conclude that simply because common understanding does not include awareness of the subtle dynamics of communication and of the actual relation of speech, word and object, these components do not exist! One must engage in careful consideration of the distinctive characteristics of factors in order to understand their true functioning.[85]

II. The Sautrāntikas

This school is called *Sautrāntika* since the followers of this school consider only *Sūtras*[86] as valid. *Sautrāntikas* admit the existence of the extra-mental phenomenal world. Only we do not have direct perception of it. We have mental presentations through which we infer the existence of external objects. The external existence exists with its own nature (*svalakṣaṇa*) and is only inferable but not amenable to our senses. They must exist because there cannot be perception without an object of perception.[87] According to *Abhidharmakoṣabhāṣya* of Vasubandhu, it is seen that *Sautrāntikas* believe in the following ontological doctrines:

i. *Aṇusañcayavāda* (conglomeration of atoms)

ii. Non-casual destruction (*ahetukavinaśvāda*)

iii. *Svalakṣaṇa* (one's own nature) as object of senses and *sāmānyalakṣaṇ* as object of inference.

Space (*ākāśa*) is not an entity but of non-obstruction state (*anāvaraṇamākāśaṃ*).[88]

Prof. Radhakrishnan provides a beautiful exposition of this theory.[89] According to this theory consciousness by itself is everywhere alike, and if it were all, the world must be one. We have, however, now blue, now red. There must be differences in the objects themselves. The variety of forms of consciousness indicates the existence of external objects. Moreover, the external world does not come into being at our will. To account for the involuntary nature of sense perceptions, we must admit that the reality of the world is able to produce sound, touch, colour, taste, smell, pleasure, pain, etc. The world is, therefore, external to consciousness. These outer objects are only momentary. *Sautrāntikas* deny any immediate knowledge of an independent world, but admit the reality of it to account for our perception and images. In this context, *Vaibhāṣikas* are on better footing. When one sees a tree, according to them he has the experience of a tree in existence. But according to *Sautrāntika,* the perception is an act of consciousness which stands in relation to a non-mental physical object. Dharmkīrti, in his *Nyāyabindu,* is of opinion that names and relations are imposed by mind, while senses reveal the objects accurately unless they are themselves perverted by organic or extraneous causes.

Vimalamitra[90], in his *Abhidharmadīpa,* criticises Vasubandhu's *Sautrāntik* approach as found in his *Abhidharmakoṣabhāṣya,* from Kaśmir *Sarvāsti-Vaibhāṣika* point of view as under:

According to Vimalamitra, the author of *Abhidharmadīpa* (herein after referred to as *Dīpikāra*), the conditioning factors, like *nāmakāya*, *padakāya*, *vyañjanakāya*, of *Vaibhāṣika* theory "have bearing only on the nature of words and meaning, as they have 'forces' that impart significance to words, sentences and letters respectively".[91]

For *Sautrāntikas nāmakāya*, etc., are not different from verbal sounds and, therefore, unreal. To this Dīpakāra (i.e.,Vimalamitra) says : verbal sound (*vāk śabda*) is synonymous with speech utterance, and is, therefore, included in the matter aggregate. The *nāmakāya*, etc., are disassociated factors, and hence are included in the aggregate of traces. The *nāmakāya*, etc., are dependent for their origin on verbal sound and manifest the meaning which is dependent on the utterance (or the individual word-shape); thus they are representative of the thing meant, as in the case of content of knowledge. Just as the five sense conditions are dependent on their corresponding five objects, so too are the *nāmakāyas*, etc., dependent for their origin on verbal sound. For this reason, it is said, "A verbal sound operates on the *nāma*, the *nāman* expresses the object."[92]

Here the *Sautrāntika* raises the following objection: You say that, along with speech, letters (like *ka*, *ca*, etc.) are produced, and by speech the *nāmakāyas* are brought into operation. But if this were the case, speech would be subject to divisibility, since it would follow each letter in turn. Therefore, there can be no such thing as *nāmakāya* functioning as meaning-conveyor (*abhidhāna*), since for this purpose a unitary entity would be required. The Dīpakāra rejects this argument by saying that when the aggregate of the sound-parts is perceived, there is possibility of its *nāmakāya* having the capacity of being a meaning-bearer. Moreover, its existence is evident from its activity, which is to convey its meaning. And it conveys its own meaning, since the relation between *nāman* and its meaning is not created by any person.

The *Sautrāntika* here brings forward the theory of *saṅketa*. He says the *nāman*, etc., are not different from verbal speech. Verbal sound alone, acting itself as the factor which gives rise to the cognition of the object, conveys the meaning to the listener when its constituent parts are grasped as a unity by memory. Why, therefore, postulate these separate *nāman*, etc.? Dīpakāra points out that verbal sounds, being atomic, are not capable of revealing the thing meant. As a collection of verbal sound can reveal only those objects with which it has come into contact, like a lamp (revealing the things around). Things which are not born or which are destroyed or are inaccessible to the senses, like heaven, are not reached by sound. Naturally, therefore, a sound cannot convey these objects.

Moreover, sounds cannot convey meaning either serially or simultaneously. .... But the words of a sentence which consist of atoms of sound, and which come into existence in series, are merely conceptual unities of the constituent parts which are received by the mind. They are, therefore, incapable of conveying meaning either individually or if taken together, since they cannot stand in unity like *balavaja* grass. Thus it is proved that the sounds do not convey the meaning serially or simultaneously.[93]

Even if we accept the theory of *saṅketa* obtaining between sound and its meaning, such a sound is still subject to the argument of seriality. If it is said that the memory of each sound conveys the meaning, then also it is subject to the same fault. And if it is maintained that the trace left by the sounds in the mind conveys the meaning, then also we deny it as it is not proved.[94]

The Dīpakāra further elaborates the drawbacks of the atomic nature of sounds. He says that sound (*ghoṣa*) cannot be a unity as it consists of several atoms. It is accepted that the diphthongs *e* and *ai* are produced in the throat and the palate. But it is not correct to say a sound consisting of only one atom operates in two different places. But this is possible in the case of aggregates of atoms. Even then the atoms cannot convey a meaning individually, for their individual existence cannot be proved. Nor can they do in collection (*saṃghāta*), for collection does not exist in reality apart from its constituent parts.

After thus showing that verbal sounds alone cannot convey a meaning, the Dīpakāra sums up his position: "The correct form of exposition," he says, "is that the letters which are past with reference to the last letter are grasped by a (single) mental effort and then cause to arise the mental concept as directed towards the relevant meaning and only in this fashion convey the meaning."

As regards the common belief that a verbal sound conveys meaning, the Dīpakāra says that this belief does not correspond to the facts. "In fact speech operates on the *nāman*, i.e., it expresses or speaks the name, i.e., it gives voice to it. The name brings to light the object. Thus the speech passing over each letter in order, speaking or giving voice to the name and at the same time giving rise to the perception of its own form, but existing only in the form of series, is said to reveal the *artha* (meaning) only by a process of metaphorical transfer. The meaning is not expressed or brought to light by sound.[95]

The translator, Padmanabh S. Jaini, offers an enlightening comment and says "The exposition of *nāmakāya* of Dīpakāra" offers several points of comparison with the *sphoṭa* theory of early grammarians. *Sphoṭa* is defined "as the abiding word, distinct from the letters and revealed by them, which is the conveyer of the meaning." [Mādhava, *Sarvadarśanasaṅgraha* (Abhayankara, *ed.,* p. 300)]. The *nāmakāya* is also distinct from letters (i.e., sound) is revealed by them, and is claimed to be the conveyer of meanings. The *vaibhāṣika* argument that sounds, on account of their seriality, cannot convey a meaning, is identical with the argument of the *Sphoṭavādins* against *Naiyāyikas* who, like the *Sautrāntikas*, maintained that verbal sounds (with the help of *saṅketa*) convey the meaning. But whereas the *sphoṭa* is called a *śabda* and described as one and eternal, the *nāmakāyas* are nowhere designated as *śabda* and are declared to be many and non-eternal.

The question raised, therefore, suggests that a similarity between the *sphoṭa* and *nāmakāya* was present in the mind of Dīpakāra.... But Dīpakāra does not accept the theory of *sphoṭa*. He examines a statement of Patañjali that *sphoṭa* (unchanging substratum) is the word, the sound being merely an attribute of the word (*Mahābhāṣya*, 1.1.7). Dīpakāra does not admit any difference between a substratum and an attribute, and therefore says that since these are identical, even sound (*dhvani*) would become eternal. For him, *dhvani*, *śabda* and *sphoṭa* are synonymous. *Sphoṭa*, being thus identical with verbal sound, was subject to the same fault of seriality and therefore incapable of conveying the meaning. Dīpakāra further confirms his rejection of the theory of *sphoṭa* by openly favoring a view, which Patañjali calls naive, that *śabda* is *dhvani*. Patañjali, in his *Mahābhāṣya*, gives two views on the nature of a word *śabda:* i) a word is that by means of which, when uttered, there arises an understanding of the thing meant; ii) a word is a sound capable of conveying a meaning. Dīpakāra does not refer to the first view, but quotes the second view, showing his preference for it. But this second view equally goes against his theory of *nāmakāya*. Dīpakāra, therefore, says that name, etc., are different from sound (*dhvani*) (i.e., from *śabda*) because they are *sarvārthanirṇaya*. The significance of this statement seems to be that whereas a sound refers to a particular thing, *nāmakāya* as a trace is capable of conveying all meanings. The translator, further opines that perhaps Dīpakāra was not aware of Bhartṛhari's

Vākypadīya which refers a view that some consider words (*śabda*) as consisting of atoms.[96] Here Dīpakāra appears to have overemphasized *śabda* in the sense of ears perceived sound as against *śabda* the mind grasps in the form of *sphoṭa*.

Dīpakāra further gives some more details about *nāmakāyas*. Some *nāmakāyas* have a definite meaning while others do not have any meaning. The former again are divided into two kinds: i) *apauruṣeya* (not created by any person) and ii) *laukika* (mundane). The *nāmakāyas*, which convey the elements, organs, and aggregates are *apauruṣeya*. They are primarily perceived only by the Buddha. It is, therefore, said, "The *nāmapadavyañjanakāyas* appear only when the *tathāgatas* appear in the world."[97]

The *laukika* (worldly) *nāmakāyas* are twofold: those which convey a particular thing (*niyata*), and those which are conventional (*yadṛccika*). Of these, the *apauruṣeya* as well as *niyatalaukikanāmakāyas* convey only those meanings for which there exists a convention (*saṅketa*).[98]

The translator further observes that – "The use of the term *apauruṣeya* for the *nāmakāyas* shows the influence of *Mīmāṃsa* philosophy, for whom, the Vedas are *apauruṣeya* and eternal. For the *Vaibhāṣika*, the Buddha-*vacanas* (i.e., *nāmakāyas*) are *apauruṣeya* but not eternal. *Vaibhāṣikas* also seem to have been benefited by arguments of early *Sphoṭavādin* (Grammarians)."[99]

III. The *Yogācāras*

Aryāsaṅga or *Asaṅga* and his younger brother Vasubandhu, the teacher of *Dignāga*, founded the

Vijñānavāda or the idealists view of the *Yogācāra*. This school is called *Yogācāras*, since it declares that the absolute truth of *Bodhi* manifested in the Buddhas is attainable by those who practice *yoga*.

The representative theory of perception adopted by *Sautrāntikas* pave the way naturally to the subjectivism of the *yogācāra*. The existence of the external world is a fiction. The external objects are only ideas in our mind. The task of *yogācāra* was like that of Berkeley to expose the baseless and self-contradictory character of the unknown absolute matter of the *Sautrāntikas*, and persuade us to drop all ideas of such an external existence. According to *yogācāra*, the matter is an idea and nothing more. Things are clusters of sensations. External objects, independent of consciousness, are not intelligible. It cannot be an atom, since it is supersensible. Besides, if the objects are momentary, then they last only an instant, and knowledge which is in effect can arise only after the cause ceases to be, and so it can never arise at all. They cannot be the causes of the mental representations of gross objects. It boils down to this that, for perceiving an object we need not have an object. Thus all the properties we know, length, size, taste, etc., are subjective. There are no objects independent of us, and when we speak of such and such thing, we use words only. Outer objects are non-existent. The apparent phenomena around us are produced by mental operations within. The so-called outward things, stars and planets are really mental experiences arising in an established order which may somehow be counted upon. We read into external nature what exists only in our own mind. All *dharmas* or things and their qualities are constituents of consciousness. The *yogācāra* traces the activity of consciousness to the beginningless instinctive tendencies working in it.[100]

The *yogācāras* are supporters of *vijñānavāda*. They deny the real existence of all except *vijñāna* or consciousness. *Sarvam buddhimayaṃ jagat*, that is, the whole world is ideal. "All that we are is the result of what we have thought; it is founded on our thought; it is made up of our thoughts."[101] Since *yogācāras* do not admit the dependence of consciousness on external objects and hold that it is self-subsistence, their view is called the *Nirālambanavāda*. The distinction of material and mental *dharmas* disappear, since all *dharmas* (elements) are mental.

The qualities and characteristics as form, etc., commonly attributed to things, may not exist, but the substratum exists. There is no matter (*rūpa*), nothing outside the thought, yet for the imaginary entities also there must be some substratum, and that, according to *yogācāras*, is *vijñāna* (consciousness).

Yogācāras is idealistic. What is merely one homogeneous *vijñāna* (consciousness), which is not an abstract, but a concrete reality. The thinking-being becomes conscious of its existence and identity of the subject only by knowing objects. The whole system of facts is placed within the individual consciousness. The *ālaya* (the storehouse of consciousness), itself with its internal duality of subject and object, becomes a little world. It is confined to its own circle of modifications.

The world of reality is deprived of its independent existence and is reduced to a mere dance of ideas or thought relations.

In short, "within this *vijñāna* arises the distinction between subject and object. The *ālayavijñāna* is the foundational fact of reality revealing itself in individual minds and things. The distinction between subject and object is a distinction made by knowledge within its own field, and not a relation between two independent entities, as the *Vaibhāṣikas* and *Sautrāntikas* assumed."

We have the *skanda vijñāna*, which is a phenomenal effect of *karma*, and the *ālaya vijñāna*, which is the ever active, continuous, spiritual energy dwelling in all.[102]

According to Vasubandhu's *Pañcaskandhaka-Prakaraṇa* (A discussion of five aggregates) "There are in *abhidharm* terminology compounds such as *nāma-rūpa* which seems to divide the individual into material and non-material aggregate, but, ...(they) always indicate a psychophysical complex not clearly divisible into the two aspects."[103] Vasubandhu uses *rūpa* as "the first aggregate of and for the object of the first consciousness, and *rūpa* is defined as a 'visible' to avoid mind-matter duality."

If so, what is "consciousness"? It is awareness of an object-of-consciousness, visible, etc. *Citta* and *manas* are the same as consciousness.[104] All the aggregate immaterialities fall within the domain of "sense-field" or "sensory domains." What are the aggregates thus designated? It is through their collectivity, i.e., various kinds of immaterialities, etc., being heaped up together that "times", "series", "aspects", "developments", and "sense-objects" seem to occur. Though *abhidharmika* systems accept *vaiśeṣika* concept that "space" is a substance yet Vasubandhu treats it as interval between immaterialities, and is thus an absence of impinging materiality.[105]

There are twelve "sense-fields": the sense-field of 1. eye (2. visible), 3. ear (4. of sounds), 5. nose (6. of smells), 7. tongue (8. of taste), 9. body (10. of the touch or tactile sensations), 11. the sense-field of "*manas*" is any aggregate of consciousness, 12. mental consciousness, e.g., feelings, cognitions, and motivating disposition. The mind is considered as the sixth sense. The sixth consciousness or mental consciousness includes in its "domain" residue of consciousness of all six varieties. A memory is explained by a sensory or mental impression remaining latent in the consciousness-"series" and subsequently, when the proper conditions are present, emerges to a conscious level. It acts as "seed."[106]

If so, what is the nature of "sound" in *yogācāra*?

Stefan Anacker, the translater, offers a beautiful elucidation of concept of "sound" in *yogācāra* school, with an example, in the contest of principles stated by Vasubandhu in his *Pañcaskandhaka-Prakaraṇa.* According to him in the act of singing, the sixth consciousness (of the mind)....includes residue consciousness of the previous audial consciousness, in continuation of present consciousness of a particular note, with a contemplation of possible consciousness of next note. It is thus a continuous process. For example an audial consciousness may arise in one moment, the mental consciousness "that note was flat", (referring to the previous audial consciousness stored in the memory), may arise in the next moment. The domain of *manas*, i.e., with any of the consciousness preceding a sixth consciousness-moment, is itself "past immediately afterwards", i.e., it is momentary. But a reflection of this *manas* (as to next note) by a succeeding sixth consciousness-moment is possible. Thus, a kind of continuity of different consciousness in a series in mind is possible, because previous consciousness-moments stored in memory of the mind, used along with the present note, in anticipation of next one. In the example, the sound itself is an audial-consciousness, and lasts for a moment. The singer might have been under some strain at that moment, since a composition requires great skill in executing musical ornaments, etc., etc., all of which are continuous upon one another and derive in part from the audial consciousness-moment which has long passed in connection with present audial consciousness.[107]

From the above explanation it is clear that for Vasubandhu "audial consciousness" is a sense of hearing grasped by ears. When someone says : "A bell is ringing"; he simply refers to the sensation of hearing in his ears accompanied by the "thought of sound of bell" from memory. Thus according to *yogācāra*, sound is nothing ultimately but "sound-consciousness" in the ear, arising from a sound of bell (recognized as sound of a bell, with the help of *ālayavijñāna*, (i.e., consciousness of mind). Thus it is the consciousness of mind and matter both, as one act. It is just like "mind-consciousness" (subjective ear-consciousness of bell) partaking "universal-consciousness" (objective consciousness of the bell-sound outside) which together ultimately constitute one consciousness called *ālayavijñāna*.

What is speech? "Speech" means "words", i.e., those special vocal emissions which communicate meanings. Verbal action is that volitions which brings forth utterances. Something is speech because it is certain sorts of syllables, or inasmuch as it expresses a desired meaning.[108]

What is the "collection of syllables"? They are the syllables of actual sound through which the other two are disclosed. What is a "collection of words"? It is the denotations for the own-beings of events. What is a "collection of phrases"? It is denotations for the particularities of events. Though all these refer to speech, through which meanings (as determined by convention) are communicated, are then dependent on words and phrases....[109] (I have already examined Vasubandhu's *Sautrāntika* theory, along with *Vaibhāṣika*.)

According to Vasubandhu, right speech, right action through good conduct and meditation reveals *Bodhisattva* the highest goal for *yogācāra* philosophy.[110]

IV. The *Mādhyamikas*

This school can be traced to the teachings of Buddha. The Buddha called his ethical teaching the Middle (*madhyama*) way, and repudiated the two extremes – an exaggerated asceticism and an easy secular life. To the Buddha the *paramārtha* or "absolute truth" is one "which cannot be preached in words." "It cannot be called void or not void or both or neither, but in order to indicate it, it is called the void." (*śūnyam iti na vaktavyam aśūnyam iti na vā bhavet| ubhayam nobhayam ceti prajñaptyartham tu kathyate* ||[111])

For Nāgārjuna *śūnyata* is a positive principle which acts as a cause for the ever-changing state of the phenomenal world, but not amenable to description in human language. He denied such extreme positions, that everything exists (*sarvāsti*), or that nothing exists (*sarva nāsti*). *Mādhyamika* philosophy tries to adopt the mean between extreme affirmation and extreme negation.[112] Nāgārjuna is the principal propounder of this theory in his *Mādhyamika Sūtra*.

The *Mādhyamika* theory of the phenomenal nature of the world follows from the doctrine of *pratītyasamutpāda* or "dependent origination." A thing is a mass of *dharmas* following one another in an unbroken succession. An individual human being is a collection of *dharmas*, since every thought, sensation or volition is a *dharma*. A carriage is the name of a collection of material and mental *dharmas*, which constitute his pseudo-individuality. Apart from *dharmas*, carriage and man have only an ideal existence, an existence of designation (*prajñāpti*) alone exist, but they are doomed to destruction. *Dharmas* are moments in a continuous series just like moment of the duration of the flame, depending on the oil, the wick, etc. Nothing exists by itself. Everything depends on something else. *Mādhyamika* do not dismiss all *dharmas* as well as their collections as unreal, though they look upon them as phenomenal and momentary. The categories through which we construct our reality or experience are unintelligible and are self-contradictory. Intelligibility is the minimum expected of reality, but the relations of experience do not possess even that. Things which are not consistent may be actual, but they are not real. This emptiness is not similar to the emptiness of *śūnyavāda* or Nihilism.[113]

A thing is known to us through qualities of substance but we do not know the substance. In Chapter V of his *Mādhyamika Sūtra,* Nāgārjuna deals with this question, with special reference to the elements of earth, water, fire, air and *ākāśa* (ether), and consciousness or *vijñāna*, and argues that there is no substance prior to attribute, for that would mean there is no attributeness without substance. Moreover neither their existence nor their non-existence cannot be proved. Qualities, like colour, hardness, softness, smell, taste, etc., are subjective. There would be no colour without the eye, no sound without the ear. The qualities then depend on conditions other than and different from themselves. They depend on our sense-organs. (For example, for deaf no sound exists.) They cannot exist in themselves....Since all qualities are appearances only, the things in which they reside cannot be real....Substance then is an abstract relation of qualities and cannot exist apart from consciousness, which is the vehicle through which it is created. Substance and quality are correlative, and neither can be applied to reality as a whole. What absolutely exists is neither substance nor quality, which are mutually dependent.[114]

A quality stands to substance in the relation of dependence. The two exist in virtue of a certain relationship. The cognition and the cognizable stand in such a relation. Absolutely, both are unreal, but relatively they seem to exist, and so long as one thing depends on another, neither is existent in itself....No objects of the universe absolutely exist. They appear to exist through relations....(Likewise).... Perception and perceived objects exist in relation to each other. If there is no vision, there is no colour; and if there were no colours, there would be no visual perceptions.[115]

According to Nāgārjuna's Theory of Negation (*Āpohavāda*), all our knowledge depend upon difference. What is cow? Not a horse, not a sheep. It means a cow is not a not-cow. Instead of saying a cow is existent; we say it is non-existent as a horse or a tree. "All our knowledge is relative and is sustained by differentiation.... We cannot know the nature of a thing apart from its distinction from others. All properties of things are relational, and not absolute. .... Truth must be equated with silence. (If so), knowledge is impossibility."[116] "Since all things are void of their own being, the incomparable. *Tathāgata* has taught the dependent origination of all things."[117] Thus, for *Mādhyamika* – Nature is appearance, yet there is the eternal foundation, infinite, from which everything springs and into which everything retires. ....The reality of the absolute involves the phenomenality of the world.... By *sūnya*, therefore, the *Mādhyamika* does not mean absolute non-being, but only a relative being. It is *Śaṅkara's* empirical existence. The *saṃvṛt*, (awareness) or worldly knowledge is the product of man's reason. It is the cause of the universe and its phenomena. It really means a covering or screen, which keeps off the truth. There is no need to prove its existence since it is its own evidence.[118] Here *saṃvṛt* is "seemingly real" as against "truly real" (*paramārthasat*).[119]

What is the nature of sound, according to the *Mādhyamikas*?

In such a system it is difficult to ascertain the exact nature of sound. By applying the concepts of this system, one can say that the sound is the sensation of soundness that arises in relation to sounding-object and the idea of sounding object arises only in relation to sound, but the nature of such relation between the two is not intelligible; and if such relation is brushed aside as unintelligible, both cease to exist. In the circumstances the "sound" is only a conventional concept useful only from practical point of view. However, I think it appropriate to take you to *Lankāvatāra Sūtra* so as to ascertain the exact nature of sound and also the nature of "word" manifested by such "sound."

Lankāvatāra Sūtra, following *Mādhyamika* tradition, discussed the nature of sound, word, letters, speech, etc., in the form of a dialogue between *Mahāmati Bodhisattva* and the Blessed One. In order to understand the reasoning behind the principles, I propose to extract the principles in that form only:

Mahāmati: Blessed One, where dost thou pronounce sound to be eternal?

Blessed One replied: According to error, *Mahāmati*; since even to the wise there is error, only that they are free from perversion. (*Lankāvatāra Sūtra* 92)

Further, Mahāmati said: Blessed One, is it not because of the reality of words that all things are? If not, for words, ... there would be no rising of things. Hence Blessed One, the existence of all things is by reason of the reality of words.

Said Blessed One: Even when there are no (corresponding) objects there are words, Mahāmati; for instance, the hare's horns, the tortoise hair, a barren woman's child, etc. (*Lankāvatāra Sūtra,* p. 105), they are not visible in the world, but words are: Mahāmati, they are neither entities nor non-entities but expressed in words....words are an artificial creation.[120]

Mahāmati, the *Bodhisattva-Mahāsattva,* said to the Blessed One: "....Why should not the *Bodhisattva-Mahāsattva* grasp the meaning from words? What are words? What is meaning?"

The Blessed One then said to him: Now, Mahāmati, how speech is produced? Depending on discrimination and habit-energy (or memory) as the cause, there is the conjunction and the disjunction of sounds and letters, which issuing from the teeth, jaws, palate, tongue, lips, and the cavity of the mouth, make mutual conversations possible. This is speech. Now, Mahāmati, what is meaning? (*Lankāvatāra Sūtra,* p. 155) The *Bodhisattva-Mahāsattva* is said to have grasped meaning well, when, all alone in a lonely place, he walks the path leading to *Nirvāṇa,* by means of his transcendental wisdom (*prajñā*) which grows from learning, thinking and meditation, causing a revulsion first at the source of habit-energy by his self knowledge (*svabuddhi*), abides at the stage of self-realisation where he leads a life full of excellent deeds.

Further, Mahāmati, the *Bodhisattva-Mahāsattva,* who is conversant with "words" and "meaning" observes that words are neither different nor non-different from meaning and that meaning stands in the same relation to words. If Mahāmati's meaning is different from words, it will not be made manifest by means of words; but meaning is entered into by words as things (are revealed) by a lamp. It is Mahāmati, like carrying a lamp to look after his property (say a pen). (By means of this light) he can say: This is my property (pen) and so it is in this place. Just so, Mahāmati, by means of the lamp of words and speech originating from discrimination, the *Bodhisattva-Mahāsattva* can enter into exalted state of self-realization which is free from speech-discrimination.

If, Mahāmati, if a man becomes attached to the (literal) meaning of words and holds fast to their agreement (convention) in regard to the original state of *Nirvāṇa* which is unborn and undying,.... he will come to cherish a view either affirmative or negative. As varieties of objects are seen in *Māyā* and are discriminated (as real), statements are erroneously made, discriminations erroneously go on. (156). It is by ignorant discriminations thus go on; it is otherwise with the wise.[121]

From the above discussion it is clear that *Mādhyamikas* hold that the sound is non-eternal and it is the manifester of artificial words which constitute speech, which the *Bodhisattva-Mahāsattva* uses as the manifester of erroneous discriminatory statements, in this transitory worldly life, so as to realize the exalted state of "self-realization" which is free from such speech-discriminations.

Is sound eternal?

Bhavya, belonging to the *Mādhymika* school, in his *Mīmāṃsātattvanirṇayāvatāraḥ*, denies the theory of *Mīmāṃsā* that the sound is eternal and words manifested by such a sound are eternal. Consequently, Vedas manifested through such words are eternal. According to Bhavya, Vedas have got to be accepted as "created by a human being, either because they are consistent with (human) understanding or because of the tradition of language (or words)."[122] "We also think that the words of the Veda must have a human author, because they give rise to ideas about the meanings that one wants to express in words. It is just like a sign".[123] "If you think the word is audible, why do you maintain that it must be expressed in sounds. [This is unnecessary and absurd.] The understanding of the (meaning of a word) depends, in our opinion, on convention. It follows as a word." (Verse 48; p. 22). "Moreover, there exists no omniscient person at all, for such a human being is not seen nowadays....(Even) the Buddha is not omniscient, for he is a human being, just like others."[124]

Notwithstanding what Bhavya says above, there is a dispute between the *Sautrāntikas* and the *Vaibhāṣikas* regarding *Buddhavacana*, similar to eternality of sound and word, consequently eternality of Veda and Vedas being *apauruṣeya*, as advocated by *Mīmāṃsākas*, as we have already seen above, under the topic dealing with the *Vaibhāṣikas*. For *Vaibhāṣikas*, *Buddhavacanas* are *apauruṣeya* but non-eternal, but for *Sautrāntikas* they are words of mundane nature (being forms of sound) and are non-eternal. Padmanābha, S. Jaini[125] has examined the nature of this kind of controversy as under:

Both (the *Sautrāntikas* and the *Vaibhāṣikas*) agreed that the words (which consisted of sounds—*śabda*) were made up of sound-atoms (*śabda–paramāṇu*) reposing on the eight dravya—*paramāṇu*. It was, therefore, only logical [for *Sautrāntikas*] to treat all sounds (*vāk*) (therefore all words) as material, and hence include them in the *rūpa-skandha*. Contrary to this *Sautrāntikas* position, the *Vaibhāṣikas* maintained that the words of the Buddha are not of the nature of *vāk* (verbal sound) but are of the nature of *nāma* (non-material). The *Vṛtti* of *Dīpa* quotes a scripture on this controversy: "While the Lord lived, his words are of the nature of speech (*vāk*) as well of the nature of *nāma* respectively in a secondary and primary sense. After his *parinirvāṇa*, however his words are only of the nature of *nāma* and not of *vāk*. For, the Lord of sages had a 'heavenly sound' (*brahmasvaravatvān*) not comparable to any mundane speech *lokavācāṃ*" (*Vṛtti* on Kārikā 12, p. 202). Commenting on this controversy, *Yaśomitra* says that, according to the *Sautrāntikas*, the *buddhavacan* is of the nature of vocal expression (*vāgvijñapti*) and hence included in the *rūpa-skandha*. Those who maintain the category of the *vipryukti-saṃskaras*, (tr. "pure forces" Stcherbatsky) include the *buddha vacana* in the *saṃskāra-skandha*. The *Abhidharmikas* however accept both these views.[126]

* * *

The Gist of the Theories of Heterodox Schools : *Cārvāka,* Jainism and Buddhism

Nāda or *Śabda* is a "mode", a "form", a "quality" or a 'potential force" of matter (Materialistic Theory of Sound)

All the three theories *Cārvāka*, Jainism and Buddhism– in one way or the other, believe that the *nāda* or sound is a product of matter. For all these three schools sound is either a matter or a quality or a mode of matter, or a sensation caused by external material sound phenomena. It is the object of cognition or perception to human ear. It is non-eternal. For them sound is not the quality of *ākāśa* as held by *Sāṅkhya*-Yoga and *Nyāya-Vaiśeṣikas*, nor is it eternal as held by *Mīmāṃsā*.

I. For *Cārvāka* philosophy all the knowledge of senses, including that of knowledge of sound, are the qualities of consciousness of the body and not directly connected to the body. It is the particular state (*svabhāva*) of all the four elements–earth, water, fire and air–working collectively to manifest sound as a quality of matter and not by any particular atom as such. *Cārvākas* do not believe in *ākāśa* since it is not available to any one of the senses, nor they accept sound as the quality of *ākāśa*.

II. According to Jaina philosophy the empirical knowledge extends to all substances. The existence or reality comprises both substance and mode. Clusters of matter possess different kinds of modes or forms like sound, integration, subtlety, grossness, shape, disintegration, darkness, shadow, heat and light. Sounds are groups (*skanda*) of atoms.

Consistent to its theory of *Anekāntvāda*, the Jaina view sound from many angles: for being modification of the matter, it is considered to be as material (*paudgalika*); for being the modification in the mode of the matter it is considered to be a quality (*guṇa*); for being non-different from substance it is regarded to be a *dravya*; in its mode of conveying the meaning in the "language form", it is considered to be a mode of soul. For being the object of senses it is considered to be a "physical sound" (*śabda*) and accordingly is *jaḍa* or material, in the sense *Sāṅkhya* uses; and when used in its language as modified sound, as a means of conveying meaning, it is used as the mode of the soul, and accordingly it is considered to be a psychic-physical modification (*cetana*). In this view of matter, "sound" in Jaina philosophy, being a modified psycho-physical sound is in fact *nāda* in the sense

Bhartṛhari has used it and it is accordingly *nāda* as accepted in this thesis.

The sound in the form of substance (*dravya*) is eternal and in its modal form, i.e., in the form of word, language or music, being temporarily available to the ears, it is non-eternal.

III. Amongst Buddhists there are four views:

1. For the *Vaibhāṣika* the external reality exists and accordingly the knowledge is nothing but awareness of external objects. Sound is material or atomic in nature, causing sensation of sound in the ear.
2. The *Sautrāntikas* believed in a screen, in between the mind and external objects, and as such they thought that the ideas would act as the media through which reality is apprehended. In that sense a "sound" is only an idea or image of our sense of hearing caused by an external substance which is indescribable.
3. *Yogācāra* denied the existence of the external world and reduced objects to a series of ideas in consciousness of the mind. Sound for them is a subjective sensation of the mind backed by memory of similar past sensation enabling it to recognize it as the sound of bell, etc.
4. *Mādhyamikas*, on the basis of their theory of "Dependent Origination", denied the absolute reality to both mind and matter; they further observed that our ideas or concepts of external world are based on such a "relation" which itself is unintelligible, and if such a relation is denied as untenable, then there

exists nothing. In this view of the matter, for them, sound is just an awareness of soundness in the mind and the human convention has named it "sound". As *Mādhyamikahṛdaya Tarkajvālā* puts it, "It is awareness that is conventionally said to see, just as we say 'a bell rings' while actually there is merely an awareness of ringing".[127]

Mādhyamikas hold that the sound is non-eternal and yet it is the manifester of artificial words and their meanings which constitute speech, which the *Bodhisattva-Mahāsattva* uses, as the manifester of erroneous discriminatory statements, in this transitory worldly life, so as to realize the exalted state of "self-realization" which emanates from such speech discriminations. Thus by means of transcendental wisdom (*prajñā*) which grows from learning, thinking and meditation with the help of such artificial speech, *Bodhisattva-Mahāsattva* walks the path leading to *Nirvāṇa*.

Notes and References

1. Tucci, G. (1994).
2. *Concise Routledge Encyclopedia of Philosophy* (2000).
3. Chattopadhyaya, Debiprasad & Gangopadhyaya, Mrinal Kanti (*ed.* & *tr.*) (1990) (Anthology) Guṇaratna's Commentary of Haribhadra's *Ṣaḍdarśana-samuccaya* (Verse 81), p. 274.
4. Cowell, E.B. and Cough, A.E. (*tr.*) (2000); pp. 3-4.
5. ____ (2000); p. 4.
6. Bhattacharyya, Ananta Kumar (1994); p. 453.
7. ____ (1994); p. 452.

8. Haribhadra's *Ṣaḍdarśana-samuccaya* with Manibhadra's Commentary; Chattopadhyaya, Debiprasad & Gangopadhyaya, Mrinal Kanti; p. 259.
9. ____; pp. 258-59.
10. Kaviraja Gopinath points out that, "Ujjvaladatta divides Svabhāva as two folds, viz., (1) *nisarga* and (2) *svabhāva*. The former is explained as habit and the latter as nature. Habit has its origin in conscious and repeated effort in the past, but nature is spontaneous and has no extrinsic source of origin at all." It is also worth bearing in mind that this '*Svabhāvavāda*' should not be confused with Yaḍracchvāda, according to which everything found in this world is either accidental or coincidence. According to Gopinath Kaviraja, "*Yaḍracchā* as defined by Śaṅkarācārya on *Śvetāśvatara Up.* as '*ākasmikaprāpatiḥ*' or coincidence (cf. Guṇaratna, p.15)... "It is very difficult to distinguish between '*Svabhāva* and *Yaḍracchā*, as both are identical so far as the rejection of the causal principle is concerned. But the distinction, however, may be taken to lie in this, that whereas in '*Svabhāvavāda*', a '*niyama*' is formally admitted which is technically known as '*Svabhāvaniyama*' in *Yaḍracchāvāda*', there is no scope for any restriction. With reference to the question–why a jar should be produced from clay and not from thread–the answer of the '*Svabhāvavādin* is a plain statement of the nature of the thing which is unchangeable; but the answer of the *Yaḍracchāvāda* would be a flat denial of the reality of any such natural principle. The observed order and regularity in our experience is due to mere chance, they would say.... " – Kaviraj, Gopinath (1994); pp. 448-49.
11. Shastri, D.R.; pp. 401-402.
12. Bhattachryya, Ananta Kumar; p. 458.
13. *Tark rahasya dīpikā* (Guṇaratna's) another commentary on Haribhadra's *Ṣaḍdarśana-samuccaya*, *Bhūtacaitanyavāda*

Chattopadhyaya, Debiprasad & Gangopadhyaya, Mrinal Kanti (*ed.* & *tr.*) (1990); p. 287.

14. Bhattacharyya, Ananta Kumar; pp. 466-67.
15. *Bhūtacaitanyavāda* (Guṇaratna's)–Chattopadhyaya, Debiprasad & Gangopadhyaya, Mrinal Kanti (*ed.* & *tr.*) (1990); p. 287-88.
16. Soni, Jayendra: *Introduction;* Potter, K.H. (2007); pp. 3-4; Vol. X.
17. Umāvasti (also called Umāsvāmi) in his work *Tattvārthasūtra* or *Tattvārthādhigamasūtra*, formulated Jaina tenets for the first time in Sanskṛt. This work has a number of commentators, and most important of them are: his own commentary *Svopajñā Bhāṣya* (recognised as authentic text by Svetāmbara sect); *Sarvārthasiddhi* by Pūjyapāda, Devanandi (recognised as authentic text of Digambara sect). Kundakunda's *Pañcāstikāya* is another text in *Prākṛt* (translated in *Sanskṛt* by Amūtacandra) also gives a good account of the principles of Jainism. (See Tatia Nathmal (2007); p. xxvii.)
18. Note *Tattvārthasūtra* means "manual of understanding" (See Nathmal Tatia (*ed.*) (2007); p. ix.).
19. Tatt. Sū. 1.4; Tatia, Nathmal; p. 6.
20. Tatt. Sū. 1.1; Tatia, Nathmal; p. 5.
21. Tatt. Sū. 1.2; Tatia, Nathmal; p. 5.
22. Tatt. Sū. 1.3; Tatia, Nathmal; p. 6.
23. Tatt. Sū. Tatia, Nathmal; p. 7.
24. Radhakrishnan, S. Prof. (1997) : *Indian Philosophy,* Vol. I; p. 319.
25. Jain, Mahendra Kumar & Ratna Lahari (*tr.*) : *Tattvārtha Sūtra Rājavārttika* - Potter, K.H. (2007); pp. 392.
26. Tatt. Sū. 1.13; Tatia, Nathmal; p. 14.
27. Tatt. Sū. 1.13; Tatia, Nathmal; p. 14.
28. Tatt. Sū. 1.15; Tatia, Nathmal; p. 16.
29. Tatt. Sū. 1.20; Tatia, Nathmal; p. 18.
30. Tatt. Sū. 1.27; Tatia, Nathmal; p. 21.

31. Of the Digambara sect, Pub. Bharatiya Jnanapitha, Delhi, (1989); cited and abbreviated as S.S. by Tatia, Nathmal at p. 21.
32. *Tattvārtha Sūtra–Rājavārttika*, Potter, K.H. (2007), Vol. X, Part I; p. 372.
33. Tatt. Sū. 5.19; Tatia, Nathmal; p. 129.
34. Tatt. Sū. 5.23; Tatia, Nathmal; p. 132.
35. Tatt. Sū. 2.15 & 2.16; Tatia, Nathmal; p. 43.
36. Tatt. Sū. 2.17; Tatia, Nathmal; p. 43.
37. Tatt. Sū. 2.18; Tatia, Nathmal; p. 43.
38. Tatt. Sū. 2.19; Tatia, Nathmal; p. 44.
39. See the commentries of *Svapajnā Bhāṣya Tīkā of Siddhasenagaṇi* of Śvetāmbara sect; Pub: Seth Devachand Lalbhai Jain Pustakoddhara Fund, and *Sarvārthasiddhi* by Pūjyapāda, Devanandi – referred to at p. 44 of Tatt. Sū. by Tatia, Nathmal.
40. *Tattvārtha Sūtra–Rājavārttika*. Potter, K.H. (2007), Vol. X, Part I; p. 408.
41. *Tattvārtha Sūtra – Rājavārttika;* Potter, K.H. (2007), Vol. X, Part I; p. 410.
42. Tatt. Sū. 5.18; Tatia, Nathmal; p. 129.
43. *Tattvārtha Sūtra–Rājavārttika;* Potter, K.H. (2007), Vol. X, Part I; p. 143.
44. Ghoshal, S.C. (*ed.*), (1989); p. 46.
45. *Tattvārtha Sūtra–Rājavārttika;* Potter, K.H. (2007), Vol. X, Part I; p. 375 (bottom).
46. *Tattvārtha Sūtra–Rājavārttika;* Potter, K.H. (2007), Vol. X, Part I; p. 391.
47. Quoted by Yogīndrānanda in *Introduction* : Jain, Sagar Mal (1996); p. 16.
48. ____ (1996); p. 16.
49. Tatt. Sū.– Tatia, Nathamal; p. 132 (see also *Jainendrasiddhāntakośa* (1944) - Part 4; p. 60).

50. Jain Sagar Mal (1996), p. 30.
51. *Jainendrasiddhāntakośa* : Jain, Hiralal (1944), Part 4; p. 60.
52. Tatt. Sū.–*Rājavārttika* : Potter, K.H. (2007) Vol. X, Part I; p. 365.
53. Tatt. Sū.–Tatia, Nathmal; pp. 132-33.
54. Jain, Sagar Mal : (1996); p. 40 (cited from *Anuyogadvāra Sūtra*).
55. Yuvācārya, Śrī Madhukaramuni (1992); p. 583.
56. Jain, Sagar Mal (1996); p. 17.
57. Tatt. Sū.–*Rājavārttika* : Potter, K.H. (2007), Vol. X, Part I; pp. 337-38.
58. Tatt. Sū.–*Rājavārttika* : Potter, K.H. (2007), Vol. X, Part I; p. 390.
59. Padmarajaiah, Y.J. (2004): pp. 281-82.
60. Tatt. Sū.–*Rājavārttika* : Potter, K.H. (2007), Vol. X, Part I; p. 341.
61. Tatt. Sū.–*Rājavārttika* : Potter, K.H. (2007), Vol. X, Part I; p. 379.
62. Bothra, Pushpa (1996) : p. 55.
63. Tatt. Sū.–*Rājavārttika* : Potter, K.H. (2007), Vol. X, Part I; p. 389. (See for comparison, *Nyāya-Vaiśeṣika* theory in Chapter 4).
64. Tatt. Sū.–*Rājavārttika* : Potter, K.H. (2007), Vol. X, Part I; pp. 338-40.
65. Tatt. Sū.–*Rājavārttika* : Potter, K.H. (2007), Vol. X, Part I; p. 406.
66. Mittal, K.K. (1974) ; p. 139.
67. March, A.C. (1986) ; p. 30.
68. Mittal, K.K. (1974) ; p. 152.
69. Mittal, K.K. (1974) ; p. 151.
70. Note: For exposition of these theories, in addition to the other books, I mainly rely on Prof. Radhakrishnan's *Indian Philosophy*, Vol I; Ch. XI (either by summarising or quoting from this text).
71. Radhakrishnan, Prof. S. : (1997), Vol. I; p. 614.

72. Radhakrishnan, Prof. S. : (1997), Vol. I; p. 614.

73. *Abhidharma Buddhism* : Potter, K.H., Vol. VII; p. 110 & p. 118.

74. Radhakrishnan, Prof. S. : (1997) Vol. I; pp. 617-19.

75. *Tattvasiddhi* of Harvarman : Potter, K.H. (2002), Vol. VIII; p. 270 (herein after referred as *Tattvasiddhi*).

76. ____ Potter, K.H. (2002), Vol. VIII; p. 272.

77. Note: There are two theories regarding Vasubandhu. Some say that there were two Vasubandhus, the brothers of Asaṅga, the founder of *Yogācāra* school. (See - Amar Singh: *Buddha's Original Logical–The Sautrantika Analytical Philosophy* (1995)). Others say that there was only one Vasubandhu who was a *Sautrāntika* who went to Kashmir to study *Vaibhāṣika* in the school run by Saṅgabhadra. After studying *Vaibhāṣika*, he delivered lectures on that subject, which were compiled in six hundred verses which constitute *Abhidharmakoṣa*. Later, not being satisfied with that *Vaibhāṣika* theory, he wrote a commentary on that *koṣa* from *Sautrāntika* point of view, called *Abhidharmakoṣabhāṣya* (commonly referred to as *Koṣabhāṣya*). But under the influence of voluminous work, entitled as *Yogācārbhūmi* of his elder brother Asaṅga, Vasubandhu converted himself to *Mahāyāna* school, and became a very famous *Mahāyāna* master. According to tradition Dignāga was his famous student. [See (i) Stefan Anacker (*ed.*) (2005). *Seven Works of Vasubandhu–the Buddhist Psychological Doctor*. General introduction; p. 1. (ii) Padmanabh, S. Jaini (*ed.*) (1958): *Collected Papers on Buddhist Studies*, Ch. 10 – On the Theory of Two Vasubandhus observes that the same has been the story of Vasubandhu in Chinese tradition also. In the circumstance I have also accepted his view that there was only one Vasubandhu.]

78. *Abhidharmakośa* of Vasubandhu : Potter, K.H. (2002), Vol. VIII; p. 488.

79. ____ (2002), Vol.VIII; p. 488.

80. *Abhidharmakośabhāṣya*: Potter, K.H. (2002), Vol. VIII; pp. 520-521.

81. ____ (2002): Potter K.H., Vol. VIII; p. 523.

82. ____ (2002): Potter, K.H., Vol. VIII; p. 523.

83. ____ (2002): Potter, K.H., Vol. VIII; p. 536.

84. ____ (2002): Potter, K.H., Vol. VIII; p. 556.

85. *Nyāyānusāra, Saṅgabhadra*: Potter, K.H. (2002), Vol. VIII; pp. 701-703.

86. The *Sūtras*, referred to here are the *Sūtras* in *Sutta Piṭaka*. The Buddhist Pāli Canon is called the *Tipiṭaka* because it consisted of three parts:

    i) *Vinaya Piṭaka*, ii) *Sutta Piṭaka* and iii) *Abhidhamma Piṭaka*. Together are called *Tipiṭaka* or Three Collections. *Vinaya Piṭaka* contains the rules of monastic discipline; *Sutta Piṭaka* contains the sermons of Buddha and a few of his foremost disciples. The third section, *Abhidhamma Piṭaka*, contains *Theravāda* canons. *Sutta Piṭaka*, which contains the sermons of Buddha and a few of his foremost disciples, is considered to be the most important of the *Tipiṭikas*. Hence the doctrines formulated and propounded, in the *Sutta Piṭaka* are grouped according to their subject, into five groups known as *nikāyas*. They are also called *āgamas*. (See Potter, K.H. (1998); Vol. VII, pp. 20-27.).

87. *Abhidharma Buddhism* : Potter, K.H. (1998), Vol. VII; pp. 24-25.

88. See - Amar Singh (1995) : p. 36.

89. Radhakrishnan, Prof. S. : (1997), Vol. I; p. 619.

90. *Abhidharmadīpa of Vimalamitra with Vibhāṣāprabhāvṛtti* : Jaini, S. Padmanabha, (*tr.*); p. 532; Potter, K.H. (2002), Vol. IX.
91. *Abhidharmadīpa* : Potter, K.H. (2002), Vol. IX; pp. 545-46.
92. *Abhidharmadīpa* : Potter, K.H. (2002), Vol. IX; p. 546.
93. *Abhidharmadīpa* : Potter, K.H. (2002), Vol. IX; p. 547.
94. *Abhidharmadīpa* : Potter, K.H. (2002), Vol. IX; p. 547.
95. *Abhidharmadīpa* : Potter, K.H. (2002), Vol. IX; p. 548.
96. *Abhidharmadīpa* : Potter, K.H. (2002), Vol. IX; pp. 548-49.
97. *Abhidharmadīpa* : Potter, K.H. (2002), Vol. IX; p. 550.
98. *Abhidharmadīpa* : Potter, K.H. (2002), Vol. IX; p. 550.
99. *Abhidharmadīpa* : Potter, K.H. (2002), Vol. IX; pp. 550-51.
100. Radhakrishnan, Prof. S. : (1997), Vol. I; pp. 624-27.
101. Radhakrishnan, Prof. S. : (1997), Vol. I; p. 627.
102. Radhakrishnan, Prof. S. : (1997), Vol. I; p. 632.
103. Anacker, Stefan (2008) ; p. 59.
104. ____ (2008); p. 71.
105. ____ (2008), Notes 28; p. 81.
106. ____ (2008); p. 85.
107. ____ (2008); See Note 52; p. 82.
108. ____ (2008); p. 119.
109. ____ (2008); p. 71.
110. ____ (2008); pp. 250-51.
111. Radhakrishnan, Prof. S. (1997), Vol. I; p. 662.
112. Radhakrishnan, Prof. S. (1997), Vol. I; p. 646.
113. Radhakrishnan, Prof. S. (1997), Vol. I; pp. 647-49.
114. Radhakrishnan, Prof. S. (1997), Vol. I; p. 650.

115. Radhakrishnan, Prof. S. (1997), Vol. I; p. 654.

116. Radhakrishnan, Prof. S. (1997), Vol. I; pp. 654-55.

117. *Sūnyatāsaptatikārikā* of Nāgārjuna : (Śloka 68); p. 80: Dragoneetti Fernando Tola Carmen (2002).

118. See Radhakrishnan, Prof. S. : (1997), Vol. I; p. 658 & p. 661.

119. Frauwallner, Erich (2010) (*ed.*); pp. 127-29.

120. Suzuki, D.T. (2003); pp. 91-92.

121. ____ (2003); pp. 133-34.

122. Lindtner, Cristian (*tr.*) (2001) : Verse 29; p. 17.

123. ____ (2001): Verse 30; p. 17.

124. ____ (2001): Verses 15 & 16; p. 13.

125. Jaini, S. Padmanābha (*ed.*) (2001); p. 201.

126. ____ (2001), *Vaibhāṣika Theory of Words and Meanings;* p. 202.

127. *Mādhyamakahṛdaya/Tarkjvālā,* Potter, K.H. (2003), Vol. IX. p. 404.

* * *

Chapter Ten

CRITICAL EVALUATION OF DIFFERENT THEORIES OF *NĀDA*

Oṃkāra or *Praṇava*, during the Vedic period, was a "cosmic principle." As I have already explained in Chapter Two, it was considered to be a creative power or a cosmic intelligence of the universe. As a physical external existence, it was called *akṣara*, and as a cosmic intelligence or cosmic consciousness, it was called *puruṣa* – two aspects of the same reality. In this view of the matter, *Muṇḍaka Upaniṣad* declared that one should know that the *Akṣara* by itself is *puruṣa* and the ultimate existence (*yenākṣaram puruṣam veda satyam*).[1] As a cosmic consciousness, it manifests itself in the form of universal principles or uniform universal laws called *ṛtam*, to regulate its own existence called *satyam*.[2] These *ṛtam* and *satyam* principles of the reality are similar to *śiva* and *śakti* principles of the pre-Vedic and subsequent *Tantrāgama* philosophy. According to the Vedic philosophy, the physical existence (*satyam*) of the cosmic consciousness (*puruṣa*) manifests itself in the form of cosmic phenomenon with universal principles called *ṛtam*. The "conscious being" (animal, insect or man), being a product of the same cosmic consciousness, can comprehend cosmic consciousness. But the "comprehension" of Man (the mundane *puruṣa*) is more advanced (yet immature)[3] than that of the animal kingdom.

Man's "comprehension", though based on sensory perceptions like other animals, is capable of being stored in his vast memory in the form of "thought" or "idea" and is also communicable in "articulate language." In other words, the inarticulate "cosmic uniform behaviour" as determined and manifested by universal laws (*ṛtam*) like "law of causality", "law of gravitation", "law of motion", etc., perceived by the senses, is comprehensible in human thought, as the "language of the universe", which Vedic *ṛṣis* called "*vāk*". With the heavy and dark clouds, accompanied by thunder in the sky, it looks as if cosmos speaks to us, that there would be rains shortly. In the words of Sāyaṇa, "this thunder of the clouds", etc., has the characteristic of a language – *vacam garjita lakṣaṇam.*[4]

Thus cosmic *vāk* is the first manifestation of "totality of an inarticulate but predictable" phenomenon of the cosmic laws (*ṛtam*) (*ṛtasya prathamajā vāk*). In this sense all the books on natural sciences–like physics, chemistry, astronomy, etc.–in effect deal with this kind of cosmic laws, and they are of the nature of the cosmic language, which Vedic seers called divine *vāk* (*devabhāṣa*). It is the language of the natural forces or cosmic bodies, personified as gods by the vedic philosophers, and it was also accordingly called *devabhāṣa*. *Ṛgveda* declares that "This *devabhāṣa* along with *devas* (cosmic forces) rests on that *ākṣara* or *oṃkāra* or *praṇava*, the ultimate reality; and if one does not understand this fundamental principle, there would not be any point in reading Veda itself."[5] As I have made it clear in Chapter Two that cosmic *oṃkāra*, having regard to their nature of this kind, neither *oṃkāra* nor *devabhāṣa* has any sound (*nirmame*) in the sense human language. As opined by Madhusūdana Sharma, an eminent Vedic scholar and others, as elaborated in Chapter Two, *devabhāṣa* is considered as a "language" or *vāk* in a metaphorical or figurative sense (*aupacārika*). But on the other hand the *vāk*, the men use, is a sound-manifested language, on the basis of *nāma-rūpa* principle (RV.10.90.4). Thus, as pointed out by Yāska, Vedic *ṛṣis* speak of *vāk* both as cosmic *vāk* (*devānām*) and as human *vāk* (*manuṣyāṇām*).[6] As we have seen in Chapter Two, they operate in different spheres and their nature is entirely different. Cosmic *vāk* and cosmic *nāda* (*praṇava* or *oṃkāra*) do not have any sound, and, as such they are soundless (*nirmame*) but human *vāk* is necessarily manifested by means of sound.

But the later learned scholars used the word *vāk* or *vacaḥ* without appreciating the difference between the two, both for cosmic and human *vāk*. May be, they were confused by the use of one and the same word *vāk* for both of them in Vedic texts; or may be that they purposely applied the principles of cosmic *vāk* or cosmic *nāda* to human *vāk* or human *nāda*, with a view of heightening the authenticity and eternality of Vedas. The second reason appears to be the strongest one. Because *ṣaḍdarśana* systems being orthodox (*āstika* or *vaidika*) systems believed in the authority of the Veda. They did not appreciate any criticism against the Veda, made by (*nāstika* or heterodoxical or non-orthodoxical) thinkers like *cārvākas*, buddhists and jaina thinkers. Hence they took upon themselves the burden of proving the validity and eternality of the Veda. Perhaps, finding that since the Vedic *mantras* were expressed in human words and sentences, the validity of the Veda could not be established, unless they established the language as an effective and authentic mode of communication of Vedic principles. A word uttered should necessarily convey the correct meaning of the Vedic injunctions. But the "sound" has been the only tool or means that is being employed in communicating thought in the form of word and language. In these circumstances, they bestowed due attention on the nature and effectiveness of sound as a means of communication of Vedic tenets in the form of "words". It is for this purpose only, that the "priority of sound" was declared by *Mīmāṃsā Sūtra* of Jaimini (*uktantu śabda pūrvatvam*).[7] Śāyaṇa, in his *Ṛgveda Bhāṣyabhūmikā* commenting on this statement of the *Mīmāṃsā Sūtra* of Jaimini, rejected the view that the Vedas are not eternal, and observed "That the sound which goes to make up the Vedas existed before men like Kaṭha....it is without beginning".[8] According to him the eternal nature of all the words and their meanings is assured by the eternality of sound. In fact Kumārila Bhaṭṭa, one of the finest exponents of *Mīmāṃsā* school, openly declared in his *Śloka Vārtika* in the chapter dealing with *Mīmāṃsā* aphorism VI to XXIII, that "It is for the sake of the validity of the Veda that we seek to prove the eternality of sound (or *śabda*)".[9] However heterodox schools, opposing these views, denied both eternality of sound and also the eternality of Veda by advocating the materialistic theory of sound.

Whatever be the reason, in my opinion, one thing is certain that six conflicting theories were advocated [as explained in Chapters Three to Nine, with the gist of the theories at the end of each chapter]. This study also reveals that, in Indian systems, (both for orthodox and heterodox schools) the concept of *śabda*, *dhvani* or *nāda* in the sense of sound, is regarded mostly as a manifester (*vyañjak*) of language, or as a means of meditation or as a means of aesthetic communication.

To the question: what is the ontological nature of *śabda*, *dhvani* or *nāda* (sound) which manifests human *vāk*? Indian philosophers have given answers, in six different ways, propounding six different theories, as under:

1. The *nāda* or *śabda* is a quality (*guṇa*) of *ākāśa* (ether) (Cosmic Theory of Sound of *Sāṅkhya*-Yoga).
2. The *nāda* or *dhvani* is a quality (*guṇa*) of *ākāśa* (ether) an extensive atom (Phenomenal Theory of Sound of *Nyāya-Vaiśeṣika*).
3. The *nāda* is Eternal substance (*dravya*) (Transcendental Theory of Sound of *Mīmāṃsā* and *Vedānta*).

4. *Nāda* is an activity (*kriye* or *spanda*) being the manifestation of "cosmic energy" or *kuṇḍalinī śakti*. (Transcendental Energy Theory of Sound of *Tantrāgamas* and Musicology).
5. *Nāda* is "sounding state", "mode, quality or potency" or "sound-sensation" of matter. (Materialistic Theory of *Nāda* of Heterodox Schools – *Cārvāka*, Jainism and Buddhism).
6. *Nāda* is an artificial sound produced by *vaikhari dhvani* of vocal chord. (Positivistic Theory of Sound of the Grammatical systems).

Keeping in view the above theories, I will now proceed to consider them to find out the acceptability or otherwise of a particular theory or theories.

Theories Nos. 1 and 2: Having regard to the similar principles I propose to consider theory numbers one and two together. According to these theories:

1. The *nāda* or *śabda* is a quality (*guṇa*) of *ākāśa* (ether) (Cosmic Theory of *Nāda* of *Sāṅkhya*-Yoga).
2. The *nāda* or *dhvani* is a quality (*guṇa*) of *ākāśa* (ether) (Phenomenal Theory of *Nāda* of *Nyāya-Vaiśeṣika*).

These two schools believe in "cosmic principles" of *nāda*. According to both of them *nāda*, *śabda* or *dhvani* (meaning sound in English) is quality or attribute (*guṇa*) of *ākāśa*. For *Sāṅkhya*-Yoga *ākāśa* is a cosmic principle, evolved out of the two primordial "cosmic principles" – *prakṛti* and *puruṣa* (which are of the nature of Vedic *satyam* and *ṛtam* principles). Sound is the evolute produced by *śabda-tanmātra*, in the course of the cosmic evolution.[10] For *Nyāya-Vaiśeṣika*, *ākāśa* is a phenomenal principle emerging out of atomic substance. It is *vibhu* (pervasive) and infinite (unlike *aṇu*) with quality of "sound" attached to it. Thus for both of them *ākāśa* is a cosmic principle. The cosmos is an extended form of phenomenon only. For both of the schools sound is the quality of such *ākāśa* which is a substance and not a vacuity as is the case with the Buddhist philosophy. Sound inheres in such *ākāśa*, and as such, the relation between *ākāśa* and "sound" is one of *samavāya*. For *Nyāya-Vaiśeṣika*, *ākāśa* is eternal and for *Sāṅkhya*-Yoga, *ākāśa* exists till the dissolution. If it is so, why should sound stand extinguished immediately after its utterance in mouth or production in the external world, when *ākāśa*, its substrate, is still subsisting? *Sāṅkhya* has no satisfactory explanation. In this respect, the case of *Nyāya-Vaiśeṣika* is still worst. They cannot plead the "non-eternality of sound" as a quality of eternal *ākāśa*. For instance, "yellowness" of gold, as its quality, subsists till the gold exists. A "quality" does not change, unless it is changed by some cause. For instance, one can say that "the green colour of the leaves" change into "yellow" owing to old age. It is not the case, in both the theories, that there could be a particular cause by which *akāśa* assumed some other quality. Moreover, they cannot plead by saying that *ākāśa* assumes some other quality, (when sound as its quality is destroyed, owing to its non-eternal status), since according to both of them, *ākāśa*, as a substance, is identifiable by the sound as its "only" quality. When, thus, the sound is the only quality of *akāśa*, it cannot take any other quality at all. Hence the statement that *ākāśa* exists and sound is destroyed would be a self-contradictory statement, just like saying that gold exists and its "yellowness" is destroyed. Hence, having admitted the *samavāya* relation between sound and *ākāśa*, they cannot prove the non-eternality of sound. *Mīmāṃsakas*, in the circumstances, rightly question them, as to how could the sound "as quality" be non-eternal of an "eternal substance" like *ākāśa*?

What, prompted *Sāṅkhya*-Yoga and *Nyāya-Vaiśeṣikas* to take sound as a quality of *ākāśa*, is the Vedic theory of communication of articulate sound[11] and also the fact that the sound requires a medium for its vibration, as also for its propagation, from the place of its source to the hearer, and such a medium should necessarily be free and obstructionless medium; and *ākāśa* assures such an obstructionless condition (*anāvaraṇa*), as specifically stated by *Sāṅkhya* scholars. (See Chapter Three.) If a bell is held by hand, while vibrating, the sound stops; because the holding of the bell causes obstruction to the sounding phenomenon. If it is so, "Can it not be said that the 'sound' is the only quality of *ākāśa*, in the sense that *ākāśa* has a special (*viśeṣa*) 'characteristic quality' of facilitating the sound to vibrate and propagate without obstruction?"

Modern science may say "No". Because even other substances like liquids, etc., also facilitate the sound to vibrate and propagate. But in that case, "sound" would not be a special (*viśeṣa*) characteristic of *ākāśa* as *Sāṅkhya*-Yoga and *Nyāya - Vaiśeṣika* thinkers take it to be, in order to identify *ākāśa* as being different from other substances. In these circumstances, the only possible conclusion would be that the relation between *ākāśa* and sound would not be one of *samavāya* (inherence), as these theories take it to be, but such a relation, being accidental, is one of *samyoga.* Moreover the modern astronomers have confirmed that in the "outer-space" beyond the atmospheric area of the earth, there is no sound nor two persons can talk and communicate each other, in spite of vast *ākāśa* all around. Veiwed from this angle, the theory of *Sāṅkhya*-Yoga and *Nyāya - Vaiśeṣika* that the sound is the quality of *ākāśa* should be failed.

But, Darśan, my grandson, a student in B.E. (Electronics), however, presents his view from another angle, and states that in neutral space, sound, in fact, is created but it is not propagated, due to lack of air or any other known medium. But scientists seem not to vouch this kind of theory as on today. One of the Website states: Sound is a series of longitudinal or compression waves that move through air or other material.... Sound waves are created by vibration of some objects like a cone in radio loudspeaker. Waves are detected when they cause a detector to vibrate.[12] According to this view sound is, in fact produced by the vibrations of the material objects, and is propagated by medium like "air" and presumably not by *ākāśa.* But what this theory overlooks is the fact that the said "material objects" can vibrate only in an obstructionless medium. Therefore, the phenomenon of obstructionless medium, is absolutely necessary for those "material objects" to "vibrate". "Vibration" as per The new Lexicon Webster's Dictionary means "to move to and fro with simple periodic motion".[13] Physics also tells us that the vibration in the inert physical body is due to its "elasticity", as in the case of strings of musical instruments or bell, etc. If that is so, such a vibration of such elasic bodies would be impossible without the obstructionless medium like *ākāśa*. In this view of the matter it is still possible to assert that sound is the quality of *ākāśa*. Here the word "quality" should be understood in a special (*viśeṣa*) sense, i.e., in the sense that it is a "necessary logical condition" for production of sound, without which vibration is impossible and consequently the production of sound is impossible. Hence it can still be argued, in support of these theories that the sound, ultimately is the quality of *ākāśa* in the sense that *ākāśa* can be known by the presence of sound in it, as its only quality. So far other media like liquids, etc., is concerned, it is theoretically possible to urge that it is *ākāśa* principles existing between two particles of the substance, like liquids, etc., that is responsible to create sound in such substances. After the sound is produced, it is transmitted through air or through such liquids, etc., as the media. Hence it is still possible that in outer space sound is created but it is not heard due to lack of the communicatory medium like "air", etc. Thus the theory of *Sāṅkhya*-Yoga and *Nyāya-Vaiśeṣika* that the sound is the quality of *ākāśa* has some substance.

Theory No. 3: The *nāda* is "substance" (*dravya*). (Transcendental Theory of *nāda* of *Mīmāṃsā* and *Vedānta*)

This third theory is that of *Mīmāṃsāka*. Of the two sub-schools of *Mīmāṃsā*, Prābhākara school propounds that the sound is the quality of eternal *ākāśa*. Prābhākaras admittedly accepted *Vaiśeṣika* theory of sound, and as such it stands covered by the above discussion regarding *Sāṅkhya*-Yoga and *Nyāya-Vaiśeṣika*. Hence, the theory of *Bhaṭṭa Mīmāṃsā* school that–the "sound is a substance"–only survives for my critical analysis.

According to Bhaṭṭās, the sound is an intangible substance. It is a quality of "air" but not a quality of *ākāśa*, as *Sāṅkhya*-Yoga and *Nyāya- Vaiśeṣika* philosophers think it to be. It manifests itself in the form of syllables (*varṇas*). These syllables manifest themselves in a mixed up form with human accents. The syllables (like *ga*) are eternal but the manifesting vocal accent (*dhvani ga*) is non-eternal and as such, there is "dual conception". But our experience does not accept this kind of theory. In fact the same sound (*nādātmaka dhvani*) takes the form of syllable *ga* (*varṇātmaka dhvani*) and as such there is no separate syllable like *ga* different from the utterance of *ga*. Thus *Mīmāṃsakas* hypothesis of existence of a separate syllable *ga* apart from the accent *ga* appears to be a myth. If they had taken "cosmic consciousness" as being similar to Vedic *praṇava*, manifesting itself in the form of eternal syllable, there could have been some justification for their theory; or they could have taken Vedic *praṇava* in the form of a syllable, as a metaphysical cause, causing phenomenal syllabic-sound, for such a theory again is permissible in philosophy. In fact, Kumārila Bhaṭṭa, admitted the existence of such a supersensuous entity different from *dhvani*, when he said : "It is by means of supersensuous power alone, that these (utterances) impart a supersensuous (power) to the sense-organs (the ear), and thereby, becomes the causes of the manifestation of words".[14] When such a "supersensuous power" could assure eternality to syllable, even if uttered in the form of the accentual syllables, their theory of eternal syllable being different from uttered syllable is unnecessary. Consequently their further theory of a "dual conception" of (the so-called eternal syllables) along with uttered vocal syllables would also be redundant. As stated by Bhavya, a bhudhist philosopher, in view of *Mīmāṃsakas* theory of the eternality of directly perceptible word (in dual conception), their further theory that "it must be expressed in vocal sounds" is unnecessary and absurd. Moreover, when an understanding of the meaning of a word is assured by an eternality of "convention" even their theory of eternality of "word" or "sound" itself was also unnecessary.[15] Apart from that, to say a word "eternal" it requires a non-eternal sound to manifest a self-contradictory statement. In addition to that if sounds were to be eternal and all-pervasive, as contended by *Mīmāṃsakas*, sound-pollution would have been a major problem in this world. Thank God! Sound is neither eternal nor pervasive. Hence this theory is also not acceptable.

However, there is some substance in the theory of *Mīmāṃsakas* when say that it is the "air" that manifests and communicates sound. The concept of *ākāśa* of *Sāṅkhya-*Yoga and *Nyāya-Vaiśeṣika* appears to refer to Vedic *salila* as I have clarified under *Nyāya-Vaiśeṣika* theory in Chapter Four. The Vedic philosophers appear to refer to *salila* in the sense of atmospheric space occupied by air (in which man lives); and this atmospheric space, as a substance, consists of "*akāśa* + air" being different from *dik* an empty space. For this kind of inference, I find support from Verse Two in the Introduction to *Ṛgveda Prātiśākhya* of Sounaka, which declares that air and *ākāśa* are equal, in the sense that Air (*vāyu*) is one with *ākāśa* (*samānata anile ca ambare*).[16] In such *ākāśa*, sound produced owing to vibrations of a material object, is communicated by surrounding "air". According to the scientists also, in outer space, there is no air (atmosphere) and because of this, sound will not be able to travel from a vibrating source to any other region in space. Therefore, since there is no air in space, there will be no medium of sound to travel. Hence, no sound will be heard in space because of vacuum. ....Astronauts communicate with each other in space, through the use of radio-wave. Radio-wave signal is sent to their head-set which then translate the signal into the form of sound.[17] Thus according to modern scientists, the sound is propagated and transmitted through air. Hence there is substance in *Mīmāṃsā* theory, to the extent that it is the "air" that communicates sound in atmospheric medium. The grammarians also accepted this "air" theory.

Theory No. 4: *Nāda* is an activity (*kriye*) - (being the manifestation of cosmic energy). (Transcendental energy theory of *nāda* of *Tantrāgama*).

For *Tantrāgama* thinkers *nāda* is an activity (*kriye*) being the manifestation of *śakti*. *Tantrāgamas* also applied "cosmic principle of *vāk*" to human *dhvani* and human language, to assure eternality and effectiveness of *mantra*, which is an object of meditation. Musicologists also followed *Tantrāgama* philosophy, in conceiving *nādabrahman* as an embodiment of *nāda* (*nāda tanu*) which is nothing but the manifestation of *śiva-śakti* principle in the form of cosmic energy, as I have already explained in Chapter Eight.

According to *Tantrāgamas*, *śakti*, in conjunction with *śiva*, manifests herself as cosmic *nādabrahman* or "*oṃ*". The same *śakti*, in the form of *kuṇḍalinī* in *mūlādhāra* of human body, manifests herself as *parā*, *paśyanti*, *madhyamā* and *vaikharī*. In *vaikharī* she becomes audible to the ear in the form of syllables *varṇamātṛkās*. Thus, it is the cosmic *nāda-śakti* that causes eternal syllabic sounds: The doer (the soul) is eternal but his deeds caused by his external energy (*śakti*) are non-eternal. Though syllables like *ga*, etc., are eternal, yet accentuated syllables, like *ga* are non-eternal. In this respect, this theory is similar to that of *Mīmāṃsakas*, though they do not plead "dual conception" like *Mīmāṃsakas*. Maybe because their "accentuated syllable" is not a substance to be perceived but only energy in action. It is true that the actions caused disappear along with the disappearance of that cause. In the circumstances "accentual syllables", caused by vocal chords, do disappear immediately after their utterance. In the circumstance, the concept of "eternal syllables", as existing different from the "accentuated syllables" is again a myth, just like the eternal syllables of *Mīmāṃsakas*. However, *Tantrāgama* thinkers may say that such a belief in the eternality of syllables arising out of *varṇa-mātṛkās* (as little mothers) is necessary for realizing *mantra-śaktī*, since the *mantras* are in the form of *vaikhari* sound. What, at the most, I can say in this context is that these are the matters belonging to "esoteric" field and a separate research is required in that direction by a scholar who is an expert in that field. In view of the fact that their further theory that the relation between "word" and its "referent" have become universal and eternal by virtue of their inseparable association with transcendental *śiva-śakti* principle, also has to be simply believed. Moreover, even the other theories, like *Nyāya-Vaiśeṣika*, as discussed above, in fact, indirectly believed in the "energy" principle as the cause of the "sound" in the form of "*avyakta* principle" in *Sāṅkhya*-Yoga; or "*adṛṣṭa* atomic power" of *Vaiśeṣikas*, etc. According to *Vaiśeṣika*, for instance, it is that *adṛṣṭa* principle that causes "conjunction disjunction," etc.[18]

However, the theory of *Tantrāgamas*, which says that the "phenomenal sound" is nothing but an energy-in-action (*kriyāśaktī*), is acceptable. Even the sound arising, while cutting the wood (in the example given by *Naiyyāyikās*, to explain conjunction, disjunction, etc.), is due to the "energy" applied in axing it. A bell sounds if some external energy is applied by striking it with a stick. The sound in the bell continues as long as the causing-energy subsists in the bell so as to make the bell "vibrate." Such a sound can be stopped also by holding the bell by hand so as to obstruct the continuation of sounding-energy (that cause vibrations) and consequently stop the "sound" in the bell. All these instances also show that such a phenomenal sound is non-eternal and such a sound also is a matter of "vibrations" (*spanda*).

Music, as I have stated above, appears to have developed as a part of *Tantrāgama* meditative technique, practically adopting their metaphysical theory of *nāda*. Music is a performing art in which it is the sound-in-action that causes aesthetic appeal, on the enjoyment side, and also spiritual appeal on the side of *nādānusandhāna*. Thus the theory of *Tantrāgamas* can be applied, at least on the phenomenal side, if not on the mystical or esoteric side meant for *sādhakas* (adepts).

Theory No. 5: *Nāda* is "sounding state", mode (quality or potency), "sound-sensation" of matter. Heterodox theories, like *cārvāka*, jainism, and buddhism, one way or the other believe that the *nāda* is a product of matter.

For *cārvākas nāda* is mode, quality or "sounding state" arising from particular conjunction of the four basic elements–earth, water, fire and air–perceived by external sense like colour, etc. It is the nature (*svabhāva*) of these elements to manifest sound. Sound is amenable to sensation of hearing.

Jaina thinkers believe that sound is one of the qualities or modes of the cluster of matter. Owing to the potency of material energy, the sound bursts out like limestone. Sound thus is the potency of energy in "sound-*pudgala*". Hence it is defined that "The transformation of matter that is perceptible to the ears is sound." It is therefore, a material substance or *kārmic* product and accordingly it is known as *paudgalika*. Sounds are groups (*skandha*) of atoms, which spread in all directions being driven by wind.

According to buddhism the atoms in mass are perceived as matter. Atom is the smallest particle of *rūpa* (form). The objects of senses are aggregates of atoms. The objects are, therefore, known to exist only through the sense-organs. Seen from this angle, it is clear that sound is sensation (awareness) of hearing caused by external objects, for *Vaibhāṣikas*, *Sautrāntikas* and *Mādhyamikas*, however, for *yogācāra*, it is a subjective sensation of "soundness" arising from "store-house of consciousness" (*ālayavijñāna*), consisting of subjective and objective sensations, together known as "universal consciousness." Sound, therefore is "*śrotra-vijñāna dhātu*" ("sound-consciousness element"), for all the schools of buddhism. In this view of the matter sound is a "psycho-physical" complex. And it is non-eternal like other physical objects. Modern science also says that sound is caused by vibration of matter and hence there is substance in these theories.

Theory No. 6: The "ultimate reality" for a grammarian like Bhartṛhari, is *śabdabrahman*. This *śabdabrahman*, being by itself a "cosmic consciousness", which is a transcendental cause for the essence of the "word" and the creation manifested by such word (*Vāka* 1.1). According to the grammarians the "word" in the form of "language" manifests the objects of the world with the help of an articulate *vaikharī dhvani*. This *vaikharī dhvani* is an artificially created "sound" in a mouth with the help of breath caused by the "energy" of the human body.[19] *Vāk* or language is the union of "sound" and syllables, which in ultimate analysis, are one and the same. *Varṇa a* is a particular "sound form" and *i* is another kind of "sound form", and a word is a group of such letter-sounds. The said conglomeration of sounds, when it conveys a particular meaning as per convention, it becomes a "word" (*śabda*). Hence, in the words of Patañjali, "the sound (*dhvani*) itself is word" (*tasmād dhvaniḥ śabdaḥ*). According to *Śabarbhāṣya*, language itself is syllable-form-group of sounds (*varṇarūpā-pada-dhvani-samūha*). Such a theory which is based on common sense and experience, is acceptable. But their further theory of *sphoṭa*, existing as a separate transcendental whole different from the meanings of syllables, words and sentence, is a myth. In fact, as opined by *Nyāya-Vaiśeṣikas*, there is nothing like *sphoṭa* different from the meanings of words and sentences. The "time factors" in a series of sounds is a matter of sound "sequencing" to constitute different words out of common sound forms (syllables).

For grammarians, *dhvani* is an airborn sound, and syllable (*varṇa*) is a "sound form" produced with the help of *vaikharī dhvani* of vocal chords. Sometimes this *dhvani* or sound is sub-divided into smaller bits. A *varṇa* may be only a *svara* (if there is no consonant in it) or a consonant. A *svara* (vowel) has one *mātrā* whereas *vyañjana* (consonant) has half a *mātrā*. This half-*mātrā* sound is taken as a *bindu*. Thus a *śabda* may consist of nine *bindus*. For instance in the word *stryarka*, there are - *sa, ta, ra, ya, a, ra, ka, ṭa*. In this combination there are seven consonants as - *sa, ta, ra, ya, ra, ka, ṭa* and one *svara a*. Seven consonants constitute seven *bindus* and *svara a* has two *bindus*; thus in all nine *bindus*.[20] From this fact it is clear that even grammarians made use of the theory of *bindu*. A *bindu* is a "sound-bit" like a drop of water. A "word" constituting of *varṇas* is created artificially by combining several *bindus*, as a means of language. Phonemes or syllables being artificially created are not eternal as the *Mīmāṃsakas* believe. Different languages have different kinds of phonemes, like *khāph* in *khūn* (blood) in Urdu, to suit the language they speak. But these non-eternal phonemes do convey meaning on the basis of convention.

This kind of theory proposed by the grammarians is based on sober common sense. It is scientific and the one practically used in the linguistic structure and hence I have accepted it.

The critical analysis of all the theories reveal that Theories Nos. 4 (Sound is the product of energy of *Tantrāgamas*), Nos. 5 (Sound is product of matter) and Nos. 6 (Sound is artificially produced in vocal chords as grammarians say) are very near to the concept of "sound", which modern science has established with the help of sophisticated instruments. But the importance of other theories: (Theory Nos. 1 and 2 that the sound is quality of *ākāśa* (ether) or (the sound requires medium like air for its propogation, vide the theory of *Mīmāṃsakas*, etc., cannot be ignored at the same time. In fact the concept of "sound" or *dhvani* has different aspects : a) it requires energy (*śakti*) as per theories Nos. 3, 4 and 5. To cause vibrations, it requires material objects (say a bell); b) these vibrations require space (*ākāśa*) as an unobstructed medium for propagation, (which is emphasized by theory Nos. 1 and 2 – if one holds the bell, vibrations stops); and c) to convey such "sound", "air" as a medium is required (as opined by theory Nos. 3, 4 and 5). In short sounding phenomena (energy-in-action) requires vibrations + space as medium for movement of vibrations + air to convey it. To put the same in a formula: sound (*dhvani*) = energy vibrations (or waves-*spanda*)+space (*ākāśa*) + air (*vāyu*).

There is substance even in Theory No. 5 of the heterodox system, like *Cārvāka*, jainism, and buddhism, according to whom sound is the product of substance constituted of the five basic elements. It is the quality, mode or potency of substance amenable to our sense of hearing. Seen from this angle, it is clear that "sound" requires a material medium for its production and propagation.

To sum up it may be said that there is some truth in all these theories. When we discuss vibrations, they are the vibrations in a material medium, like bell. Therefore, the matter itself constitutes the sounding phenomenon. When the force (energy) is applied (just like striking a bell), vibrations arise, which are carried by air in all directions in space.

Even according to *Pañcīkaraṇa* theory of Śankara since *ākāśa* is a compound of all the five elements, the sound, arising from out of such *ākāsa*, shares the characteristic of all other substances. The sound-vibrations (*spanda*), though produced due to striking (energy, or fire element) of hard substance like bell or through vocal chords (*pṛthvī* or matter element), is carried by air (*vāyu*-element) through space (*ether*-element) which may be used in music and languages, with due modifications. In this view of the matter, it may be safely concluded that matter, energy, vibrations, air and space are different aspects of sound, or sounding phenomenon, heard by ears, and accordingly every one of these theories is emphasizing a particular aspect of sound or sounding phenomena. I do not think that the modern scientific theories dispute such a position.

In terms of modern physics, as Khanna and Bedi put it, "the sound is due to vibratory movements of somebody" and "wave motion .... (is) ....one of the most important methods of energy transfer."[21] Here "sound wave" is *spanda* and energy transfer is equivalent to *śaktikriyā* in *āgamic* terminology. Physics also tells us that the vibration in the inert physical body is due to its "elasticity", as in the case of strings of musical instruments or bell, etc. When an external physical force is applied on a physical object, the object vibrates "to and fro" owing to elasticity of the substance causing sound waves, which are carried by air, but it is the nature of an inert object to return to its original position. Owing to an internal friction and owing to the obstructions of the air, the vibrations gradually die out till the whole energy is dissipated and ultimately the body comes to rest. For instance, a sound vibration in a string of a musical instrument continues long as there is energy in the body. These vibrations would be in the form of waves. For example, when the middle of the string (in *vīṇa*) is gently touched by a finger, the string vibrates on both sides of the point touched. Such a vibration may be of two or three segments. But there are points marked N which are permanently at rest, in the sense that, relatively small motions, compared to loops. Such points at rest are called "nodes", while the points, where the amplitude is maximum, are called "antinodes". The portion of the string between the two nodes is called "ventral segment" or "loop" (p. 76 *ibid.*). The authors further elucidate the nature of the "nodes" by stating that "nodes" are the points where displacement and velocity are "zero", but strain, i.e., changes in density or pressure is "maximum", a phenomenon similar to *tantrāgama's ghanībhūta śaktī* or *bindu*. *Tantrāgamas* also state that *nāda* arises from *bindu*, and *bindu* arises from *nāda* which fact is also verifiable in the sound-phenomenon, on the basis of the relation between "nodes" and "antinodes" as indicated in the Fig. 10.1 on page 328.

From this kind of description, it is clear that these "nodes" are of the nature of *bindus*. "Antidotes" are of the sound or *nāda* emanating at midway between two "nodes." These "antinodes" arising at alternative stages are points of "maximum" displacement and "maximum" velocity, but "zero" strain represents "sound" or *nāda* emanating between two nodes.[22] (*ibid.* p. 143), and "node" represents *bindu.* See the following diagram (Fig. 10.1):

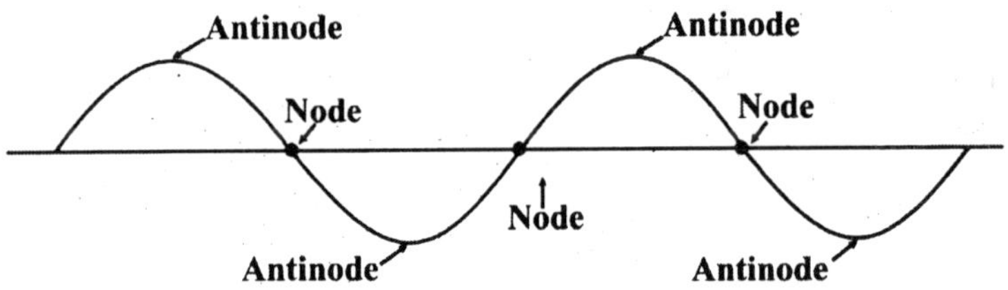

Fig. 10.1

It is also an established theory in science that "sound" is not propagated through "vacuum" (without air). If sounds were to be the quality of *ākāśa,* as *Sāṅkhya*-Yoga and *Nyāya-Vaiśeṣika* systems thought it to be, the sound should have propagated even in "vacuum". After the "air" is sucked out in "bell-jar experiment", the sound is not heard even though the hammer is striking the electrical bell inside the jar. This experiment proves the theory of the *Mīmāṃsā* and of the grammarians that the sound requires "air" or any other gaseous, liquid or solid medium, and the "sound cannot travel through vacuum or empty regions of space" (*dik*). Though the *ākāśa* of *Sāṅkhya*-Yoga and *Nyāya-Vaiśeṣika* systems is not a vacuum or empty space and is full of "*salila*" (translated as "ether"); yet this "ether", according to modern scientific experiments, cannot convey sound. As stated above, there must have been "ether" in outer space of neutral zone if it is taken as all pervasive and coextensive with *ākāśa*, but the fact is that such outer space neither has sound, nor sound can be heard even if it is produced by any artificial means like electrical bell.

The text-books on sound say that the sound is due to the vibrations of the elastic body like a string of a musical instrument. (See Khanna & Bedi; p. 9.) The movement of this elasticity is a moment of "to and fro" from the central line (rest line) of the inert body. It goes without saying that this to and fro movement of the elastic body is in space (*ākāśa*) which is an unobstructed medium. If it is so, the concept of sound as a quality of *ākāśa* as stated in *Sāṅkhya*-Yoga and *Nyāya-Vaiśeṣika* systems is acceptable as a necessary logical condition for propagation and perception of sound or a series of sounds.

How about time?

Though there are varied divergent views regarding the concept of "time" in Indian systems[23], yet regarding the nature of the process as to how sound travels from the mouth of the speaker and reaches the ears of the listener, there appear to be not much difference among them. It is in the nature of the human mouth that it utters only one sound at a time and that there is selectivity in the ears of the listener too. Therefore, both the utterance and perception of sound follows a "time-sequence", i.e., one at a time or one after the other, both in speech and music. In order to constitute a word, the sound-syllables (phonemes) have to be conveyed a "time-sequence." The sequence of sounds in the words *nadī* (river) and *dīna* (poor) are different, and as such they are different words (morphemes) conveying different meanings, as per convention, even though the syllabic-sounds (phonemes) that constitute these words are the same. Even in a sentence, it is the sequence of "words" (morphemes), as per linguistic syntax, that convey the meaning of the whole sentence. In this view of the matter, in terms of this kind of process of "sound-sequencing", I may redefine "language" as a "conscious sequencing of phonemes (syllables) and morphemes (words) in a sound-patterns (sentences) according to the rules of syntax and semantics, so as to convey a thought or meaning according to the rules of convention." Even in music the same *svaras* with different sequences produce different *rāgas*. Therefore, "time" like "space" is also an inevitable condition for constituting a "meaningful sound" (= a meaningful word) or an aesthetic sound (in music). Therefore, it can be said that though neither time nor space (*ākāśa*) is a part of sound as "quality" but they are necessary conditions for propagation and perception of sound or *dhvani*, so as to convey some meaning in language or aesthetic-sense in music. This kind of "meaningful" sound in language or an aesthetic-manifesting-sound in music is generally called *nāda* and as such "time" becomes a necessary element in *nāda* that distinguishes it from "an unrelated unorganized physical sound." To put it in a propositional formula: If physical sound is taken as S and time sequencing process as T, then *nāda* = S+T.

Then a question arises – What is the nature of *nāda*? How is it different from *dhvani*?

As I have highlighted in Chapter Two, Vedas used the word *nāda*[24], but they used it only in the sense of *dhvani* or "voice". Subsequent Vedic-literature, used the word *śabda* sometimes in the sense of sound and sometimes in the sense of a word.

Some of the systems like *Sāṅkhya*, *Nyāya*, *Vaiśeṣika*, *Mīmāmsā* and *Vedānta* used the word *śabda* both for the "word" and "*dhvani*." Quite often there would be confusion and it would be difficult to ascertain whether the author of a particular book used *śabda* in the sense of "sound" or "word" when both the senses would be permissible in the context. Hence, some authors translated the same word as sound and, others as word. For example, *śabda pūrvatvam* of *Mīmāṃsā Sūtra*-1.1.29, some have translated it as a "priority of word", and some others as a "priority of sound."

Many of the systems used *nāda* and *dhvani* as synonyms, one in the place of the other. However, broadly speaking, the word *nāda* was preferred by the systems which emphasized the application of sound, as a sound only (*nādātmaka dhvani*) like *tantrāgamas* and musicologists; and those who used "sound" as the manifester of "word" with a meaning opted for the word *dhvani* (*varṇātmaka dhvani*). However, the credit should necessarily go to Bhartṛhari, who for the first time, clearly distinguished between *dhvani* and *nāda*.

For Bhartṛhari and other grammarians, an "idea" (in the form of *madhyamā vāk*) is primary and the same is expressed in *vaikhari vāk* in the form of syllabic sounds. The meaningful word, say *ghaṭa*, is first conceived in the mind before it is uttered. In this form, the word is without any change and while uttering it in the context of language it appears to change. In the sentence *ghaṭamānaya* (bring the pot) the word *ghaṭa* becomes *ghaṭam* and along with the word *ānaya* it becomes *ghaṭamānaya*. Likewise, the word *vada* (to speak) becomes *vadāmi* (I speak), etc. Thus, according to Bhartṛhari, the word, which is without change, is *prakṛta dhvani*, and when it changes, in terms of the gross sound (or *nāda*) amassed (*pracīyamāne*), in the process of articulation, it is *vaikṛta dhvani*.

Bhartṛhari uses three terms to explain his theory and they are: *vṛtti-śabda* (meaningful word), *dhvani* and *nāda*. According to Bhartṛhari, when a sound is uttered with the help of vocal chords, it is *prākṛta dhvani* (original physical sound)[25], and while uttering a meaningful-word (*vṛttī-śabda*), the *prākṛta dhvani* (original physical sound) gets modified in the air and becomes short and long as *vaikṛta dhvani*, according to the intention of the speaker; and it is this *vaikṛta dhvani* that continues in the air for sometime and reaches the ears of the listener and causes meaning in the form of *sphoṭa* in the mind of the speaker. This *vaikṛta dhvani* is *nāda*, according to Bhartṛhari.[26] The *vaikṛta dhvani* may contain irrelevant, idiosyncratic sound, and may also contain certain non-linguistic sounds. The word *gau* may become *gavi* in *vaikṛta dhvani* of certain pronunciations. However, it remains *gau* as per its *prākṛta dhvani*.

What happens to *prākṛta dhvani* (original physical sound) after it is modified into *vaikṛta dhvani*? To this Bhartṛhari replies that the *prākṛta dhvani* gets modified (*vikāra*) and also gets merged in *vaikṛta dhvani* and continues as an important constituent of *vaikṛta dhvani*. According to him, when there is an effort on the part of the speaker to utter something, the air strikes the speech centers in the mouth and vocal organs produce different sounds.[27] The impact caused by *prākṛta dhvani* (original physical sound) is such that it produces other secondary sounds or vibrations in the air called *vaikṛta dhvani* (*nāda*) which cause modifications (*vṛtti*, like *drut*, etc.); and *vaikṛta dhvani* (*nāda*), in fact, arises after the cessation of movements of the vocal organs[28] just like flames arising in the burning fuel.[29] In other words, after cessation of the vocal movements, the sound uttered continues for sometime, just like a fan rotates for sometime, even after the current is switched off.

On the basis of this analysis, I find that Bhartṛhari's *nāda* is a "modified and prolonged sound in the air." The importance of this theory consists in emphasizing *nāda* as a "modified or modulated sound" by human effort to convey a certain idea. If it is so, the sound a railway engine produces cannot be described as *nāda*. Even when the strings of a musical instrument vibrate and make sound, owing to the fall of some object on them, cannot make that sound a *nāda*. Therefore the distinguishing factor that differentiates *nāda* from other "sound" (*dhvani*) is the effort, on the part of the human mind to achieve certain objects (of conveying idea in linguistic application or aesthetic experience in musical application, etc.), by sequencing the sounds. Thus in sequencing of sounds (of *Varṇātmaka dhvani*) there is participation of human mind (or consciousness) but the same is not required in a mere physical sound (*śabda* or *dhvani*). In fact *Praśastapāda* of *Navya-Nyāya* school, while commenting on Vai. Sū.2.1.27 and 2.2.21, divided physical sound (*śabda*) into : 1) *varṇātmaka* (of the form of letters) and 2) *dhvanyātmak* (of the form of noise in general) and further observed: the former is in the shape of *a* and other letters, and the latter in the shape of noise produced by blowing of the conch and such things. Sound of the former kind proceeds from the contact of the mind and soul as influenced by remembrances.[30] In this way "the contact of the mind and soul" is a necessary element in the concept of *nāda*. *Pāṇini Śikṣā* reiterated this principle by stating that "....for articulation of sound the faculties of soul (*ātman*), mind, intelligence (*buddhi*) and body *kāya* are required to be used" (Pā. Śi. 1.6). According to Pārśvadeva, a Jaina *muni* and musicologist, the "lifeless musical instrument" produces beautiful music only because of "human effort" (*puruṣa prayatna*) and an accidental *dhvani* arising due to fall of a stick on the strings of a musical instruments cannot be said to be a "musical *svara*."[31] Thus the human psychic element is a necessary constituent of *nāda*. This idea can be explained in the form of a formula as under:

Let "S" be taken for sound and "N" for *nāda* and the psychic effort as "P". Then N = S + P or S = N – P.

The time sequencing process in the earlier formula given above is nothing but the same mental or psychic element that is responsible for the sequencing of the sound. Thus the concept of *nāda* is a psychophysical concept, different from mere physical sound, in the sense of *śabda*.

Bhartṛhari's *nāda* accordingly is a psychophysical entity in the form *vaikṛta dhvani* different from mere *dhvani* which is a physical entity. Even the other systems like *Sāṅkhya*-Yoga, *Nyāya-Vaiśeṣika* and *Mīmāṃsā* and *Vedānta*, etc., when they speak of *dhvani* as a manifester of word (*śabda*), etc., in fact, they mean *nāda* in the sense Bhartṛhari used it as *vaikṛta dhvani* (modified or modulated sound), but not in the sense of physical sound (*prākṛta dhvani*). However, it should be noted that this "physical sound" constitutes the raw material for obtaining *nāda*. *Nāda* is a processed and modified (*vaikṛta*) sound so as to apply and use it for different human purposes, just like a potter or sculptor requires a "seasoned" mud or "chiseled" stone to create a piece of art. *Nāda* is, likewise, processed sound for its application. Thus *nāda* is different from sound having regards to its metamorphosis (*vikāra*) caused by human intellect. Even in lifeless musical instruments, when music is created by suitable "modification" of sound, by a human intellect, that sound becomes *nāda*. In short, *nāda* is consciously modulated and regulated physical sound (*śabda*).

The question, whether there is modification of sound or not, appears to be the bone of contention since the time of Vedic *Prātiśakhyās*. *Prātiśakhyās* believed that in *saṃhitāpāṭha* when two words are joined to save time (since pronouncing them separately would take longer time) there is a modification of the sound due to joining of the last syllable of the first word and the first syllable of the second word. Before conjunction a word is known as *padaprakṛtiḥ*, and after conjunction it is called *vikṛti padaḥ*. *Ṛgveda Prātiśākhya* called such a science dealing with modifications of sound as *vikāraśāstra*.[32] Tribhāṣyaratna, the commentary on *Taittirīya-Prātiśākhya*, accepted the theory of modification of sound (as per Tai. Prā.51 – api *vikṛtam*). While commenting on Tai. Prā.56 (*varṇasya vikāralopau*), he stated that even in the case of *lopa-sandhi* (e.g. *īm mandra* = *īma'ndra*), there is no omission of the syllable (*m*), but there is modification of sound. But for those who believed in the eternality of sound, the syllable *m* is not pronounced (or kept silent). He further observed that some have maintained the eternality of sound, in order to confutation of that doctrine, this rule (of *lopa* or omission) has been uttered, in conformity with the general grammar. .... Even *Pāṇini* also said "omission is disappearance from view" (Aṣṭa.1.60) as done by *Taittirīya-Prātiśākhya*.[33] In these circumstances, Tribhāṣya-ratna, who says that those who believed in the eternality of sound did not accept the theory of modification of sound, appears to be correct. Since *Mīmāṃsakas* accepted the eternality of "sound", they did not accept the modification of sound. For instance, for Kumārila Bhaṭṭa letters are eternal and non-changing ".... letters having no parts and as such being like *ākāśa*, they cannot undergo either an increase or decrease...."[34] *Naiyyāyikas* (Nyā. Sū.2.2.40-41; 50) also did not accept the modification of sound on the ground that the sound being the quality of the eternal *ākāśa* there cannot be any modification. According to both *Mīmāṃsaka* and *Naiyyāyikas*, in the case of *dadhyatra* (*dadhi* + *atra*), the opposite sounds–*i* in *dadhi* and *a* of *atra*–do not get modified into *ya*, but this *ya* of *dadhyatra* is substitution (*ādeśa*) for the sound-letters (*varṇa*) *i* and *a*.[35] But, on the contrary, in Bhartṛhari's theory of modification, the sounds *i* and *a* get modified into *ya*. In my opinion there is justification for this view. The phonetic form of *i* + *a* in conjunction (*sandhi*) would be *ia* and in its final metamorphosis it takes the shape as *ya*.

Thus, from phonetic point of view, there is modification sound *i+a* into *ya*. It must be noted that the phonetic form *i+a* cannot take any other form except *ya*. Hence the sound *ya* cannot be a matter of mere accidental substitution. In fact, this kind of controversy, with regard to *prākṛta dhvani* and *vaikṛta dhvani*, has been going on since generations. It appears that having regard to this kind of background only Bhartṛhari did not define *prākṛta dhvani* and *vaikṛta dhvani*, in his *Vākyapadīyam*, perhaps, he might have thought it to be unnecessary. Only because he did not define these terms, it cannot be concluded that he borrowed these concepts from

Sāṅkhyakārikā, which said "The *mūla prakṛti* is unmodified" and "modification" or "no modification" does not apply to *puruṣa*[36]; and also it cannot be said that from the concept of *śabdatanmātrā*, Bhartṛhari developed these concepts as opined by Johannes Bronkhorst.[37] In fact, the learned author proceeded on the basis of his statement – "The important thing is that the *tanmātras* are perceptible" (p. 29). But, in fact, these *tanmātras* are matters of inference only as per *Sāṅkhya Sūtras* (Sā. Pr. Sū.1.63) and, as such, they are not perceptible just like *prākṛta dhvani* of Bhartṛhari along with *vaikṛta dhvani*. Moreover, *śabdatanmātrās* first modify into *akāśa*, a gross substance, whose quality is "sound". This sound of *sāṅkhya*, being, thus, the last evolute (i.e., not being an evolvement), does not undergo any further modification. Hence, I beg to differ with Johannes Bronkhorst.

According to Bhartṛhari, thus *prākṛta dhvani*, which causes *sphoṭa*, continues in the air, for some more time, as a modulated or modified sound form, as if suspended in "sound-breath-phenomenon", which he calls *vaikṛta dhvani* or *nāda*. In other words, what is generally called *dhvani* is, in fact, Bhartṛhari's *prākṛta dhvani* (physical sound), and *nāda* is his *vaikṛta dhvani*, translated as a "modulated and regulated sound". This kind of theory of sound, in my opinion, is quite sound and acceptable, and I am going to demonstrate the same in the next Chapter.

Now the next question would be: How does this *nāda* become an epistemological means to human knowledge?

When the human soul as a conscious entity, with the instrumentality of mind, cognizes an object or objects, presented to it through senses, by means "sound" (*nāda*) as the "sign" (*cihna*), in the form of "syllables", "words" and "sentences", that *nāda* would become an epistemological means to human knowledge. "Sound" is commonly used as a "sign" (*cihna* - Vā.1.20) in all the languages in the world. According to Wittgenstein, "A sign is what can be perceived of a symbol".[38] For example, the word like "cow", etc., is expressed in "sound" by using "sound" as a "sign." This sound-word "cow" as a sign is perceived by the ears. The said sign "cow" is used to refer to the object-cow. In other words, the word "cow" is used as a symbol (*saṃjña*) to refer to the object-cow. Here "sound-cow" is used as a "sign" to refer to cow as its symbol, i.e., sound sign-cow is a symbol (*saṃjña*) for object cow. "In order to recognize a symbol by its sign we must observe how it is used with a sense" (*Tractatus* 3.326). This sense would be "dependent on the meaning that our arbitrary conventions have given...." (*Tractatus* 3.15). Thus, the word "is" used in the place of "exist" but the former indicates "something" and the latter "something is happening." "These words do not merely have different meanings: they are different symbols." (*Tractatus* 3.323). According to Wittgenstein the "word" is a "symbol" standing for the meaning cow. A symbol "characterizes its sense" as an expression (*Tractatus* 3.31). But for Indian grammarians, in all such instances, "sound" is a manifester (*vyañjaka*) of a "word."

In this kind of linguistic structure, the letters, according to Kunjunni Raja, are the smallest acoustic units of sounds called phonemes. "The phoneme in a language remains the same even when uttered by different people at different speeds and intonations" (p.105). .... Kumārila Bhaṭṭa says that even the individual letters should be considered as a "linguistic pieces" (*śabda*), though they do not convey any meaning (p. 106).[39] Bharata Miśra, one of the eminent grammarians goes to the extent of saying that "It is the sounds, not phonemes, that manifest the *sphoṭa*."[40] Koṇḍa (or Kauṇḍa) Bhaṭṭa also maintains a position almost similar to that of Bharata Miśra "that sounds perceived by the listeners are not different from *sphoṭa*. The *sphoṭa* is cognized in the form of the distinctive sounds *g-h-a-ṭa*." Koṇḍa Bhaṭṭa holds the view that the object of cognition is the indivisible word-*sphoṭa*, but its form is nothing else than the "phonemes" auditorally perceived. The phoneme *g* manifested by "sound" is identified with the phoneme *g*, which appears to be a part of indivisible *sphoṭa* word.[41] In this respect, a "syllable" is, in fact, a "particular sound-form" indicated by the word "phoneme." A "word" is a group of sequential phonemes ("morphemes") conveying an "idea" or meaning (*ghaṭa* = pot). In the words of Shabara Swamin, "An ear perceptible, meaning bearing sound, (*śabda*) is acknowledged as word in the world." (*śabda*)[42] ("*śrotragrahaṇe hi arthe loke śabdaśabdaḥ iti prasiddhaḥ*" – *Śabara* in his *Bhāṣya* on *Mīmāṃsā Sūtra*, 1.1.5.)

Among Buddhists Vasubandhu, representing *Sautrāntika* theory, stated that "sound" by itself conveys meaning according to convention and the concept of syllable and word is not necessary. But Saṅghabhadra of *Sarvāsti-Vaibhāṣika* School of Kaśmir, in his *Nyāyānusāra* refuted this theory by observing that "Syllables cause an utterance to be remembered by the speaker after the sound has passed away and such syllables thus allow the utterance to be transmitted to another." If this is so, even according to Saṅghabhadra the syllables serve only as memory devices to remember and to be transmitted such sound-manifested utterances (see *Vaibhāṣika* theory in Chapter Nine). According to the *Bhāṣya* of *Vātsyāyana*, and *Vārtika* of Uddyotakara (on Nyā. Sū.2.2.38), "a particular kind of sound takes the shape of a particular letter (*varṇa*)". According to him, *a, ka, ma, ya*, etc., represent particular sounds and a "word represents a particular combination of sounds" or a group of sounds denoting (the object). For example, the word "lamp" is "a group of particular sounds", i.e., lamp. *Vārtika* of Uddyotakara further adds that in the perception of a word there is a series of sounds, and the first of the series is produced by conjunction and disjunction and from that initial sound proceed other sounds in all directions and from each of these sounds there proceeds another, each being weaker than the previous until there is an obstacle, or the last sound becomes too weak to produce any further sound, and such a series comes to an end. Of these series of sounds that alone which approaches the *ākāśa* in the ear-cavity of the listener becomes apprehended.[43] Thus there are multitudes of words like *nadi* (river), *dīna* (poor), *jarā* (old age), *rāja* (king) and the like. But such a sound by itself being without meaning is mere shouting only, as Kayyaṭa puts it. (*nādo'rtharahitatvād ghoṣamātrameva*).[44] Hence, as explained by D.D. Sharma, ".... a mere aggregate of sounds does not form the basic linguistic unit called word, which has been defined as a minimum meaningful unit by modern linguists."[45] To the question: what constitutes the "meaningfulness" of the meaning, *Kātyāyana* striking a golden mean explains that the employment of *śabda* with and according to *śastric* knowledge (of *pratyaya* and *prakṛti*) brings merit, as does the study of Vedic *śabdas*. (*śāstrapūrvake prayoge bhyudayasta-ttulyaṃ vedaśabdena*) (p. 81) "When *śruti* says – *śabdajñāne dharmaḥ*, it means the knowledge of *śabda* acquired through necessary precedent, namely, the knowledge of *apaśabdas* which have to be eliminated from the former" (p. 83).[46] Wittgenstein, a modern Western philosopher also emphasized the knowledge in the "use" of the word in linguistic practice. "In order to recognize a symbol (word) by its sign (sound) we must observe how it is used with a sense" (*Tractatus* 3.326).

A sentence likewise is a group of words conveying a "unit of meaning", e.g. "It is a cow"; or "Devabhaṭṭa cooks rice", etc. The earliest definition of "sentence" appears to be that of Jaimini "By reason of the unity of sense there is one sentence; on division it is dependent on other factors (like syntactical structure, etc.)."[47] In fact, our day-to-day language consists of such sentences.

If we analyze the language in terms of "sign" language (of sound), we find that it stands for a conglomeration of sequential sounds in the form of "phonemes" (syllable), "morphemes" (words), and in the form of a sentence as a "sound pattern", what Kunjunni Raja calls a "sonematic pattern".[48] Thus, "language in its spoken form is a sequence of sounds, articulated with certain speed and with half-pauses and pauses at predetermined junctures. The listener perceives these sounds and maps them into meaningful units in order to receive message."[49]

In the West also there are many linguistic philosophers who thought of language in terms of "sound forms" or "sound patterns", etc. For example, Jerrold J. Katz notes one such a linguistic school which believes in taxonomic conception according to which the significant features of a language are exposed to perceptual view in the phonetic surface of sentences which can be classified as segments of the utterances as phonemes, morphemes and sentence, etc. "A particular phoneme is thought of as a class of linguistically equivalent, significant sounds, ...(p. 35).... Morphemes, which are the minimal syntactic units, are therefore classes of sequences of phonemes. Thus, another way of characterizing a phoneme is to say that it is a feature of the sound pattern of a language that differentiates morphemes .... two distinct morphemes must differ by at least one phoneme; for example, as the English morphemes bin and pin do (similar to the example of *nadī* and *dīna* as seen above).... The constituents of a sentence, its syntactic parts, are continuous segments of the sequence of morphemes that comprise it...."[50] From the substance of that theory so provided by Katz, it is clear that the said Western modern theory is similar to the one advocated by Indian linguistic philosophers about two thousand years back.

From the above discussion, it is clear that such a "sonematic pattern" of language has been the only major means to human knowledge. Even though our senses enable us to see a cow yet it is through linguistic apparatus that we recognize it as a cow. When a child sees a "cow" for the first time, he recognizes it only as "some animal"; and such cognition would be vague and indefinite. Such cognition is described as an indeterminate perception (*nirvikalpakam pratyakṣa*). But later being informed by his parents that such an animal, with these characteristics, is called *gau* (in *Sanskṛt* language) and such a cognition is called a determinate perception. (*savikalpakam pratyakṣa*). "Perception" according to *Nyāya Sūtra*, "is that knowledge (*jñānam*) which arises from the contact (*sannikarṣe*) of a sense with its object, which is determinate (*avyabhicāri*), unnameable and non-erratic un-erroneous" (*indriyārthasannikarṣotpanna jñānamavyapadeśyamavyabhicāri vyavasāyātmakaṃ pratyakṣam*–Nyā. Sū.1.4)".[51] Thus it is clear that the "perception" is the "cognition", "produced by the contact of the sense-organ with the object".[52] In case of perception of "sound" the contact of the sense-organ (ear) with sound would be of the nature of *samaveta-samavāya* relation as I have explained in Chapter Four.

If somebody were to utter sound *gha* the same is heard by the listener because the sound *gha* that inheres in *ākāśa* (in *samavāya* relation as its quality) produces the soundness (that inheres in sound, by way of *samaveta-samavāya* relation) in the *ākāśa* of the ear-cavity of the listener. As a result the listener "perceives" the sound *gha* that inheres in the *akāśa* of his ear-cavity. This sound *gha* in linguistic convention is recognised as a letter-sound (*varṇa*). This letter-sound along with another letter-sound takes the form of a word-*ghaṭa*, and, according to convention it means a "pot". If a person knowing the meanings of these words, utters a sentence–*ghaṭaḥ asti* (there is a pot) – it would be a means of valid knowledge. In this manner "....the means by which or the process through which the valid knowlege is derived is called verbal testimony (*śabda pramāṇa*)....Any knowledge derived from a speech is called verbal knowledge (*śabda-bodhaḥ*)."[53]

According to *Mīmāṃsakas* like *Kumārila*, knowledge is partly determinate and partly indeterminate. "Just as one, who has been well instructed in music, is able to discriminate between its different notes, both ordinary and Vedic, such as the *ṣadja*, *ṛṣabha* & c.; and those, who have not been so instructed, know all notes merely as music; ...."[54] and it cannot be said that such knowing it as only music is false.

But *Navya Nyāya* philosophers like Gangeśa and Gadādhara and others have different and more complicated explanations. According to Gangeśa's *Nirvikalpavāda*, such a cognition is a complex process, in which an indeterminate perception (*Nirvikalpam pratyakṣam*) of "cowness" as a qualifier, on the basis of imposed properties of mind (*upādhi*) (with the help of memory), on qualificand "cow", a "determinate sense perception" (*svikalpa pratyakṣam*) "cow" (is obtained), named by convention by the word "cow", occurs, due to intrinsic relationship (*sannikarṣa*) between "cowness" and the cow. Here the perception of the qualifier "cowness" and the qualificand "cow", according to Gangeśa, overlap alright, but they are not repetitions. Indeterminate perception is with fewer properties of the object of perception than determinate perception.[55] But according to Gadādhara's theory of objectivity (*viṣayatvāda*), the epistemological cognition (or knowledge) of "cowness possessing" in a cow has become possible because of the particular ontological "relation" (*sambandhaviśeṣaḥ*) between the qualifier (cowness-posing) and the qualificand ("cow").[56]

However, in both these theories, in my opinion, it cannot be disputed that such "perception" or knowledge of "cow" arises, through the instrumentality of "visual perception" of cow (in case of Gadādhar) or through the instrumentality of "ear perception" of "sound-word cow" (in case of Gangeśa), on the basis of "convention." It is the convention that determines the relation between the word (*saṃjñā*) and the object (*saṃjñin*). In order to understand what the speaker says, the listener also should belong to the same convention by necessary teaching. When "Mr. A" utters a proposition that "This is a cow", then, Mr. B the listener, belonging to the same convention, understands the proposition and says, "Yes it is a cow". Thus, as Wittgenstein said, a language is like a game; it has its own rules that take care of both the sides of players, provided the players are competent and well-versed with the rules.[57]

A thought is clothed in "language". Such a language may be spoken or written. As observed by Sibjiban Bhattacharyya, "spoken language is logically prior to written language".[58] Whatever it may be, as Wittgenstein observed...."from the outward form of the clothing, it is possible to infer the form of the thought beneath it" (*Tractatus* 4.002 at p. 35). According to him, "Man possesses the ability to construct a language capable of expressing every sense, without having any idea how each word has meaning or what its meaning is – just as people speak without knowing how the individual sounds are produced. Every language is a part of the human organism and is no less complicated than it." (*Tractatus* 4.001). Patañjali put the same idea in a more graphic way, when he said: If one has to do with a jug, he goes to the potter's house, and says : "Make a jug that I have something to do with it." But wishing to use word, he does not go to the grammarian and say: "Make a word. I wish to use it. But he takes whatever objects he likes and uses words."[59]

But one thing has to be admitted that every language, in the world, uses "sound" as the only basic mode of linguistic expression, but in accordance with its own linguistic rules, which Tucker calls "phonetic laws." "A phonetic law of a particular language is a statement of a regular practice of that language at a particular time in regard to the treatment of a particular sound or a group of sounds in a particular setting."[60] In other words, sound is the only extensive epistemological means to human knowledge. The same fact is emphasized by

Śabara in his commentary on *Mīmāṃsā Sūtra* - (1.1.5), when he says - "In the day-to-day transaction of the world, 'the ear-perceptible-word' is in the shape of 'syllable-form group sounds', denotes the facts and things of the external world. The denoted entity is something different from the 'group of sounds'; and such a 'sound-form' denoting process is called language."

According to Bhartṛhari, the human consciousness (*caitanyam*) is preceded by speech or language (Vā.126). He further declares that "In this world no knowledge is possible except accompanied by *śabda* (or word). All types of knowledge (due to perception inference, etc.) shine as permeated by speech".[61] "The human reasoning is the power of *śabda*. *Tarka-śāstra* adopts words and sentences in its reasoning and conclusions."[62]

If the "word" is nothing but a "sound-form", as we have seen above, then knowledge, in the ultimate analysis, would be the one manifested by *nāda* and *nāda* alone. Having regard to this kind of role of *nāda* in human knowledge, both Vedic *paṇḍits* and modern grammarians praised it as *śabdabrahman* and *nādabrahman*. To highlight this kind of importance of sound-phenomena in linguistic communication, Dāmodara Paṇḍit said:

Nādena vyañjate varṇaḥ padaṃ varṇāt padādvacaḥ
Vacaso vyavahāro'yaṃ, nādādhīnamato jagat.

"From sound manifest syllables, from syllables word; and from words language; thus the entire (human linguistic) transaction is dependent on sound".[63]

Notes and References

1. *Muṇḍaka Upaniṣad*-1.2.13.
2. R.V. 10.190.1.
3. R.V. 1.164.21.
4. R.V. 1.164.37.
5. R.V. 1.164.39.
6. *YāsakaNirukta*-13.9 - *asmād brāhmaṇā ubhayīṃ vācam vadanti yā ca devānām yā ca manuṣyānām.*
7. Jai. Sū. 1.1.29.
8. Peterson Peter (*tr.*) (1974) ; p. 40.
9. *Śloka Vārtika* of Kumārila Bhaṭṭa; Aphorism VI to XXIII, 7. Jhā, Gangānāth; p. 410.
10. Dasgupta, Surendra (2001); p. 88.
11. R.V. 1.164.41.
12. Ron Kurtus (2009) : Retrieved on 05-05-2011.
13. *The New Lexicon Webster's Dictionary of the English Language* (1987); p. 1095.
14. Śl. Vā. - 'Aphorism VI to XXIII. 45' ; Jhā, Gangānāth. p. 417.
15. Lindtner Christian (*tr.*) (2001) : *Mīmāṃsātattvanirṇayāvatāraḥ* (Verses 48 & 49).
16. See *Ṛgveda Prātiśākhya*, Varma, Virendra Kumara. p. 16,
17. Edmondson, R. (2005) : Retrieved on 05-05-2011.
18. Vai. Sū. 5.2.17.
19. *Kāyāgni - Pāṇini Shikṣā*; 3.
20. Refer to Sharma Madhusūdana (1969); p. 55.
21. Khanna and Bedi (1992); p. 1, 36 & 76.
22. ____; page 9.
23. a. Balslev Anindita Niyogi (1999).
    b. Mandal Kumar Kishore (1968).
24. R.V. 10.11.2 and A.V.19.34.3.
25. Vā. 1.76.
26. Vā. 1.77.
27. Vā. 1.108.

28. Vā. 1.105 - *kampetūparate jāta nāda vṛttiviśeṣakaḥ.*
29. Vā. 1.106.
30. Jhā, Gaṅgānātha (*tr.*) (1982) : *Padārthadharmasaṅgraha of Praśastapāda*, p. 611-612 - on Sound.
31. San. Sam. Sā. - Bṛhaspati (1977) : *Verse* 2.20; p. 27.
32. *Ṛgveda Prātiśākhya* : 2.5; p. 130 - Varma, Virendra Kumāra.
33. Wittney, D. William (*tr.*) (1973); pp. 37-40.
34. Sl.V. 213-216; Jhā.; pp. 430-45.
35. *Nyāya-Sūtras* of Gautama (Jhā.) II; p. 988 regarding *Naiyyāyikas.*
36. *mūla prakṛtiḥ avikṛtiḥ....na prakṛtiḥ na vikṛtiḥ puruṣaḥ* - Verse No. 3 of *Sāṅkhya Kārikā* - Satri Suryanarāyana (1948); p. 7.
37. Bronkhorst, Johannes (1999), Vol. 27; pp. 22-33.
38. Pears D.F. & McGuinness B.F. (*tr.*) (1961) : 3.32.
39. Raja, Kunjunni K. (1977); pp. 105-106; Kumārila Bhaṭṭa also says *tasmācchrotraparicchinno yady arthaṃ na vā, sarvathā tasya śabdatvaṃ lokasiddhaṃ na hīyate* - Śl. Vā.; p. 106 (Jha, Ganganath).
40. Miśra, Bharata : Potter, K.H. (1990), Vol. V; p. 231.
41. Kauṇḍa, Bhaṭṭa : Potter, K.H. (1990), Vol. V; p. 303.
42. *śrotragrahaṇe hi arthe loke śabdaśabdaḥ iti prasiddhaḥ* - Śabara in his Bhāṣya on *Mīmāṃsā Sūtra*, 1.1.5.
43. Jhā (1999), Vol II; pp. 985-87.
44. Chatterji, Kshitish Chandra (1957); p. 104.
45. Kumar, Pushpendra, (1984); p. 15.
46. Sarma, Krishna Madhava K. (1968); pp. 81 & 83.
47. *arthekatvādekaṃ vākyaṃ sākāṅkṣaṃ cedvibhāge syāt* Mi. Su.2.1.46. (Jha)
48. Raja, Kunjunni K. (1977); p. 105.
49. Misra, B.G., Dr. (1980).
50. Katz, J. Jerrold; Ch. 4, p. 31.
51. Sihha, Nanda Lal and Vidyabhūṣaṇa, Satisa Chandra (*tr.*). (1990); p. 3.

52. Jhā, Gangānāth (1999), Vol. I; p. 133.
53. Vidyabhūṣaṇa, Satisa Chandra (2002); p. 444.
54. Sl. V.237-41 – Jha, Ganga Nath, p. 110.
55. Bhattacharya, Sibjiban (1993), Part II; p. 11.
56. ____ (1990) Part II; pp. 6-12.
57. Pitcher, George (1964); pp. 247-50.
58. Bhattacharyya, Sibjiban (1998); p. 22.
59. Dasgupta, Surendranath (*tr.*) (1991); p. 38.
60. Aiyar, Ramachandra T.K. (1987); p. 68.
61. *jñānenam sarvam śabdena bhāsate* – Vā.1.123.
62. Vā.1.138; Korada, Subramanyam (*tr.*).
63. Bhaṭṭa, Viśvambhara Nātha (*tr.*) (1975); 1.14.

* * *

Chapter Eleven

VOCAL APPLICATIONS OF THE ACCEPTED THEORY OF *NĀDA*

In previous chapter, I have already examined a number of theories regarding the concept of *nāda*, and have also found that the one propounded by Bhartṛhari– "*nāda* is a modulated or modified sound"–is acceptable. The efficacy of a theory consists in its effective applications. This aspect can easily be demonstrated with the help of musical sound. For example, the part of *shahanāi* called "mouth piece", if blown separately, it makes a "quak" sound, it is *prakṛti dhvani* (original physical sound). But by connecting it to the other part, which has holes, and by opening and closing of the holes on the instrument, when music is produced, the original physical sound gets modified or modulated according to the need, and this sound in the form of music is called *vaikṛti dhvani* or *nāda*. See Fig. 11.1.

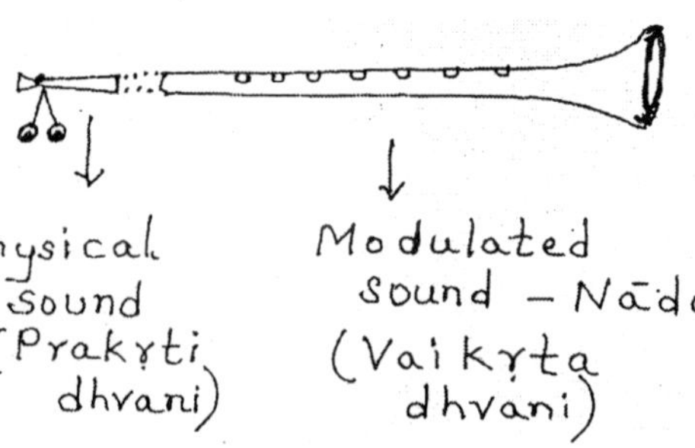

Fig. 11.1

Almost similar is the process of producing sound in human throat. With the help of air coming from lungs, the sound created at vocal chords, is the original physical sound (*prākṛta dhvani*), just like the sound produced by the "mouth-piece" of the *shahanāī*. The said sound, after entering the cavity of the mouth, gets modified, as per one's desire, into linguistic syllables (*varṇas*) or the musical *svaras* (tones, like *sa, re, ga, ma,* etc.). This modified sound is called *vaikṛta dhvani* or *nāda*. (See Fig.11.2.)

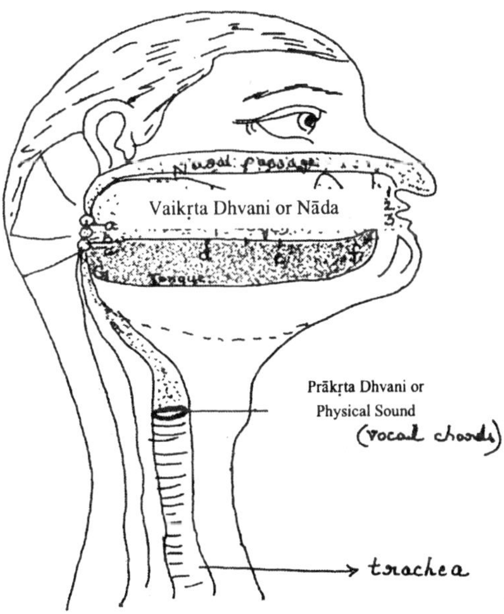

Fig. 11.2

Now I proceed to consider the nature of the vocal application of *nāda*. In fact, the concept of *nāda*, different from *dhvani*, has developed in its applications only. The word *prayoga* was used for "application" in ancient classical literature (*prayujyata iti prayogaḥ*; *prayuj* = use, or employ). For instance, according to *Taittirīya Prātiśākhya*, the sound *oṁ* is pronounced differently, sometimes as *udātta*, sometimes as *svarita*, sometimes as *anudātta* and sometimes with three *mātrās* and sometimes with four *mātrās*, etc., etc., as per the need of its applications.[1] Sometimes the word *viniyoga* also was used to indicate an application or use. For example, a person desirous of knowing the efficacy of a *mantra* should know the *svara*, arising in different combinations (*yoga*), *varṇa* (sound-syllables), *mātrā*, *devatā*, *ṛṣi* and *viniyoga* (application).[2] It should be noted that nobody thinks of a futile application. Who will be attracted to the study of a science (*śāstra*) or a work (*karma*), unless its use is explained to him?[3] *Uvvaṭa*, the commentator of *Ṛgveda Prātiśākhya*, stated in his prelude that : "the matters pertaining to a science are required to be understood only after knowing its use and applications."[4] In fact, Patañjali Maharṣi had declared the use of grammar by stating that the study of grammar, enabling one to avoid corrupt words (*duṣṭa śabdaḥ*), leads to *mokṣa*. According to *Maitrī Upaniṣad*, one can attain Brahman (*śabdabrahmāṇi niṣṇātaḥ paraṃ brahmādhigacchati*) by mastering the technique of *nāda* and its manifestations.[5]

The "vocal application" mentioned in the subject matter of the thesis means a "conscious" human vocal application. In birds also we find the vocal application of sound for inviting the mate for co-habitation, warning their species in the presence of the predators, or for ensuring the presence of the group-mate, etc. However, such an application is instinctive and involuntary, and there cannot be any scope for any suggestion or any effort, for improving their vocal sound, by any external agency. Hence, such a vocal application of sounds by birds would be outside the scope of my thesis, except for the purpose of comparison, analogy, if need be. Thus I am, in fact, concerned with the "conscious" application of *nāda*, produced in vocal organ of the human body, for human purposes.

According to Śārangadeva, "The body of human beings is most suitable for the manifestation of *nāda*." (*tatra nādopayogitvāt mānuṣaṃ dehamucyate*)[6]. The "voice" (*svara*), which the human body utters, is described as *śārīra* by Bharata.[7] *Nāradīyaśikṣā* described human body as *gātravīṇā* (body - *vīṇā*). In this kind of background, *Śārangadeva* defined "human voice" as – "A *dhvani*, born along with the body, having inherent capacity, without any practice, to present *rāga* is called *śārīram* or (voice)."[8] "The concept of *śārīra* is perhaps unique to musicological thinking in India....what is meant by *śārīra* is the original and natural capability of the voice of a person".[9] The nature of the "voice" of a person depends on the totality of sound producing factors in the body, viz., the size of the mouth, the nature of vocal chords, larynx, the sex, and the age of a person, etc. For instance, "The larynx in the case of man is larger while vocal chords are thicker and bigger than in the case of a woman and children. The pitch of the note produced by a man is lower than that of the note produced by a woman or a child."[10] Thus, *śārīra* represents the "innate voice" of a person. It is the "sound" arising out of the built-in capacity of an individual, and accordingly is the product of the entire organism, including the nature of the structure of the mouth. The timber, pitch and loudness are part of this *śārīra* and it is this *śārīra* only what Strawson, a Western philosopher, calls "master sound".[11] The man is also capable of producing different kinds of voices in different occasions. Thus, the nature of the production of the voice varies according to the intended applications. For instance, when a person wants to call a man standing at some considerable distance, he has to increase the loudness and intensity of his voice (so as to shout louder); and this kind of voice is not required to talk to a person by his side. Thus, voice is produced differently for different applications. In these circumstances, how exactly is *nāda* produced in human vocal organ, broadly speaking, there are two theories:

1. Theory No. 1 is the one expounded by phoneticians, like *śikṣās* and *prātiśākhyas* and grammarians for linguistic application; and
2. Theory No. 2 is advocated by musicologists and *Tantrāgamas* for the purpose of applying *nāda* for musical and meditational purposes.

The object of these two methods is to process the *dhvani* produced at vocal chords, differently for different purposes, just like a potter and an artist seasons the mud or stone for producing artistic pieces. By regulating the breath and the vibrations caused at vocal chords, man is capable of producing "different kinds of voices" by suitably modifying or modulating such a mixture of those two in vocal organs. Pāṇini called this mixture *anupradāna*. (*Anupradāna* means the resultant product caused by an effort.) It is the resultant "sound-breath-material".[12] It is to that "sound-breath-mixture" emitted by the larynx (vocal chord), the musicologists called *dhātu*, and *prātiśākhyas* as *dravya*. It is called *dhvani* in common parlance. It is caused by the effort in the mouth (*āsyaprayatna*). The nature of this "sound-breath-material" would be slightly different in linguistic applications and in musical applications. In aesthetics applications, there would be additional modified voices and tones, to express emotions and feelings, which Bharata called *kāku*. Thus, on the basis of the intended application of *nāda*, the nature of the production of "sound-breath-material" depends. With this introduction, let me now proceed to consider the vocal applications of *nāda*.

There are mainly four kinds of vocal applications of *nāda*:

A. Linguistic Applications
B. Musical Applications
C. Aesthetic Applications
D. Spiritual Applications.

A. Linguistic Applications

As we have seen in the last chapter, a language, in substance, is a mode of expression of thought or ideas by means of sequencing of articulate sounds. The grammarians, and the authors of *prātiśākhyas* and *śikṣas* provide the mode of production of articulate sounds for Linguistic Applications –colloquial (*laukika* or *bhāṣik*) and Vedic (*ārcik*).

(a) Coloquial (*laukika* or *bhāṣik*) applications

THEORY NO. 1: "VOICE PRODUCTION" FOR LINGUISTIC APPLICATIONS

Pāṇini Śikṣā, for instance, excluding mystical elements of *Tantrāgamas*, stated that "The soul (*ātmā*) in conjunction with intellect (*buddhi*), having cognized the objects, directs the mind's intention to speak and the mind impels the vital fire (vital force or energy) in the body, which in turn produces soft tone (*mandra svara*), (for morning *savana*=prayer) at the chest (*urasi*); middle tone (*madhya svara*) at the throat (for noon *savana*); and high tone (*tāra svara*) at the roof the mouth (*mūrdhani*) (for evening *savana*); thereby are created all the articulate sounds (*varṇas*) called differently letters, letter-sounds or sound-syllables, etc. According to *Ṛgveda Prātiśākhya*, the union of breath (*śvāsa*) and sound (*nāda*) becomes the cause (*prakṛtayaḥ* = *mūla kāraṇa*) for the syllables (*varṇānām*). When one and the same sound-breath-material takes the pronunciation mode in the mouth, it causes multiple sounds (*ekaḥ śrutīḥ karmaṇāpnoti bahvīḥ*) in the form of syllables."[13]

From different combinations of such sound-syllables, "words" (*pada*) are formed; and from words "sentences" (*vākya*) are created, with the help of "internal effort" (*abhyantara prayatna*) and "external effort" (*bāhya prayatna*).[14]

The original natural voice so produced is called *vaikharī* in Vedic tradition because it undergoes modulation or modification (*vikāra*) in linguistic and musical applications. We have already seen that *nāda* itself is a modified (*vaikṛta*) *dhvani*, as against *prākṛta dhvani* (original voice) of the vocal chord. After being produced at larynx, when such a *prākṛta dhvani* enters the mouth, it is controlled by the muscles in the vocal organs, and as per the desire of a person, it is made to pass through eight different places[15] in vocal organs, producing different *varṇas*. The most important point in determining the quality of sounds is the resonance of the cavity of the mouth. By altering the position of the jaws, tongue, etc., the form and size of the cavity of the mouth can be greatly modified, thus, forming a quickly and completely controllable resonator....No musical instrument is such as can produce a vowel tone.[16] The muscles of the upper and lower jaws play a very important role in producing different vowel "tones". Even in the Vedic tradition, the use of the jaws, while chanting *mantras*, was very much emphasized for correct and melodic intonation.[17] Likewise, *prātiśākhyas* also emphasized the use of jaws in producing *varṇas*. They considered, for instance, "a *varṇa*" as being produced at the root of the jaws (*hanūmūla*). Such a muscular control in the jaws of the vocal organs is called *yama* by our ancient phoneticians (*svaraśāstrajña*). For instance, in the words "*paddma, rukkma*" there is muscular control of the jaws by holding two syllables together, e.g., *pad+dma* and *ruk+kma*, etc. *Yama* literally means "restraining" or "controlling".[18] The *yamas*, according to me, are the muscular-controlled syllabic utterances. In musical *svaras*, for longer continuity of *svaras*, "longer duration" of muscular control is required. It is in this sense only that the ancient scholars treated musical tones – *sa, re, ga, ma*, etc. also as *yamas* (*sapta svarā yamāste*).[19]

The sound that causes different linguistic syllables or musical *svaras* is nothing but "sounding breath", and this "sounding breath", is called *dhvani* in *Sanskṛt*. In other words, the vibration caused by breath in vocal chords, emerging together out of the mouth is *dhvani*. The total mass of sound emitted from throat, while taking different syllables or musical *svaras*, takes different volume and different qualities – sometimes more "hard", sometimes more "soft", sometimes more volume, sometimes less volume, as per the need. This kind of variations of sound-breath-material in volume and intensity is called *saṃyoga piṇḍa*. According to *Apiśāli Śikṣā*, there are three kinds of such *saṃyoga piṇḍas*: *Ayaḥpiṇḍa* (hard like iron e.g. *agniḥ, tanacmi, yakknā* etc. 2) *Dārupiṇḍa* (hard like wood), e.g. *aśvaḥ, sūryyaḥ,* 3) *Ūrṇapiṇḍa* (soft like wool), e.g. *kṣṇaḥ, āsmmin,* etc.[20] *Yājñavalkya Śikṣā* states seven kinds of *saṃyoga piṇḍas* : *āyaḥ piṇḍa, dāru piṇḍa, ūrṇa piṇḍa, jvāla piṇḍa, mṛt piṇḍa, vāyu piṇḍa, vajra piṇḍa*.[21]

Thus, the *prākṛta dhvani* (physical sound arising in vocal chords while passing through different places (*sthānat*) in the vocal cavity gets modified (*vaikṛta dhvani* or *nāda*) into the speech-sounds. Such speech-sounds are called *varṇas*, translated differently as syllables, letters or letter-sounds or syllabic sounds, etc., as stated above. According to Pāṇini, these letter-sounds take their shapes in five ways: (1) as per their accentuating sounds (*svarataḥ*), (2) as per the time they take (*kālataḥ* – *laghu, guru* and *pluta*) (in pronunciation), (3) as per the places they touch or pass through (*sthānāt*) (in the mouth), and (4) as per internal and (5) external efforts required (to utter them).[22]

To utter a syllable or *varṇa* (say *ka*), some effort is required. Here effort means the control of the movement of the vocal organs in utterance or accentuation. Such efforts are of two types: internal effort (*ābhyantara prayatna*) and external effort (*bāhya prayatna*).

Internal effort is the one that takes place within the mouth for producing linguistic syllables, and it is also called *āsyaprayatna* or *mukha prayatna*. According to *Kāśikā Vṛtti* on Pāṇini,[23] there are four kinds of internal efforts – *spṛṣṭatā*, (contacted or touched), *īśat spṛṣṭatā* (slightly contacted), *saṃvṛtta* (closed), *vivṛttā* (open). Internal effort is very important in uttering syllables, since it is with the help of this effort only that different parts of the mouth are regulated in such a way that the sound-breath-material strikes different parts of the mouth producing different linguistic syllables. The places in vocal cavity, from the throat (producing *kaṇṭhya svaras* like *akāra*) to the lips (producing *oṣṭya o*) are considered parts of mouth (*mukham* or *āsyam*), (*ākākalakād oṣṭhaparyantam mukham āsyam*) by the experts in *śikṣāśāstra*.[24]

External effort consists in the control of the opening and closing of vocal chords with the help of breath. When one wants to speak, the air, while passing through vocal chords produces breath in open (*vivṛt*) position, and *nāda* or sound in closed position (*saṃvṛt*).[25] On the basis of this process, as explained by *Āpiśāli Śikṣā*[26] different accentuating activities are obtained. They are *saṃvāra*, *vivāra*, *nāda*, *svāsa*, *ghoṣa*, *aghoṣa*, *mahāprāṇa*, *udātta*, *anudātta*, and *svarita*. From these descriptions, it is clear that this external effort is mainly concerned with the processing of the sound-breath-material, into different articulate sounds.

Thus, with the help of these two efforts, all the 63 or 64 syllables called *varṇasamāmnāya* are produced. These syllables (the last units of language) are produced, according to Pāṇini, *svarataḥ* and *kālataḥ*. *Svarataḥ*, means as per *svaras* (tones), and *kālataḥ* means as per time-measure, in terms of *hrasva* (of one *mātra*), *dīrgha* (of two *mātrās*) and *pluta* (of three *mātrās*), etc.

Svarataḥ concept requires some more elaboration. The word *svara* is derived from the root *śvṛ* (to utter a sound or to sound, make sound, etc.). In the linguistic structure, *svara* in the sense of voice or tone is the basic element. In fact, a *vyañjana* (consonant) is an "obstructed *svara*". A *vyañjana* has no independent existence without *svara*. Hence it is considered to be a limb of *svara*, (*svarāṅga*) since it is pronounced with the help of *svara* only. Thus *svara* (vowel) is basically a regulated "sound-shape", produced at vocal organ, for the purpose of its use in linguistic applications in the form of syllables (*varṇātmaka dhvani*).

What exactly is the nature of vowel-sounds? There are two theories in the West, as noticed by Khanna and Bedi. They are called the "Fixed pitch" and the "Relative pitch" theories. Helmholtz believed in the fixed pitch theory, according to which each vowel is characterized by one or two restricted regions of "given pitch", which are independent of the fundamental tone of the vowel. On the relative pitch theory, each vowel has a series of partials or overtones, the frequencies of which have a certain "definite relation" to the fundamental.... Recent experiments of Wills and Miller are in favor of fixed theory. If theory be true, it would be possible to change the vowels in a phonograph by running the instrument at a speed higher or lower than the original. If the vowels depend upon the "relative" frequencies (Relative pitch theory), quality should not change; while if they are dependent upon "absolute" frequency (Fixed pitch theory), vowels should change. A number of investigators applied this test to the phonography and it was seen that "vowels" are changed, thus proving the results in favour of the fixed theory.[27] According to me, this kind of theory is not explicit and clear. A "vowel sound", according to Indian phoneticians, has nothing to do with higher or lower "pitch", etc. In one "pitch", say in *ṣaḍja-svara*, all the vowels can be uttered.

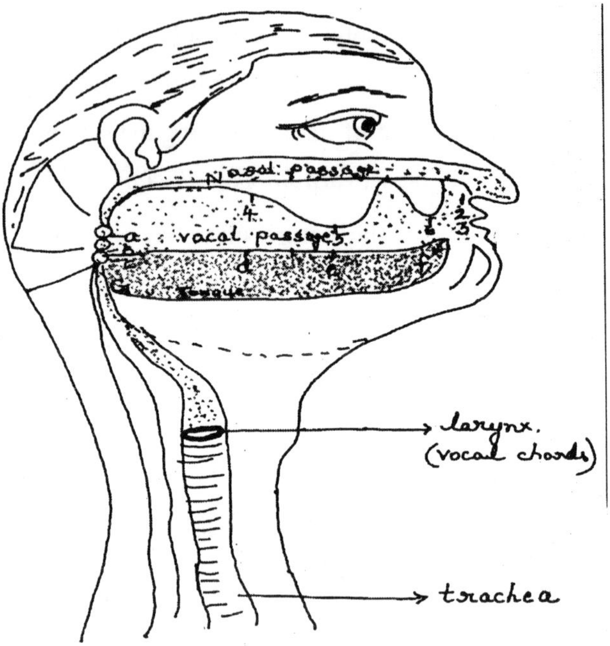

Fig. 11.3

(*Courtesy*: A sketch in Sanskṛt Text – *Madhusūdana Śarma, Pathyāsvasti*, p. 43, with my own modifications.)

Colour indications: ▒ = Tongue

■ = Sound-breath-material (*anupradāna*)

According to Pāṇini, the sound of a syllable is fixed to the place (*sthānāt* - Pā. Śi., 1.10) where it is produced in mouth. Thus, the vowel sound of *a* is taken as chest sound (*uras*) or throat sound (*kaṇṭhya*) and the one produced at the root of the tongue (*jihva mulīya*); the sound of *i*, *e* and *ai* are taken as palatal (*tālavya*), and *o* and *u* as labials (*oṣṭhaya*), etc.

Breath, while passing through trachea, enters vocal chords by causing their vibrations, as a result, sound-breath-material (*anupradāna*) is produced. This sound-breath-material after entering into the vocal passage gets modified into different sound-syllables (*varṇas*) by striking different parts of mouth, with the help of tongue, before exiting from vocal cavity. Such sound-syllables (*varṇas*) are named by the places of their production. As discussed above, sometimes they are named differently by some grammarians by taking different part of mouth as their places of production.

The syllables and their places of production, as indicated by William Dwight Whitney[28], are as follows:

Vowels : simple	short	long	name - place
	a	ā	gutturals (*kaṇṭha* - throat)
	i	ī	*tālu* (palatal)
	u	ū	*oṣṭha* (labial)
	ṛ	ṛū	*mūrdhā* (lingual)
	lṛ	lṛū	*danta* (dental)
dipthongs	e	ai	*tālu* (palatal)
	o	ou	*oṣṭha* (labial)
Visarga	ḥ	*kaṇṭha* (throat) (Aspiration)	
Anusvāra	ṅ, ṃ	*nāsikya* (nasal)	

Mutes:

surd	surd asp.	sonant	son. asp.	nasal	place
ka	kh	g	gh	ṅ	gutturals *kaṇṭha* (throat)
c	ch	j	jh	ñ	*tālu* (palatal)
ṭ	ṭh	ḍ	ḍh	ṇ	*mūrdhā* (lingual)
t	th	d	dh	n	*danta* (dental)
p	ph	b	bh	m	*oṣṭha* (labial)

Semivowels	y	*tālu* (palatal)
(antastha)	r	*mūrḍhā* (lingual)
	l	*danta* (dental)
	ḷa	(as substitute to ḍa - Whitney p. 19, e.g., iḍe = iḷe)
	v	*oṣṭha* (labial)
Sibilants	ś	*tālu* (palatal)
	ṣ	*mūrdhā* (lingual)
	s	*danta* (dental)
Aspiration	h	*kaṇṭha* (throat)

The important parts of the mouth, producing different sounds, as indicated in Fig. 11.3 are:

Root of the chest (*uromūla*) (aspirate *visarga*) ḥ-(ha or ḥa):

a. Beginning of throat (*kaṇṭha mūla*), (*kaṇṭhya*) (a, ka)

b. & c. Root of the tongue, (*jihva mūlīya*), (ka)

d. Middle of the tongue (*jihva madhya*), (ya)

e. Front of the tongue (*dantya*) (*ta, da*)

f. Tip of the tongue (*jihvāgra*) (*ra, la*).

When sound-breath-material passes through

1. *Kaṇṭhya*–at middle of vocal cavity–*ha* sound
2. Between two lips (labials) – *oṣṭya* (*pa, ma* sounds)
3. Between teeth (sibilants) – (*śa, sa, ṣa* sounds)
4. At the roof of mouth – (*mūrdhā*) (*mūrdhanya*) (*ṭa, ḍa* etc.)
5. At hard palate (*tālavya*), *i*
6. At palatals (root of teeth) *c, cha, ja,* etc.

The nasal passages produce nasal sounds (*nāsikya*) and sonant nasals (*ṅa, ña, ṇa, na, ma*), etc., etc.

Vowels are matters of sound-shapes. A vowel itself is *svara* (*a iti, ā, iti svarāḥ,* (*Ṛktantra*-1.2). A consonant is an obstructed *svara.* For instance, *ka* is obstructed *a,* and *pi* is an obstructed sound of *i,* etc. Sound *ā* and the sound *ī* are opposite sounds in mouth structure (as discussed in Chapters Four and Five under the issue as to modification of sound). The sound *ā* is pronounced at the lower jaw at A-B line, (Fig.11.4), whereas the sound *ī* is pronounced at the centre of the palate at C. If point A of A-B line and point B of A-B line is joined with point C at the palate, it takes a "a triangular form phenomenon" in the mouth. The sound *ū* is at the middle of the triangle or mouth; and other syllables are placed as indicated in the triangle. The vowel-sounds also get modified in euphonic combination (or conjunction) with other vowels resulting in dipthongs, like *e, o, ai, au,* etc. Thus, the vowel-sounds get distributed between those two opposite *svaras ā* and *ī* in the triangle phenomenon as indicated in Fig.11.4 :

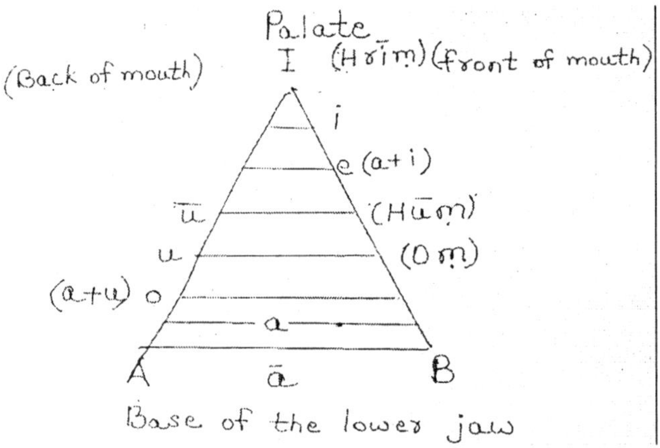

Fig. 11.4

In a technical sense, *svara* is used in three contexts, as pointed out by *Nāradīyaśikṣā* : *ārcika svara, sāmika svara,* and *gāthika svara.*[29] Of the three, (1) *ārcika svaras* are the one used in accentuating *ṛcas* (*Ṛgvedic* hymns). (2) *Sāmika svaras* are used in singing *ṛcas* (*Ṛgvedic* hymns) and such *ṛcas* are called *sāmans* (or melodic hymns). (3) *svaras* used in music (*gītī*) are called *gāthika svaras.* Of the three, *ārcika svara,* as stated above would be discussed as part of linguistic or colloquial (*bhāṣātmaka*) applications of *nāda,* and the other two, namely, *sāmika* and *gāthika svaras,* in substance being of musical nature, can be taken together as part of musical applications.

(b) Vedic (*ārcika*) applications

Aārcika svaras:

The principle and practice of three *svaras* (*traiśvarya*) (*udātta*, *anudātta*, and *svarita*) appear to be very much in vogue during the Vedic and *brāhamaṇa* period, under different phrases like *tisraḥ vācaḥ* or *traiśvarya*, etc. *Ṛgveda* described them as *tisraḥ vācaḥ*[30].

While commenting on *Sāmaveda Saṃhita*, (Sā. V. 1.5.2.471),[31] Griffith observed that, though Sāyaṇa had commented on it, as three praises in three Vedas, yet this phrase may mean the three tones (*udātta, anudātta* and *svarita*). He further said that even Prof. Ludwig suggested the three vocal tones under the phrase *israḥ vācaḥ*. I think Griffith appears to be right in view of further elaboration of the phrase *israḥ vācaḥ* in *Sāmaveda* (2.5.1 (2).1206)[32] : "At your effusion upward rise three voices fresh and strong....". Griffith commenting on the phrase "three voices" fresh and strong stated that "....Three different tones of voice may be intended." The three tones are *udātta, anudātta* and *svarita*.

Even in *brāhamaṇas*, the importance of these "three-tones-mode accentuation" is very much stressed. It appears that this method of using "three tones" was considered by itself a science, known as *Niṣkaivalya Śastra*. In the words of Pingale, Pratibha M., "A passage from the *Aitareya brāhmaṇa* ....explains the way of recitation of the *Niṣkaivalya Śāstra*....The passage tells us about the four different tones *ucca*, *nīca*, *madhyma*, and *svaravat*." *Svaravat* here means that "It is to be recited with sonorous speech.... (Ait. Br.iii. 2.24)."[33] From these *brāhmaṇas*, it is clear that the recitation of Vedic *mantra* should be not only with three *svaras* – *udātta*, *anudātta* and *svarita*, but it should also be "sonorous" with sweet voice (*svaravat*).

But a fundamental question raised among the scholars is: What exactly is the nature of these *svaras* – *udātta*, *anudātta* and *svarita*?

It is pointed out by *Yudhiṣṭhira Mīmāṃsaka* that "The delicate and intricate nature of Vedic accentuation is found to be lost. It may still be possible to find old persons, in certain families traditionally following *Ṛgvedic* practices, knowing the intricacies of such *udāttādi svaras*."[34] It appears, by the time *śikṣās* and *prātiśākhyās* were written the persons well-versed in these *svaras* (*svaraśāstrajñas*) had become scares. Hence, it appears, with the help of a few chanters available at that time, the writers of *śikṣās* and *prātiśākhyās* made a serious attempt to ascertain the nature of pronunciation of these *svaras*, and after knowing them they reduced them to writing in the form of "rules" for the guidance of future progeny, hoping that, in case they are lost completely, some persons would be able to reproduce them with the help of these rules. But to my surprise, I find that so far we have not been lucky enough to find such a person or persons, who can chant the Vedic *mantras*, according to the rules found in *śikṣās* and *prātiśākhyās*, inspite of all possible efforts on the part of Indian and foreign scholars. Human experience tells us that it is the attempt and the attempt alone that has helped the science to grow from vague ideas to more and more concrete principles. In this view of the matter, the theory that the earth was flat has not gone futile, since it has paved the way for the correct theory later.

There is no dispute that *ārcika svaras* are mainly three: *udātta, anudātta*, and *svarita*. Regarding the nature of these *svaras*, as stated by me above, there is considerable dispute among Vedic scholars.

Some have identified *udātta* as acute or high tone, on the basis of the rule–*uccairudāttaḥ*, and *anudātta* as low tone (or grave tone), taking the clue from the rule–*nīcairanudāttaḥ*. But they could not ascertain decisively *svarita* which the rule describes as *samāhāraḥ svaritaḥ* (the mixture of the two is *svarita*). Pāṇini's *Aṣṭādhyāyī* also gave the same description of *udātta, anudātta* and *svarita*. D. Whitney, by taking the dictionary meaning of *samāhāra* as combination, translated *svarita* as "circumflex", yet could not help but surmise: "This rule is so far ambiguous that it does not tell us in what order the acute and grave tones are to be combined to produce the circumflex accent, whether acute and grave, or grave and acute; but we may perhaps assume that the treatise consciously intends them to be taken in the order in which they are defined by the two preceding."[35] From this statement, it is clear that, on the basis of mere dictionary meaning of these words, it is difficult to ascertain the nature of these *svaras*. According to me the clue as to the nature of these *svaras* lie in understanding what *svarita* is, since admittedly, according to all the texts, it is the combination (*samāhāra*) of *udātta* and *anudātta svaras.* Owing to the failure to comprehend the true nature of this *svarita* has resulted in not getting the true nature of the other two *svaras*, namely, *udātta* and *anudātta* and, consequently lead to different theories.

My survey of relevant literature suggested to me that, broadly, there are about three theories regarding the nature of these "three *svaras*":

1. They are three tones, according to Strangways – "The raised" (*udātta*) and "not raised" (*anudātta*) sounds, represent the two main pitches of the speaking voice, this is the prose accent of *brāhmaṇas*.... "In addition to these two there was, for the reciting voice, the 'sounded' tone (*svarita*)...."[36]

2. They are of predominantly musical *svaras* referable to three *svaras* of music:

   a. According to Siddheśvara Varma[37] and Vidhāta Miśra[38], in the ascending order–equal to modern *svaras–re, ma, pa,* etc. as in musical *svaras.* (At the same time the possibility that they refer also to linguistic accents cannot be excluded.)

   b. But according to Rājeśvara Miśra[39] and G.H. Tarlekar[40], they are musical *svaras* in descending order – *pa, ma, re,* or *sa, ni, dha,* etc. as in *sāmagāna* practice.

3. They are linguistic accents arising at three places of mouth; as if the mouth is divided into three parts.[41] The same is the opinion of *Uvvaṭa*.[42]

But, in my opinion the learned scholars, who advocated the Theories No. 1 and 2, have not properly appreciated the type of schemes as proposed by *Nāradīyaśikṣā*, on which they heavily rely. As *Nāradīyaśikṣā* puts it, there are three kinds of *svaras* in Indian phonetics (*svara śāstra*): 1) *ārcika svara*, 2) *sāmika svara* and 3) *gāthic svara*. Broadly speaking, in fact, there are only two kinds of *svaras* (*dhvani viśeṣataḥ*) : one accentuating type (used in *ārcika*) and the other singing *svaras* used in *sāmika* and *gāthic*. So far as *sāmika* and *gāthic svaras* are concerned, they are the same seven *svaras* used under two sets of names with different order. *Sāmika svaras* like *kṛṣṭa*, etc., were used in the descending order, and *gāthic svaras* like *ṣaḍja*, *ṛṣabha*, etc., were used in the ascending order. But the fact remains that both of them accepted seven *svaras* with different names and in different orders. But the use of three *svaras*, like *uras* (chest-*mandra*), *kaṇṭha* (throat-*madhya*) and *śiras* (palate-*tāra*); and also three *svaras* like *udātta*, *anudātta* and *svarita*, etc., were only in *pravacana vidhi* (the mode of pronunciation of prose).[43] To make such a pronunciation beautiful (*kaṇṭha-kalā-pravṛtteṣu*), *Nāradīyaśikṣā* suggests the reciting of *Ṛgveda* and *Sāmaveda*, in *prathamā svara* (*madhyama svara* of music); and it further says that the use of *dvitīya* (*gāndhāra*) and *tritīya* (*ṛṣabha* of music *svaras*), etc., such recitation becomes more enjoyable and great (*pārthivaḥ*).[44] While singing, as cautioned by *Nāradīyaśikṣa*

(1.8.5), the distinction between *udātta*, etc., *svaras* and seven musical *svaras* has to be maintained by listening to musical *svaras* by the right ear and *udātta*, etc., *svaras* by the left ear (1.8.5).

Thus, it is clear that the three *svaras* (as *udātta*, etc.), were linguistic and not musical. Moreover, those who take *udātta*, etc., as musical *svaras* cannot explain *svarita* as a mixture (*samāhāra*) of the other two. Because in music it cannot be said that a particular *svara*, say *gāndhāra*, is a mixture of *madhyama* (a preceding *svara*) and *ṛṣabha* (the succeeding *svara*).

In this view of the matter, I think the third view is acceptable. According to this view, the three *svaras* are linguistic and accentual, and are identified with the place of their pronunciation at three different parts of the vocal organs. All the rules pertaining to these "three *svaras*" can be satisfactorily explained and applied and demonstrated on the basis of this view. For instance, *Ṛgveda Prātiśākhya* defines these three *svaras* – *udātta*, *anudātta* and *svarita*, as follows:

"The *svaras* are three: *udātta*, *anudātta* and *svarita*. They arise at higher place, with muscular tension (*āyāma*), at lower place with relaxed muscular tension (*viśrambha*) and at middle (*ākṣepa* = drawing together)".[45] Commenting on this verse Uvvaṭa stated as follows:

"The *svaras* that arise on account of (vocal muscles drawing up) (*āyāma*) (and accordingly) the breath flowing at upper part of vocal organs is called *udātta*, e.g., *e*, *i*, etc. The *svara* that arises on account of relaxed vocal organ (*viśrambha*), the breath flowing at the lower part of vocal organs is called *anudātta*, e.g., *naḥ*, *nau*, etc. A *svara*, drawing together or going together (*ākṣaipaḥ*) (with the other *svaras*, namely, *udātta* and *anudātta*) due to the breath flowing horizontal in the middle (*tiryak*) of the (vocal organs), is called *svarita*."[46]

Even Patañjali uses the words "high" and "low" with reference to various parts of vocal organs.[47] His commentator Kayyaṭa clarified that *ucca* meant "the higher part of the articulating organ, by coming into contact with breath, is called into play."[48] Nāgeśa's commentary thereon also stated that it meant "the conjunction of breath at the upward part of (vocal organs).[49] According to these authorities, it is a particular part of the articulating organs that constitutes a fixed standard for determining whether the accent is high or low, and that is invariable factor of the production of accent." [50] In other words, these three *svaras* are matters of their respective accent, taking place at a particular part of the vocal organs. They are mainly three *svaras* accented at three places of the vocal organ – *udātta* at the upper part, *anudātta* at the lower part and *svarita* at the middle of the mouth. These *svaras* are due to the special effort of controlling the vocal organ (*āyāma gātrāṇāṃ nigraha*) that a *svara* is produced at a particular place of the mouth, that effort consists in making the "breath-sound-material" to pass through at a particular place in the vocal organs. It is an effort of placing the voice at the upper, lower and middle of the mouth. In other words, it is that part of vocal organ with which a particular *svara* is associated. *Udātta* is not only the higher part of the vocal organ but it is a sound arising at the higher part of the vocal organ. *Uccairudāttaḥ* means a *svara* arising at the higher part of the vocal organ. In fact, both "tones" and "particular part of the mouth" go together in the production of these *svaras*. When a tone is placed at the higher part of vocal organ, it is called *udātta* and when a tone is placed at the lower part of the mouth, it is called *anudātta*, and when it is placed at the middle of the mouth, it is called *svarita*. Therefore, *uccairudāttaḥ* cannot be understood as "higher tone", and *nīcairanudāttaḥ* also cannot be understood as a "lower tone", as mistakenly thought of by both Indian and Western scholars. In fact, our ancient scholars repeatedly warned against such a possible mistaken notions arising from these *sūtras*. *Nāradīyaśikṣā* (1.8.6 and 7), among others, clearly declared that "Though we call *udātta* as high *svara* and *anudātta* as low *svara*, still there is nothing higher than the high *svara* nor lower than the low *svara*. Know that these are special (*vaiśvarya*) *svaras* (*dhvanis*) only are (used as) signs (*saṃjña*). Therefore (*kim*), the place (*sthānaṃ*) itself is taken as *svara* (*dhvani* or *śruti*) – *sthānaṃ svara ucyate*."[51] *Yājñavalkyaśikṣā* puts the same idea differently, and says – "When it is said high, it is not higher; when it is said low, it is neither lower, these *svaras* go along with the accents of the syllables (Yā. Śi.58)". In other words, these *svaras* (*udātta*, etc., are the *svaras* of three places), go along with the eight places of pronunciation of syllable in the mouth as per rules of *Pāṇini* (*kaṇṭhya*, *oṣṭya*, etc., eight places).[52]

What is required to be emphasized here is that one and the same syllable is called *udātta*, if it is placed at the higher part of the vocal organs, and it is called *anudātta* if it is placed at the lower part of vocal organs, and it is called *svarita* if it is placed at the middle of the vocal organ. According to *Nāradīyaśikṣa*, in fact, they are uttered in the same tone (*śruti-sādhāraṇa*-1.8.7) common to *udātta* and *anudātta* and *svarita*. In other words, they are uttered in one and the same tone (voice) as a person has, or in any one of the musical *svaras* (say in *ṣaḍja*). Hence, the concept of "high", "low", etc., used in this context, has nothing to do with "pitch" in the sense musicians use.

When *udātta* and *anudātta* join (*samāveśa*) in a syllable, there emerges a third *svara* called *svarita*.[53] *Svarita* is a new *svara* arising due to the dual effort (*dviyaman*) of lower and upper part of the vocal organs.[54] It is the joining (*samāhāra*) of two efforts in one place. When a syllable is uttered at the middle of the mouth, it is uttered in *svarita svara*. The upper half of *svarita* sounds like *udātta* and the lower half like *anudātta*.[55] Thus, being the mixture of two *svaras*, *svarita* has the characteristics of both *udātta* and *anudātta*. But what kind of mixture is it? According to Uvvaṭa it is not mixture like milk and water but it is like mixture of *til* (sesamum indicum) and rice. In other words, it is not an inseparable mixture like milk and water (*nīra-kṣīra*) but separable like wood (*kāṣṭa*) and lac or gum (*jat*). In other words this mixture gives rise to a new *svara* alright but not a new substance like brass (*kānsyakam*), being the mixture of lead (*trapu*) and copper (*tāmra*). That means, they are separable with little effort.

It is in this sense *Atharva Prātiśākhya* and Pāṇini's *Aṣṭādhyāyī* stated *samāhāraḥ svarītaḥ* (*svarita* is mixture of the two, viz. *udātta* and *anudātta*) generally translated as "circumflex". In the Fig. 11.5 the top red line represents *udātta svara* and the down blue line represents *anudātta* and the middle "parallel lines" of "red and blue" represent *svarita* (the mixture of *udātta* and *anudātta*).

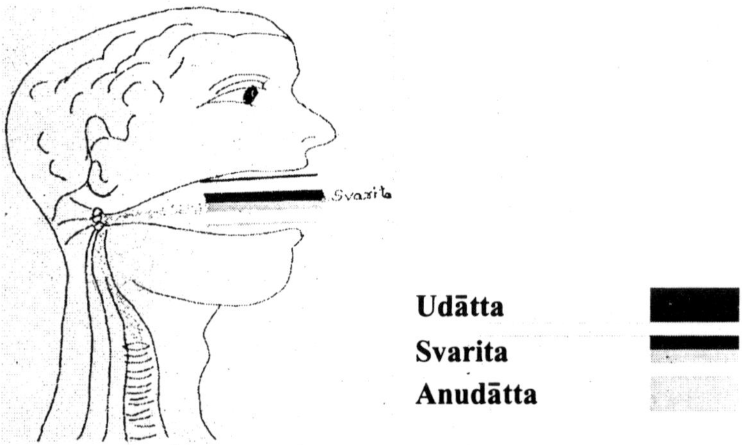

Fig. 11.5

These *udātta*, etc., *svaras* are basically only three.[56] But in *saṃhitā-pāṭha* (euphonic combination) owing to modifications (*vikāra*), they assume more than three forms. Presumably in this sense, *Nārada* considers them, ultimately, to be of five varieties as *udātta*, *anudātta*, *svarita*, *pracita*, and *nighāta*.[57] Of these, *pracita* or *pracaya* is another name of *ekaśruti*, whereas *nighāta* is lower than *anudātta*. However, according to other scholars, *nighāta* is the same as *anudātta*.

For some, the *pracaya* is formed out of *svarita* and *anudātta*. A *svara* lower than *anudātta* is called *sannatara* in *Aṣṭādhyāyī*,[58] which Patañjali calls *anudāttatara*.

In fact, Patañjali considered them to be of seven varieties as *udātta*, *udāttatara*, *anudātta*, *anudāttatara*, *svarita*, *svaritoudātta* (as forming a part of *svarita* differing from the other *udātta*), *ekśruti*.[59] *Nārada* clarified by saying that the second *udātta* (which comes after *svarita*, as per Patañjali) is itself called *pracaya* by the experts[60] and it is not an independent *svara* as such.

Fig. 11.6
Udātta

Fig. 11.7
Anudātta

Fig. 11.8
Svarita

If that is so, the so-called five varieties or eight varieties of *svaras*, in fact, arise out of the basic three *svaras* – *udātta*, *anudātta* and *svarita*. Hence we can safely take it for granted that there are only three *svaras* as *udātta*, *anudātta* and *svarita* and these *svaras* can be explained with reference to their places in the mouth with the help of Figs.11.6, 11.7 and 11.8, as above.

Such three tier *svaras* can be produced with vocal chords, neither too wide (*vivṛt*) nor too closed (*saṃvṛt*). When the vocal chords are too close, tone is created and when they are wide open, breath is produced. (*samvṛt kaṇṭe nādaḥ kriyate, vivṛte svāsaḥ*)[61] The "tone" (*śabdaḥ*) is the basic physical sound (*prakṛtiḥ*) of all the syllables (*śabdaḥ prakṛtiḥ sarvavarṇānām*).[62] The tension (*āyāmaḥ*), hardness (*dāruṇyam*), smallness of aperture (*aṇutā*), are the producers of high tone (*ucca svara* or *udātta*).[63] Relaxation (*anvavasargaḥ*), softness (*mārdavam*), wideness of aperture (*urutā svasya*) are the producers of low tone.[64] With the help of these techniques, the three Vedic *svaras* (*traīsvarāḥ*)–*udātta, anudātta* and *svarita*–are uttered. *Ṛgveda-Prātiśākhya* further cautions that while producing the *udātta svaras,* etc., there should not be any tremor in voice. *Udātta* should not be too high and *anudātta* should not be too low in the mouth, and *svarita* should not be stretched too much low, (i.e., it shall be retained at the middle). In other words, the opening of the mouth should be moderate and neither should it be too wide nor too approximated.[65]

Thus, unanimously accepted *svaras* are only three – *udātta, anudātta* and *svarita,* and accordingly we may take these three *svaras* for the purpose of our application. The nature of these tripartite *svaras* (*traisvaryam*) are based mainly on the vowels of the syllables. They are not dependent on "tone" or "pitch",[66] but are dependent on syllables (*akṣarāśrayāḥ*).[67] These *svaras* follow the accent of syllables. These *svaras* can be demonstrated with reference to a *vedic mantra,* by taking the clue from the signs assigned to the syllables, in the Veda. The composers of Veda have indicated *udātta,* etc., *svaras* with different types of "signs". I propose to adopt the one followed in *Ṛgveda.* In *Ṛgveda,* no sign is assigned to *udātta*. *Anudātta* is indicated by a horizontal line below the syllable, and *svarita* is indicated by a verticle line above the syllable. Let us take a part of Vedic hymn for demonstration with such signs as under:

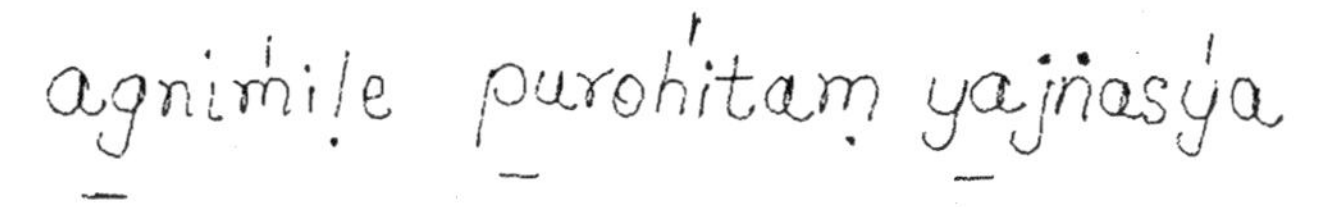

Fig. 11.9. (R.V.1.1.1)

"I glorify Agni the high priest of the sacrifice".[68] This *mantra* can be explained in terms of *udātta*, etc., *svaras* by arranging the syllables in a tabular form as per the accentuations of the syllables, indicated by the signs, at different parts of the mouth, as under:

Udātta -		gni				ro		*taṃ*		*jña*	
Svarita -			mi	ḷe			hi				sya
Anudātta -	a				pu				ya		

Fig. 11.10

The object of such *udātta*, etc., *svaras* like that of grammar has been primarily to preserve the Vedic texts and their correct pronunciations by utilizing all the parts of the mouth, so as to pronounce syllables, words and sentences clearly; and to avoid the calamities arising out of erroneous utterances like *Indraśatru*. "When the word *Indraśatru* is recited as having an accent on its final member, it becomes a *bahuvṛhi* compound, meaning Indra, who is the destroyer (of demons). If the word is recited as having the accent on its initial member, it becomes a *tatpuruṣa*.... It will then mean the destroyer of Indra. ....Since the demons, while chanting *mantra* employed the wrong accent (in *bahuvṛhi*) meaning Indra, who is the destroyer (of demons), accordingly they met with disaster".[69]

B. Musical Applications - *Sāmika* and *Gāthic svaras*

According to our ancient phonetic texts (Nā. Śi.8.8 & Pā. Śi.11), the musical *svaras* arise out of the three Vedic *svaras*, viz., *udātta*, *anudātta* and *svarita*. From *udātta* arises *gāndhāra* and *niṣāda*, from *svarita* – *ṣaḍja*, *madhyama* and *pañcama*, and from *anudātta* – *ṛṣabha* and *dhaivata*. As I have explained above, *udātta*, etc., *svaras* are matters of three places in the human mouth – *udātta* at the upper part, *anudātta* at the lower part and *svarita* in the middle. It means that the musical *svaras* arise at these three places. The same can be explained with the help of a diagram at Fig.11.11.

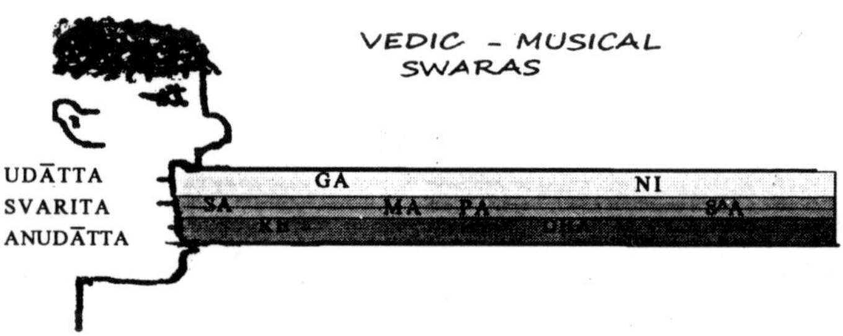

Fig. 11.11

The voice required for musical applications would be slightly different from the voice required for linguistic communications. For musical applications it has to be more "tenacious" and "resonant". With sustained breath for long, one can stretch a *svara* for a long duration. According to our music *paṇḍits* and *ustāds*, the long stretching of the voice would enable the artist to create varieties of melodic patterns and as per our ancient seers, such sustaining breath for a long duration ensured longevity of life also.[70]

Musical voice should also be 'resonant' (*anuraṇātmaka*). Resonance, according to Khanna and Bedi, is "forced vibrations greatly exceeding those which would be due to the pressure changes actually occurring and resulting from the accumulated pressure impulses...called 'sympathetic or resonant forced vibrations......"[71] It is like prolonged vibrating sound that of a *veeṇa* after being struck with a finger. The *Sanskṛt* word *anuraṇana*, in a literal sense, means the sound that follows; in musicology it means 'harmonics' or 'overtones', for instance, when violin strings are made to vibrate, they produce overtones. According to our ancient phoneticians, the five kinds of vital airs viz. *prāṇa*, *apāna*, *samāna*, *udāna*, and *vyāna*, that are present in the human body, make it a resonant body.[72] Such a human body does the same function as a pumpkin does to a *sitāra* or *tambūrā*. See Fig. 11.12.

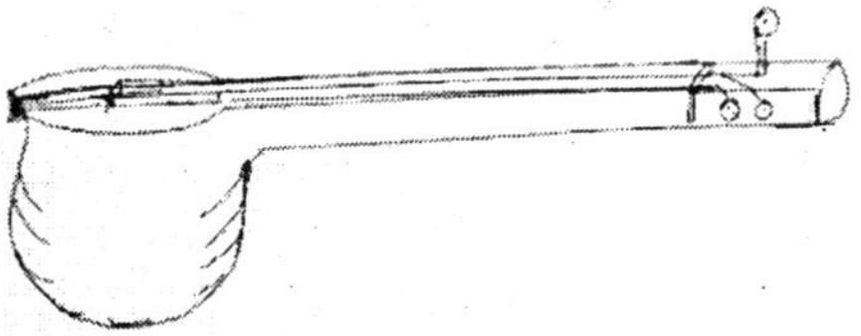

Fig. 11.12

Fig. 11.13

The frogs too have an air-sack just below the jaws, and such "Vocal sacks have been considered primarily as sound resonating chambers for sound production...."[73] (Fig. 11.13).

To make the voice resonant, our ancient phoneticians suggested certain methods. Nānyabhūpāla suggests a simple method. According to him, while uttering a nasalized *ākāra* with a slightly closed mouth by allowing sound-breath material to pass through bottom of the teeth, it sounds like *alābuveeṇā.* With regulated loose muscular-control the nasalised *ā* breath while making its exit it would present a sonorous and soft (*mridu*) voice.[74] In Shatapatha *brāhmaṇa*, still a simpler method of producing resonance voice is suggested: "before reciting enkindling verses, one has to pronounce the *hūṃkāra* (the sound *hūṃ*); but it must be pronounced inaudibly."[75] "One should mix *rica* and *oṃ* just like parched grains are mixed with honey".[76] Such a voice with *oṃ* becomes resonant.

This meaningless *hūṃ* sound also consists of breath in the form of *ha* and nasal sound *ṃ* plus *ū.* The nasal tinge in the form of *anusvāra* with *ṃ* makes the voice resonant. However, there is always the danger of its becoming fully nasalized (*nāsikya*), and that would be one of the defects in voice, according to both phoneticians and musicians, that should be avoided. *Anusvāra* is different from *nāsikya* in the sense that in *nāsikya*, the voice "finds its exit from the nasal passage, the mouth being almost closed. In *anusvāra*, on the other hand, the mouth-organs are not wholly closed, but the intonated breath finds exit through the mouth and the nasal cavity, simultaneously."[77] The *anusvāra ṃ* should be used only as a flavor in a very small quantity. To indicate this nature of *ṃ* sometimes half moon symbol (*m̐*) is used. Without *m̐* also one can sing, but such a voice is considered to be defective, as it would be dry (*śuṣka*).

Om̐ by itself is the modification *hūm̐*.[78] Both *hūm̐kāra* and *om̐kāra* make the voice *rakta* (lit. coloured) enchanting, loving, and enjoyable. Because of its composition A+U+M, it starts as *bindu* at the middle of the mouth, between two lips; and with the help of resonants generated by the nasal cavity, it occupies the whole of mouth, and it becomes versatile in its applications for different purposes. (See Fig. 11.14.)

Fig. 11.14

This idea has been beautifully carved on a marble stone, placed at the ceiling, at the main entrance of a Jaina temple, in Raṇakpur in Rajasthān. This piece of art is described as *Kalpa Lata* (heavenly creeper) by Mahopadhyaya Lalitprabha

Sagar.[79] But as per my interpretation, it is *oṃ* resonant-phenomenon starting from *bindu*, in the lower middle of the mouth; indicated by the smallest circle at the bottom of the architecture. (See Fig. 11.15.)

Fig. 11.15

Courtesy: Temple authorities of Raṇakpur (Rajasthan); 1439 A.D.

Having noticed its quality that it adds melody to the Vedic text *Vājasaneyī Prātiśākhya* (or *Śuklayajurprātiśākhya*) has laid down a rule that the word *om* is to be employed while studying or reciting the Veda.[80] A Buddhist text *Bṛhaṭ Purascaryārṇava* (1972) (p. 218), found in Kaṭhamaṇḍu also advocates the employment of *hūṃ* – *hūṃantaḥ stambhane mantraḥ*, (a *mantra* ending in *hūṃ* indicates a chant for imposing motionlessness on someone).[81] *Vājasaneyī Prātiśākhya* (or *Śuklayajurprātiśākhya*) also laid down another rule that, before reading prose, one should start with *athakāra-athakāraṃ bhāṣyeṣu* (Vāj. Prā.1.19). There is a wisdom behind these rules – *om vedeṣu* and *athakāraṃ bhāṣyeṣu*. In *a* and *aum*, there is one common element and that is *a-kāra*. This *a* has to be uttered by either "upper jaw" or "lower jaw" – one at a time, as per one's own choice. When the lower jaw is used to utter *a* or *ā*, one feels as if the lower jaw has grown wider than the upper jaw. Conversely, when one is using the upper jaw, there would be a feeling that the lower jaw has shrunken. It is also a fact that when one jaw moves quickly in utterances of syllables or *svaras*, it does so, with the muscular support of the other jaw. There would be a feeling that the other jaw is fixed and static, and acting as the controller of the former. That is a sheer biological phenomenon in which the mouth would take a shape of a "bow", which can easily create a triangular sound phenomenon in the vocal cavity. The wider jaw would become the base for which the shrinking jaw would create a point in the middle, so as to create a triangle. There can also be an utterance with both jaws held together, but such an utterance produces a "monotone". But for the utterance of multiple letters, one has to revert back either to the lower jaw or to the upper Jaw. Sri G.U. Thite in his book "Music in the Vedas – Its Magico-Religious Significance", has given an instance, by referring to *Śatapathabrāhmaṇa* which highlighted the use of these jaws in *darśapūṇamāsa* sacrifices.[82]

In the case of pronunciation of either *a* or *auṃ*, either with the lower jaw or the upper jaw, a triangular phenomenon automatically gets manifested, and this phenomenon enables the human mouth to produce a variety of sounds.

This *oṃ*, according to the Indian traditions, is a manifester of *trikoṇa* or triangle. It is believed, as Daivarāta, the author of *Vedārthakalpalatā* puts it, that *Praṇava* as *Oṁkāra*, in a triangular form, manifests three *vyāhṛties-bhūr*, *bhuvaḥ* (*bhuvar*), *svaḥ* (*svar*).[83] According to *Tantrāgama* philosophers also, out of the triangle form, that is emerged out of *oṃkāra*, all creation and all the words to describe them arise concomitantly. *Parā*, *paśyanti* and *madhyamā* are born out of this triangle. Cidvalli, the commentary on *Kāmakalā Vilāsa*, while commenting on Verse 25 stated that 'It is ancient (*purāṇa*) and is the *Praṇava* itself. It can be known by three lines (*rekhātraya*) (or *trikoṇa*) (which compose it). It is pure knowledge (*saṃvit mātra*) and is of the nature of Śiva.[84] From all these texts it is clear that *oṃ* manifests "triangle", a source of *nāma-rūpa* principle manifesting the objects and the words. My vocal experiment also reveals to me that while pronouncing *oṃ*, automatically, a "triangular phenomenon" gets manifested in the mouth.

For Aumāpatam, by the grace of Śaṃbhu, Devi becomes the cause of *nāda* at *mūlādhāra* taking a triangle form, and out of the said metaphysical triangle arises a triangular-phenomenon in the mouth, out of which emerge *dhvani* (sound), *śabda* (word), and *udātta*, etc., *svaras* and all other musical *svaras*.

Musical voice should be capable of producing all the seven *svaras* easily. The human throat is the most suitable for that purpose. Of all the animals, no other animal except birds, especially songbirds, appear to be nearer to human's singing ability. In this context, it would be appropriate to note the observations made by an eminent ornithologist, Donald E. Kroodsma–"Vocal learning appears to have reached a pinnacle in humans and in (song) birds, the parallels in ontogeny, nervous control, and population consequences of vocal learning between humans and birds are intriguing" (p. 2). "The phenomenon of vocal learning seems pervasive among birds, but it is especially pronounced among song birds" (p. 18).[85]

But the question is, "Why is it so?" All along the scientists were making all kinds of attempts to find out the principles responsible for that kind of ability with the necessary sophisticated instruments. But those attempts have not yielded any satisfactory results. In fact, another ornithologist by name John H. Brackenbury opined that they still remained unsolved problems. He observed that, "On the problem of active sound modulations: what if any, is the role of extralyringeal structures such as the trachea, pharynx, and hyoid apparatus? What is the structural basis of the "three" and "four voice" phenomena? All these areas are in the need of experimental investigation. ....The difficult problems await solution."[86] Perhaps, keeping the difficulties in answering these and other intricate questions in view, C.G. Beer suggested an alternative, "To understand the communication system we have to go beyond what our senses and sensory adjuncts tell us to what the animals register and differentiate as signals" (at p. 290).

He also suggested the area of investigation – "The surprising discovery of lateralization of neutral control of the larynx in songbirds (Nottebohm, 1970), and subsequent developmental study showing functional plasticity in this vocal system before a certain age, helped to turn attention towards other hitherto unsuspected possibilities of parallels between birds song and human speech" (at p. 283).[87]

Taking the clue from these ornithologists, I have to answer two questions: "What is the structural basis of the 'three' and 'four' voice phenomena? (John H. Brackenbury). What are the possibilities of parallels between birds' song and humans' speech? (C.G. Beer)"

Aumāpatam's triangular theory in my opinion, satisfactorily explains the structural basis of the "three" and "four" voice phenomenon (to use John H. Brackenbury's phraseology) found in humans, and the same can be applied to song-birds, on the basis of certain "possibilities of parallels between birds' song and humans' speech."

THEORY NO. 2: VOICE PRODUCTION FOR MUSICAL APPLICATIONS

Aumāpatam explained a special mode of the production of *nāda* in the body composed of *pañca bhūtās*, and stated that, as desired by *Mahādeva*, (in the form of the soul) *nāda* arises in *mūlādhāra* in *trikoṇa* form; and this *nāda*, being pushed by air, passes through an "air-struck *trikoṇa* agni cave" (=*pavanāhata-koṇāgni-jvālāpūrita-kandaraḥ*), a narrow lane or a cave formed as if it is a "triangle", stuffed with air and fire (energy).[88] There sprouts *dhvani* with *bindu* (*ghanasvara*) at the heart. Having obtained the support from veins (*nāḍi*), the said *dhvani* rises higher; and with the help of mind, it ultimately gets the name *śabda* (*dhvani*) or *svara*, which is the generator of *śruti*, and obtains different *svaras* like *udātta*, etc. From out of these *udāttādi svaras*, there arise *ṣaḍja*, etc., seven *svaras*[89], and *niṣāda* arises as if the one born at the end of a triangle (*koṇāvasānabhāvāttu niṣādaḥ*).[90] Explaining the creative power of that "triangular phenomena", Śankarācārya praised Devi in his *Soundaryalaharī*: "O Devi! Because of the function of three lines (*rekhāstisro gati*) (forming *trikoṇa*) in your throat, made you an expert in *gamaka*, and *gīta*, and made you shine in varied forms of sweet *rāgās* of all the three *grāmas* of music, manifesting your unlimited existence." [91]

The close observation of human mouth reveals that the internal part of the mouth is such that it can create a phenomenon of triangular form. One can draw a straight horizontal line at the lower jaw.

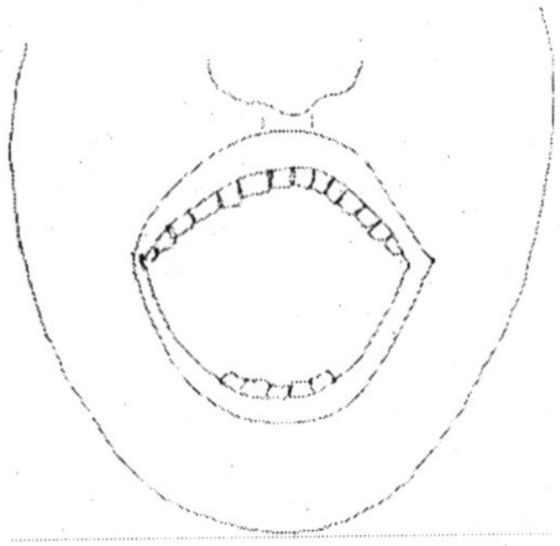

Fig. 11.16

The semi-circular shape at the upper part of the jaw (palate) has a central point where refracted and reflected sound waves can create a "central point", and the said central point can be joined with the two ends of the horizontal line at the lower jaw. Thus it takes the shape of a triangle. Even the semi-circular shape of the lower jaw also is helpful in creating such triangular phenomenon of the reverse shape. See Fig.11.16. But one has to choose either the upper jaw or the lower jaw at a time for the purpose of singing. This triangle shape phenomenon enables the human mouth to produce varied tones by modifying the volume of the "sound-breath-material". Elastic muscles enable us the modification of the sound-breath-material, in the triangular "phonetic-structure" created in the mouth, so as to produce different tones. In musical *svaras* (tones) this "sound-breath-material" gradually gets reduced under the muscular pressure, in upward movements, in between the tongue and the palate. It cannot be disputed that one particular flexible mass (of sound-breath-material) can produce vibrations of a particular frequency. If the volume or mass of this medium is reduced gradually in upward movement, it produces a sound of higher frequencies with higher muscular pressure, that means a higher *svara*. By reducing the volume of the given mass in a particular proportion in the ascending order, we can produce the *svaras* of higher and higher frequencies until we reach the seventh *svara* – in the order of *sa, re, ga, ma, pa, dha, ni*; and this becomes possible, because of the triangular phenomenon, created in mouth.

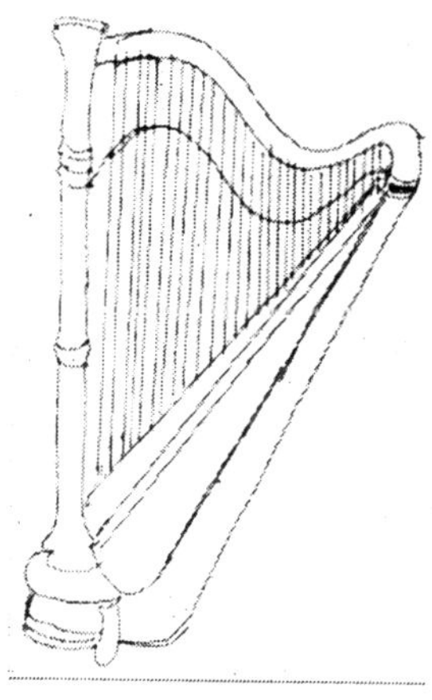

Fig. 11.17. Harp

(*Courtesy:* Jean-Claude Corbeil, The Facts on File, Visual Dictionary; Facts on File Publications, p. 464; (1986); New York.)

All the musical instruments apply this triangular phenomenon in different forms. For example, "harp" is made on the basis of this principle only. (See Fig.11.17.)

In parrots also comes the same position, but with fewer options of lesser quantity and quality, and with better ease, because of its natural triangular shape of its mouth. Parrots' mouth being of a triangular shape both in lower jaw and upper jaw (similar to diamond shape) enables it to produce different tones by squeezing the sound-breath-material with the help of the jaws and the tongue between the upper and the lower beaks; starting with larger volume of sound-breath-material at the lower jaw and ending with a very small volume of such material at the top of the mouth. The birds (including "songbirds") have this kind of mouth. Other factors like necessary development in brain, genetic factors and good ears for feedback, etc., cannot be ignored at the same time. It is also a fact that the process of tone production and sound modulation, both in birds and in human beings is not available for perception with eyes or with the help of any sophisticated instrument; and accordingly, what transpires in the mouth, only the singer feels and knows, just like the wearer knows where the shoe pinches.

The human mouth being bigger in size, with more effective muscular control is highly sophisticated and versatile than that of the birds. Those animals with projected and long mouth like buffaloes and horses, etc., cannot get the triangle phenomena in their mouth since they can produce only "monotones" with the help of their vocal chords and two jaws forming a "single resonant tube."[92] Hence, the ability to create triangular phenomenon in mouth is, thus, responsible for the musical ability of man and song birds. (See Fig. 11.18 and 11.19.)

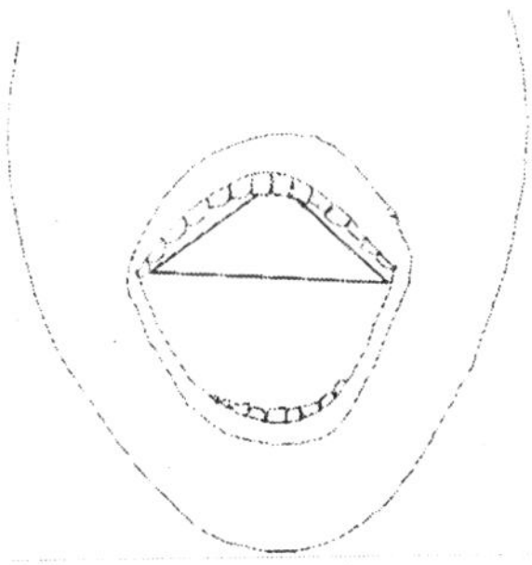

Fig. 11.18

Fig. 11.19

Such a triangular or a diamond shape in the mouth provides the structural basis for the "three" and "four" voice phenomena both in man and in birds. This kind of phenomena is helpful in producing both syllabic *svaras* and musical *svaras*. However, the nature of these two *svaras* would be different. Syllabic *svaras* are uttered with relaxed muscular tension generally in one tone (*śruti*) by modifying *svaras*, with the help of the tongue by diverting the sound-breath-material, through different parts of mouth, in order to have different kinds of sound syllables. Whereas in the case of musical *svaras* the sound-breath-material is reduced by squeezing it, in between tongue and palate, in the ascending order with proportionate muscular control (*yama*) so as to produce different pitches called musical *svaras*. The sounds *ā* and *ī* are opposite sounds even as per *Nyāya Vaiśeṣika*.[93] The phonetic value of linguistic *svara*, *ā* and musical *svara sā* is almost the same, at the base of the mouth at A-B line. Likewise, the phonetic value of linguistic *svara-ī* and musical *svara-nī* at point C is the same. However, in between these two points, the sound-breath-material is processed differently for linguistic and musical purposes.

For linguistic purpose, one uniform sound-breath-material is used by passing it through different parts of mouth (to produce different syllables) with the help of tongue, whereas for musical *svaras*, sound-breath-material is squeezed, in the ascending order to produce different tones. What is important to be noted is that for both the purposes, such variations of sounds take place in a triangular phenomenon in mouth. (See Fig. 11.20.) I have elaborated this idea of triangular sonic phenomena vide Fig. 11.21 & 11.22, by separating triangle from mouth.

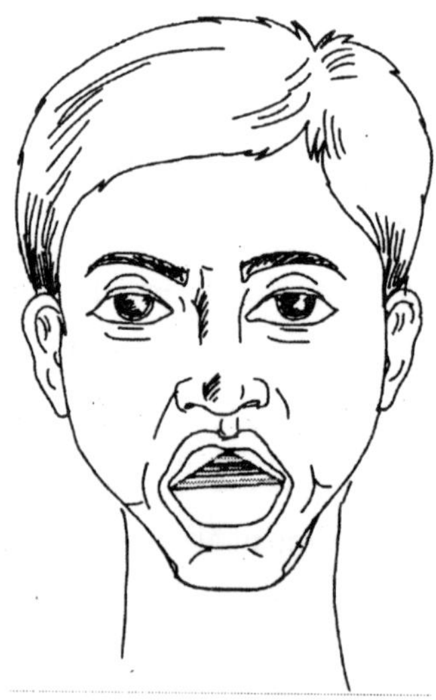

Fig. 11.20

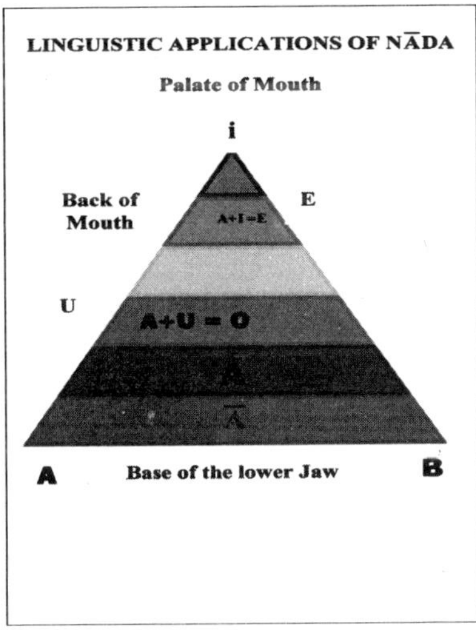

Fig. 11.21

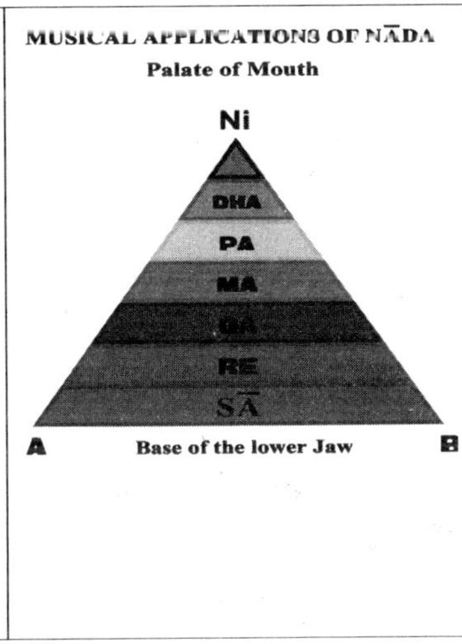

Fig. 11.22

The same is the mode of sound production, both for Vedic langauge or for *laukika* language. On the musical side also, the same is the mode of sound production in both Vedic and *laukika* music.

Vedic music was predominantly vocal. The *Ṛgvedic ṛc-s* (verses), with certain modifications (*stobhas*, by way of embellishments), were sung in melodic tones. The majority of *Sāmavedic* verses (*Sāmans*) were nothing but *ṛc-s* used for singing. They were generally called *Sāmans*. A *sāmn* is nothing but *ṛc* + melody or *svara*.

The utterance of *om* and *hūṃ* added resonance to the *Sāman* singing."The beautiful voice for the priest was considered his property. Some of the *brāhmaṇas* described such sweet voice as gold."[94] Such priests of toneful voice (*svarasampannyāṛtvijyaṃ kuryāttasmādyajñe svaravantaṃ*, etc.) were always in demand, and they used to make huge property while performing "sacrifices".[95] At any rate, by singing *Sāmans*, methodically and studying it attentively, according to *Yājñavalkya Smṛti*, one attains Brahman.[96]

I have already stated that in music, *svara* is the smallest unit of sound. There are seven such units named *ṣadja, ṛṣabha, gāndhāra, madhyam, pañcama, dhaivata* and *niṣāda*. Musicologists and the phoneticians have tried to equate these *svaras* with the voices of certain animals and birds, a sample of which I have given as under:

The peacock utters *ṣaḍja*, the bulls utter *ṛṣabha*, the sheep and goats' voice is *gāndhāra*, the bird *krauñca*, utters *madhyamā*, the voice of cuckoo is *pañcama*, the horse utters *dhaivata* and the elephant utters *niṣāda*.[97]

As opined by a number of musicologists, though there is no scientific basis for such theories, yet in my opinion these *svaras* give a rough idea about the nature of the tone, a *svara* represents, to a beginner in music or at least give him an idea that these tones indicate high and low pitch tones. The "stone" pillars in Hampi (Tq. Hospet in Bellari Dist.), producing different *svaras*, serve almost the same kind of purpose.

Music is nothing but a series of sequential *svaras* regulated by "time-patterns" called beat (*tāla*). In *laukika saṅgīta*, seven *svaras* (called *śuddha svaras*) are used along with five modified *svaras* (*vaikṛta svaras*), in different patterns for musical renderings, called *rāgas*. The *laukika saṅgīta* is used mainly for worldly enjoyment; yet by adopting it as a meditational technique, one can have both *bhukti* (enjoyment) and *mukti* (salvation).[98]

C. Aesthetic Applications of *Nāda*

Different "voice variations" can be employed for creating certain aesthetic appeal, both in the linguistic context and also in the context of musical renderings. My attempt, here, is only to show that *nāda* (sound), by itself, can cause *rasa* (aesthetic experience).

What is aesthetics?

Rasa, according to Indian philosophers, stands for 'aesthetic delight' (*anubhāva*) by which the abiding emotions (*sthāyibhāvās*) of the appreciator (*sahṛdaya*) are roused, resulting in his different moods (*vyabhicāri bhāva*). There is no art without *rasa*, nor is there *rasa* without *bhāva*. In metaphysical (*aloukika*) terminology, *rasa* itself is Brahman (*raso vai saḥ*).[99]

In India, aesthetics is known as *rasaśāstra* or *alankāraśāstra*. Indian theory of *rasa* is very much acclaimed even in the West for its delicate analysis of the shades of sentiments, which are experienced (*anubhāva*) by the spectator. According to Bharata, this *anubhāva* (a mental state) results in the *sthāyībhāva* of a particular stable sentiment called *rasa* (say a "sentiment of love" in *śṛṅgāra*). Therefore, a good artist is one who presents such *rasas* (which are eight according to Bharata and nine according to some others). The names (*saṃjña*) of such *rasas* are: *śriṅgāra*, *karuṇa*, *raudra*, *vīra*, *bhayānaka*, *bibhitsa*, *adbhuta*.[100] According to Bharata, the meaning (of the text) would not be explicit (*na hi rasādrute kaścidarthaḥ pravartate*).[101] Rasa is the cumulative result of *vibhāva* (stimulus), *anubhāva* (involuntary reaction) and *vyabhicāri bhava* (voluntary reaction). When various condiments, sauces, herbs and other materials are mixed, a taste is produced; in the same way with different *bhāvās* (emotions), the *sthāyībhāva* becomes a "taste" (*rasa* or flavour, feeling). What is this thing called *rasa*? Bharata's reply to this question is: "Because it is tasted, it is called *rasa*."[102] In day-to-day worldly life, *bhāva* is the feeling, or sentiment or disposition of the mind. *Rasa* is the product of *bhāva*. It is the *rasa* that acts as the seed of all *sthāyībhāvas* (of the spectators).[103] A *sthāyībhāva* is a lasting or durable state of mind or feeling (representing one or more of eight *rasas* and according to some, plus ninth–*śānta rasa*–the state of tranquility). Explaining the content of such an experience Prof. K.J. Shah (my respected professor, for my M.A. in Philosophy) said: "The emotional content voice variations can effectively manifest *vybhicārī bhāvā* that is the state of mood of a person (as presented in the text or poetry (or *bandhiś* in music) which causes an occasion for response (*vibhāva*) and also response in the listener (called *anubhāva*)".[104]

I wish to consider the concept underlying the phrase "the emotional content voice variations" found in the statement of Prof. Shah.

Variations of "voice-intonations", according to the *rasa* to be presented in a *rāga* of music or in dramatic presentation, is important. Such variations of the voice are called *kāku* by

Bharata Muni, and the same is being followed even today. According to Bharata, these *kākus* should be (artificially) produced to express various emotions and feelings in dramas.[105] For example, grief or distress is required to be expressed in a feeble voice[106] and the voice has got to be moderate (*mandra*), with speed (*druta*), for soothing the children (by women, etc.).[107]

Bharata Muni applied even Vedic *svaras* – *udātta*, etc., in prose-dialogues of the dramas in order to express different sentiments (*rasas*). He named the syllable (*varṇa*) by a particular *svara* which it accompanies – as *udātta varṇa*, etc. Thus according to him "there shall be four types of *varṇas* (accentuated syllable), namely, *udātta varṇa* (acute arising at the upper part of the mouth), *anudātta varṇa* (grave arising at the lower part of the mouth), and *svarita varṇa* (circumflex – arising at the middle of the mouth), and *kampita varṇa* (quivering-vacillating between two *svars*)."[108] In *hāsya* (humour) and *śṛṅgāra* (amorous), *svarita* and *udātta* syllables are to be employed in the dialogues. In *vīra* (heroic), *raudra* (terror) and *adbhūta* (wonder) *rasas*, the accents suitable are the *udātta* and *kampita*. In the *karuṇa* (pathos), *bībhatsa* (disgust) and *bhayānaka* (fear), the accents required would be *anudātta* (acute), *svarita* (circumflex) and *kampita* (quivering).[109] Thus, the utility of Vedic *udātta*, etc., *svaras* cannot be ignored even in general *Sanskṛt* language (*laukika bhāṣā*).

There are *svaras* which are part and parcel of natural human voice. A "sound", combined with articulation, is the origin of voice (*varṇāpṛktaḥ śabdaḥ vāca utpattiḥ*).[110] There are seven qualities of "voice", and they are: inaudible, murmur, whisper, mumbling, soft, middle and loud. There are also three other kinds of voices: "soft" in the chest, "middle" (*mandra*) in the throat, "loud" (*tāra*) at the (top of the mouth). They are called registers in modern musicology. There can be further variations of these tones (or voice) in different intonations with the help of muscular control (*yama*) of the breath, with the help of tongue and the jaws. Such variations of voice or tone differ as per the need of the situations to express sentiments or feelings in linguistic texts.

There are some natural voices which by themselves express certain sentiments. According to Aumāpatam, there are seven such natural voices a person employs on certain occasions, and they are: *mārgam* (a tone used in requesting or soliciting favour or guidance; or begging, *ānanda* (voice indicating happiness), *hāsyaṃ* (voice used in cracking jokes), *sambhāṣyaṃ* (conversational voice), *kaladhvaniḥ* (murmuring voice), *śokaḥ* (voice indicating distress or sadness), *kalahaḥ*, (quarreling voice).[111] In addition to the above, there are some more intonations mixed with syllables, and they can be used in communicating feelings and emotions. For instance, the three *svaras* arising at the chest (*uras*) at the throat (*kaṇṭha*) and at the top of palate (*śira*) (or the roof of the mouth) can be used for these purposes. The voice that arises at the top of the mouth can be employed for beckoning or to address a person who is far-off the voice arising at the throat can be used to address a person who is not far-off and a person who is by the side can be addressed in a voice arising at the chest (low bass voice).[112] From all these examples, it is clear that a language communicates thought, but these voice variations or intonations communicate the feelings and emotions of that thought.

Such voice variations are equally important in musical applications. Pārśvadeva has defined *kāku* as the typical tone-variations in the voice,[113] which can manifest the shades of emotions presented in language,[114] and found in the poetic compositions (called bandhish) for being presented (by the artist).

According to musicologists, such *kākus* are six: 1. *rāgakāku* (the speciality of *rāga* itself), 2. *kṣetrakāku* (the special quality of the voice manifested by the singer, 3. *yantrakāku* (the voice resembling an instrument like *shahanāi*, *veeṇā*, etc.), 4. *svarakāku* (the special nature of the voice of the singer), 5. *deśakāku* (the speciality of the *rāga* presentation or voice modulation prevalent in a particular area), 6. *anyarāgakāku* (mixing the shade of the other *rāga* in a particular *rāga*).[115]

Music by itself is an aesthetic presentation of *svaras*. A *svara* by itself is a voice variation or a voice modulation. In isolation, a *svara* has no effect. It becomes enjoyable in combination with other *svaras* by taking a melodic pattern in relation to *vādi* (dominant *svara* on which the form of *rāga* rests) and its complementary *svara* (called *samvādi*). In such combination, every *svara* presents its own "sentiment" (*rasa*). According to Pārśvadeva, a) the repeated use of *madhyama* and *pañcama* gives rise to sentiment of love (*śṛṅgāra*) and humour (*hāsya*); b) the repetitive employment of *ṣaḍja* and *ṛṣabha* produces the sentiments of valour (*vīra*), the sentiment of fury (*raudra*) or the sentiment of wonder (*adbhuta*); c) excessive use of *gāndhāra* and *niṣāda* presents the sentiment of pity or compassion (*karuṇa*); d) using *dhaivata* repeatedly causes the sentiment of disgust (*bibhitsa*) or the sentiment of terror (*bhayānaka*).[116]

The *Nāṭyaśāstra* of Bharata has also equated different *rasas* with different colours as : a) *sṛṅgāra* (sentiment of love) –dark, blue; b) *hāsya* (sentiment of humour)–white; c) *raudra* (sentiment of horror)–red; d) *karuṇa* (sentiment of compassion)–pigeon colour; e) *vīra* (sentiment of heroic) – yellowish; f) *adbhūta* (sentiment of wonder) – yellow; g) *bibhatsa* (sentiment of repulsion) – blue; *bhayānaka* (sentiment of fear) – dark.[117] *Nāradīyaśikṣā* also follows Bharata in this respect.[118] Thus in our ancient texts, there is an attempt to equate *svaras* with sentiments on the one hand and colours on the other. For example, in *rāga Shuddha Sāraṅga*, in which *madhyama* and *pañcama svaras* dominate, there can be an effective presentation of the sentiment of love (*śṛṅgāra*). The sentiment of pity or compassion can be effectively presented in *Rāga Jog* in which *gāndhāra* and *niṣada svaras* are used repeatedly. The use of colours along with *svaras* would definitely heighten the manifestation of *rasa*. I am aware that some of the modern writers have criticized such equations as unscientific and arbitrary, but, according to me, such opinions appear to be a bit hasty, without further scientific verifications. We see, day in and day out, in TV programmers, that is, in a bull fight, the bulls are roused by holding a red flag before them. This experience tells us that there appears to be some causal relationship between colour and emotions. The greenery of forest, for other instance, makes one feel sublime, relaxed and at peace. If it be so, the theory of ancient scholars in this respect cannot be said to be totally unfounded. Can it be said that the modern dance theaters using colour lights during dance performances is a useless exercise? According to me, "No". As a spectator, I myself felt a different aesthetic effect of the dance, in different lights and in different colours projected from the top.

Fig. 11.23. Rāga Lalita in Rāgamālā Painting

(*Courtesy*. The Central Library Jaipur)

From the above discussion, it is clear that according to our ancestors, there is some relation between "*svara* and sentiment" and "sentiment and colours".[119] In the Rāgamāla Paintings of Rajasthan, attempts were made during the 14th and 16th century to picturise the emotions, which *rāgas* present. For instance, Rāga Lalit can manifest *vipralambha alankāra*. This *alankāra* stands for the sentiment of a deceived and dejected lover. The said *alankāra* was presented in Ragamāla Painting. This sentiment can also be presented by adopting voice-variations (*kāku*); or there can be simultaneous presentation of both. (See Fig.11.23.)

According to Vedic literature music has curative effect both on mental and physical ailments.[120] Music has the effect of inducing sleep among the children and the elderly both. It can also wake up a person from "coma". It is said that "The protestant reformer, Martin Luther was brought to a state of wakefulness with the help of music."[121] Even in modern days music is amply being used as a therapy.[122]

D. Spiritual Applications of *Nāda*

Almost all the Indian philosophical systems advocate the practicing of *yoga* as an effective means to self-realization. Of course, there are different methods of practicing such *yoga*. Some *yogis* meditate on *nirākāra brahman* and some on *sākāra brahman*, etc. It may be possible for *yogis* to concentrate on *anāhata nāda* or on *niṣkala brahman*, but as stated by Śaraṅgadeva, for ordinary people, it is not possible to concentrate on *anāhata nāda*, since there is no emotional colour and enjoyment (*raktivihīnatvāt, manorañjakaḥ*) in it.[123] Hence from time immemorial, a large number of people employed *nāda* in the form of *mantra* or in the form of music or in the form of *bhajans*, for spiritual realization. Many found it easier to practice *mantras* like *pañchākṣara mantra* (consisting of five syllables) *"Namaśśivāya"* or *ṣaḍakṣara mantra* (consisting of six syllables) – *om namaśśivāya* or some others as *om namo nārāyaṇāya*, etc. There can be a practice of meditating on certain other syllables (*varṇadhyāna*), like *dāṃ, diṃ, doṃ,* etc., as advocated by *Rudrayāmala Tantra*,[124] or meditating of syllables like *hrīṃ, krīṃ, śrīṃ*, etc., as preached by certain *Śākta Tantras*.

So far as the subject matter of my thesis is concerned what is required to be emphasized is that in all such chanting whether in the form of *mantra* or syllable, there is a common element, i.e., sound or *nāda* by means of which such a syllable (*varṇa*) or a group of syllables, constituting *mantra* are uttered. This aspect is clearly explained by *Lakṣmī Tantra*, by stating that: "A *mantra* is sound (*dhvani*), which (the adept invariably) associates (with the belief that) 'This protects me', and 'secret purport always protects me from fear'."[125] In *Lakṣmī Tantra*, Devi said: "Knowledge (insight, *bodha*) appears as identical with sound, and sound (as) identical with the object connoted. Considering that knowledge (insight) is one of my aspects, it follows that all the above mentioned sounds (are projections) of myself."[126] If it is so, in practice, meditating on *mantra* is as good as meditating on *nāda* as the manifestation of the reality, with the belief that it protects me.

In this view of the matter, *mantrānusandhāna* is nothing but *nādānusandhāna*. By means of such a practice (*sādhana*), the adept attains all eight *siddhis* (*aṇimā, garimā*, etc.), and ultimately liberation. Different forms of *mantra* are considered to be different forms of God or Goddess according to the religious belief, and they are prescribed according to the nature of the belief of the adept (*bhāvanā tāratamya*).

There have been a number of spiritual *gurus*, who advocated chanting with devotion the syllable *om* as part of once meditation (*praṇavopāsana*). As we have already seen, the chanting of syllables like *oṃ* or *hūṃ* has been in practice in India right from Vedic times. In fact, in *Agra Gharānā* music, with which I associate myself, through my *guru*, Ramrao Naik, before starting with *khyāl* singing, they sing *ālāpa* with the *mantra om namo nārāyaṇāya* for at least half an hour. Hence this *gharānā* is popularly known as *om tom gharānā*. This by itself is a *nāda* yoga.

Nādabindu Upaniṣad explains the nature of another kind of *nāda* yoga. According to it, one should practice *dhvani* or *nāda* as if it has been manifested by Brahma in order to reach the highest spiritual state (*turyīya padam*). In such a practice, one hears different kinds of sounds, sometimes loud and sometimes subtle; sometimes sounds of drums and sometimes the sounds of bells, etc. At the last stage of the practice one hears pleasing jingling sounds, or the sounds of *veeṇā* or flute. In such a practice, by forgetting the entire external world, one merges with *nāda*, just like water merges with milk. This *brahma-praṇava-oneness nāda* looks all luminous. The soul merging with such light attains the highest state of *viṣṇupada*. The mind would be steady, and independent, as if it is an embodiment of *nāda* (*Nādarūpa* or God) itself.[127] In this state, according to *Dhyānabindūpaniṣat, kuṇḍalinī śakti* at *bhrahmarandhra* shines like the sun in the sky. The soul or *puruṣa* attains liberation and becomes one with *brahman*.[128]

Emphasizing the importance of *nādopāsana*, Nīlakaṇṭha said that by *yajña, dāna*, etc., one can attain only *thrivarga*, namely, *dharma, artha* and *kāma* but through the knowledge of science of music (*saṅgītavijñānaṃ*), one can attain all the *caturvarga* : *dharma* (religious merit), *artha* (wealth), *kāma* (desires) and *mokṣa* (salvation). (*trivargaphalpradāḥ srve dānayajñastavādayaḥ / ekaṃ saṅgītavijñānaṃ caturvarga-phalapradam*)[129] and that is the ultimate goal of all Indian philosophical systems.

Notes and References

1. *yathāprayogaṃ vā sarveṣāṃ yathāprayogaṃ vā sarveṣāṃ*; Tai. Prā.18.7 – Whitney; p. 357.
2. Uvvaṭa in his introduction to *Ṛgveda Prātiśākhya* stated *svaro varṇā'kṣaraṃ mātrā daivaṃ yogarṣameva ca, mantraṃ jijñāsamānena veditavyaṃ pade pade* – Varmā, Veerendra Kumār, Dr. (*tr.*) (1999): (Hindi); p. 9.
3. *sarvasyaiva hi śāstrasya karmaṇo vāpi kasyacit / yāvatprayojanaṃ noktaṃ tāvattatkena gūhyatām* || Rig. Prā.– Varmā, Veerendra Kumār (1999); p. 15.

4. *śāstrāvatāraṃ sambandhaṃ viṣayaṃ ca prayojanam, jñātvā grāhyaṃ bhavecchastramiti śiṣṭānuśāsanam"*–Rig. Prā.–Varma, Veerendra Kumār (1999); p. 7.
5. Maitr. Up. 6.22.
6. S.R. 1.2.17.
7. Nā. Śā. Chap. 28.13.
8. S.R. III.82; Vol II; pp. 169-71.
9. Shringy, R.K. and Sharma, Prema Latā, Commenting on this definition of *śārīra* (voice) given by Shārangadeva.
10. Saighal, R.L. (1990) ; p. 188.
11. Strawson, P.F. (1959), Chapter on 'Sound'; p. 85.
12. Ghosh, Manmohan (1991) : Pā. Śi. 1.10; pp. 56-57.
13. Rig. Prā. 13.13 (*śikṣā paṭala*).
14. Pā. Śi. 1.3-10.
15. *aṣṭau sthānāni* - Pā. Śi. 13.
16. Khanna and Bedi (1992) ; p. 288.
17. Thite, G.U. (1997) : (ŚB.XI.4.1.13); p. 363.
18. Apte, V.S. (2000) ; p. 78.
19. Rig. Prā. 13.43 (*Śikṣā Paṭala*).
20. Sharma, Dr. Śrīkṛṣṇa (1993); p. 137.
21. Yājñ. Śi. ; pp. 94-97.
22. Pā. Śi. 10.
23. *Kāśikā Vṛtti* on Pāṇini 1.1.9.
24. Sharma, Dr. Shrikṛṣṇa, (1993) ; p. 129. Note: *Aāpiśāliśikṣā* is included at Apendix 2; at pp. 168-74.
25. Rig. Prā. 13.1 - Varma, Veerendra Kumār (1999); p. 679.
26. *Aāpiśāliśikṣā* 8.25-26; Sharma, Srikṛṣna (1993); p. 174.
27. Khanna, D.R. and Bedi, R.S. (1992); p. 289.
28. Whitney, William Dwight (1997) ; pp. 8-9.
29. Nā. Śi. 1.1.2.

30. R.V. 9.97.34 Wilson (at p. 153 of Vol. 4); Note: Sā.V., Verse 859 (Part II, Book II, Chapter II, (1) and Griffith (2001) : *Sāmaved Saṃhitā*, p. 219); see also R.V. 9.33.4 Wilson's at p. 39 of Vol. 4); Sā. V. 471, (Part I, Book V, Chapter II, (5) and Griffith's *translation*, notes at the bottom; p. 124).
31. Sā. V. 471, (Part I, Book V, Chapter II, (5)-Griffith); p. 124.
32. Sā. V. - Part II, Book V, Chapter I (2) (S.N.1206); p. 297 of Griffith – *rasave ta udīrate tisro vāco mukhasya uvaḥ; yadavya eṣi sānavi.*
33. Pingale, M. Pratibha (2005) ; p. 128-29.
34. Yudhiṣṭira Mīmāṃsāk, (*Samvat* - 2042)
35. Whitney, D. William (1973) (*tr.*); p. 3.
36. Strangways, A.H. (1989); p. 246.
37. Varma, Siddheśvara (1961); pp. 164-65.
38. Mishra, Dr. Vidhāta, (1972) ; p. 225.
39. Mishra, Sri Rājeśvara, (1978) (*tr.*) , p. 17 & 26.
40. Tarlekar, G.H. (1995) ; p. 23.
41. Ojha, Madhusudana (1995) ; p. 102; has described *Udātta*, etc., as *bhāgalakṣaṇasvaraḥ*.
42. *Uvvaṭa* : Commenting on *Ṛgveda Prātiśākhya* 3.1 - See Varma, Veerendra Kumār (1999); p. 213.
43. Nā. Śi. 1.1.8.
44. Nā. Śi. 1.1.10. & Nā. Śi. 1.1.11-13.
45. *udāttaścānudāttaśca svaritaśca trayaḥ svarāḥ āyāmaviśrambhākṣapairata ucyante* - Rig. Prā.3.1.
46. (Note): 1) Apte, V.S. : The Practical Sanskṛt-English Dictionary - '*tiryak*', '*tiryac*'= oblique, transverse, horizontal, winding, lying in the middle or between; an animal (going horizontally as distinguished from man who walks erect);.... crooked etc. p. 475; 2) Williams, Monier Monier : *ākṣaipa* = drawing together,

shaking about the hands, convulsion (= contortion due to the contraction of the muscles of body); p. 128.

47. Pat. M. Bhā. on Pāṇini 1.2.29-30.
48. *ekasmiṃstālavādikesthāne ūrdhvādharabhāgayukte ūrdhva bhāgenocyāryamāṇaudāttaḥ, adharabhāganiṣpannonudāttaḥ.... evamuccairityanena ūrdhvabāgaḥgruhyate, nīcairityadhobhāgaḥ.*
49. *ūrdhvabhāgāvacchivāyusaṃyogenetyartha.*
50. Mishra, Vidhata; p. 224.
51. *svāra saṃjñāyāṃ kiṃ* therefore *sthānaṃ svāra ucyate* = Why '*svārā*' is sign (*saṃjñā*); because the place (*sthānam*) itself is taken as '*svārā*' (*dhvani* or *śruti*) (here) - Nā. Śi.1.8.6 & 7. Note: here 'kiṃ' is used in the sense of 'or', or 'wherefore or for that reason', - as in "Is it not in this sense the place taken as *svara*"? See Williams, M.M. - at page 282 - kiṃ = what?, how?, whence?, wherefore? why?
52. in the sense of '*sthānāt*' - Pā. Śi. 10.
53. Rig. Prā. 3.3.
54. *dvi yamau* - Taittirī. Prā.19.3; 23.17; 19.4 - Whitney.
55. Rig. Prā. 3.4 & 5.
56. Rig Prā. 3.6.
57. Nā. Śi. 1.7.19.
58. *Aṣṭādhyāyī* 1.2.40.
59. Pat. M. Bhā. 1.2.33.
60. Nā. Śi. 1.8.2 - Bhise, R. Usha (*tr.*) (1986); p. 103.
61. Taitta. Prā. 2.4 - Whitney (*tr.*); p. 51.
62. Taitta. Prā. 22.1 - Whitney (*tr.*); p. 395.
63. Taitta. Prā. 22.9 - Whitney (*tr.*); p. 398.
64. *nīca svara, or anudātta* - Taitta. Prā. 22.10, Whitney (*tr.*) ; pp. 55 & 62.
65. Rig. Prā. 3.31-33; Varma, Veerendra Kumār (1999); (*tr.*); p. 242.

66. Nā. Śi. 2.5.3 - Bhise, Usha (1986) (*tr.*); p. 122.

67. Rig. Prā. 3.2.

68. R.V. 1.1.1 - Wilson, H.H. (*tr.*).

69. Bhise, Usha (1986) on Nā. Śi. 1.1; p. 76.

70. Thite, G.U. (1997) : (TMB XII.11.17; JB. III.79); p. 228.

71. Khanna and Bedi (1992) ; p. 191.

72. (See for details *Uvvaṭa Bhāṣya* to Verse 13.1 in *Śikṣā Paṭala*, Varma, Veerendra Kumar (1999); p. 679. Of these 'airs' *prāṇavāyu* and *apānavāyu* are amenable to our experience. It is *prāṇavāyu* that prompts lungs to pump air and causes vibrations of our vocal chord that produces sound in the form of our voice. *Apānavāyu* is the one that goes downwards and out of the anus. While exiting from it, it also 'makes sound' but of unpleasant type. An unknown Sanskṛt poet, for the sake of humour, has described such unpleasant sound, as '*ṭaraka purakañca madhyamā*, *ṭiskāre mahāghorān*, *nisśabdaṃ prāṇasankaṭam*'. (The sound '*ṭarak* and *purak*' is of ordinary bad smell but the sound '*tiskāra*' is terrible (in its bad smell), however, the one without sound is highly suffocating.)

73. Hiremath, C.R. (1992).

74. Desai, Puṇḍarīka Chaitanya (1976) ; 2.38-39.

75. Thite, G.U. (1997): *Its Magico-Religious Significance* (SB, I.4.3.1); p. 332.

76. ____ (1997); p. 345.

77. See the explanation of Whitney on verse 2.30 of Taittirīya Prā.; p. 67.

78. *huṃkārāt prasavaścaiva yathā vedasya omiti* : *Nārada Samhita In* Simha, Bipin Guru (1990), (Vol. I, Verse 2822; p. 208). (Hindi tr.).

79. Sagar, Lalitprabha Mahopadhyaya (2000) ; p. 3.

80. *om vedeṣu* - Vāj. Prā.1.18.

81. Joshi, M.C. (1999); p. 79.

82. "In the *darśapūṇamāsa*-sacrifices, after uttering the invitatory formula, one offers with the offering-formula. Therefore, the lower teeth grow first (= a feeling that the lower jaw is wider than upper jaw). Similarly inasmuch as after uttering *gāyatrī*-verse as an invitatory-formula, one offers with *triṣṭubha*-verse (which is bigger than the *gāyatrī*-verse) therefore the lower teeth are smaller (= feeling that lower jaw is lesser wide, and the upper one is broader) and in as much as the two *saṃyājyā*-verses are in the same metre; therefore the molars are of equal size. (=feeling that both jaws are of equal size)" (SB.XI.4.1.13) - Thite, G.U. ; p. 363. (Bracketed explanations are my own, by way of clarifications.)

83. *tasmād bindau praṇavākṣaraḥ oṃkāraḥ triṣu koṇeṣu tisrao vyāhrutayaśca lekhanīyāḥ iti* – Devarāta (1962) ; under *trikoṇatatvam,* p. 111.

84. Dwivedi, Ramayana Prasad, Prof. & Malaviya, Sudhakara (2004) ; pp. 79-80.

85. Kroodsma, E. Donald (1982) ; (Ch. 1), Vol. 2

86. Brackenbury, H. John (1982) ; p. 71 (Vol. 1).

87. Beer, C.G. (1982) ; p. 279 (Vol. 2).

88. Aum. - 1.17 ; *pavanasyāgnisaṃyogānnādotpattiriti sthitiḥ pavanāhatakoṇāgnijvālāpūritakandaraḥ.*

89. Aum. 8.88.

90. Aum. 9.107.

91. Sou. Lah. 69.

92. The phrase is borrowed from Brackenbury, H. John (1982). (Vol. 1). (Vol. 1, page 67), vide Sl. No. 86 above.

93. See Vātsyāna on Nyā. Sū. - 2.2.39-40; Jhā, Ganganatha Vol. II; p. 988.

94. *svara eva suvarṇam* - Pāṇḍeya, Devendra Nātha and Jhā, Bodhakumāra (*ed.*) (1997) ; p. 145.

95. See - *svarasampannayā vācā ārtvijyaṃ kuryāt asmādyajñe svaravantaṃ....*, etc., of *Bṛhadāraṇyaka Upaniṣad* 1.3.25.

96. Yā. Smṛ. 3.112.

yathāvidhānena paṭhansāmagāyamvicyutam /

āvadhānastanaṇdabhyāsātparaṃ brahmādhigacchati //

97. Nā. Śi. 1.5.2-3.

98. S.R. 2.163.

99. Tai. Up. 2.7.1.

100. Nā. Śā. 6.16.

101. Nā. Śā. 6.33.

102. Nā. Śā. 6.31-34 - Adya, Rangacharya (*tr.*) (1996); p. 55.

103. Nā. Śā. 6.39.

104. Shah, Prof. K.J. (1987); page 115.

105. Nā. Śā. 19.44-59.

106. Nā. Śā. 19.52-55.

107. Nā. Śā. 19.51. Board of Scholars (*tr.*) (1996) ; pp. 269-70.

108. *udāttaścānudāttaśca svaritaḥ kampitastathā/ varṇāścatvāra eva syuḥ pāṭhyayoge tapodhanāḥ* || Nā. Śā. 19.41.

109. Nā. Śā. 19.41-42.

110. Taitti. Prā. 23.15.3. Whitney (*tr.*); (*pṛkta* = mixed or mingled with, see also Williams; Monier Monier (1997), p. 645.

111. *mārgamānaṇdahāsyaṃ, ca sambhāṣyaṃ ca kaladhvaniḥ / śokaśca kalahaścaiva hīyete saptabhedanam* || Aum. 8.83.

112. Nā. Śā. 19.40-42.

113. *dhvaniśārīra sañjātaṃ vicitraṃ svaravartanam chāyā tadāśrayāc-āryyaiḥ gītamityabhidhīyate* - San. Sam. Sā. 2.44; p. 33.

114. *bhāvanā bhāṣā chāyāraktiḥ samarthavān* - San. Sam. Sā. 3.96; p. 66.
115. San. Sam. Sā. 3.96-102; p. 66.
116. San. Sam. Sā. 1.49-50. (The same idea is found in Nīlakaṇṭha's *Saṅgītārṇavacandrikā at* 1.158-159; p. 25.)
117. Nā. Śā. 6.42-45.
118. Nā. Śi 1.4.1-2 Bhise (*tr.*); p. 88.
119. *Saṅgīta* means and includes vocal music, instrumental music and dance. (*gītaṃ vādyaṃ tathā nṛtyaṃ trayaṃ saṅgītamucyate*) - S.R. 1.5.21.
120. Thite, G.U. (1997) ; p. 190 and chapter on 'Music and Medicine'; p. 221.
121. ____; p. 311.
122. Sharma, Manorama, (1996).
123. S.R. 2.165-167; Vol. I; p. 104.
124. Ru. Yā. Tan. 45.39-43; p. 447.
125. *Lakṣmī Tantra* 18.44-45 ; Gupta, Sanjuka (*tr.*); p. 102.
126. *Lakṣmī Tantra* 19.45; Gupta, Sanjuka (*tr.*); p. 108.
127. Nā. Bin. Up. 32-56, Paṇḍit Jagadiś Śastri.
128. Dhyā. Bin. Up. 104-105 - Paṇḍit Jagadiś Śastri.
129. Panigrahi, Nila Madhav (1995), 1.48; p. 8.

* * *

Chapter Twelve

CONCLUSION

The contribution of this thesis consists in analyzing the concept of *nāda* as found in Indian philosophical systems right from pre-Vedic and Vedic period, and also in highlighting the techniques of *nāda*, developed and experimented by Indian *ṛṣis*, for nearly two and a half thousand years back, so as to make them available for the use of present day generation, as a means to linguistic, musical, aesthetic and spiritual applications. I hope that my analysis of the subject and certain findings I have recorded would be useful to the society:

The entire Indian philosophy of *nāda* can be epitomized in one sentence in the words of *Maitri Upaniṣad*

"A person who is an expert in sound-*brahman* (*śabdabrahman*) attains the supreme reality (*parabrahman*), (*śabdabrahmaṇi niṣṇātaḥ paraṃ brahmādhigacchati*"[1] – it means that *nāda* (sound) in the form of word is itself *śabdabrahman*. (The word *śabda* stands for both sound and word.) *Śabdabrahman* is another name for *brahmajñāna* (the knowledge of the supreme reality). According to the Indian philosophers, there is inseparable relation between the word (language) and knowledge of the reality. Language is an epistemological means to knowledge. Even according to Bhartṛhari speech exists within and outside all living beings in the form of "consciousness"[2] (Vā. 1.126). That consciousness manifests itself in the form of speech. In this view of the matter for Bhartṛhari, ".... no knowledge is possible except as accompanied by *śabda* (word or language)."[3] We have seen that word or language in the ultimate analysis is the one that is manifested by *nāda* or *dhvani* (sound). It should also be noted in this context that those who emphasized the language (*vāk*) aspect of *dhvani*, (*varnātmakam dhvani*), on the basis of word and meaning relation, as a means of attaining the supreme reality, described the reality as *śabdabrahman*, and those who emphasized the *nāda* aspect of *dhvani* (*nādātmakam dhvani*), as an object of meditation (*upāsana*) as the means of self-realization, described it as *nādabrahman*. At any rate *nādānusandhāna*[4] (meditation on *oṃ*) is considered to be the highest means of "liberation."

According to the Indian traditions, *oṃkāranāda*, or *praṇava* is a metaphysical category that stands in between man and the reality: it is a manifester of the reality (*oṃ iti ekākṣaram brahman*) and it is also a means to comprehend that reality (*tasya vācaka praṇavaḥ*). Thus *oṃkāra* is both *vācya* (the object of knowledge) and *vācaka* (his description in human language). Thus the syllable *oṃ* is used both in transcendental sense, and in the sense of phenomenal *nāda*.

During the period of *brahmaṇas* and *upaniṣads*, the concept of "cosmic *oṃkāra*" was taken as a transcendental cause for the phenomenal world and phenomenal *oṃkāra*-sound. The human body (*piṇḍāṇḍa*) is taken as a miniature "cosmic phenomenon" (*brahmāṇḍa*). On the basis of such metaphysical relation between the two, the word *oṃkāra* was used to refer to both *oṃkāra-brahman* and the vocal phenomenal *oṃkāra*-sound. The result, an ambiguity, was introduced in the concept of *oṃkāra*. For instance, in the statements "*Om* is *brahman*; *om* is this all" (*omiti brahma, omitidam sarvaṃ*)[5] of *Taittirīya Upaniṣad*, the word *oṃkāra* is used to refer it to the ultimate reality. *Chāndogya Upaniṣad*, on the other hand, takes *omkāra* for a syllable, and mandates that "one should meditate on this syllable, as *udgītam*" (*aum ity etad akṣaram udgītam upāsīta*).[6] The confusion was so much that in certain circumstances it was difficult to appreciate the meaning of *oṃkāra* (or *praṇava*), whether the text meant *oṃkāra-brahman* or *oṃkāra*-sound syllable, unless one deciphered the intent of the text.

My reading has revealed me that, during the *upaniṣadic* time, attempts were also made to differentiate "transcendental *nāda*" from "phenomenal *nāda*". The following broad guidelines could be among others to distinguish them:

1. Whenever *oṃkāra* is used to indicate the Ultimate Reality or *Brahman*, we can safely take it as a transcendental *oṃkāra nāda*. For instance the statement that "The single syllable *Aum* by itself is

brahman (*om iti ekākṣaraṃ brahma*)[7], or the statement "*Om* by itself is that Ultimate Reality (*om tat sat iti*)"[8] etc., are the instances in which the concept of *oṃkār* is used in a "transcendental sense."

2. Whenever *Aum* is taken for being the one sublime and beyond the phenomenal world or beyond human comprehension, it is clearly a transcendental concept. For instance, see the statement in *Māṇḍukya Upaniṣad* "*Aum*", this syllable is all this. An explanation of that is (the following): "All that is the past, the present and the future; all this is only the syllable *Aum*. And whatever else there is beyond the three-fold time, that too is only the syllable *Aum*."[9] Here the word *Aum* relatable to present, past and future and to all "this" and "that", etc., is phenomenal. The phrase "this" and "that" refers to all physical objects around us on the basis of Ṛgvedic *nāma-rūpa* principle[10] and *Aum* referable to the statement, in that *Upaniṣad* – "whatever else there is beyond the three-fold time, that too is only the syllable *Aum*, is transcendental *nāda*."

3. Whenever the syllable *Aum* is referred to as the "end" or "goal" of human knowledge, it is taken as a transcendental concept, and whenever it is taken as a means to realize *Brahman*, it is taken as a phenomenal concept. For instance, see a statement in *Kaṭhā Upaniṣad*– "But the word which all the Vedas

declare, which all the austerities proclaim ....in brief is *Aum*....This syllable is, verily, the everlasting spirit. This syllable, indeed, is the highest end; knowing this very syllable, whatever any one desires will, indeed, be his."[11] But, to the question, what is the means of knowing this syllable? *Praśna Upaniṣad* replies,"....If he meditates on the highest person with three elements of the syllable *Aum* (a, u, m), he becomes one with the light ...."[12] In these two instances, *Aum* referred to as the goal or the end by *Kaṭhā Upaniṣad*, is "transcendental *nāda*", and the syllable *oṃ*, thought of by *Praśna Upaniṣad* as a means of contemplation and meditation, is a "phenomenal sound." The same principle is summed up graphically by *Muṇḍaka Upaniṣad* when it said: "Thus the syllable *Aum* (like a bow), can be used to meditate upon *brahman*, to attain *Brahman* (the target), and get merged with Him (in the manner the arrow does with its target)."[13] In other words, "phenomenal *oṃkāra*", in the form of "words" and "language", becomes the means to realize the "transcendental *nāda*", the target of human knowledge.

During later years when Patañjali's *Yogasūtra* stated that "His description is *Praṇava*" (*tasya vācaka praṇavaḥ*),[14] it referred to "phenomenal *oṃkāra*" or phenomenal sound, used in human language, to describe *Brahman* or the Reality. When

Bhartṛhari said, "Almost all Indian (schools), without contradiction, accepted that the God's creation is capable of being grasped through one word in the form of *Praṇava* (*Aum*)"[15]. He meant phenomenal sound manifesting syllables and words, and sentences, etc., used in human language. But, on the other hand, when *Mīmāṃsā* philosophers said that the sound "pronounced and uttered" by human vocal organ is the manifester of the "eternal syllable", they take the existence of transcendental *nāda* (in the form of eternal syllable) as different from phenomenal *nāda*. But they have not succeeded, as I have already clarified (in the Chapter Ten on Critical Review). Their concept of "eternality" of sound (in the form of syllable *varṇa*) is misconceived. Because there is nothing like a separate eternal "syllable" *ga* different from the "sound-form" *ga* produced in the vocal organ. If *Mīmāṃsā* thinkers had conceived the "eternal *nāda*" as an *adṛṣṭa* or *avyakta* principle, in the sense of a transcendental cause for phenomenal sound, as *Sāṅkhya*-Yoga and *Nyāya-Vaiśeṣika* have done, there could have been some justification for the existence of a separate "eternal transcendental sound" different from phenomenal sound, but the fact is that they have not done so. Their theory of "dual conception" makes the eternal syllable perceivable along with the phenomenal syllable, which our experience does not support.

Majority of the Indian philosophers just like their Western counterparts, in fact, accepted the concept of "transcendental cause" for phenomenal world. They conceived such "ultimate cause" or the "cause of causes" (*satyasya satyam*)[16] to avoid the principle of "regressio ad infinitum". But the nature of such "ultimate cause" varied from system to system. For Vedic thinkers, the cause of causes is *puruṣa*, for *Sāṅkhya*-Yoga it is *avyakta*-principle, for *Nyāya-Vaiśeṣika*, it is *adṛṣṭa*-principle, and for *Tantrāgamas* it is *Nāda-Brahman*, (consisting of *shiva-shakti* principle), etc. According to them, these are the matters of only inferences and the immediate cause (*nimitta kāraṇa*) for phenomenal world, and phenomenal *nāda* is *ākāśa* (ether) according to *Sāṅkhya*-Yoga and *Nyāya-Vaiśeṣika*, *vāyu* (air), according to *Mīmāṃsā*, and *agni* (energy), according to *Tantrāgama* philosophers. *Ākāśa* (ether), Air (*vāyu*) and *Agni* (energy), etc., being part of *pañcamahābhūtas*, are phenomenal entities only. Thus, for the Indian systems, "sound" is that which is used and applied. Being the manifestation of the *pañcamahā-bhūtas*, it is phenomenal. Our experience also supports their further theory that this phenomenal sound is a manifester (*vyañjaka*) of syllables, words and sentences. These syllables, words and sentences as manifested forms (*vyaṅgya*) of sound or *nāda* serve as a "epistemological means" to our knowledge.

It is important to note in this context, that irrespective of their respective metaphysical theories, when *ṣaḍdarśana* philosophers wanted to prove the eternality of Veda, they ultimately relied upon the relation between the phenomenal word and its meaning only. They concluded that on the basis of such an eternality of relation between word and its meaning as per convention, the authenticity and the eternality of Veda is established. So far as, the acceptance of any philosophical or religious scriptures, on the basis of such relation between word and meaning, is concerned; even the heterodox systems have not disputed it. For *Vaibhāṣika* school of *Buddhism*, for instance, *Buddha-vacanas* are *apauruṣeya* and eternal, even though they are expressed in "sound-words" that are phenomenal and non-eternal.

As we have already seen in Chapter Eleven, that it is the "phenomenal sound" of the vocal organ that undergoes modifications in human applications, in the form of syllables, words, musical *svaras*, etc., and such modified or modulated *dhvani* or sound called *vaikṛta dhvani* or *nāda* by Bhartṛhari, is different from mere vocal physical sound (*prakṛti dhvani*). But Bhartṛhari takes the root form (*dhātu-rūpa*, say *vada*) of the word as *prakṛti dhvani*[17] and its tense form (*vadāmi* or I speak, etc.,) as modified *dhvani*. Likewise, musicologist take seven "basic *svaras*" as *śuddha svaras* (*prakṛti dhvani*). "The other five modified *svaras* are *vaikṛta dhvani*. It may be so, for their immediate purpose of explaining their subjects, grammar in the case of Bhartṛhari and music in the case of musicologists; but a further analysis of the word *prakṛti dhvani* itself indicates that it stands for the original physical sound." *Prakṛti* means anything original or primary substance, cause or original source, etc.[18] Therefore, according to me, it would be reasonable to take the sound arising in the vocal chord itself as *prakṛti dhvani* out of which the root (*dhātu rūpa*) (*vada* = to speak) arises. Vyādi, in his work *Saṃgraha*, also states the same. It is said by one of the commentaries on *Vākyapadīya* by name *Vṛtti* (of Vṛṣabha), that Bhartṛhari had borrowed these concepts, *prakṛti dhvani* and *vaikṛta dhvani*, from this *Saṃgraha* of Vyādi, which reads as under:

Varṇasya grahaṇe hetuḥ prākṛto dhvanir iṣyate
Vṛttibhede nimittatvaṃ vaikṛtaḥ pratipadyate

(The "sound" (*dhvani*) that is meant to manifest audible syllable (*varṇa*) is "primary sound" (*prakṛti dhvani*), and due to modification (*vṛtti bheda*, as long short, etc.), it becomes *vaikṛta dhvani*.[19] Here *prakṛti dhvani* is the "original sound" that is meant to manifest syllables, and after taking different forms into syllables, etc., it becomes *vaikṛta dhvani*. Therefore, according to me, *prakṛti dhvani* exists even before the syllable is formed. In view of this matter, I do not accept Bhartṛhari's view that this *prakṛti dhvani* arises along with root or *dhātu rupa* of a word which is continued in *vaikṛta dhvani*. Of course Bhartṛhari is correct when he says that, after *vaikṛta dhvani* comes into existence, *prakṛti dhvani* does not cease to exist, and, in fact, it itself gets modified into *vaikṛta dhvani*. Moreover, even the musicologists also have expressed similar views. According to them, as it has been already seen in Chapter Eight, that different number *śrutis* (microtones) arising in *dhvani* (*prakṛti dhvani*) gets modified into different *svaras* (*vaikṛta dhvani*), just as the milk gets modified into curds.

Vaikṛta dhvani also takes the form "time-sequential sounds" for purposes of linguistic, musical, aesthetic and spiritual applications. I have explained all these aspects in detail in Chapter Eleven on Vocal Applications. However, I would like to highlight, here, how one and the same sound (physical sound) as a "raw material", takes different forms or modifications in different human applications. The same physical sound (*śabda*), by human effort, becomes a regulated sound or *nāda*, in the form of syllables in language or in the form of *svaras* in music, etc. To put in Vedic language, *śabda* represents *satyam* principle, i.e., the physical (or *bhautika*) existence, and *nāda* represents its *ṛtam* aspect, being a regulated sound. In fact Mahārṇā Kumbha stated that a *rāga* manifests a pleasing melody because of an *apūrva* principle.[20] This *apūrva*, as I have highlighted in Chapter Two, is the same *ṛtam* regulatory mechanism of the physical existence.

Being regulated differently in different human applications the concept of *nāda* emerges as an independent concept, different from sound (*śabda*). This *nāda* has different aspects in its different kinds of applications: as linguistic aspect, musical aspect, aesthetic aspect and mystic aspect.

Linguistic Aspect of *Nāda* : *Nāda*, as we have seen in Chapter Ten, is a modified and modulated sound (*vaikṛta dhvani*). For such a modulation or modification (*vikāra*) of sounds and their sequential arrangement, it is the mental faculty (what *praśastapāda* calls "the contact of the mind and soul"[21] that is responsible. A musical instrument is a lifeless object. An accidental fall of a hard substance on a stringed instrument causes only "bang" sound. But because of the application of human intellect, it produces beautiful music.

Likewise, human vocal organ is a phonic instrument. A child born produces that original unmodified physical sound (*prākṛta dhvani*), when it utters its first sound *ā* in its crying. That is why some of the scholars take *a* or its long form *ā* as a basic syllable and the rest of the syllables as its modifications only.

As and when a child grows, with the help of his or her elders, he or she learns syllabic sounds and their modifications to employ them in different situations to convey what he or she intends. The modification and arrangement of sounds is not a mere casual or accidental phenomenon. It is a matter of conscious arrangement of sounds with a design to convey certain ideas. As I have already explained in Chapter Seven, that the uttered sound-word (cow) becomes *saṅketa* (sign), and the word "cow" becomes a symbol (*saṃjña*) for the idea cow, referring to the object "cow" as per long convention (*sanskāra*). For example, to mean "river" one may utter *nadī* consisting of two "sound-syllables" – *na* and *dī*. To mean a "poor man", one may utter *dīna* consisting of two sound-syllables – *dī* and *na*. In these two words syllables are the same but they convey different meanings, because of different arrangements of the sounds' syllables. It is so because the speaker "intended" to convey two different ideas with two different sequencing of the syllables. The sequencing of sounds results in conscious modification of sound in the vocal organs. (See Figs.11.1 and 11.2.) Hence there is, this "psychic or mental element", in *vaikṛta dhvani* or *nāda*. In the form of a formula, it may be explained as under:

Nāda = sound + mental element;

or sound = *nāda* – mental element.

Thus, according to me, *nāda* is a psycho-physical concept. The psychic element not only modifies the sound but also introduces "time factor" in between two unrelated sounds to constitute them into words and sentences.

The nature of the vocal organ is such that only one sound can be uttered at a time. In the word *nadī, na* is uttered first and then *dī*. In other words both the sounds cannot be uttered simultaneously. There is also selectivity in perception in the ear of the listener. *Nyāya-Vaiśeṣika, Mīmāṃsā* and the grammarians believe in this kind of sequencing of syllables in the utterance of the speaker and perception by the listener in the same sequential order. When the word *nadī* is uttered in a time sequence as *na* and *dī*, the listener also hears them in the same sequential order and understands its meaning as "river" on the basis of "convention". Likewise in uttering the word *dīna* time sequencing of the sound is reversed to convey a different meaning (poor man). If it is so, then time also becomes an important constituent of the concept of *nāda* in human applications. In music, the nature of *rāga* depends on the sequencing of *svara* within the framework of time units called *tāla* (beat). Hence the concept of *nāda* can be defined as an act of "conscious sequencing of sounds to convey a thought or to communicate an aesthetic experience." Hence *nāda* = sounds + conscious time sequencing;

or sound = *nāda* – conscious time sequencing.

Ancient Indian thinkers took all the care to see that a "word" is also "uttered" properly in a clear voice in order to convey its meaning. As explained by *Taittirīya Prātiśākhya*, a voice is a 'sound combined with articulation....." (*varṇaprikta sabdo vāca utpattiḥ*).[22] In other words, the "voice" of a person is nothing but a combination of vocal-sounds (or tone) in articulation. In fact, "tone" is prior to articulation; it is material (*dravya*) of all the articulate sounds called "syllable", "letter" or "letter-sound" (*varṇa*). "Tone is the original source of all "syllables" (*śabda prakṛtiḥ sarva varṇānāṃ*)".[23] A "syllable" is the "smallest tone" or "sound unit". The "word" itself is a phonetically altered (*vikṛtam*) tone or sound.[24] Modern phoneticians call it "morpheme." A word is the smallest meaningful unit or form in a language (Webster's Electronic Dictionary). Hence, for employment of voice (tone), in the pronunciation of word and sentences, whether Vedic hymns, or other prose texts, our ancient scholar insisted on the "correct utterance" in the vocal organs. In this respect, they laid down two rules to be followed, as mandated by *Vājasneyi Prātiśākhya*.

Rule One: While reciting Vedic hymns one should start with *om* (*omkāra vedeṣu*)[25].

Rule Two: While reading a prose, like the commentaries on different *sūtras*, one should start with *athakāra* (*athakāraṃ bhāṣyeṣu*)[26], i.e., with *a-kāra* or "a-mode" in the mouth.

In view of the discussion in Chapter Eleven on Vocal Application, the wisdom behind the "Rule One" becomes clear. Some of the scholars are of the opinion that all syllables are born out of *oṃkāra.* Others say that, in the utterance of *oṃ*, the voice becomes balanced. May be because *oṃ* is produced at the middle of mouth. It is commonly believed that the utterance of *oṃ* in the beginning provides resonance to such "voice or tone". According to our ancient tradition such a "resonant" tone or voice is necessary to have melody in Vedic recitation. Vedic recitation should be not only correct but it should be "sonorous" and pleasing also. The sweet voice (in Vedic recitation), is considered to be as valuable as gold (*svara eva suvarṇaṃ*).[27] Therefore, the priests using "sonorous golden voice" were in very much in demand in times of sacrifices. Having regard for this principle, only *Nāradīya Śikṣā* prescribed that "First, the *oṃkāra* should be employed, then *vyāhṛtis.* (*om bhūḥ, bhuvaḥ, svaḥ*). After the muttering of *gāyatri* stanza, the practice of recitation should begin."[28]

The Rule Two states that the recitation of a prose-text should be started with *atha* or *a.* Ancient Indian phonetic philosophers believed that the syllable *a* or *ā* is the basic syllable, and other syllables are its modifications. For example, according to *Aittareya Āraṇyaka,*[29] *a-kāra* is the source of all other *svaras.* It says, "Know that the entire language is the modification (*vikāra*) of that *a-kāra.* It is this *svara* that takes different forms (of other *varṇas*) due to the obstruction (*sparśa*) of *ha* (or the breath) (in the different part of the mouth)" – (*yo vaitāṃ vācaṃ veda yasyā eṣa vikāraḥ sa samprativit, akāro vai sarvā vāk saiṣā śparśoṣma bhirvyajyamānā vahvī nānārūpa bhavati*).[30]

Hence the wisdom behind Rule Two is that one should start reading or speaking with voice in *a*-mode for clear pronunciation of the words. The music teachers also advise their students to utter *ṣaḍja,* i.e., *sā* with mouth wide open.

One more aspect to be borne in mind is that for effective and correct pronunciation one has to bear in mind the three *svaras* – *udātta, anudātta* and *svarita.* While pronouncing words, one should adhere to the places of syllables in the mouth. *Udātta* syllable has got to be pronounced at the upper part of the mouth, *anudātta* at the lower part and *svarita* at the middle. Such pronunciation is necessary for the words to convey correct meanings. The ultimate object of any language is to convey meaning. A word can convey the correct meaning if each syllable constituting the word is uttered at its proper place in the mouth, keeping in view the three places of accents – *udātta, anudātta,* and *svarita* and also the eight places of production of syllables like chest (*uras*), throat (*kaṇṭha*), the roof of the mouth or palate (*śiras*), etc., as prescribed by Pāṇini.[31] I have explained this aspect in detail in Chapter Eleven on Vocal Application. As a general rule, it is prescribed that one should utter a word, just like a tigress carries her cub by holding it between the jaws without hurting it. In other words, such pronunciation of the word should be lucid, and it should be neither too hard nor too soft.[32]

Vedic scholars have also sternly warned against the evils of wrong accents. An improper accent may even convey a meaning quite contrary to the one intended. *Nāradīyaśikṣā* provides one such instance:

"If the Vedic text (employed in the sacrifice) is defective in the (pitch) accent, or sounds (*svara*), it does not yield the correct meaning. Then it becomes just like a 'thunderbolt' in the form of speech, and kills the master performing the sacrifice, i.e., an undesirable result is brought about by the incorrect accent of (the compound) *indraśatru*."[33] If the word *indraśatru* is recited as having an accent on its final member, it becomes a *bahuvrīhi* (meaning Indra who is the destroyer of (of the demons). If the word is recited as having the accent on its initial member, it becomes *tatpuruṣa* .....it will mean then (demon), a destroyer of Indra. But while reciting (*mantra*) the demons accented *Indraśatru* as *bahuvrīhi* and they met with disaster.[34]

The object of all these rules is to see that all the potentialities of vocal chord are utilized in reciting the Vedic text properly, correctly in order to convey its correct meaning. Prior to the script was invented, the Vedic text was transmitted from the teacher to his students by word of mouth of the teacher to the ears of the students. The students followed the same practice when they themselves became teachers and so on, for generations. To maintain the correctness of the Vedic texts with correct accents, in such oral tradition, such rules were very much required. Hence, for correct pronunciations, the *śikṣās* and *prātiśākhyas* (written texts on phonetics), and for maintaining linguistic structure and the meanings of the Vedic texts, grammar and *nirukta* (etymological science) were devised. As we have seen even Darśanakāras have also tried their best to maintain the authority and purity of the Vedic texts by advocating the eternality between the Vedic words and their meanings. *Mīmāṃsā* philosophers presumed the priority of the transcendental sound in the form of eternal syllables manifested by non-eternal vocal sounds in order to prove the eternality of Vedic injunctions. According to them, "the priority of sound" is already spoken of, as an accepted principle, on the basis of which the eternality of Veda *ipso facto* stands established (*uktantu śabdapūrvāt, ākhyā pravacanam*).[35] In fact, Kumārila Bhaṭṭa, one of the strongest exponents of *Mīmāṃsā* school, in his *Śloka Vārttika*, (in the Chapter dealing with Mīmāṃsā Aphorism VI to XXIII), openly declared that "It is for the sake of the validity of the Veda that we seek to prove the eternality of sound (*śabda*)." Whether we accept *Mīmāṃsā* theory or not, one thing is certain that the language we speak, as a matter of fact, is uttered in phenomenal sound (*nāda*); and the entire linguistic structure has been manifested by this *nāda* and *nāda* alone, as Dāmodara Paṇḍita puts it:

"The syllables (*varṇas*) are manifested by *nāda*, the word is manifested by syllables; and the sentence is manifested by words and the language is manifested from sentences; and the entire day to day transactions take place in language. Hence the entire world is subject to *nāda*":

Nādena vyañjate varṇaḥ padaṃ varṇāt padādvacaḥ
Vacaso vyavahāro' yaṃ, nādādhīnamato jagat.[36]

Musical and aesthetic aspect of *Nāda*

Svara is the basic unit in music. As we have seen in Chapter Eleven, the muscular control of the jaws plays a very important role in channelising the sound-breath material through the mouth. If the vocal chords are open, they simply produce breath; and if they are very close to each other, they produce sound. According to *Atharva Prātiśākhya*, the breath that produces sound is called *nāda*.[37]

According to Aumāpatam, when this sound-breath material (called *anupradāna* by Pāṇini) passes through triangular phenomena, in the vocal cavity, it produces *dhvani* along with *bindu*. In such triangular phenomena, *niṣāda*, the seventh *svara* appears, as if it is at the end of the triangle. My experiments also revealed to me that such triangular phenomena could be easily felt by pronouncing the syllable *oṃ* at the lower jaw with the mouth neither too open nor too close. In such an utterance the voice becomes resonant. All the seven *svaras* can be uttered with ease in the ascending order, with proportionate muscular control as if they arise in a triangular framework. Each *svara* is a result of the necessary muscular control. Hence the seven *svaras* are called *yamas* in ancient literature. A *svara* is defined as a source of *rāga*.[38] Saṅgītaratnākara defines *svara* as the one that shines itself. Thus *svara* in music is the smallest unit. There are seven *svaras* in music.

Even in music, the *svara ṣaḍja* is uttered with *ā-kāra* as *sā*. It is also believed by the musicologists that "In its pure form *svara* is only one (and) it takes many forms as *ṣaḍja*, etc". (.....*tatra niṣkalarūpeṇaika eva svaraḥ ṣaḍjādirūpāṇāneka svaraḥ*),[39] that is, basically there is one *svara*, namely *ā-kāra*, and because of its modification it becomes *ṣaḍja, ṛṣabha, gāndhāra*, etc.

Bharata for the first time established, on the basis of demonstration with the help of four *vīṇas*, that the same *prakṛti dhvani* gets modified into different *svaras* with different combination of microtones (*śrutis*) out of twenty-two *śrutis* of the *śaptak*. The *svaras* like *ṣaḍja, madhyama, pañcama,* take four *śrutis* each, *gāndhāra* and *dḥaivata* take three *śrutis* each, and *ṛṣabha* and *niśāda* take two *śrutis* each. I had raised a query, which musicologists did not answer: If *svaras* like *ṣaḍja, madhyama, pañcama,* take four *śrutis* each, how is that they produce different pitches? I myself found an answer in the "Triangle theory of Aumāpatam" that they produce different pitches owing to the squeezing of the volume of the sound-breath material in ascending order. The frequency of vibration of smaller volume of the mass would be higher than the one with more volume or more mass. Hence, notwithstanding the same number of *śrutis*, (for example *ṣaḍja, madhyama, pañcama*, with four *śrutis* each), they produce different pitches, in view of their relative volumes. I have also discussed in detail in Chapter Eight on Musicology that because of the adjustment of *śrutis* amongst *svaras* (*śrutyantarabhāvi*) as per the need, musician can glide from one *svara* to another with ease, in order to produce different melodic patterns for the purpose of aesthetic appeal. In addition, the artists also make use of voice variations generally known as *kākus*. Even in linguistic communication such a variation of *svara* is adopted to convey emotion and feelings. There are also natural voices like those that the one used in sorrow, happiness, etc. The text expresses a thought and voice variations express the emotional content of that thought. This emotional content (*bhāva*) is itself considered to be *rasa* by our *alaṅkāra paṇḍits*. According to Vedic literature, music has curative effect both on mental and physical ailments. Even in modern days music is amply being used as a therapy.

Thus *nāda* itself takes the form of *svara* and *svaras* together constitute a *rāga*, and from all the *rāgas* music emerges as an art with an aesthetic appeal. Hence it is rightly said:

na nādena vinā gītaṃ na nādena vinā svaraḥ
na nādena vinā rāgastasmāt nādātmakaṃ jagat

"There is no music without *nāda*, there is no *svara* without *nāda*, nor is there *rāga* without *nāda*. Hence this world is the manifestation of *nāda*."[40]

Mystic aspect of *Nāda*

One more aspect, which I had just hinted in Chapter Six (on *Tantrāgamas*), is regarding mystic aspect of *nāda*. There are a number of "mystic sound-syllables." The word mystic stands for an esoteric principle, which is understood only by few inner groups of disciples or initiates, and which is beyond the comprehension of ordinary human beings. *Oṃ* is one such mystic syllable. There are innumerable statements in *upaniṣads*, highlighting the mystic significance of *Aum* or *Praṇava*. Likewise even the letter *a* or *a-kāra* is a mystic syllable. In *Bhagavadgīta*, Lord Kṛṣṇa declares that of all the letters I am the letter "A".[41]

In *Tantrāgamas*, there are innumerable mystic syllables. They are matters of esoteric principles. For instance, according to them, *nāda* is a manifestation of *śiva-śakti* principle. The Divine Energy, in the form of *Kuṇḍalinī śaktī*, manifests Herself as *parā, paśyanti, madhyamā* and *vaikharī*. From *vaikharī*, arise all sound-syllables, (*varṇas*), from *a* to *kṣa*, what Vedic tradition calls *varṇasamāmnāya*. These syllables are the manifested state of that "hissing *dhvanī*" of *kuṇḍalinī śaktī* (in the form of a sleeping snake). She is the substance of all letters.

> *a-kāraḥ sarva-varṇāgrayaḥ prakāśaḥ paramaḥ śivaḥ*
> *ha-kāro' ntyaḥ kalārūpa vimarśākhyaḥ prakīrtitaḥ*

(*A-kāra* is the Supreme Śiva, the source of all letters and *Ha-kāra* is a manifestation of *śaktī* in the form of varied *vidyās* as a means to grasp those syllables (as per *nāma-rūpa* principles.).[42] These letters are called *mātṛkas* (little mothers) for the reason that these letters embody the sound (*nāda*) produced by Mother-*Kuṇḍalinī śaktī*. According to the mystic theory of *Tantrāgamas*, these syllables (*varṇas*) are not only the "sound-units" (*mātṛkās*) but the "energy-units" (*śaktī-bīja*) also. It is because of this intrinsic nature that these *varṇas* are capable of being the components of *mantra* which, by itself, is the source of energy called *mantra śaktī*.

Mother-*Kuṇḍalinī śaktī* takes the form of three *bindus* or three *guṇas–satva, rajas* and *tamas*. Māheśvara Puṇyānanda Nātha in his *Kāmakalāvilāsa* states that Devi is *triguṇa svarūpiṇī* and She manifests herself in a Triangle (*trikoṇarūpam*) (Verse 25). *Chidvalli*, a commentary written by Nityānanda Nātha, clarified that this "triangle" represents three *Śaktis*, viz., *icchā, jñāna* and *kriyā* which change into *paśyanti, madhyamā* and *vaikharī* respectively, symbolised as three *puras* and indicated by three letters – *A, Ka, Tha*. Each *bindu* represents a *pura* (a town or a country). Hence Devi is called *Tripura Sundarī*. Devi manifests herself in these three *bindus*, manifested by the syllable *AUM*. In other words, as I have already explained in Chapter Eleven, according to the Indian esoteric theory, the triangle arises out of *oṃ* or *praṇava*. "The beautiful Triangle" (*Śṛngāṭa*) .....is *praṇava* itself (*praṇavātmakam*). It is known by three lines (*rekhatrayāvagantavaya*) (which composes it).[43]

If one utters or pronounces *aum* with the lower jaw, the syllable "*A*" takes the horizontal base at the lower jaw with syllable "*Ka*", resulting in, say, "*A* - *Ka*" line. From this line a triangle phenomenon is formed with a meeting point at the upper part of the mouth, say, at "*Tha*". Thus there would be an *A, Ka, Tha*-triangle. (See Fig. 12.1.) From the description of *Śrīcakra* in *Kāmakalāvilāsa* of Māheśvara Puṇyānanda Nātha (p.75), it is clear that it is composed of nine triangles of which four are upward (representing *śaktī*-triangles) and five downward (p. 77), (*śiva*-triangles) ending with square (71). My experiment revealed to me that if *Oṃ* is uttered by lower jaw, a triangle–*A.Ka.Tha*–is formed (as per Fig.12.1); and if one pronounces the syllable AUM with upper jaw the triangle stands reversed (See Fig.12.2) as "a q r" (see Fig. 12.4). And if the syllable *AUM* is pronounced by both the jaws then these two triangles get mixed resulting in a phenomena of 'nine angles' in a square phenomena, and it is described as *Śrīcakra*. (See Fig. 12.3 and Fig. 12.4.) (Even the angles in square are required to be counted to account for nine angles.)

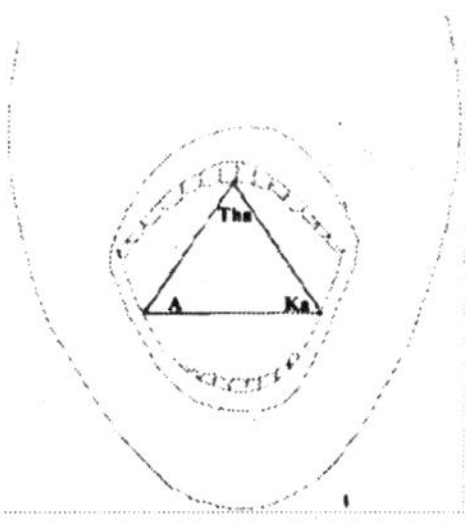

Fig. 12.1

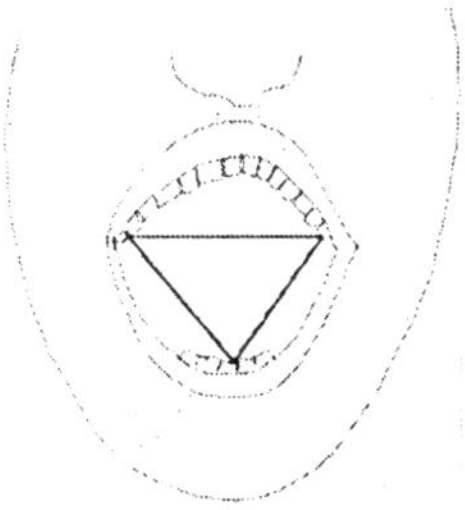
Fig. 12.2

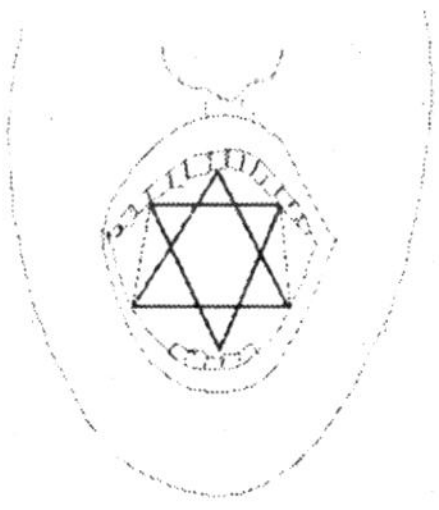
Fig. 12.3

In high muscular tension this phenomenon can result in innumerable triangles and ultimately all can merge in a single *bindu*.

In this phenomena of "nine angles" Devi manifests herself at the centre, (at ninth angle) as *bindu* called *Mahābindu*, in the form of "bliss and other spiritual powers (*siddhis*)", if the *sādhaka* (spiritual practitioner) meditates on Her with strong belief (*bhāvanā*) that, Devi, so manifesting, protects him. See Fig.12.4.

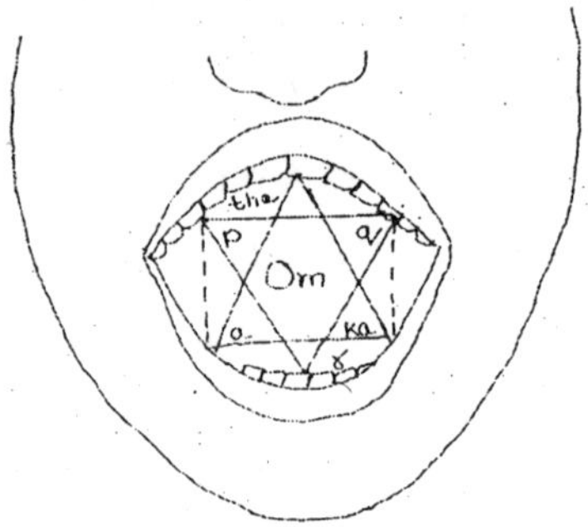

Fig. 12.4

In this view of the matter, according to me, these concepts of "triangle" and "*śrīcakra*",[44] etc. refer basically to such sonic phenomenon in the mouth. These esoteric ideas are camouflaged in a language that can be understood only with the help of *guru* (teacher), who is an expert in the subject, as pointed out by Sir John Woodroffe (Arthur Avalon).[45] The intention behind this principle appears to be that a person who is not initiated by a competent *guru* is not entitled to know this *vidyā*. Otherwise, he may misuse it. *Tantrāgama* texts have also warned that there would be negative and harmful results which may ruin the person, if he attempts to practice it, on the basis of his book-learning only.

Thus the syllable *aum* or *oṃ* is the sacred and mystic syllable both in the Vedic traditions and also in the *Tantrāgama* traditions. *Chāndogya Upaniṣad* also mandated that *oṃ*-meditation on the entire *sāman* is good (*oṃ samastasya khalu sāman upāsanaṃ sādhu* (Chā. Up.2.1.1). Even the non-vedic philosophers of Buddhism, Jainism, etc., also believe in *oṃ* as a sacred syllable. Buddhist's *Hūṃ* is another form of *oṃ*. In the majority of the Hindu religions in India, even as on today, irrespective of their propitiating *devatā* (deity), they chant *oṃ* with their prayer or with the *mantra* of that deity. Thus the syllable *oṃ* is common to all religious sects in India. If it is so, in order to assure better social harmony, there can *a* be a non-sectarian temple, only having *AUM* as a symbol of worship.[46]

I also find that the entire mystical philosophy of *nāda* of India stands epitomized in the following duet:

> *Na nādena vīnā jñānaṃ na nādena vinā śivaḥ*
> *Nādarūpaṃ paraṃ jyotirnādarūpī svayaṃ hariḥ*

"Without *nāda* there is no knowledge, without *nāda* there is no Śiva. Hence the all-luminous eternal Reality is an embodiment of *nāda*. Even Hari himself is in the form of *nāda*".[47]

With the above summary of my findings, I state that the contribution of this thesis consists of the following:

1. In projecting the evolution of the concept of *nāda*, right from the Vedic period, in different systems of Indian philosophy, with all its multi-facets, as an independent subject.

2. In highlighting the ontological and the epistemological status of *nāda* as *śabda* or *dhvani*, in

relation to speaker's utterances and cognition of listeners.

3. In critically analyzing and comparing different theories of the Indian systems, and suggesting an acceptability of particular theory of *nāda*.

4. In highlighting the Indian concept of *nāda* as a modulated and modified psycho-physical sound different from *dhvani* or *śabda* (a physical sound), which is the subject matter of physics.

5. In identifying the Vedic *svaras* like *udātta, anudātta* and *svarita* as *bhāgalakṣaṇa svaras*. These *svaras* refer to the places of accenting syllables at the higher or the lower or the middle part of the mouth. Such accents of the syllables could be with one common intonation (*svara sādhāraṇa*) or *śruti*; and as such they are not high, low and middle tones, as taken by majority of modern scholars.

6. In projecting the "triangular theory" of production of sound which is useful in linguistic, musical and spiritual applications.

7. In redefining the language as a system of "conscious sequencing of phonemes (syllables) and morphemes (words) in a sound-patterns (sentences) according to the rules of syntax and semantics, so as to convey a thought or meaning according to the rules of convention." In effect, it is the sound in the form of

language, at the base, that functions as an epistemological means to human knowledge.

8. In highlighting various techniques of production and application of *nāda* in the form of human voice, experimented and used right from the Vedic period, for nearly two and a half thousand years, in India, so as to make them available for the use of the present day generation, as a means to linguistic, musical, aesthetic and spiritual applications.

9. In deciphering the mystic symbols like *Trikoṇa* and *Śrīcakra*, etc., which are basically sonic phenomena in the mouth.

Notes and References

1. Maitr. Up. 6.22.
2. Vā. 1.126.
3. Vā. 1.127.
4. *sadā nādānusandhānāt kṣīyante pāpasañcayāḥ*
   nirañjane vilīyate niścitaṃ cittamārutau (Verse 104) - By practising the *nāda* all the accumulations are destroyed and the mind and the life do certainly get merged in the Unseen (Paramātman) : Sinh, Pancham (*ed.*) (1992).
5. Tai. Up. 1.8.1 - Radhakṛṣna, Prof. (1994); p. 535.
6. Chā. Up. 1.1.1.
7. *Bhagavad Gītā* 8.13.
8. *Bhagavad Gītā* 17.23.
9. Māṇḍ. Up. - Verse 1 : Radhakṛṣna, Prof. (1994).
10. R.V. 10.71.1-6.
11. Kaṭha Up. 1.2.15-16; Radhakṛṣna, Prof. (1994).

12. Pras. Up. 5.5; Radhakṛṣna, Prof. (1994).
13. *Muṇḍaka Up.* 2.2.3 and 4. (*Upaniṣad Sangraḥ*)
14. Patañjali's *Yoga Sūtra-Samādhipāda* 27.
15. Vā. 1.9.
16. Br. Up. 2.3.6.
17. Vā. 1.76 & 77.
18. Williams, M.M. (1997); p. 654.
19. *Tr.* by Raja, Kunjunni (1977).
20. Sharma, Premalata (1963) Vol. I; under *Gitaratnakośaḥ* - Verse 443; p. 587.
21. Jhā, Gangānātha (1982), p. 612.
22. Tai. Pr. 13.3; Tr. by Whitney.
23. Tai. Pr. 22.1; Tr. by Whitney.
24. Tai. Pr. 1.51.
25. Vāj. Prā. 1.18.
26. Vāj. Prā. 1.19.
27. Thite, G.U.; p. 355.
28. Nā. Śi. 1.6.4, Bhise, R. Usha (1986).
29. Ait. A 2.3.6. Phadke, Babashastri (*ed.*), (1992).
30. Ait. A. 2.3.6. Phadke, Babashastri (*ed.*), (1992).
31. Pā. Śi. Verses 11 and 12, Ghosh, Manmohan, (1991).
32. Pā. Śi. 25.
33. Nā. Śi - Bhise, Usha (*tr.*); p. 76.
34. Nā. Śi - Bhise, Usha (*tr.*); p. 76 (with certain modifications of my own).
35. Mī. Sū. 1.28-29.
36. Paṇḍita Dāmodara : 1.14.
37. *nādoghoṣavatsvareṣu* – Ath. Prā.1.2.
38. *rāgajanako dhvaniḥ svaraḥ* - Br.1.4.15.

39. *Saṅgītasamayasāra* - Pārśvadeva : 1.38; p. 11.
40. *Saṅgītadāmodara* of Śubhaṅkara - Acharya Hariram, p. 58 - *Nāda*.
41. *akṣarāṇāmakāro'smi* - *Gītā* -10.33.
42. *Kāmakalāvilāsa* - Dwivedi, Rāmāyana Prasad, Prof. and Malviya Dr. Sudhakara (*tr.*); p. 23.
43. *Kāmakalāvilāsa;* pp. 80-81.
44. Bhattacharyya, Narendra Natha (1999) : *Śrīyantra* ; p. 150.
45. Woodroffe, Sir John (2006); p. 385.
46. *Aum* the essence of the Vedas; p. 25; Kendra Worker; (1995).
47. Acharya, Hariram (1998), Ch. 2; under sub-heading '*Nāda*'; p. 58.

* * *

BIBLIOGRAPHY

Primary Sources

Abhidharmadīpa of Vimalamitra *with Vibhāṣāprabhāvṛtti* : Jaini, Padmanabha S. (*tr.*); (2003); *In* Potter, Karl H. : Encyclopedia of Indian Philosophies, Vol. IX; p. 532; Delhi, Motilal Banarsidass.

Abhidharmakośa of Vasubandhu : Potter, Karl H. (2002); *In* Encyclopedia of Indian Philosophy, Vol. VIII; p. 486 ; Delhi, Motilal Banarsidass.

Abhidharmakośabhāṣya of Vasubandhu : Potter, Karl H. (2002) : *In* Encyclopedia of Indian Philosophy; Vol. VIII; p. 516; Delhi, Motilal Banarsidass.

Abhinavabhāratī : Abhinavagupta (1994); Delhi, Parimal Publications.

Advaitasiddhi of Madhusudana Saraswati : Jhā, Gaṅgānātha (1990), p. 146; Delhi, Sri Satguru Publications.

Aitareya Aaraṇyaka (*Sāyaṇa Bhāṣāsametam*); p. 146 : Phadke, Babashastri (*ed.*) (1992); Puna, Anandashrama.

Aṣṭādhyāyī of Paṇini (1991) : Vāsu, Śirīśa Chandra : Delhi, Motilal Banarsidass.

Atharva-Veda-Prātiśākhya or *Shounakīya Caturādhyāyikā* (*tr.*): Whitney, William, D. (1994); Delhi, Parimal Publication.

Aumāpatam of Umāpaṭiśivārya : Chandrasekharan (1957); Madras, Government Oriental Manuscripts Library.

Bhagavadgīta (1986) : Mumbai, The Bhaktivedanta Book Trust.

Bhāvaprakāśanam of Śāradatanaya : Agrawal, Madan Mohan (1983), Varanasi, Chaukhamba Surabharati.

Bṛhaddeśī of Śrī Mataṅga Muni, Vol. I : Sharma, Prema Lata Assisted by Beohar Bihari (1991); New Delhi, Indira Gāndhi National Centre of Arts & Delhi, Motilal Banarsidass.

Bṛhadāraṇyaka Upaniṣad : *In* Paṇḍit Jagadiśaśastri (1996) : *Upaniṣad Saṅgraḥ;* Delhi, Motilal Banarsidass.

Chāndogya Upaniṣad : *In* Paṇḍit Jagadiśaśastri (1996) : *Upaniṣad Saṅgraḥ* ; Delhi, Motilal Banarsidass.

Dhyanabindhu Upaniṣad : *In* Paṇḍit Jagadiśaśastri (1996) : *Upaniṣad Saṅgraḥ* ; Delhi, Motilal Banarsidass.

Hymns of the Ṛgveda : Griffith R.T.H. (*tr.*) (1999), Delhi, Motilal Banarsidass.

Kāmakalāvilāsa of Māheśvara Puṇyānanda Nātha, along with Cidvalli of Śrī Naṭānanda Nātha : Dwivedi, Ramayana Prasad & Malaviya, Sudhakar (*ed.* & *tr.*), (2004); Delhi, Chowkhamba Sanskrit Pratishthan.

Katha Upanishad : Radhakrishna, S. Prof. (1994) : *The Principal Upaniṣads*, New Delhi, Harper Collins Publishers (India).

Lakṣmī Tantra (A Pāñcarātra Text) : Gupta, Sanjukta (*tr.*) (2000); Delhi, Motilal Banarsidass.

Mādhyamakahṛdayakārikā and Tarkajvālā of Bhavya : Potter, Karl H. (2003) : *Encyclopedia of Indian Philosophy* (Vol. IX), p. 397; Delhi, Motilal Banarsidass.

Mahābhāṣya of Pantañjali (Aahnikas, I–IV) : Dasgupta, Surendranath (*tr.*) (1991); New Delhi, Indian Council of Philosophical Research.

Mahānirvāṇa Tantram : Misra, Baladeva Prasad (2004), Mumbai, Khemarāj Srīkṛṣṇadāsa.

Maitri Upanishad: *In* Paṇḍit Jagadiśaśastri (1996) : *Upaniṣad Saṅgraḥ*; Delhi, Motilal Banarsidass.

Mānameyodaya of Nārāyaṇa : Raja, Kunhan C. & Sastri, Suryanarayana S.S. (1975); Chennai, The Adyar Library and Research Centre.

Māṇḍūkya Upanishad – Radhakrisna, S. Prof. (1994) : *The Principal Upanishads*, New Delhi, Harper Collins Publishers (India).

Māṇḍūkya Upanishad with Gaudapāda-Kārikā: *In* Dave, Jayantkrishna, H.(1990) : *Thirteen Principal Upaniṣads*, Bombay, Bharatiya Vidya Bhavan.

Muṇḍaka Upaniṣad : Radhakrisna, S. Prof. (1994) : *The Principal Upanishads* : New Delhi, Harper Collins Publishers (India).

Mīmāṃsa Sūtra of Jaimini : Sandal Mohanlal (*tr.*), (1999); Delhi, Motilal Banarsidass.

Nāda Bindu Upaniṣad : *In* Paṇḍit Jagadiśaśastri (1996) : *Upaniṣad Saṅgraḥ* ; Delhi, Motilal Banarsidass.

Nāradīyāśikṣā with the Commentary of Bhaṭṭa Śobhākara: Bhise, Usha R.(*tr.*), (1986); Poona, Bhandarkar Oriental Research Institute.

Nāṭyaśāstra : Adya Rangacharya (*tr.*) (1996); New Delhi, Munshiram Manoharlal.

Nāṭyaśāstra of Bharatamuni with commentary of Abhinavagupta: Ravishankar & Joshi, K. L. (*ed.*) (1996); Delhi, Parimala Publications.

Nāṭyaśāstra of Bharatamuni : Board of Scholars (*tr.*) (1996); Delhi, Sri Satguru Publications.

Nayasaṅgītaḥ: In *Luptāgama Saṅgrahaḥ*–Vol. II; (1983), p. 98; Varanasi, Sampūrṇānanda Sanskṛt Viśvavidyālaya.

Netratantram with the commentary of Kṣemarāja: Dwivedi, Vrajavallabha. (*ed.*) (1985); Delhi, Parimala Publications.

Nighaṇṭu & *Nirukta* of Yāska : Sarup, Lakshman (1998); Delhi, Motilal Banarsidass.

Nyāyānusāra of Saṅgabhadra : Potter, Karl H. (*tr.*), p. 650, *In* Encyclopedia of Indian Philosophy, Vol. VIII, (2002); Delhi, Motilal Banarsidass.

Pañcīkaraṇam of Śaṅkarācārya's (2004), Kolkata, Advaita Ashrama.

Pañcīkaraṇam (*Śaṅkarācārya's*) with 1. Sureśvara's *Vārtika*, 2. Nārāyaṇa's *Vārtikābharaṇa*, 3. Ānandagiri's *Vivarṇa*, 4. Rāmatīrtha's *Tattvacandrikā*, 5. Śāntyānanda's *Advaitāgamahūdaya*, 6. Gaṅgādhara's *Pañcīkaraṇacandrikā* : Mishra, Kameshwara Nath (*Hindi tr.*). (1962), Introduction; p. 7 : Varanasi, Chaukhambha Sanskrit Sansthana.

Pāṇini Śikṣā : Ghosh Manmohan (1991); Delhi, V.K. Publishing.

Paramalaghumañjūṣā of Nāgeśa or Nāgoji Bhaṭṭa : Raja Kunjunni K; p. 324; *In* [Potter Karl H. (*Gen. Ed.*)]; Goward Harold G. & Raja Kunjunni, K. (1990): *The Encyclopedia of Indian Philosophies*, Vol. V ; Delhi, Motilal Banarsidass.

Praśna Upaniṣad : Radhakrishnan S. Prof. (1994) *Principal Upaniṣads;* New Delhi, HarperCollins Publishers India.

Ṛgveda Bhāṣyabhūmikā (Sāyaṇa's) : Varma, Veerendrakumar, Dr. (*Hindi tr.*); (1980); Varanasi, Chaukhamba Orientalia.

Ṛgveda-Prātiśākhya of Śaunaka with *Uvvaṭa Bhāṣya* : Varma, Veerendrakumar, (*Hindi tr.*) (1999); Delhi, Chaukhamba Sanskṛt Pratishthan.

Ṛgveda-Saṃhita with *Bhāṣya* of Sāyaṇa : Wilson, H.H. (*tr.*), (2001), Delhi, Parimala Publications.

Ṛgveda-Saṃhitā (With Sāyaṇa's Commentary) : Muller, Max, F. (1983), Varanasi, Krishnadas Academy.

Ṛktantram (*A Prātiśākhya of Sāmaveda*) : Dr. Suryakanta (1970); Delhi, Meharchand Lachhmanadas.

Rudra Yāmalam Tantram (*Uttaratantram*) (*Prthamobhāgaḥ*) : Tripāṭhī, Śrīrāmaprasāda (1991); Vāraṇāsi, Sampūrnānanda Sanskrit University.

Śābarabhāṣyam of Śabara Swami (*Hindi tr.*) : Musalagāṉvakar, Gajānana Shāstri (2004); Varanasi, Chowkhamba Sanskrit Series Office.

Śabda Kausthubha of Dikṣita Bhaṭṭojji (1990) : p. 241, *In* [Potter Karl H. (*Gen. ed.*)], Goward, Harold G. & Raja Kunjunni : Encyclopedia of *Indian Philosophy,* Vol. v. (1990); Delhi, Motilal Banarsidass.

Ṣaḍdarśana Samucchayaḥ of Haribhadra : Murthy, Sacchidananda, K. (*tr.*) (1986); Delhi, Eastern Book Linkers.

Ṣaḍdarśana Samucchayaḥ of Haribhadra with Commentary of Maṇibhadra: *In* Chattopadhyaya, Debi Prasad & Gangopadhyaya, Mrinal Kanti (*ed.* & *tr.*) (1994): *Cārvāka / Lokāyata* – An Anthology of Source Materials and Some Recent Studies, New Delhi, Indian Council of Philosophical Research.

Sāmaveda : Ganapati, S.V. (*tr.*) (1992); Delhi, Motilal Banarsidass.

Sāmaveda Saṃhitā (*tr.*) : Griffith, R.T.H., (2001); Delhi, Parimala Publications.

Saṅgītaratnākara of Śāraṅgadeva : Shringy, R.K. and Sharma, Prem Lata (*tr.*) (1991); New Delhi, Munshiram Manoharlal.

Saṅgītaratnākara of Śāraṅgadeva with the Kalānidhi of Kallinātha & Sudhākara of Simhabhūpāla (1992) : Sastri Subramanya; Madras, Adyar Library and Research Centre.

Saṅgīta Samaya Sāra of Pārśvadeva: Acharya Brihaspati (1977); Delhi, Shri Kundanakundana Bharati.

Śārada Tilaka Tantram : Board of Scholars (1988); Delhi, Sri Satguru Publications.

Ślokavārtika of Kumārila Bhaṭṭa : Jhā, Gaṅgānātha : (1983); Delhi, Sri Satguru Publications.

Soundarya Laharī of Śaṅkara Bhagavatpada : Śastri, Subrahmanya S. & Ayyangar, Srinivasa T.R. (2000); Chennai, The Theosophical Publishing House, Adyar.

Sphoṭasiddhi of Bharata Miśra : Palsule, G.B., p. 231; [Potter Karl H. (*Gen.ed.*)], Goward, Harold G. & Raja, K. Kunjunni : The Encyclopedia of Indian Philosophies, Vol. V (1990); Delhi, Motilal Banarsidass.

Sphoṭasiddhi of Maṇḍana Miśra : Subramania Iyer, K.A. (1966); Poona, The Deccan College Postgraduate and Research Institute.

Śuklayajuḥ Prātiśākhyam athavā Vājasneyi-Prātiśākhyam : Rastogi Indu (1967) Vaṛanasi, Chaukhamba Sanskrit Series Office.

Śuklayajurveda Prātiśākhyam or *Vajasneyi Prātiśākhyam* : Varma, Veerendra Kumar : (*Hindi tr.*) (2001); Delhi, Chaukhamba Sanskrit Pratishthana.

Sūnyatāsaptatikārikā (Śloka 68) of Nāgārjuna; p. 53: *In* Dragoneetti, Fernando, Tola Carmen (2002) : On Voidness (A study on Buddhist Nihilism); Delhi, Motilal Banarsidass.

Taittirīya Upaniṣad : Radha Krishna (1994) – Principal Upaniṣads; New Delhi, Harper Collins Publishers India.

Tarka Sangraha of Annam Bhatta (*tr.*) : Bhattacharya, Jivananda Vidyasagara (1992); Varanasi, Chowkhamba Sanskrit Series Office.

Tattvārtha Sūtra of Umāsvāti/Umāsvāmī, (with the combined commentaries of Umāsvāti / Umāsvāmī, Pujyapāda and Siddhasenagaṇi) : Tatia, Nathmal (*tr.*) : (2007), Delhi, Motilal Banarsidass.

Tattvārtha Sūtra-Rājavārttika of Bhaṭṭa Akalaṅka : Jain, Mahendra Kumar & Lahari Ratna (*tr.*); p. 305-06; *In* [Potter, Karl H. (*Gen. ed.*)], Dalsukh Malvania & Jainendra Soni (2007) : Encyclopedia of Indian Philosophy, Vol. X ; Part I; Delhi, Motilal Banarsidass.

Tattvasiddhi of Harvarman ; p. 255, Potter , Karl H. (2002); Encyclopedia of Indian Philosophy (Vol. VIII); Delhi, Motilal Banarsidass.

Upaniṣad Saṅgraḥ : Paṇḍit, Jagadiśśastri, (1996); Delhi, Motilal Banarsidass.

Vaiyākaraṇabhūṣaṇa of Koṇḍa (or Kauṇḍa) Bhaṭṭa : Joshi S.D., p. 255; *In* [Potter, Karl H. (*Gen. ed.*)], Goward, Harold G., & Raja, Kunjunni, K. : *The Encyclopedia of Indian Philosophies*, Vol. V ; (1990); Delhi, Motilal Banarsidass.

Vājasneyi Prātiśākhya, Part I : Ghosal S.N. (*tr.*) (1964); Calcutta, Indian Studies – Past & Present.

Vākyapadīyaṃ of Bhartṛhari (Brahmakāṇḍa) : Korada Subramanyam (*tr.*) (1992); Delhi, Sri Satguru Publications.

Vākyārtha-Mātṛkā; Avasthī, Brahāmitra (*Hindi tr.*) (2036 V.); Delhi, Indu Prakāśana.

Vedanta Explained – Śaṅkara's Commentary on *Brahma Sūtras* (*tr.*): Date, V.H. (1973); New Delhi, Munshiram Manoharlal.

Yājñavalkyaśikṣā : Jhā, Naresha (*Hindi tr.*) (1999); Varanasi, Chaukhamba Surabharati Prakashana.

Yājñavalkyaśikṣā : Jhā, Udayanāth (Ashok), (*Hindi tr.*) (1986); Varanasi, Chowkhambha Orientalia.

Yājñavalkya Smṛti: Miśra, Śrī Nārāyaṇa (1994); Varanasi, Chaukhamba Sanskrit Sansthan.

Yāska Praṇīta Nighaṇṭu tathā Nirukta : Yogi, Satyabhūṣaṇa (*Hindi tr.*) (1985); Delhi, Motilal Banarsidass.

Secondary Sources

Abhyankar, Kāshinath Vasudev (1967) : Pāribhāṣasaṇgraḥa (1967); Poona, Bhandarkar Oriental Institute.

Abhyankar, Kāshinath Vasudev and Shukla, J.M. (1986) : *A Dictionary of Sanskṛt Grammar;* Baroda, Oriental Institute.

Acharya Hariram (*ed.*) (1998) : *Sangita Damodar* of Shubhankara ; Jaipur, Publication Scheme.

Agrawal, Madan Mohan (2001) : *Six Systems of Indian Philosophy* (*Sūtras* of Six Systems of Indian Philosophy); Delhi, Chaukhamba Sanskrit Sansthan.

Aiyar, Ramachandra, T.K. (1987) : *Comparative Philology* (of Indo-European Languages); Palghat, R.S.Vadhyar & Sons.

Allyn, Miner (1998) : *Saṅgītopaniṣad Sāroddhāra* of Sudhākalaśa; New Delhi, Indira Gandhi National Centre for Arts; Delhi, Motilal Banarsidass.

Anacker, Stefan (2008) : A Discussion of Five Aggregates (*Pañcāskandhaka Prakarṇa*); p. 49; *In* Seven Works of Vasubandhu; Delhi, Motilal Banarsidass.

Apte, Vaman Shivaram (2000) : *The Practical Sanskrit English Dictionary*; Delhi, Motilal Banarsidass.

Avalon, Arthur (Woodroffe, John) (2006) : *Śakti and Śākta* ; Delhi, Oriental Book Centre.

____ (*ed.*) (2001) : *Śārada Tilka Tantram;* Delhi, Motilal Banarsidass.

____ (*tr.*) (2000) : *Kulārṇava Tantra*, Delhi, Motilal Banarsidass.

Balslev, Anindita Niyogi (1999) : *A Study of Time in Indian Philosophy*; New Delhi, Munshiram Manoharlal Publishers.

Bandopadhyaya, S. (1986) : *Saṅgīta Bhāṣya* (Terminology of Musical Terms); Delhi, B.R Publishing Corporation.

Basu, Manoranjan (1986): *Fundamentals of the Philosophy of Tantras*; Calcutta, Mira Basu, 50B, Haldarpara Road.

Baumer, Bettina (*ed.*) (1996) : *Kalātattvakośa*–A Lexicon of Fundamental Concepts of the Indian Arts ;Vol. III; New Delhi, Indira Gandhi National Centre for the Art and Delhi, Motilal Banarsidass.

Beer, C.G. (1982) : *The Conceptual Issues in the Study of Communication;* Ch. 9; p. 279; *In* Kroodsma, Donald E.; Miller Edward H. & Ouellet, Henri : *Acoustic Communication in Birds* (Vol. II); London, Academic Press.

Bharatamuni : *Nāṭyaśāstra* – Board of Scholars (*tr.*) (1996); Delhi, Sri Satguru Publications.

Bhatt, Govardhan, P. (1962) : *Epistemology of the Bhaṭṭa School of Pūrva Mīmāmsā*; Varanasi, Chowkhamba Sanskrit Series Office.

Bhaṭṭa, Viśvambhara Nātha (*tr.*) (1975) : *Saṅgītadarpaṇa* of Dāmodara Paṇḍita; Hatharasa, Sangeet Karyalaya.

Bhattacharyya Ananta Kumar : *Cārvāka Darśana*, p. 452, *In* Chattopadhyaya, Debi Prasad & Gangopadhyaya, Mrinal Kanti (*ed.* & *tr.*) (1994),

Cārvāka / Lokāyata, An Anthology of Source Materials and Some Recent Studies : New Delhi, Indian Council of Philosophical Research.

Bhattacharyya, Narendra Nath (1999) : *History of the Tāṇtric Religion* – An Historical, Ritualistic and Philosophical Study; Delhi, Manohar Publishers.

____ (1999) : *A Glossary of Indian Religious Terms and Concepts*; New Delhi, Manohar Publisher.

Bhattacharya, Sibjiban (1993) : *Gangeśa's Theory of Indeterminate Perception*; Part II; p.11; New Delhi, Indian Council of Philosophical Research.

____ (1990) : *Gadhādhara's Theory of Objectivity* (*Viṣayatvāda*), pp. 6-12; Part II; New Delhi, Indian Council of Philosophical Research.

____ (1998) : *Language Testimony and Meaning*; New Delhi, Indian Council of Philosophical Research.

Bhaṭṭācāryya, Tārānātha Tarka Vācaspati (2003) : *Vācaspatym* (Sanskrit Dictionary); Varanasi, Chowkhamba Sanskrit Series Office.

Bhise, Usha R. (*tr.*) (1986) : *Nāradīyāśikṣā* with the Commentary of Bhaṭṭa, Śobhākara; Poona, Bhandarkar Oriental Research Institute.

Bothra, Pushpa (1996) : Jaina Theory of Perception; Delhi, Motilal Banarsidass.

Brackenbury, John H. (1982) : *The Structural Basis of Voice Production and Its Relationship to Sound Characteristics* ; Ch. 2 (p. 53); *In* Kroodsma Donald E., Miller, Edward H. & Ouellet Henri : *Acoustic Communication in Birds* (Vol. I) ; London, Academic Press.

Chakravarty, H.N. (1992) : *Bindu* (Ch. I); *In* Baumer Bettina (*ed.*): *Kalātattvakośa*; Vol. II; New Delhi, Indira Gāndhi National Centre of Arts & Delhi, Motilal Banarsidass.

Chatterji, Kshitish Chandra (*tr.*) (1957) : *Patañjali's Mahābhāṣya*; Calcutta, A. Mukharjee & Co.

Chattopadhyaya, Debi Prasad & Gangopadhyaya, Mrinal Kanti (*ed.* & *tr.*) (1994), *Cārvāka / Lokāyata* – An Anthology of Source Materials and Some Recent Studies : New Delhi, Indian Council of Philosophical Research.

Chattopadhyaya, Sudhakar (1979) : *Ethnic Elements in Ancient Hinduism* ; Calcutta, Sanskrit College.

Concise Routledge *Encyclopedia of Philosophy* (2000); London, Routledge, 11 New Fetter Lane.

Cowell, E.B. & Cough, A.E. (2000) : *Sarvadarśana Saṅgraḥ* of Mādhavāchārya; Delhi, Motilal Banarsidass.

Dasgupta, Surendranath (1997) : *A History of Indian Philosophy* (Vol. I-V); Delhi, Motilal Banarsidass.

____ (2001) : *A Study of Patañjali*; New Delhi, Indian Council of Philosophical Research.

____ (2001) : *Natural Science of the Ancient Hindus*; New Delhi, Indian Council of Philosophical Research.

____ (*tr.*) (1991) : *Mahābhāṣya of Pantañjali* (*Aahnikas,* I-IV) : New Delhi, Indian Council of Philosophical Research.

Date, V.H. (*tr.*) (1973) : *Vedanta Explained* - Śaṅkara's Commentary on *Brahma Sūtras*; New Delhi, Munshiram Manoharlal.

Desai, Caitanya Puṇḍarīka (1961) : *Bharatabhāṣyam* of Nānyabhūpāla ; Khairgaḍ, Indirā-Kalā-Sangīta-Viśvavidyālaya.

Devrāta (1962) : *Vedārtha Kalpalatā*; Varanasi, Hindu Vishwa Vidyalaya.

Dragonetti, Fernando Tola Carmen : *The Sūnyatāsaptatikārikā* of Nāgārjun (Śloka 68), p. 80, *In "On Voidness" A Study on Buddhist Nihilism* (2002) : Delhi, Motilal Banarsidass.

Dwarakanatha C. (1996) : *Lectures on Tanmātras and Pañcamahābhūtas*; Varanasi, Chowkhamba Sanskrit Series Office.

Dwivedi, Ramayana Prasad & Malaviya, Dr. Sudhakar (*ed.* & *tr.*), (2004); *Kāmakalāvilāsa* of Māheśvara Puṇyānanda Nātha, along with Cidvalli (Sanskṛt Commentary) of Śrī Naṭānanda Nātha : Delhi, Chowkhamba Sanskrit Pratishthan.

Dwivedi, Vajravallabha (*ed.*) (2004) : *Svacchandatantram* (Vol. II) with the commentary of Kṣemarāja : Delhi, Parimala Publications.

____ (1985) : *Netratantram* with the commentary of Kṣemarāja : Delhi, Parimala Publications.

Frauwallner, Erich (2010) : *Philosophy of Buddhism (Die Philosophie des Buddhismus)* – Translated by Sangpo Gelong Lodro; Delhi, Motilal Banarsidass.

Gangopādhyāya, Anantlal (1984) : *Paṇḍitarāja Jagannātha on Aesthetic Problems*, Calcutta, Sanskrit Pustaka Bhandar.

Ghate, V.S. (1981) : *The Vedānt* – A Study of the *Brahma-Sūtra* with *Bhāṣyas* of Śaṃkara, Rāmānuja, Nimbārka, Madhva and Vallabha; Poona, Bhandarkar Oriental Research Institute.

Ghosh, Manmohan (1991) : *Pāṇini Śikṣā*; Delhi, V.K. Publishing House.

Ghoshal, S.C. (*ed.*) (1989) : Nemichandra Siddhānta Chakravarttī's *Dravya-Saṃgrah;* Delhi, Motilal Banarsidass.

Goswaṃy, Ashok Kumar (1991) : *Critique of Śabda* (Based on Viśvanātha's *Bhāṣāpariccheda*); Delhi, Sri Satguru Publications.

Griffith, R.T.H. (2001) : *Sāmaveda Saṃhitā* (*tr.*); Delhi, Parimala Publications.

Gupta, Abhinava : *Parā-triśikā-vivaraṇa* – Singh, Jaideva (*tr.*) (2005); Delhi, Motilal Banarsidass.

Gupta, Sanjukta (*tr.*) (2000); *Lakṣmī Tantra* (A *Pāñcarātra* Text) : Delhi, Motilal Banarsidass.

Hiremath, C.R. (1992) : *Acoustics and Reproductive Biology of Some Anurans* – A thesis submitted to Karnatak University, Dharwar for the award of Doctor of Philosophy in Zoology.

Hiriyanna, M. (1995) : *The Essentials of Indian Philosophy*, Delhi, Motilal Banarsidass.

____ (1994) *Outlines of Indian Philosophy*, Delhi, Motilal Banarsidass.

Hassan, Nazir & Koul Omkar, N. (1980) : *Urdu Phonetic Reader*, Mysore, Central Institute of Indian Languages.

Ingalalli, R.I., Prof. (1988) : *Shabda Pramāṇa* – An Epistemological Analysis (1988); Delhi, Sri Satguru Publications.

Iyer, Subramania K.A. (*tr.*) (1977) : *Vākyapadīya* of Bhartṛhari; Delhi, Motilal Banarasidass.

Iyengar, Srinivasa P.T. (1909): *Outlines of Indian Philosophy*; Adyar, Madras, Theosophical Publishing Society.

Jain, Hiralal & Upadhyaya, A.N. (1944) : *Jainendra Siddhānta Kośa;* New Delhi, Bharatiya Jnanapith.

Jain, Mahendra Kumar and Ratnalahari : *Tattvārtha Sūtra - Rājavārttika* of Bhaṭṭa Akalaṅka, p. 305-06; *In* [Potter Karl H. (*Gen. ed.*)] Dalsukh Malvania & Jainendra Soni (2007) : Encyclopedia of Indian Philosophy, Vol. X; Part I; Delhi, Motilal Banarsidass.

Jain, Sagar Mal (1986) : *Jain Bhāṣā Darśana*; Delhi, Bhogilal Leharchand Institute of Indology.

Jaini, Padmanābha S. (2001) : The *Vaibhāṣika Theory of Words and Meanings*; p. 201: *In* Jaini, Padmanābha S. : *Collected Papers on Buddhist Studies*; Delhi, Motilal Banarsidass.

Jha, Gaṅgānātha (1982) : *Padārtha Saṅgraha of Praśastapāda*; Varaṇasi, Chowkhamba Orientalia.

____ (*tr.*) (2004) : *Yoga-Sāra-Sangraha of Vijnānabhikṣu*; Delhi, Parimal Publications.

____ (1999) : *Nyāyasūtras of Gautama* with the *Bhāṣya* of Vātsyāyana and the *Vārtika* of Uddyotkara (*tr.*); With notes from Vācaspati Mishra's *Nyāya Vārttika-Tātparyatīkā,* Udayana's *Parishuddhi* and Raghūttama's *Bhāśyachandra* : Delhi, Motilal Banarsidass.

____ *Ślokavārttika* of Kumārila Bhaṭṭa (1983); Delhi, Sri Satguru Publications.

Jhalakīkara, Bhīmācārya (1996) : *Nyāyakośa*; Pune, Bhandarkar Oriental Research Institute.

Joshi, M.C. (1999) : *The Conceptual Aspects of Sound in Śāktism;* p. 79; *In* Malik, S.C. : *Dhvani—Nature and Culture of Sound;* New Delhi, Indira Gāndhi National Centre for the Arts, & D.K. Print World.

Joshi, Laxmanshastri : *Dharmkośaḥ*; Vol. I; Part I—*Upaniṣatkāṇḍa*; p. 349; (1950); Wai, Prajña Pāṭhśalā Maṇḍala.

Joshi, Shivaram Dattatreya (1993) : *Kauṇḍa Bhaṭṭa on the Meaning of Sanskrit Verbs*; *In* Saṃbhāṣā : *Nagoya Studies in Indian Culture and Buddhism;* Japan, Department of Indian Philosophy, University of Nagoya.

Karmarkar, K.V. (*ed.*) (1967) : *Pāribhāṣāsaṅgraḥ* (Introduction); Poona, Oriental Research Institute.

Karmkar, Raghunātha Damodar (1973); *Gauḍapāda Kārikā* : Poona, Bhandarkar Oriental Research Institute.

Katz, Jerrold, J. : *Linguistic Philosophy*, Ch. 4, p. 31, *The Underlying Syntactic Reality of Language ; In* Arthur C. Danto (*ed.*) : *Essays in Philosophy;* London, George Allen & Unwin.

Kavi, Ramakrishna, M. (1951) : *Bharatakośaḥ*; (1951); New Delhi, Munshiram Manoharlal.

Kaviraj Gopinath (1994) : *Lokāyata and the Doctrine of Svabhāva*, p. 441, *In* Chattopadhyaya, Debi Prasad & Gangopadhyaya Mrinal Kanti (*ed. & tr.*) *Cārvāka / Lokāyata* – An Anthology of Source Materials and Some Recent Studies ; New Delhi, Indian Council of Philosophical Research.

Keith, A.B. (1924): *Taittirīya Samhita*, Part II – *Kaṇḍa* vi. 18; p. 495; Delhi, Motilal Banarsidass.

Kendra Worker : *Auṃ* – The Essence of the Vedas (1995); Kanyākumari, Vivekananda Kendra Prakashana.

Khanna, D.R. and Bedi, R.S. (1992) : *Textbook of Sound;* Delhi, Atma Ram & Sons.

Koṇḍa (or Kauṇḍa) Bhaṭṭa : *Vaiyākaraṇabhūṣaṇa* : Joshi, S.D., p. 256; *In* [Potter, K.H. (*Gen. Ed.*)] Goward, Harold G. & Raja, K. Kunjunni Raja : *The Encyclopedia of Indian Philosophies,* Vol.V; (1990); Delhi, Motilal Banarsidass.

Korada, Subramanyam (*tr.*) (1992); *Vākyapadīyaṃ* of Bhartṛhari (Brahmakāṇḍa) : Delhi, Sri Satguru Publications.

Krishnamacharya (*ed.*), (1977) *Sphoṭavāda* of Nāgeśa Bhaṭṭa, Introduction at p. 6; Madras, The Adyar Library and Research Centre.

Kroodsma, Donald E. (1982) : *Learning and the Ontogeny of Sound Signals in Birds*, Ch. 1 at p. 1; *In* Kroodsma, Donald E. & Miller Edward H. & Ouellet Henri : *Acoustic Communication in Birds* (Vol. II); London, Academic Press.

Kumar, Pushpendra (*ed.*) : *Linguistic Thought in Ancient India ;* p. 15, *In* Sharma, D.R. (1984); *Linguistic Speculations of Sanskrit Rheotoricians;* Delhi, Nag Publishers.

Larson & Bhattacharya (Gauḍapāda on the Subtle and Gross Elements); *In* Potter, Karl H. : Encyclopedia of Indian Philosophy, Vol. IV, pp. 219-20; Delhi, Motilal Banarsidass.

Lindner, Christian (*tr.*) (2001) : *Bhavya on Mimāṃsā* (*Mīmāṃsātattva-nirṇayāvatāraḥ*) ; Chennai, The Adyar Library and Research Centre.

Mackay, Earnest (1938) : *Further Excavation At Mohenjodaro;* New Delhi, Government of India Press.

Mandal, Kumar Kishore (1968) : *A Comparative Study of the Concepts of Space and Time in Indian Thought*; Varanasi, Chaukhamba Sanskrit Series Office.

March, A.C. (1986) : The Glossary of Buddhist Terms; Delhi, Sri Satguru Publications.

Marshall, Sir John (1931) : *Mohenjodaro and the Indus Civilization*; London, Arthur Probsthain.

Mīmāṃsak, Yudhiṣṭira (Saṃvat 2042) : *Vaidika-Svara-Mīmāṃsā;* Bahālgaḍ (Sonipat - Haryāṇā), Srī Rāmlāl Kapūr Trust.

Miśra, Bharata : *Sphoṭasiddhi* ; p. 231; *In* [Potter, K.H. (*Gen. ed.*)], Goward, Harold G. & Raja, Kunjunni K. : *The Encyclopedia of Indian Philosophies*, Vol. V (1990); Deḷhi, Motilal Banarsidass.

Misra, B.G., Dr. (1980) : Preface, In *Urdu Phonetic Reader :*Nazar, Hasan & Koul, Omkar, N.; Mysore, Central Institute of Indian Languages.

Miśra, Rājeśvara (1978) : *Vaidik paramparā me sāmagāna* : (Bangalā-Hindi Trans. by Madanlāl Vyās) : Vārāṇasi, Aananda Prakāśana.

Mishra, Vidhāta (1972) : *Critical Study of Sanskrit Phonetics*; Vārāṇasi, Chowkhamba Sanskrit Series Office.

Mittal, K.K. (1974) : *Materialism In Indian Thought*; New Delhi, Munshiram Manoharlal.

Muller, Max K.M. (1998) : *The Six Systems of Indian Philosophy*; Varanasi, Chowkhamba Sanskrit Series Office.

Muller, Max F. (1988) : *Science of Thought* – Three Introductory Lectures; New Delhi, Asian Educational Services.

____(1983) : *Ṛgveda-Saṃhitā* (With Sāyaṇa's Commentary), Varanasi, Krishnadas Academy.

Musulgaonkar, Gajananashastry (*Hindi tr.*) (2000) : *Sāṃkhyatattvakaumudi* of Vācaspati Misra; Varanasi, Chaukhamba Sanskrit Sansthan.

____ (2004): Śabara Swamy's *Śābhara Bhāṣyam* (*Hindi tr.*), Varanasi, Chaukhambha Sanskrit Series Office.

Natarajan, Kanchana (1995) : *The Vidhi Viveka* of Maṇḍana Miśra– Understanding Vedic Injunctions; Delhi, Sri Satguru Publications.

New Lexicon Webster's Dictionary of the English Language (1987); New York, Lexicon Publications, INC.

Oza, Madhusudana (1995) : *Varṇa Samīkṣā*; Jayapur, Rajasthan Oriental Research Institute.

Padmarajiah, Y.J. (2004) : *A Comparative Study of the Jaina Theories of Reality and Knowledge*, Delhi, Motilal Banarsidass.

Pāndeya, Umesh Chandra (1994) : *Yājñavalkya Smṛti*, Varanasi, Chowkhamba Sanskrit Samsthan.

Pāṇḍeya, Devendranātha and Jhā, Bodhakumāra (*ed.*) (1997): *Brāhmaṇa Vijñāna Saṅgrahaḥ*, p. 45; Jaipur, Boharā Prakāśana.

Pandita Damodar (1975) : *Sangita-Darpaṇa*, Hathras (India), Sangeeta Karyalaya.

Panigrahi, Neelamadhav (1995) : *Saṅgītārṇavacandrikā* of Nīlakaṭha; Bhuvaneshwar (Orissa), Sangita Natak Academy.

Pansikar, Wasudeva Laxmana Shastri (*ed.*) (1985); *Lalitā Sahasranāma* (Part II – *Brahmāṇḍa Purāṇa*) with the commentary–*Saubhāgya Bhāskara* of Bhāskararāya ; Delhi, Nāga Publishers.

Pears, D.F. & McGuiness, B.F. (*tr.*) (1961) : Ludwig Wittginstein's *Tractatus Logico-Philosophicus*, 3.32; London, Routledge & Kegari Paul.

Peter, Peterson (*tr.*) (1974) : Sāyaṇa's Preface to the *Ṛgvedabhāṣya* (*Ṛgvedabhāṣyabhūmikā*) ; Poona, Bhandarkar Oriental Research Institute.

Pillai Raghavan, K. (1971); *Vākyapadīya* ; Delhi, Motilal Banarsidass.

Pingle Pratibha, M. (2005) : *The Concept of Vāc in the Vedic Literature*, Delhi, Sri Satguru Publications.

Pitcher, George (1964) : *The Philosophy of Wittgenstein*, New Delhi, Prentice-Hall of India.

Potter, Karl H. (*Gen. ed.* for Entire Series) : *Encyclopedia of Indian Philosophy;* Delhi, Motilal Banarsidass.

___(2003): *Mādhyamakahṛdayakārikā and Tarkajvālā of* Bhavya, p. 397; *In* Encyclopedia of Indian Philosophy (Vol. IX) ; Delhi, Motilal Banarsidass.

Prasād, Rāma (*tr.*) (1995) : Pātañjali's *Yoga Sūtras* with the commentary of Vyāsa, and the gloss of Vāchaspati Miśra : New Delhi, Munshiram Manoharlal.

Purani, A.B. (1963) : *Studies in Vedic Interpretation;* Varanasi, Chowkhamba Sanskrit Series Office.

Radhakrishnan, Prof. S. (1997) : *Indian Philosophy*; Delhi, Oxford University Press.

____ (1994) : *The Principal Upaniṣads*; New Delhi, HarperCollins Publishers India.

Raghavan, V.K.S.N.(*tr.*) : *Mahābhāṣyapradīpoddyota* of Nāgeśa or Nāgoji Bhaṭṭa, Vol. V ; p. 340; *In* Potter, Karl H. (1990) : *Encyclopedia of Indian Philosophy;* Delhi, Motilal Banarsidass.

Raja, Kunhan C. & Sastri, Suryanarayana, S.S. (1975) : *Mānameyodaya* of Nārāyaṇa : Chennai, The Adyar Library and Research Centre.

Raja Kunjunni, K. (1977) : *Sangraha* of Vyadi, p. 101, *In* Indian Theories of Meaning; Madras, The Adyar Library and Research Centre.

____ (1990): *Paramalaghumañjūṣā* of Nāgeśa or Nāgoji Bhaṭṭa (1990): p. 324; *In* [Potter, K.H. (*Gen. ed.*)] Goward, G. Harold & Raja Kunjunni, K. : *The Encyclopedia of Indian Philosophies*,Vol.V; Delhi, Motilal Banarsidass.

Ramanathan, A.A. (1989) : *Amarakośa* with *Amarapadavivṛti* of Liṅgayasūrin and *Amarapadapārijāta* of Mallinātha; Madras, The Adyar Library and Research Center.

Rāya, Rāmakumāra (1986) : *Gandharva Tantram*, Vārāṇasī, Kṛṣṇadāsa Academy.

Rukmani, T.S. (1981) : *Yogavārttika* of Vijñānabhikṣu (Vol. I-IV) : New Delhi, Munshiram Manoharlal.

Sagar, Mahopadhyaya Lalitprabh (2000) : *World Renowned Jain Pilgrimages Reverence and Art*, Jaipur, Prakrit Bharti Academy.

Saighal, R.L. (1990) : *A Textbook of Sound*; New Delhi, S. Chand and Co.

Sandal, Mohanlal (*tr.*) (1999) : *Mīmāṃsa Sūtra* of Jaimini : Delhi, Motilal Banarsidass.

Sarkar, Bharati (1999): *Communication Through Sound in Animals* at p. 31; *In* Malik S.C (*ed.*) : *Dhvani* – Nature and Culture of Sound; New Delhi, Indira Gandhi National Centre for Arts.

Śarma, Madhava Krishna K. (1968) : *Pāṇini, Kātyāyana and Patañjali*; Delhi, Shri Lal Bahadur Shastri Rashtriya Sanskrit Vidyapeeth.

Śastri, D.R. : *A Short History of Indian Materialism, Sensationalism and Hedonism*, p. 398, *In* Chattopadhyaya, Debi Prasad & Gangopadhyaya, Mrinal Kanti (*ed.* & *tr.*) (1994), *Cārvāka / Lokāyata* – An Anthology of Source Materials and Some Recent Studies : New Delhi, Indian Council of Philosophical Research.

Śastri, Subramanya P. S. & Ayyangar, Srinivasa, T.R. (1944) : *Lectures on Patañjali's Mahābhāṣya* (Vol. I); Annamalai Nagar, Annamalai University.

Śastri, Suryanarayana S.S. (*tr.*) (1948). : *Sānkhya Kārikā of Iśvara Kṛṣṇa*; University of Madras.

Śastry, Ananthakrishna (*tr.*) (1988) : *Lalitā Sahasranāma* : Madras, The Adyar Library and Research Centre.

Shah, K.J. Prof. (1987) : *The Theory of Rasa* – Its Conceptual Structure; p. 115; *In* Daya Krishna (*ed.*) : *India's Intellectual Traditions;* New Delhi, Indian Council of Philosophical Research and Delhi, Motilal Banarsidass.

Sharma, B.R. (1991) : *Vedic Heritage of India*; Tirupati, Rashtriya Sanskrit Vidyapeetha.

Sharma, Chandradhara (2000) : *A Critical Survey of Indian Philosophy*; Delhi, Motilal Banarsidass.

Sharma, D.D. (1984) : *Linguistic Speculations of Sanskrit Rhetoricians*, p.15; *In* Pushpendra Kumar, Dr. (*ed.*) : *Linguistic Thought in Ancient India;* Delhi, Nag Publishers.

Sharma, Madhusūdana (1996) : *Pathyāsvasti*; Jodhapur, Rajasthan Oriental Institute.

Sharma, Manorama (1996) : *Special Education : Music Therapy;* New Delhi, S.B. Nangiya, A.P.H Publishing Corporation.

Sharma, Prema Lata (1963) : *Saṅgītarājaḥ* of Mahāraṇā Kumbhā, Vol. I, Varanasi, Banaras Hindu University.

Sharma, Prema Lata and Beohar, Bihari, Anil (1991): *Būhaddeśī* of Śrī Mataṅga Muni, Vol. I ; New Delhi, Indira Gāndhi National Centre for Arts & Delhi, Motilal Banarsidass.

Sharma, R.N. (*tr.*) (1987); *Vākyārtha-Mātṛkā* of Sālikānatha Miśra with his own Vṛtti : Delhi, Sri Satguru Publications.

Sharma, Shrikṛṣṇa (1993) : *Aachārya Aapiśāli Ki Kṛtiyoñ kā Samīkṣātmaka Adhyayana*, Kurukshetra, Nirmal Book Agency.

Shastri, Babulal (1972) : *Nāṭakalakṣaṇaratnakoṣaḥ* of Sāgaranandi; Varanasi : Chaukhamba Sanskrit Series Office.

Shringy, R.K. and Sharma, Prem Lata (1991); *Saṅgītaratnākara* of Śāraṅgadeva; New Delhi, Munshiram Manoharlal.

Ṡimha, Guru Bipin (1990) : *Vaiṣṇava-Sangītaśāstra*, Varanasi, Chaukhamba Orientalia.

Singh, Amar (1995) : *Buddha's Original Logical – The Sautrantika Analytical Philosophy*, New Delhi, Dharma Cakra Publication.

Singh, Fatah : Vedic Etymology; Kota, Sanskrit Sadana (Rajasthan).

Singh, Jaideva (*tr.*) (1994): *Spanda Kārikās* (The Divine Creative Pulsation) with Spanda Nirṇaya – The commentary by Kṣemarāja ; Delhi, Motilal Banarsidass.

_____ (2005) : *Parā-triśikā-vivaraṇa* of Abhinava Gupta (2005); Delhi, Motilal Banarsidass.

Sinha, Nandalal (2003) : *Sānkhya Philosophy* – Containing (1) *Sānkhya-pravacana-sūtram* with *Vṛtti* of Aniruddha, and the *Bhāṣya* of Vijñānabhikṣu and Extracts from *Vṛttisāra* of Mahādeva Vedāntin;

(2) *Tatvasamāsa*; (3) *Sāmkhyakārikā*; (4) *Pancaśikhāsūtram* ; New Delhi, Munshiram Manoharlal.

Sinha, Nandalal & Vidyabhushana, Satish Chandra (*tr.*) (1990) : The *Nyāya Sūtras of Gotama;* Delhi, Motilal Banarsidass.

Sinha, Pancham (*tr.*) (1992) : *Haṭha Yoga Pradīpikā*; New Delhi, Munshiram Mañoharlal.

Strangways, A.H. (1989) : *Sāman Chant*; p. 246. In *Features Principles of Technique of Indian Music* ; Delhi, Kanishka Publishing House.

Strawson, P.F. (1959) : *Individuals;* In *An Essay in Descriptive Metaphysics*; Chap. on *"Sounds"*; pp. 59-86; London, Methuen & Co.

Suzuki, D.T. (2003) : The *Laṅkāvatāra Sūtra*, New Delhi, Munshiram Manoharlal.

Swami, Harshananda (2000) : *Hindu Symbols*; Bangalore, Ramakrishna Math.

Swami Madhavananda (1996) : *Bhāṣā-Pariccheda* of Viśvanātha Nyāya Pañcānana ; Calcutta, Advaita Ashrama.

Swami Prajñananda (1973) : *The Schools of Indian Philosophical Thought*; Calcutta, Firma K.L. Mukhopadhyaya.

Swami, Virupākṣānanda (*tr.*) (2004) : *Tarka Saṅgraha* (with the *Dīpika* of Annambhaṭṭa); Madras, Sri Ramakrishna Math.

Tarktirtha, Amarendramohan (2003) : *Nyāyadarśanaṃ* with Vātsyāyana's *Bhāṣya*, Uddyotkara's *Vārtika*, Vācaspati Miśra's *Tātparyaṭīkā* & Viśvanātha's *Vṛtti;* New Delhi, Munshiram Manoharlal.

Tarlekar, G.H. (1995) : *Sāman Chants* – In theory and Present Practice; Delhi, Sri Satguru Publications.

Tatia, Nathmal (*tr.*) (2007): *Tattvārtha Sūtra of Umāsvāti / Umāsvāmī*, (With the combined commentaries of Umāsvāti/Umāsvāmī, Pujyapāda and Siddhasenagaṇi); Delhi, Motilal Banarsidass.

Thite, G.U. (1997) : *Music in the Vedas*–Its Magico-Religious Significance; Delhi, Sharada Publishing House.

Tripathi, Rama Shankar (1992) : *History of Ancient India*; Delhi, Motilal Banarsidass.

Tripathi, Kedarnatha (1974) : *Sānkhya Yoga Kośaḥ* : Varanasi, Tripathi Veerendra & Tripathi, Vijayakumar, F.F.18, Banaras Hindu University.

Tucci, G. (1994) : *A Sketch of Indian Materialism*, p. 384; *In* Chattopadhyaya, Debiprasad and Gangopadhyaya Mrinal Kanti: *Cārvāka/Lokāyata* – An Anthology of Source Materials and Some *Recent Studies*; New Delhi, Indian Council of Philosophical Research.

Varma, Siddheśvara (1961) : *Critical Studies in the Phonetic Observations of Indian Grammarians*; Delhi, Munshiram Manoharlal.

Varma, Veerendra Kumar (*Hindi tr.*) (1999) : *Ṛgveda-Prātiśākhya* of Śaunaka with Uvvaṭa *Bhāṣya* : Delhi, Chaukhamba Sanskrit Pratishthan.

Vidyabhūṣaṇa, Satisa Chandra, M.M. (1990) : *Nyāya Sūtras of Gautama:* (Edited by Sinha, Nandalal), Motilal Banarsidass.

____ (2002) : *A History of Indian Logic, Ancient, Medieval & Modern Schools* ; Delhi, Motilal Banarsidass.

Webster's New World Dictionary (Electronic C.D.).

Whitney, William Dwight (1997) : *Sanskrit Grammar*; Delhi, Motilal Banarsidass.

____(1973) : *Taittirīya Prātiśakhya with its Commentary the Tribhāshyaratnakar* ; Delhi, Motilal Banarsidass.

____ (1994) : *Atharvaveda Prātiśākhya* or *Shounakīya Caturādhyāyikā* (*tr.*); Delhi, Parimala Publication.

Williams, Sir Monier Monier (1997) : *A Sanskrit-English Dictionary*; Delhi, Motilal Banarsidass.

Wilson, H.H. (*tr.*) (2001) : *Ṛgveda Samhitā* with *Bhāṣya* of Sāyaṇa ; Delhi, Parimala Publications.

Wittgenstein, Ludwig (1961) : *Tractatus Logico – Philosophicus*; Pears, D.F. & McGuinness, B.F. (*tr.*); London, Routledge & Kegan Paul.

Woodroffe, Sir John (1998) : *The Garland of Letters* (Studies in Mantraśāstra); Madras, Ganesh & Co.

____ (*tr.*) (2001) : The Great Liberation (*Mahānirvāṇa Tantram*), pp. 25-27; Madras, Ganesh and Company.

____ (*tr.*) (2002) : *Principles of Tantra* (*The Tantratattva* of Śriyukta Śivacandra Vidyārṇava Bhattacārya Mahodaya); Avalon Arthur (Woodroffe John); Delhi, Shivalik Prakashana.

____ (2006) : *Śakti and Śākta*, Delhi, Oriental Book Centre.

Woodworth, Robert S. and Marquis, Donald G. (1955) : *Psychology*; London; Methuen & Co.

Yuvacharya, Shri Madhukar Muni (1992): *Sthānāṅgasūtra*(1992), p. 583, Rajasthan, Byavara.

Journals

Ingalalli, R.I. Prof. (2003) : *Referential Theory of Meaning in Navya-Nyāya System*; p. 1; *In* Shiva Nath Prasad, Patna: *Journal of Bihar Philosophical Research* (Part : III-IV).

Bronkhorst, Johannes (1999) : *Studies on Bhartṛhari* – Prākṛta Dhvani and the Sāṅkhya Tanmātras, p. 23; In *Journal of Indian Philosophy*, Vol. 27, pp. 22-33; Kluwer, Academic Publishers.

Article – Website

Edmondson R. (2005) : Can-you- hear- me- sound-in- space = Retrieved on 05-05-2011 - from : http://www.myuniversalfacts.com/2005/07/can-you-hear-me-sound-in-space-html

Ron Kurtus (2009) : 'Overview of Sound Waves' (revised 1 December 2009);

Retrieved on 05-05-2011 - from :

http://www.google.com.in/search?hl=&aq=f&source=hp&q=www.science.sound+in+space&btnG=Serch&meta=&aq=f&aqi=&aql=&oq=Andhttp://www.school-for-champions.com/science/sound.htm.

WORD INDEX